First World War

and Army of Occupation

War Diary

France, Belgium and Germany

23 DIVISION
Headquarters, Branches and Services
Commander Royal Artillery
1 June 1915 - 31 August 1916

WO95/2170/2

The Naval & Military Press Ltd
www.nmarchive.com
Published in association with The National Archives

Published by

The Naval & Military Press Ltd

Unit 10 Ridgewood Industrial Park,

Uckfield, East Sussex,

TN22 5QE England

Tel: +44 (0) 1825 749494

www.naval-military-press.com

www.nmarchive.com

This diary has been reprinted in facsimile from the original. Any imperfections are inevitably reproduced and the quality may fall short of modern type and cartographic standards.

Contents

Document type	Place/Title	Date From	Date To
Heading	WO95/2170/2		
Heading	23rd Division Divl Artillery C.R.A. 1915 Aug-1916 Aug		
Heading	23rd Divn H.Q. 23rd Division Staff Capt To C.R.A. Vol 1 Sept 15		
War Diary	London	21/08/1915	21/08/1915
War Diary	Folkestone	22/08/1915	22/08/1915
War Diary	Boulogne	22/08/1915	22/08/1915
War Diary	St Omer	22/08/1915	26/08/1915
War Diary	Tilques	27/08/1915	05/09/1915
War Diary	Renescure	06/09/1915	06/09/1915
War Diary	Merris	07/09/1915	15/09/1915
War Diary	Croix Du Bac	16/09/1915	30/09/1915
Operation(al) Order(s)	Operation Order No. 1 By Brigadier General D Fasson, C.B. Commanding Royal Artillery 23rd Division.		
Miscellaneous	23rd Divisional Artillery	21/09/1915	21/09/1915
Miscellaneous	Appendix 1 21st September Artillery bombardment		
Heading	23rd Div H.Q. 23rd Div: Staff Capt R.A. Vol 2 Oct 15		
Miscellaneous	A.G. Office Base	01/11/1915	01/11/1915
War Diary	Croix Du Bac	01/10/1915	31/10/1915
Heading	Staff Capt: To C.R.A. 23rd Div Vol 3 Nov. 15		
War Diary	Croix Du Bac	01/11/1915	28/11/1915
War Diary	23rd Division Headquarters 23rd Div C.R.A. Vol I		
War Diary	Boulogne	25/08/1915	25/08/1915
War Diary	Tilques	26/08/1915	31/08/1915
Heading	23rd Division H.Q. 23rd Division C.R.A. Vol: II June To Sept 15		
War Diary	Tilques	01/06/1915	06/09/1915
War Diary	Merris	07/09/1915	14/09/1915
War Diary	Croix Du Bac	15/09/1915	25/09/1915
War Diary	Rolanderie Farm	25/09/1915	26/09/1915
War Diary	Croix Du Bac	27/09/1915	30/09/1915
Operation(al) Order(s)	23rd Division Operation Order No 1 App I	05/09/1915	05/09/1915
Miscellaneous	March Table For 6th September App I		
Operation(al) Order(s)	23rd Division Order No. 2 App II	06/09/1915	06/09/1915
Miscellaneous	March Table For 7th Sept		
Miscellaneous	Operation Order No 1 By Brigadier General D. Fasson, C.B. Commanding Royal Artillery, 23rd Division. App III	07/09/1915	07/09/1915
Miscellaneous	March Table	08/09/1915	08/09/1915
Miscellaneous	To The Officer Commanding, 104th Brigade R.F.A.	07/09/1915	07/09/1915
Miscellaneous	Alarm Signals. App IV	15/09/1915	15/09/1915
Operation(al) Order(s)	23rd Division Operation Order No 3 App V	12/09/1915	12/09/1915
Miscellaneous	To All Formations And Units Of Divisional Troops.		
Operation(al) Order(s)	Operation Order No. 2 by Brig. General D. Fasson, C.B. Commanding 23rd Div Artillery. App VI	13/09/1915	13/09/1915
Operation(al) Order(s)	Operation Order No. 3 By Brigadier General D. Fasson, C.B. Commanding Royal Artillery, 23rd Division.	14/09/1915	14/09/1915
Miscellaneous	Headquarters "A" Group, 23rd Division Arty. App VIII	15/09/1915	15/09/1915

Operation(al) Order(s)	Operation Order No. 1 By Brigadier General D. Fasson, C.B. Commanding Royal Artillery, 23rd Division. App X	20/09/1915	20/09/1915
Miscellaneous	Appendix 1. 21st September Artillery bombardment		
Miscellaneous	23rd Divisional Artillery	21/09/1915	21/09/1915
Miscellaneous	R.A. 23rd Division. During 4 Days Bombardment App XII		
Operation(al) Order(s)	Report On Operation. App XI	21/09/1915	21/09/1915
Miscellaneous	23rd Divisional Artillery App XIII		
Miscellaneous	Report On Operations App XIV	22/09/1915	22/09/1915
Miscellaneous	Headquarters, "A" & "B" Groups & No. 2 Mountain Batty. App XV	23/09/1915	23/09/1915
Miscellaneous	R.A. G.384 23rd		
Miscellaneous	23rd Divisional Artillery. App XVI		
Miscellaneous	Report On Operation 23rd Divisional Artillery.	23/09/1915	23/09/1915
Miscellaneous	23rd Divisional Artillery. App XVII		
Miscellaneous	23rd Divisional Artillery. App XVIII	24/09/1915	24/09/1915
Miscellaneous	23rd Divisional Artillery. Report On Operations. App XIX	25/09/1915	25/09/1915
Miscellaneous	Headquarters, 102 & 104 Brigade, R.F.A. App XX	25/09/1915	25/09/1915
Miscellaneous	Royal Artillery, 23rd Division. App XXI	26/09/1915	26/09/1915
Miscellaneous	23rd Divisional Artillery. App XXII		
Operation(al) Order(s)	Operation Orders No. 4 By Brigadier General D Fasson. C.B. Commanding Royal Artillery, 23rd Division. App XXIII	27/09/1915	27/09/1915
Operation(al) Order(s)	Operation Order No. 5 By Brigadier General B. Fasson, C.B. Commanding Royal Artillery, 23rd Division App XXIII	28/09/1915	28/09/1915
Miscellaneous	Dispositions 23rd Divisional Artillery. App XXIV		
Heading	23rd Division War Diary Of General Staff Branch Headquarters 23rd Divisional Artillery. From October 1st. 1915 To October 31st. 1915 Vol 3		
War Diary	Croix Du Bac	01/10/1915	01/10/1915
War Diary	W. Estaires	02/10/1915	07/10/1915
War Diary	Croix Du Bac	08/10/1915	31/10/1915
Miscellaneous	Headquarters,	15/10/1915	15/10/1915
Miscellaneous	Defensive Arrangements. 23rd Divisional Artillery.	14/10/1915	14/10/1915
Miscellaneous	To Col. Henning, R.F.A.	13/10/1915	13/10/1915
Miscellaneous	Battery Positions. 23rd Divisional Artillery.	20/10/1915	20/10/1915
Miscellaneous	Night Lines.	02/10/1915	02/10/1915
Miscellaneous	D.A. 530 23rd Divisional Artillery. Alternative Positions.		
Miscellaneous	Alternative Observation Stations.		
Miscellaneous	Estimate Of Ammunition Required By 23rd Div. Artillery.	24/10/1915	24/10/1915
Miscellaneous	Headquarters, 23rd Division.	26/10/1915	26/10/1915
Miscellaneous	R.A. Divisional Hdqtrs. 23rd Division.	26/10/1915	26/10/1915
Miscellaneous	Result Of An Inspection Of Battery Positions Made To-Day By The Royal Flying Corps.	26/10/1915	26/10/1915
Miscellaneous	R.A. Divisional Headquarters, 23rd Division.	30/10/1915	30/10/1915
Miscellaneous	Table Showing Batteries Which Can Be Concentrated On Each British Trench.		
Heading	H.Q. 23rd Div C.R.A. Vol 4 Nov 15		
War Diary	Croix Du Bac	01/11/1915	30/11/1915
Heading	C.R.A. 23rd Div Vol 5 121/7931		
Heading	War Diary December Original 23rd Divl Arty		

War Diary	Croix Du Bac	30/11/1915	31/12/1915
Heading	C.R.A. 23rd Div Vol 6		
War Diary	Croix Du Bac	01/01/1916	31/01/1916
Miscellaneous	Routine Order No. 89 By Brigadier General D Fasson, C.B. Commanding Royal Artillery, 23rd Division.	17/01/1916	17/01/1916
Miscellaneous	Routine Order No. 98 By Brigadier General D Fasson, C.B. Commanding Royal Artillery, 23rd Division.	30/01/1916	30/01/1916
Miscellaneous	Routine Order No. ?? By Brigadier General D Fasson, C.B. Commanding Royal Artillery, 23rd Division.		
Heading	C.R.A. 23rd Div Vol 6		
Heading	H Q R A 23 Div		
War Diary	Croix Du Bac	01/02/1916	18/02/1916
War Diary	Lynde	19/02/1916	23/02/1916
War Diary	Estaires	24/02/1916	25/02/1916
War Diary	Lynde	26/02/1916	28/02/1916
War Diary	Pernes	29/02/1916	29/02/1916
Miscellaneous	Routine Order No. 101. By Brigadier General D Fasson, C.B. Commanding Royal Artillery 23rd Division.	05/02/1916	05/02/1916
Miscellaneous	Royal Artillery, 23rd Division. App II	07/02/1916	07/02/1916
Miscellaneous	Table "A"		
Miscellaneous	Ref: Sheets 36 And 36a 1/40,000. Table "B"		
Miscellaneous	Ref: Sheets 36 And 36a 1/40,000 Table "B" 3.		
Operation(al) Order(s)	Operation Order No: 30, By Brig: General D.J.M. Fasson C.B. Commanding R.A. 23rd Division. App III	29/02/1916	29/02/1916
Miscellaneous	March Table.		
Heading	C.R.A. 23 Div Vol 8 War Diary For March		
War Diary	Pernes	01/03/1916	07/03/1916
War Diary	Chateau De La Haie	08/03/1916	19/03/1916
War Diary	Bruay	20/03/1916	23/03/1916
War Diary	Boyeffles	24/03/1916	31/03/1916
Miscellaneous	O.C. 102nd Brigade R.F.A. App IV	03/03/1916	03/03/1916
Miscellaneous	Notes On The French Positions.	03/03/1916	03/03/1916
Operation(al) Order(s)	Operation Order No: 31 By Brigadier General D.J.M. Fasson C.B. Commanding R.A. 23rd Division App V	04/03/1916	04/03/1916
Miscellaneous	March Table.		
Miscellaneous	Addenda		
Operation(al) Order(s)	Operation Order No. 32 By Brig: General D.J.M. Fasson C.B. Commanding R.A. 23rd Division App VI	06/03/1916	06/03/1916
Miscellaneous	March Table. (A)		
Miscellaneous	March Table. (B)		
Operation(al) Order(s)	Operation Order No. 33 By Brig General D.J.M. Fasson C.B. Comndg R.A. 23rd Division. App VII	12/03/1916	12/03/1916
Operation(al) Order(s)	Operation Order No. 34 By Brigadier General D.J.M. Fasson C.B. Commanding R.A. 23rd Division. App VIII	16/03/1916	16/03/1916
Miscellaneous	Table "A"		
Miscellaneous	Table "B"		
Operation(al) Order(s)	Operation Order No. 35. By Brigadier General D.J.M. Fasson C.B. App IX	21/03/1916	21/03/1916
Miscellaneous	Table Of Reliefs. (1)		
Miscellaneous	Table Of Reliefs. (2)		
War Diary	Boyeffles	01/04/1916	19/04/1916
War Diary	Le Vielfort	20/04/1916	30/04/1916
Operation(al) Order(s)	Operation Order No: 36, by Lt: Colonel W.A. Nicholson R.F.A. C.R.A. 23rd Division. App X.	03/04/1916	03/04/1916

Miscellaneous	Addenda To R.A. 23rd Division Operation Order No: 36 Of 3rd April, 1916	07/04/1916	07/04/1916
Operation(al) Order(s)	Operation Order No: 37 By Br: General D.J.M. Fasson C.B. Commanding R.A. 23rd Division. App XI	17/04/1916	17/04/1916
Miscellaneous	Table Of Reliefs.		
Operation(al) Order(s)	Routine Order No: 136 By Lieut: Colonel W.A. Nicholson. Commanding Royal Artillery, 23rd Division.	04/04/1916	04/04/1916
Operation(al) Order(s)	Routine Order No. 137 By Lt. Colonel W.A. Nicholson, Commanding Royal Artillery, 23rd Division.	05/04/1916	05/04/1916
Operation(al) Order(s)	Routine Order No. 138. By Lieut. Colonel W.A. Nicholson, Commanding Royal Artillery, 23rd Division.	06/04/1916	06/04/1916
Operation(al) Order(s)	Routine Order No. 139. By Brigadier General D Fasson, C.B. Commanding Royal Artillery, 23rd Division.	12/04/1916	12/04/1916
Operation(al) Order(s)	Routine Order No. 142. Brigadier General D Fasson, C.B. Commanding Royal Artillery, 23rd Division.	17/04/1916	17/04/1916
Miscellaneous	Routine Order No: 143 By Brigadier General D.J. Fasson, C.B., Commanding Royal Artillery, 23rd Division.	18/04/1916	18/04/1916
War Diary	Le Vielfort	01/05/1916	14/05/1916
War Diary	Boyeffles	15/05/1916	31/05/1916
Operation(al) Order(s)	R.A. 23rd Division Order No: 38 Appendix XII	10/05/1916	10/05/1916
Miscellaneous	Table Of Reliefs.		
Miscellaneous	C.O.C. R.A. IVth Corps.	10/05/1916	10/05/1916
Operation(al) Order(s)	R.A. 23rd Division Order No. 38 Appendix XII	10/05/1916	10/05/1916
Miscellaneous	Table Of Reliefs.		
Operation(al) Order(s)	Routine Order No. 153. By Brigadier General D Fasson, C.B. Commanding Royal Artillery, 23rd Division.	01/05/1916	01/05/1916
Miscellaneous	Routine Order No. 160 By Brigadier General D.J.M. Fasson C.B. Commanding Royal Artillery, 23rd Division.	16/05/1916	16/05/1916
Operation(al) Order(s)	Routine Order No. 161. By Brigadier General D.J.M. Fasson C.B. Commanding Royal Artillery 23rd Division.	17/05/1916	17/05/1916
Operation(al) Order(s)	Routine Order No. 162 By Brigadier General D.J.M. Fasson, C.B. Commanding Royal Artillery, 23rd Division.	19/05/1916	19/05/1916
Operation(al) Order(s)	Routine Order No. 163 By Brigadier-General D.J.M. Fasson, C.B. Commanding Royal Artillery 23rd Division.	21/05/1916	21/05/1916
Operation(al) Order(s)	Routine Order No. 168 By Brigadier-General D.J.M. Fasson, C.B. Commanding Royal Artillery, 23rd Division.	28/05/1916	28/05/1916
Operation(al) Order(s)	Routine Order No. 169 By Brigadier General D.J.M. Fasson, C.B. Commanding Royal Artillery, 23rd Division.	30/05/1916	30/05/1916
Operation(al) Order(s)	IVth Corps Order No. 109 Appx XIII	22/05/1916	22/05/1916
Operation(al) Order(s)	47th (London) Division Operation Order No. 63	22/05/1916	22/05/1916
Map			
Operation(al) Order(s)	47th Divisional Artillery Operation Order No. 20	22/05/1916	22/05/1916
Operation(al) Order(s)	IVth Corps Order No. 110 Appx XIVa	22/05/1916	22/05/1916
Miscellaneous	23rd Div Arty. Appx XIV	22/05/1916	22/05/1916
Operation(al) Order(s)	47th Divisional Artillery Operation Order No. 21 Appx XVa	23/05/1916	23/05/1916

Operation(al) Order(s)	47th (London) Division Operation Order No. 64 Appx XV	23/05/1916	23/05/1916
Operation(al) Order(s)	23rd Divisional Artillery Order No. 39 Appx XVI	23/05/1916	23/05/1916
Miscellaneous	R.A. 23rd Division-Table Of Tasks.		
War Diary	Boyeffles	01/06/1916	15/06/1916
War Diary	Clarques Chateau	16/06/1916	25/06/1916
War Diary	Belloy Sur Somme	26/06/1916	29/06/1916
War Diary	Allonville	30/06/1916	30/06/1916
Miscellaneous	23rd Divisional Artillery Special Operation Report. App XVII	02/06/1916	02/06/1916
Operation(al) Order(s)	R.A. 23rd Division Order No. 42 App. XVIII	12/06/1916	12/06/1916
Miscellaneous	Table Of Reliefs.		
Miscellaneous	Addenda To R.A. 23rd Division Order No. 22	12/06/1916	12/06/1916
Miscellaneous	O.C. X/23 T.M. Battery. App XIX	13/06/1916	13/06/1916
Operation(al) Order(s)	Routine Order No. 170 By Brigadier-General D.J.M. Fasson, C.B. Commanding Royal Artillery, 23rd Division.	01/07/1916	01/07/1916
Operation(al) Order(s)	Routine Order No. 171. By Brigadier-General D.J.M. Fasson, C.B. Commanding Royal Artillery, 23rd Division.	02/06/1916	02/06/1916
Operation(al) Order(s)	Routine Order No. 172 By Brigadier-General D.J.M. Fasson, C.B. Commanding Royal Artillery, 23rd Division	03/06/1916	03/06/1916
Operation(al) Order(s)	Routine Order No. 173 By Brigadier-General D.J.M. Fasson, C.B. Commanding Royal Artillery, 23rd Division.	04/06/1916	04/06/1916
Operation(al) Order(s)	Routine Order No. 174 By Brigadier-General D.J.M. Fasson, C.B. Commanding Royal Artillery, 23rd Division.	05/06/1916	05/06/1916
Operation(al) Order(s)	Routine Order No. 175 By Brigadier-General D.J.M. Fasson, C.B. Commanding Royal Artillery, 23rd Division.	06/06/1916	06/06/1916
Operation(al) Order(s)	Routine After Order No. 176 By Brigadier-General D.J.M. Fasson, C.B. Commanding Royal Artillery, 23rd Division.	06/06/1916	06/06/1916
Operation(al) Order(s)	Routine Order No. 176 By Brigadier General D.J.M. Fasson, C.B. Commanding Royal Artillery, 23rd Division.	07/06/1916	07/06/1916
Operation(al) Order(s)	Routine Order No. 177 By Brigadier General D.J.M. Fasson, C.B. Commanding Royal Artillery, 23rd Division.	08/06/1916	08/06/1916
Operation(al) Order(s)	Routine Order No. 178 By Brigadier General D.J.M. Fasson, C.B. Commanding Royal Artillery, 23rd Division.	09/06/1916	09/06/1916
Operation(al) Order(s)	Routine Order No. 179 By Brigadier General D.J.M. Fasson, C.B. Commanding Royal Artillery, 23rd Division.	10/06/1916	10/06/1916
Operation(al) Order(s)	Routine Order No. 180 By Brigadier General D.J.M. Fasson, C.B. Commanding Royal Artillery, 23rd Division.	12/06/1916	12/06/1916
Operation(al) Order(s)	Routine Order No 181 By Brigadier General D.J.M. Fasson, C.B. Commanding Royal Artillery, 23rd Division.	15/06/1916	15/06/1916
Operation(al) Order(s)	Routine Order No 182 By Brigadier General D.J.M. Fasson, C.B. Commanding Royal Artillery, 23rd Division.	17/06/1916	17/06/1916

Operation(al) Order(s)	Routine Order No. 183 By Brigadier General D.J.M. Fasson, C.B. Commanding Royal Artillery, 23rd Division.	18/06/1916	18/06/1916
Operation(al) Order(s)	Routine Order No. 184 By Brigadier General D.J.M. Fasson, C.B. Commanding Royal Artillery, 23rd Division.	20/06/1916	20/06/1916
Operation(al) Order(s)	Routine Order No. 185 By Brigadier General D.J.M. Fasson, C.B., Commanding Royal Artillery, 23rd Division.	21/06/1916	21/06/1916
Operation(al) Order(s)	Routine Order No. 186 By Brigadier General D.J.M. Fasson, C.B., Commanding Royal Artillery, 23rd Division.	22/06/1916	22/06/1916
Operation(al) Order(s)	Routine Orders No. 187 By Brigadier General D.J.M. Fasson, C.B., Commanding Royal Artillery, 23rd Division.	27/06/1916	27/06/1916
Operation(al) Order(s)	Routine Order No. 186 By Brigadier General D.J.M. Fasson, C.B., Commanding Royal Artillery, 23rd Division.	28/06/1916	28/06/1916
Heading	23rd Divisional Artillery C.R.A. 23rd Division. July 1916		
War Diary	Allonville	01/07/1916	01/07/1916
War Diary	Baizieux	02/07/1916	05/07/1916
War Diary	Moulin Vivier	06/07/1916	25/07/1916
War Diary	Albert	26/07/1916	29/07/1916
War Diary	W 27 C. 5.5	30/07/1916	31/07/1916
Operation(al) Order(s)	R.A. Order No. 44 App XIX	01/07/1916	01/07/1916
Miscellaneous	Historical Section (Military Branch),		
Operation(al) Order(s)	R.A. 23rd Division Order No. 40 App XX	06/07/1916	06/07/1916
Miscellaneous	Table A. Bombardment From 7.20 A.M. To 8 A.M.		
Miscellaneous	Table B.		
Miscellaneous	Table C		
Miscellaneous	102nd Bde: App XXI	10/07/1916	10/07/1916
Miscellaneous	Barrage "A"		
Miscellaneous	Barrage "B"		
Miscellaneous	Barrage "C"		
Miscellaneous	Barrage "D"		
Miscellaneous	Barrage "E"		
Miscellaneous	Barrage "F"		
Operation(al) Order(s)	R.A. 23rd Division Order No. 47 App XXII	13/07/1916	13/07/1916
Miscellaneous	Table To Commence At 3.0 A.M. 14th July.		
Map			
Operation(al) Order(s)	R.A. 23rd Division Order No. 48 App XXIII	14/07/1916	14/07/1916
Miscellaneous	Table Of Bombardment		
Operation(al) Order(s)	R.A. 23rd Division Order No. 49 App XXIV	16/07/1916	16/07/1916
Miscellaneous	Left Flank Barrage.		
Miscellaneous	Front Line Barrage.		
Miscellaneous	Support Line Barrage.		
Operation(al) Order(s)	R.A. 23rd Division Order No. 50 App XXV	22/07/1916	22/07/1916
Miscellaneous	Preliminary Fire.		
Miscellaneous	Bombardment.		
Miscellaneous	First Lift.		
Miscellaneous	Second Lift.		
Miscellaneous	Final Barrage.		
Operation(al) Order(s)	R.A. 23rd Division Order No. 51 App XXVI	24/07/1916	24/07/1916
Miscellaneous	Bombardment.		
Miscellaneous	Lift.		

Miscellaneous	Final Barrage.		
Operation(al) Order(s)	R.A. Order No. 52 App XXVII	26/07/1916	26/07/1916
Operation(al) Order(s)	Routine Order No. 189 By Brigadier General D.J.M. Fasson, C.B. Commanding Royal Artillery, 23rd Division.	02/07/1916	02/07/1916
Operation(al) Order(s)	Routine Order No. 190 By Brigadier General D.J.M. Fasson, C.B., Commanding Royal Artillery, 23rd Division.	03/07/1916	03/07/1916
Operation(al) Order(s)	Routine Order No. 191 By Brigadier General D.J.M. Fasson, C.B., Commanding Royal Artillery, 23rd Division.	06/07/1916	06/07/1916
Operation(al) Order(s)	Routine Order No. 192 By Brigadier General D.J.M. Fasson, C.B., Commanding Royal Artillery, 23rd Division.	10/07/1916	10/07/1916
Operation(al) Order(s)	Routine Order No. 193 By Brigadier General D.J.M. Fasson, C.B. Commanding Royal Artillery, 23rd Division.	13/07/1916	13/07/1916
Miscellaneous	After Orders. By Brigadier General D.J.M. Fasson, Commanding Royal Artillery, 23rd Division.	13/07/1916	13/07/1916
Operation(al) Order(s)	Routine Order No. 194 By Brigadier General D.J.M. Fasson, C.B. Commanding Royal Artillery, 23rd Division.	15/07/1916	15/07/1916
Operation(al) Order(s)	Routine Order No. 195 By Brigadier General D.J.M. Fasson, C.B. Commanding Royal Artillery, 23rd Division.	17/07/1916	17/07/1916
Operation(al) Order(s)	Routine Order No. 196 By Brigadier General D.J.M. Fasson, C.B. Commanding Royal Artillery, 23rd Division.	20/07/1916	20/07/1916
Operation(al) Order(s)	Routine Order No. 197 By Brigadier General D Fasson, C.B. Commanding Royal Artillery, 23rd Division.	21/07/1916	21/07/1916
Operation(al) Order(s)	Routine Order No. 198 By Brigadier General D.J.M. Fasson, C.B. Commanding Royal Artillery, 23rd Division.	23/07/1916	23/07/1916
Operation(al) Order(s)	Routine Order No. 199 By Brigadier General D. Fasson C.B. Commanding Royal Artillery, 23rd Division.	27/07/1916	27/07/1916
Operation(al) Order(s)	Routine Order No. 200 By Brigadier General D.J.M. Fasson C.B. Commanding Royal Artillery, 23rd Division.	28/07/1916	28/07/1916
Operation(al) Order(s)	Routine Order No. 201 By Brigadier General D Fasson, C.B. Commanding Royal Artillery, 23rd Division.	29/07/1916	29/07/1916
Operation(al) Order(s)	Routine Order No. 202 By Brigadier General D Fasson, C.B. Commanding Royal Artillery, 23rd Division.	31/07/1916	31/07/1916
Miscellaneous	Routine After Order By Brigadier General D Fasson, C.B. Commanding Royal Artillery, 23rd Division.	31/07/1916	31/07/1916
Heading	23rd Divisional Artillery. C.R.A. 23rd Division August 1916		
War Diary	W 26 C 5.5 (W Of Albert)	01/08/1916	07/08/1916
War Diary	W 26c 5.5.	08/08/1916	14/08/1916
War Diary	Behencourt	15/08/1916	16/08/1916
War Diary	Fletre	17/08/1916	17/08/1916
War Diary	Eecke	18/08/1916	20/08/1916
War Diary	Steenwerck	21/08/1916	28/08/1916
War Diary	Bailleul	29/08/1916	31/08/1916
Operation(al) Order(s)	R.A. 23rd Division Order No. 53 App XXVIII	02/08/1916	02/08/1916
Miscellaneous	Bombardment. Lift.		
Miscellaneous	O.C. 175th Brigade R.F.A. App XXIX	03/08/1916	03/08/1916

Operation(al) Order(s)	R.A. 23rd Division Order No. 54 App XXX	04/08/1916	04/08/1916
Miscellaneous	Bombardment.		
Miscellaneous	Lift.		
Miscellaneous	Final Slow Barrage.		
Miscellaneous	O.C. 102nd Brigade R.F.A. App. XXXI	05/08/1916	05/08/1916
Operation(al) Order(s)	R.A. 23rd Division Order No. 55 App XXXII	06/08/1916	06/08/1916
Miscellaneous	Adjutant 103rd Bde. R.F.A. App XXXIII	07/08/1916	07/08/1916
Miscellaneous	15th Division. App XXXIII	08/08/1916	08/08/1916
Operation(al) Order(s)	R.A. 23rd Division Order No. 56 App XXXIV	10/08/1916	10/08/1916
Miscellaneous	First Relief.		
Miscellaneous	Second Relief.		
Miscellaneous	Subsequent Reliefs.		
Miscellaneous	App XXXV	16/08/1916	16/08/1916
Miscellaneous	Fifth Relief.		
Miscellaneous	Sixth Relief.		
Miscellaneous	Seventh Relief.		
Miscellaneous	Eight Relief.		
Miscellaneous	15th Division. App. XXXVI	11/08/1916	11/08/1916
Miscellaneous	App. XXXVII		
Miscellaneous	Ninth And Last Relief.		
Operation(al) Order(s)	R.A. 23rd Division Order No. 57 App XXXVIII	11/08/1916	11/08/1916
Miscellaneous	Bombardment.		
Miscellaneous	Lifts.		
Miscellaneous	Final Barrage.		
Operation(al) Order(s)	R.A. 23rd Division Order No. 58 App XXXIX	12/08/1916	12/08/1916
Miscellaneous	Table Of Reliefs.		
Miscellaneous	R.A. 23rd Division Order No. 60 App XL	18/08/1916	18/08/1916
Miscellaneous	Table Of Reliefs.		
Miscellaneous	O.C. Right Group. App XLI		
Miscellaneous	Report Of Operations Of 23rd Divisional Artillery From 4th July To 14th August 1916 App XLII	16/08/1916	16/08/1916
Operation(al) Order(s)	Routine Order No. 203 By Brigadier General D Fasson, C.B. Commanding Royal Artillery, 23rd Division.	02/08/1916	02/08/1916
Operation(al) Order(s)	Routine Order No. 204 By Brigadier General D Fasson C.B. Commanding Royal Artillery, 23rd Division.	04/08/1916	04/08/1916
Operation(al) Order(s)	Routine Order No. 205 By Brigadier General D Fasson C.B. Commanding Royal Artillery, 23rd Division.	05/08/1916	05/08/1916
Operation(al) Order(s)	Routine Order No. 206 By Brigadier General D Fasson, C.B. Commanding Royal Artillery, 23rd Division.	07/08/1916	07/08/1916
Operation(al) Order(s)	Routine Order No. 207 By Brigadier General D Fasson, C.B. Commanding Royal Artillery, 23rd Division.	08/08/1916	08/08/1916
Operation(al) Order(s)	Routine Order No. 208 By Brigadier General D Fasson, C.B. Commanding Royal Artillery, 23rd Division.	09/08/1916	09/08/1916
Operation(al) Order(s)	Routine Order No. 209 By Brigadier General D Fasson, C.B. Commanding Royal Artillery, 23rd Division.	11/08/1916	11/08/1916
Operation(al) Order(s)	Routine Order No. 210 By Brigadier General D Fasson, C.B. Commanding Royal Artillery, 23rd Division.	18/08/1916	18/08/1916
Operation(al) Order(s)	Routine Order No. 211 By Brigadier General D Fasson C.B. Commanding Royal Artillery, 23rd Division.	19/08/1916	19/08/1916
Operation(al) Order(s)	Routine Order No. 212 By Brigadier General D Fasson, C.B. Commanding Royal Artillery, 23rd Division.	22/08/1916	22/08/1916
Operation(al) Order(s)	Routine Order No. 213 By Brigadier General D Fasson, C.B. Commanding Royal Artillery, 23rd Division.	24/08/1916	24/08/1916
Operation(al) Order(s)	Routine Order No. 214 By Brigadier General D Fasson, C.B. Commanding Royal Artillery, 23rd Division.	25/08/1916	25/08/1916

Operation(al) Order(s)	Routine Order No. 215 By Brigadier General D Fasson C.B. Commanding Royal Artillery, 23rd Division.	26/08/1916	26/08/1916
Operation(al) Order(s)	Routine Order No. 216 By Brigadier General D Fasson C.B. Commanding Royal Artillery, 23rd Division.	27/08/1916	27/08/1916
Operation(al) Order(s)	Routine Order No. 217 By Brigadier General D.J.M. Fasson C.B. Commanding Royal Artillery, 23rd Division	28/08/1916	28/08/1916
Operation(al) Order(s)	Routine Order No. 218 By Brigadier General D Fasson C.B. Commanding Royal Artillery, 23rd Division.	29/08/1916	29/08/1916
Operation(al) Order(s)	Routine Order No. 219 By Brigadier General D Fasson C.B. Commanding Royal Artillery, 23rd Division.	30/08/1916	30/08/1916
Operation(al) Order(s)	Routine Order No. 220 By Brigadier General D. Fasson, C.B. Commanding Royal Artillery, 23rd Division.	31/08/1916	31/08/1916
Heading	Commander Royal Artillery		

WO 95/2170/2

23RD DIVISION
DIVL ARTILLERY

C. R. A.

~~AUG 1915 DEC 1916~~

1915 AUG – 1916 AUG

23rd Divn

121/7198

H.Q. 23rd Division

Staff Capt. to C.R.A.

Vol 1.

Aug & Sept 15

Instructions regarding War Diaries and Intelligence Summaries are contained in F. S. Regs., Part II. and the Staff Manual respectively. Title pages will be prepared in manuscript.

WAR DIARY
or
~~INTELLIGENCE SUMMARY.~~
(Erase heading not required.)

Army Form C. 2118.

Place	Date	Hour	Summary of Events and Information	Remarks and references to Appendices
LONDON	26.8.15	[illegible] a.m.	Proceeded, as one of advanced billeting party of 23rd Division, to FOLKESTONE	WP
FOLKESTONE	22.8.15	10 a.m.	Proceeded to BOULOGNE	
BOULOGNE	22.8.15	3 p.m.	Proceeded to ST. OMER [illegible] G.H.Q. [illegible] and [illegible]	
ST OMER	22.8.15	6.30 p.m.	[illegible] the next morning	
ST OMER	23.8.15	9 a.m.	The Division was instructed to billet in the area TILQUES – AUDR[illegible] – WATTEN – LOUCHES.	WP
			SCHEME. That of 37th Division. 3 Brigade Areas. HQ Group Area. Artillery Area. Artillery was billetted	
			10[illegible] Bde RUMINGHEM. 10[illegible] Bde POLINCOVE. 10[illegible] Bde [illegible] 10[illegible] Bde BO[illegible]	WP
			Div Art[illegible] TOUAFQUES. HORSES in FIELDS. MEN in BARNS & FARM OUTBUILDINGS	
			As area was 9 miles from St. OMER and extended over 7 miles, detail could not be worked out. Lists of billets and accommodation for each unit [illegible] available	
ST OMER	24.8.15	9 a.m.	[illegible] of Billets changed. 3 Brigades + HQ group. Artillery with Brigades	WP
			HQ group. HQ GRA [illegible] (DA[illegible])	
			Billeted HQ group [illegible] TILQUES and SERQUES	
			[illegible] of 9th [illegible] (Pioneers) [illegible]	
			Divisional Train, Divisional Supply Column, [illegible]	WP
			[illegible]	
			[illegible]	

2353 Wt. W2544/1454 700,000 5/15 D. D. & L. A.D.S.S./Forms/C. 2118.

Reference [illegible]

Army Form C. 2118.

Instructions regarding War Diaries and Intelligence Summaries are contained in F. S. Regs., Part II. and the Staff Manual respectively. Title pages will be prepared in manuscript.

~~WAR DIARY~~ *or* ~~INTELLIGENCE SUMMARY.~~

WAR DIARY

(Erase heading not required.)

Place	Date	Hour	Summary of Events and Information	Remarks and references to Appendices
ST OMER	24/8/15	6 pm	It is decided Staff Captain R.A. [illegible] Artillery Units & units of H.Q. Group.	
ST OMER	25/8/15	[illegible]	~~[illegible]~~	WJS
		9 am	Proceed to TILQUES. [illegible] 23794 [illegible] TILQUES	
		12.30 pm	[illegible] Bde R.F.A. arrive [illegible] CAUES [illegible] Guides from Battery [illegible] to lead succeeding battery. A similar system of guides [illegible] was used for all succeeding batteries.	
			A list of billets was handed over to the O.C. of the first battery to be given to each battery on arrival.	WJS
			The Mayor of the village was informed of the arrival of [illegible]. The village [illegible] used as guides to billets. A.S.C. [illegible] billets at TILQUE	
ST OMER	26.8.15	11 am	Advanced Party of [illegible] arrive [illegible] proceed to TILQUE [illegible]. [illegible] Billets [illegible] handed out to [illegible] party.	WJS
			103rd Bde arrive. ADRIGHEM 1st Battery [illegible] by Brigade [illegible] Batteries arriving [illegible] all one day's ration [illegible].	
TILQUES	27.8.15		105th Bde R.F.A. arrive at ST OMER 13 miles from billets at BOSSARGUES. Are conducted as other brigades.	WJS
			H.Q. [illegible] TILQUES [illegible]	
	28.8.15		104th Bde continue to arrive followed by 106 Bde at ST OMER [illegible] conducted to [illegible] at TOURNEHEM.	WJS

2353 Wt. W2514/1454 700,000 5/15 D. D. & L. A.D.S.S./Forms/C. 2118.

Ref BELGIUM [illegible] HAZEBROUCK

Instructions regarding War Diaries and Intelligence Summaries are contained in F. S. Regs., Part II. and the Staff Manual respectively. Title pages will be prepared in manuscript.

WAR DIARY
or
~~INTELLIGENCE~~ SUMMARY.
(Erase heading not required.)

Army Form C. 2118.

Place	Date	Hour	Summary of Events and Information	Remarks and references to Appendices
TILQUE	29.8.15	—	Cable Sect. & H.Q. R.E. [illegible] billeted at TILQUE	
	29.8.15	—	10th [illegible] complete arrival.	
			Sanitary Section, Mobile Vet. Section arrive and are billeted at TILQUES	WP
			23rd Div. Cavalry [illegible] billets at SERQUE.	
			23rd Div. Am. Col. commence to arrive at AUDRICQUES [illegible] billets at ZOUAFQUES	
TILQUE	30.8.15		D. A. C. complete and billeted at ZOUAFQUES	
			[illegible]	
			28-29 [illegible]	
			Four cars for division for D.A.Q.M.G, D.A.D.O.S, & Staff [illegible]	
			[illegible]	
			[illegible]	
			It is [illegible]	WP
			necessary for H.Q. Group.	
			The senior supply officer must [illegible] the [illegible]	
			[illegible] should be informed [illegible]	
			REFILLING POINT.	

2353 Wt. W2544/1454 700,000 5/15 D. D. & L. A.D.S.S./Forms/C. 2118.

Instructions regarding War Diaries and Intelligence Summaries are contained in F. S. Regs., Part II. and the Staff Manual respectively. Title pages will be prepared in manuscript.

WAR DIARY
or
~~INTELLIGENCE SUMMARY.~~
(Erase heading not required.)

Army Form [illegible]2118.

Place	Date	Hour	Summary of Events and Information	Remarks and references to Appendices
TILQUES	31.8.15	—	Ammunition was drawn by 23rd DIV. Sub Park from ARQUES and delivered to 23rd D.A.C at ZOUAFQUES to complete.	
TILQUES.	1.9.15	—	No Report	
	2.9.15	—	Ditto	WJP
	3.9.15	—	Ditto	
	4.9.15	—	Ditto	
TILQUES	5.9.15	—	Exchange of 18 Pr Shrapnel for H.E. by 103, 104 Bdes. Orders for march and billet ~~[illegible]~~ ARQUES — HAZEBROUCK received.	
RENESCURE	6.9.15	—	Division billeted from ARQUES to HAZEBROUCK. Tram arrangements caused wandering of baggage vehicles	WJP
MERRIS	7.9.15	—	ARTILLERY billeted BORRE – PRADELLES – STRAZEELE – VIEUX BERQUIN – NEUF BERQUIN CAUDESCURE – Le Gd. HASARD. Billeting officers were met at HAZEBROUCK, after seeing area in early morning, and areas were allotted to Brigades & D.A.C. Units moved in during afternoon. Orders to 102nd Brigade re Batteries to be attached to 27th Division for instruction, to 103rd re personnel for instruction, to 104 Bde re Batteries attached for instruction, to 105th Bde re 3 batteries to 27th Div for instruction, to 105th Bde re one battery to 20th Division for instruction were delivered. Supplies to be arranged for between S.S.O of divisions.	WJP
" "	8.9.15	—	Batteries moved off into areas as arranged. 102nd Brigade reported almost complete lack of supplies owing to wandering of supply vehicles. Sub Park placed under direct orders of 3rd Echelon	WJP
" "	9.9.15	—	3 Batteries of 105th Brigade joined 27th DIV for instruction. 1 batt. 105th Bde joined 20th DIV for instruction. 2 Batteries each of 102nd Bde + 104th joined 27th DIV for instruction. Personnel amounting 2 officers and 12 men of each battery of 103rd Bde also joined for instruction. Supply arrangements made by 27th DIV.	
" "	10.9.15		No report	WJP
" "	11.9.15		No report	
" "	12.9.15		Sections of each battery from 23rd DIV not yet in area of 27th DIV relieve one section from battery of 27th DIV and take over corresponding waggon line	
" "	13.9.15		No report	
" "	14.9.15		Remaining sections, with brigade ammunition columns relieve 27th DIV. 23rd DAC relieves 27th D.A.C.	

Army Form C. 2118.

WAR DIARY
or
~~INTELLIGENCE SUMMARY.~~
(Erase heading not required.)

Instructions regarding War Diaries and Intelligence Summaries are contained in F. S. Regs., Part II. and the Staff Manual respectively. Title pages will be prepared in manuscript.

Place	Date	Hour	Summary of Events and Information	Remarks and references to Appendices
MERRIS	15.9.15	9.am	With Brigade major went to CROIX DU BAC to take over from R.A 27th DIVISION. Time was spent in getting information of positions of units and ideas for forthcoming operations.	WJP
CROIX DU BAC	16.9.15	a.m.	G.O.C. R.A took over command from G.O.C. R.A 27th DIVISION. Preliminary arrangements made with regard to ammunition supply for operations. A distribution of rounds had to be made as shown in SCS 19.	WJP
" " "	17.9.15	—	Ammunition was drawn from park as ordered in corps letter and distributed to brigades.	
" " "	18.9.15	—	Special Ammunition was drawn for operations. It was not found that any 18 Pr. H.E. shell should be exchanged.	WJP
" " "	19.9.15	—	A special dump of the whole of the contents of the sub park was ordered. This was dumped at H.Q. 23rd D.A.C and Colonel Drury placed in charge.	WJP Special Orders No 1
" " "	20.9.15	—	No allotment of ammunition was made by the army. The brigades were ordered to draw up to a fixed maximum unless otherwise ordered.	WJP
" " "	21.9.15	—	Those batteries which had wagon lines north of the river LYS were ordered to remove their wagon lines south of the river. Steady bombardment of enemy's position commenced this day. Ammunition expended being replaced from earlychurch.	WJP
" " "	22.9.15	—	Reports as to prematures with 18 Pr. H.E. were ordered and also the observation of the 100 fuze were 4.5 H.E. The bombardment continued	WJP
" " "	23.9.15	—	The wagon lines of one brigade were removed south of the river. The position of the ammunition column of 102nd Bde was moved nearer the guns. The bombardment continued	WJP
" " "	24.9.15	—	The wagon lines and column of 104 Bde were moved. The wagon lines south of the river. The S.A. A sections of the columns were advanced to positions south of the river. This the fourth day of the bombardment. The headquarters of the R.A. 23rd DIV moved to battle headquarters. Staff Captain for ammunition and supply remaining at CROIX DU BAC.	WJP
" " "	25.9.15	—	Success of Division on our right and of French reported. First prisoners seen to march through CROIX DU BAC. The supply of ammunition to D.A.C. good	WJP

2353 Wt. W2544/1454 700,000 5/15 D. D. & L. A.D.S.S./Forms/C. 2118.

Army Form C. 2118.

WAR DIARY

or

~~INTELLIGENCE SUMMARY.~~

(Erase heading not required.)

Instructions regarding War Diaries and Intelligence Summaries are contained in F. S. Regs., Part II. and the Staff Manual respectively. Title pages will be prepared in manuscript.

Place	Date	Hour	Summary of Events and Information	Remarks and references to Appendices
CROIX DU BAC	26.9.15	—	Supply of ammunition readjusted. Owing to advance and retirement of division on our right expenditure of ammunition was heavy. A readjustment was therefore necessary. The amount of rounds for the remaining operations being revised. The amount of ammunition expended was reduced to a minimum	[illegible]
	27.9.15	—	Nothing of note. The staff left battn. HQ returned to CROIX DU BAC.	[illegible]
	28.9.15	—	Nothing of note to report	[illegible]
	29.9.15	—	Readjustment of proportion in 18 Pr Ammunition.	[illegible]
	30.9.15	—	8 Wagon lines north & south of RIVER LYS ordered. In event of retirement these wagon lines south could be near for guns in advanced positions. The bridges would also be kept more free from traffic. Ammunition columns changed their positions to north side of river.	[illegible]

Staff Copy

SECRET.   This order is not to be taken into the trenches.

OPERATION ORDER NO.1   Copy No. 9

BY

Brigadier General D. Fasson, C.B.

Commanding Royal Artillery, 23rd Division.

Ref. 1/10000 Map.sheet 36

1. Offensive operations are to be carried out by the 3rd Corps, beginning on the 25th September, as part of the operations of the First Army. The Eighth Division is going to capture the hostile trenches between the CORNER FORT N.6.d.1.6 and BRIDOUX FORT I.31.d. both inclusive.
   The further objective of the 8th Division is to be the capture of BAS MAISNIL, LE BRIDOUX and Fme HOUSSAIN with a view to bringing under effective fire the FROMELLES - RADINGHEM road and preparing the way for a subsequent advance of the whole Corps on to the AUBERS - RADINGHEM RIDGE, should such an advance be ordered.

2. The 23rd Division will co-operate by Artillery, Machine Guns, Rifle fire and Search Lights against the enemy's trenches between I.32.a.5.5 and I.21.c.5.2 and be prepared to take advantage of any success to assault the trenches on their front.

3. A timetable of operations to be carried out by the 23rd Division to assist the 8th Division is given in attached Appendix 1. (Artillery programme Appendix 2)

4. The general outline of operations will be as follows:-
   21st, 22nd, 23rd and 24th September Artillery bombardment which will continue night and day.
   25th September assault by 8th Division at daylight.

5. As the enemy is certain to employ gas shells special care will be taken by all commanding officers that gas helmets are carried by all ranks and are eff in efficient condition.

6. The attacking brigade of the 8th Division will mark the position of their bombers and their advanced Infantry in the German trenches by means of RED FLAGS.

7. The Artillery will be under the immediate orders of the C.R.A. but Infantry Brigadiers may call on them in case of necessity.

8. A programme of Artillery targets for each day will be issued the evening before - being arranged as far as possible so as to have fire on some part of the enemy's line during most of the day. The two principal points in front trenches which will be bombarded are salient at I.26.b.8.5. and salient at I.26.c.8.1 - and in front of both these wire will be cut - in the latter case by the 8th Division.
   The other targets will be support trenches, M.G. emplacements, cross roads, etc. Infantry Brigades are requested to inform H.Q. R.A. or their R.A. Group Commander of any suitable targets they know of.

9. During these operations the S.ec of C/104 at I.14.a.6.6., the Sec. of D/104 at I.13.c.4 6 and D/102 will come under the orders (tactically) of O.C. "A" Group.

10. Sould any alterations in the daily programme become necessary Group Commanders will at once notify them to Infantry Brigade Commanders concerned and Headquarters R.A.

11. The amount of ammunition allowed for the operations has not yet been finally approved.
For the 21st inst the following will be the maximum expenditure -

Four batteries shooting at the two salients	30 rounds per gun	H.E.
	12	Shrap.
For other batteries	12 rounds per gun	H.E.
	50	Shrap.
C/102 Counter battery	30 rounds per gun	Shrap.

Except as regards the number of rounds to be fired at the two salients, the number of rounds to be fired at each target on the programme, and any other targets which it may become necessary to engage during the day, will be fixed by Group Commanders.

12. At least one day's supply of ammunition on the above basis will be dumped at the guns and replenished each night. Should it be possible to dump more (up to 2 days supply) this will be done.

13. At the conclusion of the shooting on each target a telephonic report of the effect obtained will be sent through Group Commanders to H.Q.R.A.

14. Reports to CROIX DU BAC until 4 p.m. September 24th after which time they will be sent to ROLANDERIE FARM H.11.c.

Charles Bruce
Capt.
Brigade Major, R.A.
23rd Division.

Issued at 1.30 a.m. by Motor Cyclist.

Copy No.1 A Group
... 2 B Group
... 3 23 Div.
... 4 8th Div.Arty.
... 5 50th Div. Arty
... 6 3 Corps
... 7 B-G.R.A.
... 8 B.M.R.A.
... 9 S.C.R.A.
... 10 - 11 - 12 Filed.

SECRET

23RD DIVISIONAL ARTILLERY.

Tuesday 21st Sept.1915.

TIME	TARGET	BATTERY SHOOTING	AMMUNITION.
9-0 a.m. to 9-45 a.m.	Parapet Salient I.26.b.8.5.	A/102	H.E.
10-10 a.m. to 11-35 a.m.	(Support Trench I.27.a	Sec.D/104 near Moat-Farm.	Shrap.
	(Brewery Support (trench I.22.c.	Do. Do.	Shrap.
	(German House	B/104	H.E.
11-55 a.m.	Salient I.26.c.8.1	D/102	H.E.
12-57 p.m. to 2-20 p.m.	Trench at LE QUESNE	B/102	Shrap.
	Salient I.26.c.8.1.	B/102	H.E.
2-50 p.m. to 3-45 p.m.	(M.G. in I.27.b.2.5	B/104	H.E.
	(Support Trench I.27.a	Sec.D/104 Nr.Moat Farm	Shrap.
	(Distillery trenches	B/104	Shrap.
4.5 p.m. to 5-30 p.m.	(Parapet I.26.b.8.5	A/102	H.E.
	(M.G. I.27.c.0.1	A/102	H.E.

NIGHT.

8 p.m. to 4 a.m.	Parapet I.26.b.8.5 40 rounds in bursts of 2.	A/102	Shrap.
8 p.m. to Midnight	Parapet I.26.c	D/102	Shrap.
Midnight to 4 a.m.	ditto. 20 rounds each in bursts of 2.	B/102	Shrap.

APPENDIX 1.

21st September	Artillery bombardment.
22nd September	ditto
23rd September	ditto
	The 69th and 70th Bdes. will send up two rockets each at 8 p.m. and the men will cheer as if they were going to attack.
24th September	Artillery bombardment. Rifle and Machine Gun Fire from front trenches along the front of the 69th and 70th Brigades on points which have been previously bombarded. Night firing by Machine Guns on enemy's lines of approach and where the wire has been cut. The Search Lights are to assist the fire of the Naval Guns at 10 p.m. Their position will be arranged by the C.R.E
25th September	The 8th Division will attack the enemy at daylight. Infantry and Machine Guns will open rapid fire on enemy's trenches and communications at an hour which will be given later and support 8th Div. attack.

D

23rd Div.

121/7595.

H.Q. 23rd Div: Staff Capt: R.A.

Vol 2

Oct 15

nil

Cn.

A. G. Office
Base

Herewith War Diary
October 1915

Staff Captain
RA 23rd Division

W. J. Smith [illegible]
Staff Captain
RA 23rd Division

1. 11. 15

Army Form C. 2118.

Instructions regarding War Diaries and Intelligence Summaries are contained in F. S. Regs., Part II. and the Staff Manual respectively. Title pages will be prepared in manuscript.

WAR DIARY
or
~~INTELLIGENCE SUMMARY.~~
(Erase heading not required.)

Staff Captain RA 23rd DIV

Place	Date	Hour	Summary of Events and Information	Remarks and references to Appendices
ROIX DU BAC	1.10.15		Work commenced on construction of horse standings shelters etc	
	2.10.15		Nothing of note to report	
	3.10.15		" " "	
	4.10.15			
	5.10.15		" " "	
	6.10.15			
	7.10.15			
	8.10.15			
	9.10.15		" " " "	
	10.10.15			
	11.10.15			
	12.10.15			
	13.10.15		Ammunition supply for defence scheme was drafted	
	14.10.15		Nothing of note to report	
	16.10.15		" " " " "	
	17.10.15		" " "	
	18.10.15		Ammunition dumps returned to railhead	
	19.10.15		Nothing of note to report	
	20.10.15		Area of forest at LAMOTTE allotted. Working parties detailed for wood cutting and obtaining [illegible] for [illegible]	
	21.10.15		Areas for brigades and Divisional Ammunition column allotted	
	22.10.15		Cutting commenced by parties from each brigade and Divisional Ammunition Column	
	23.10.15		The wood from Forest of Nieppe was carted to build shelters for horse lines	
	24.10.15		No report	
	25.10.15		" "	
	26.10.15		" "	
	27.10.15		Positions of emergency wagon lines south of the river LYS were allotted.	
	28.10.15		No report	
	29.10.15		No report	
	30.10.15		" "	
	31.10.15		"	

2353 Wt. W2544/1454 700,000 5/15 D. D. & L. A.D.S.S./Forms/C. 2118.

Staff Capt: 15 C.R.A.
23rd Div:
Vol: 3

121
1761

Nov. 15

Army Form C. 2118.

Instructions regarding War Diaries and Intelligence Summaries are contained in F. S. Regs., Part II. and the Staff Manual respectively. Title pages will be prepared in manuscript.

WAR DIARY
or
~~INTELLIGENCE SUMMARY.~~

(Erase heading not required.)

Staff Captain
RA 23rd Division

Place	Date	Hour	Summary of Events and Information	Remarks and references to Appendices
CROIX DU BAC	1.11.15		Advance parties of 2 Battys Hows. 50th Division were brought into billets in area near proposed battery positions. The material necessary was hauled at night to the positions to make gun emplacements. Arrangements were made to ration these parties from the 4th Bde	WP
	2.11.15		Wagon lines were allotted to 5" How Batteries of 50th Divn	WP
	8.11.15		Arrangements made for wagon lines to have subsidiary huts erected by artificers of the battery. The construction of shelters for the horse lines continues. The timber cutting party at work at LAMOTTE have very adverse conditions. Endeavour is to be made to billet the men. The exchange of 200 mules of the 23rd D.A.C for infantry transport horses of the MEERUT DIVISION was completed.	WP
	9.11.15		The greater proportion of the men working in the forest were put in billets	WP
	10.11.15		Billetting of men in the forest completed. A return was called for of all gun spares deficient in brigades. A distribution of spares available in the D.A.C was made. Indents for the large number outstanding are to be rendered and a letter sent drawing attention to the large deficiency.	WP
	13.11.15		Captain Broad reports departure on appointment as STAFF OFFICER RA ~~3rd~~ Corps	WP
	14.11.15		Captain CLIBBORN reports arrival as BRIGADE MAJOR RA 23rd DIVISION	
	28.11.15		Owing to bad weather, lack of experience in officers, very large number of horses had to be evacuated. Possibly the long journey to LAMOTTE is a contributory cause. The wagon lines show need of care in planning on low lying ground which is easily flooded. Work of constructing subsidiary huts for ablution rooms, latrines ~~and~~ dining rooms and drying rooms continues.	WP
			[illegible]	
			[illegible]	

2353 Wt. W2544/1454 700,000 5/15 D. D. & L. A.D.S.S./Forms/C. 2118.

23rd Division

Headquarters 23rd Div: C.R.A.

Vol: I

Ind

Instructions regarding War Diaries and Intelligence Summaries are contained in F. S. Regs., Part II. and the Staff Manual respectively. Title pages will be prepared in manuscript.

WAR DIARY
or
~~INTELLIGENCE SUMMARY~~.
(Erase heading not required.)

Army Form C. 2118.

1

Place	Date	Hour	Summary of Events and Information	Remarks and references to Appendices
BOULOGNE	1915 Aug 25		Left LIPHOOK Stn at 5.50 pm with DIV HQ and 10th 5th Fusiliers. Arrived FOLKESTONE 9.30 pm BOULOGNE 11.30 pm. Put up for night at LOUVRE HOTEL. Motored next morning to ST OMER.	
TILQUES	Aug 26th		Met Lt Smith Staff Captain RA at S. MARTIN. Div HQ RA billetted at Chateau de TAFFIN TILQUES. Accommodation good. About ½ mile to DIV HQ at Chateau de HOGUET. But 6-7 miles away from F.A. Bdes. 102 Bde arrived 25th. 103 Bde arrived 26th. Train all late. Lieut Pritchard R.E joined us today to run our communications. Communication opened with Div HQ at 3 pm.	
"	Aug 27th		105 Bde arrives. Decided to organize correspondence as follows. General correspondence continuous serial numbers. Kept in one Central Registry No DA etc. Secret do " " " Two Registers B.M S and S.C S. Field message book Daily serial numbers. F etc for CRA } carbon copies BM — BM } are registered. S.C — S.C }	
"	28th		1. All Brigades arrived & billetted as follows. 102 FA Bde RUNNINGHEM, 103 " " POLINCOVE, 104 " " Tournehem (last batteries arrive during night), 105 " " BONNINGUES. All on the St LOUIS RIVER.	Billets 28th
			2. Orders are issued by Div HQ to the "Group" in which each Brigade lies. It remains to be seen if this is entirely satisfactory, as in Routine matters much of the responsibility will eventually fall on the Div Arty & the responsibility for respective orders lies with Inf. Brigadiers. CB	Orders when billetted in "Groups"

2353 Wt. W2544/1454 700,000 5/15 D. D. & L. A.D.S.S./Forms/C. 2118.

Instructions regarding War Diaries and Intelligence Summaries are contained in F. S. Regs., Part II. and the Staff Manual respectively. Title pages will be prepared in manuscript.

WAR DIARY
or
~~INTELLIGENCE~~ SUMMARY.
(Erase heading not required.)

Army Form C. 2118

2

Place	Date	Hour	Summary of Events and Information	Remarks and references to Appendices
TILQUES	29/8		1. D.A.C is arriving + billetting at ZOUAFQUES	D.A.C
		6 pm	2. Visit from G.H.Q in the afternoon about ammunition. 16 rds H.E per 18 pr is now allowed but fuze is still unsafe. Shrapnel for 4.5 not available so 100% Lyddite may be expected. Proper How. proportion is now 70 to 30.	Amtn.
			3. The amtn sub-Park will always be with us unless the Corps require its amtn for another division when they may take it	
			4. The number of rounds available in action is therefore 26256 or about 410 per gun.	
"	30/8		1. No entry.	
"	31/8		1. No entry	

Charles Brand
Capt RA
Reaching 28 Div

2353 Wt. W2544/1454 700,000 5/15 D. D. & L. A.D.S.S./Forms/C. 2118.

23rd Division

121/6991

H.Q. 23rd Division C.R.A.

Vol: II

June? to Sept. 15

Aug 15
to
Dec 16

Instructions regarding War Diaries and Intelligence Summaries are contained in F. S. Regs., Part II. and the Staff Manual respectively. Title pages will be prepared in manuscript.

WAR DIARY
or
~~INTELLIGENCE~~ SUMMARY.
(Erase heading not required.)

Army Form C. 2118.

Place	Date	Hour	Summary of Events and Information	Remarks and references to Appendices
TILQUES	June 1st	1915	1. Divisional Field day. Touch rather lost as commanders did not report their positions. Officers patrols good & improving.	
			2. Started "Secret" Register with 3 files (a) Tactics (b) Technical matter (c) Spies & information.	
"	2nd		1. Div: Arty Tactical Day. All batteries out. Scheme Bombardment of a line of Trenches. Batteries registered points during the morning & sent in identification Traces of zones of fire. Dead ground was in most cases forgotten. Communication worked well on the whole except that duplication by visual means was neglected. The identification Traces show the capabilities of each Brigade. These should be combined with a list of Targets showing the batteries that have registered that Target. Then Div: Hd RA knows exactly what its power is on every target at a glance. These "Div" Targets are allotted high numbers so as not to confuse them with targets of only Brigade or Battery interest. System will be further tried next Monday.	
"	3rd		1. No entry.	
	4th		1. Laying competition held. Won by 104 - second 103 third 102 Bde	
	5th		1. Orders received to march on 6th	

2353 Wt. W2544/1454 700,000 5/15 D. D. & L. A.D.S.S./Forms/C. 2118.

Instructions regarding War Diaries and Intelligence Summaries are contained in F. S. Regs., Part II. and the Staff Manual respectively. Title pages will be prepared in manuscript.

WAR DIARY
or
INTELLIGENCE SUMMARY.
(Erase heading not required.)

Army Form C. 2118.

2

Place	Date 1915	Hour	Summary of Events and Information	Remarks and references to Appendices
TILQUES	Sept 6th		1. Marched East & billetted in depth as follows. 102 Bde HAZEBROUCK 103 Bde SERCUS 104 Bde 105 Bde BANDRINGHAM DAC RENESCURE AIRA RENESCURE. March Table attached.	app I
			2. Changed from marching in groups to "fighting formation". Artillery was scattered over 12 miles distance - orders received about 5 pm & out to Bdes by 8 am. Delivered personally by BM in car & S.C. on horseback.	
MERRIS	7th		1. March of RA delayed by infantry straggling. all Bdes billetted by 7 pm as follows. 102 CAUDESCURE 103 Pt Sec Bois 104 STRAZEELE 105 BORRE DAC LE TIR ANGLAIS - see app II	app II
			2. Orderlies from each Bde reported by 7 pm.	
			3. Visited 20th & 27th Div HQ RA and arranged for attachment of batteries & issued orders see app III	app III
MERRIS	8th		1. Four miles an hour just about the correct rate to allow for artillery concentrating on a starting Point.	
			2. Batteries in app III moved up a section each during night 8/9th and occupied positions as follows. Ref. 1/20000 sheet 36. see app IV	app IV
			3. Most batteries started at noon & got into pits by 10 pm.	

2353 Wt. W2544/1454 700,000 5/15 D. D. & L. A.D.S.S./Forms/C. 2118.

Instructions regarding War Diaries and Intelligence Summaries are contained in F. S. Regs., Part II. and the Staff Manual respectively. Title pages will be prepared in manuscript.

Army Form C. 2118.

WAR DIARY
or
INTELLIGENCE SUMMARY.
(Erase heading not required.)

3

Place	Date	Hour	Summary of Events and Information	Remarks and references to Appendices
MERRIS	1915 Sept 9th		1. Visited batteries in action - all defences have been greatly improved since last winter - Gun emplacements look as safe now as the turret of a battleship - The men live in the big dugouts behind the guns and all are lined with wood & have water proof ~~[illegible]~~ roofs. There is not much doing. The E exit to ARMENTIERES is shelled frequently but the battery positions are apparently mostly undiscovered.	
"	10th		1. Visited HQ RA 27 Div and got maps showing position of all guns in 27th Div zone i.e. BOIS GRENIER - TOUQUET road to ARMENTIERES LILLE road. This zone is divided into 2 groups as only 2 Inf Bdes are in first line. Two Inf Bdes are thus unemployed which seems a waste but no solution is forthcoming at present. Also saw maps of 2nd line & the "GHQ" rear line. The latter is apparently not yet properly dug in. All concentration of fire appears to be left to the Group Commanders. No tables were available showing the "gun power" for concentration on different parts of the front. Visited [illegible] HQ of 12th RA Bde and found there that no real information was available for concentration of fire - concentration is all very well but it seems that for a big show the CRA must know exactly what every battery can do all along the front.	

2353 Wt. W2544/1454 700,000 5/15 D. D. & L. A.D.S.S./Forms/C. 2118.

Army Form C. 2118.

4

Instructions regarding War Diaries and Intelligence Summaries are contained in F. S. Regs., Part II. and the Staff Manual respectively. Title pages will be prepared in manuscript.

WAR DIARY
or
INTELLIGENCE SUMMARY.
(Erase heading not required.)

Place	Date	Hour	Summary of Events and Information	Remarks and references to Appendices
MERRIS	11th		1. Arrangements for taking over from 27 Div hastened. All batteries in action to remain & five additional sections sent up today from A/103 B/103 C/103 A/102 A/104 batteries.	
			2. Taking over just before an attack is contemplated made things rather complicated.	
	12th		1. The last three remaining half batteries ordered up today. The batteries are now located as follows, i.e. those sections in action.	

A/102	I 13 b 2 9	A/103	I 19 a 2 1	A/104	I 7 b 4 5	A/105	I 19 d 8 8
B/102	H 18 b 6 7	B/103	H 24 a 6 7	B/104	I 13 b 1 9	B/105	H 18 [illegible] 0 5
C/102	I 8 d 0 3	C/103	H 24 b 8 8	C/104	H 12 b 8 4	C/105	[illegible]
D/102	I 1 d 6 5	D/102	H 30 a 6 6	D/104	I 13 c 4 5	D/105	H 29 b 2 6

The grouping of the batteries to fit the [illegible] will be completed tomorrow – 103 & 105 are definitely under orders of 8th Div for offence.

23 Div Operation Order No 3 attached — App V

2353 Wt. W2544/1454 700,000 5/15 D. D. & L. A.D.S.S./Forms/C. 2118.

Army Form C. 2118.

5

Instructions regarding War Diaries and Intelligence Summaries are contained in F. S. Regs., Part II. and the Staff Manual respectively. Title pages will be prepared in manuscript.

WAR DIARY
or
INTELLIGENCE SUMMARY.
(Erase heading not required.)

Place	Date Sept	Hour	Summary of Events and Information	Remarks and references to Appendices
MERRIS	13th		1. Issued orders for all AC's to exchange billets with AC's 27 Div on 14th	
			2. Issued orders for all remaining sections to move up on night 14/15 so that 23 Div Arty (less C/105) will all be in action then.	app VI
			3 Traces not yet got in from batteries in action – slowness no doubt due to first time in action.	
			Guns have been grouped temporarily as follows but without traces it is probably not the best grouping that could have been made.	
			Rt Group A/102, B/102, D/102 — Left Group 104 Bde, C/102	
			103 & 105 Bdes remain attached to 8th Div but we may call on them in case of emergency.	
MERRIS	14th		1. Batteries grouped into two groups see App VII	app VII
			2. The handing over except for HQRA will be complete tonight. It has been much hindered I think by lack of system.	
			3. The handing over has been complicated by the movement of batteries into 8th Div area. But if all available information as to battery positions, wagon lines, observation station etc had been tabulated in one file & a map prepared for it, the handing over would have been easier for us. Another file showing suggested moves for us with a second map would have further helped us. No general scheme showing the stages of relief	

2353 Wt. W2544/1454 700,000 5/15 D. D. & L. A.D.S.S./Forms/C. 2118.

Instructions regarding War Diaries and Intelligence Summaries are contained in F. S. Regs., Part II. and the Staff Manual respectively. Title pages will be prepared in manuscript.

WAR DIARY
or
INTELLIGENCE SUMMARY.
(Erase heading not required.)

Army Form C. 2118.

6

Place	Date	Hour	Summary of Events and Information	Remarks and references to Appendices
			was prepared; and the supply arrangements could only straight[?] of day by day. The enemy has been quiet so that nothing untoward has occurred except that the rations & forage have been short in many cases & often very late.	
CROIX DU BAC	Sept – 15	10 am	Took over from 27th Div Arty	
	16		1. Spent the day in classifying papers & registering aerial photos. 2. Batteries were finally grouped into two groups to correspond to 2 / Bdes. See app. 3. S.O.S. call at night but a false alarm.	App VIII IX
	17		1. Another day in office – issued orders for night arrangements & began to make a Divisional Register of Targets. 2. The Groups are very slow in getting in their arcs of fire & panoramas which delays all preparation for divisional control of fire.	
	18		1. Allotment of ammn for operation is 112 HE & 336 Sh for 18 pr. All our 4.5 are with 8th Div.	
	19		1. Considerable difficulty in deciding how to use the ammn for the 10 days battle as there is very little data to go on. More information may be forthcoming at the conference tomorrow.	

Instructions regarding War Diaries and Intelligence Summaries are contained in F. S. Regs., Part II. and the Staff Manual respectively. Title pages will be prepared in manuscript.

WAR DIARY
or
INTELLIGENCE SUMMARY.
(Erase heading not required.)

Army Form C. 2118.

7

Place	Date	Hour	Summary of Events and Information	Remarks and references to Appendices
CROIX DU BAC	Sept ~~?~~ 20th		1. Reconnoitred in morning for position to enfilade B Group & found one in Rue CHARLES. Old pits in good repair - observation in the CONVENT RUE GRENIER.	
			2. Visited CRA 50 Div and arranged details for artillery cooperation at junction of division. Two batteries on each side told off to help. Both Group Cmdrs to arrange all details.	
			2. Conference in the evening to arrange targets for tomorrow's bombardment. 1st day of 1st Army Offensive. Total allowance of ammn for 4 days to the div. & 1st days Targets attached.	App X
	~~?~~ 21st		1. First day. Programme carried out - See attached Report - Hostile gun fire feeble. Communication are still bad. It is impossible to be certain of being able to talk. Reports were slow in coming in.	App XI App XII App XIII
	22nd		1. Second day. Enemy produced very little artillery. One large shell fell in the night & did not explode so it affords indication of whereabouts of battery.	
			2. Both parapets were well knocked about & I 27 d breached in 8 places. Various M.G. have been located (?) & knocked out. The wire at I 27 b has been well cleared out but the grass & trees prevent details being seen. An officers patrol last night gave no really definite information.	
			3. Got a very necessary big cable & began to work out details for our advance if it takes place. The objectives are BOIS BLANCS and TROIS FETUS. The identification traces of the Boches are I fancy unreliable so sent round for the ~~[illegible]~~ bearing of	

2353 Wt. W2544/1454 700,000 5/15 D. D. & L. A.D.S.S./Forms/C. 2118.

Instructions regarding War Diaries and Intelligence Summaries are contained in F. S. Regs., Part II. and the Staff Manual respectively. Title pages will be prepared in manuscript.

WAR DIARY
or
INTELLIGENCE SUMMARY.
(Erase heading not required.)

Army Form C. 2118.

8

Place	Date	Hour	Summary of Events and Information	Remarks and references to Appendices
			of extreme right switch of each battery. We now possess aerial photos of all the ground that we shall want to go over in the first advance.	appx XIV
			4 Last night was quite quiet.	
Sept 23rd			1. Bombardment carried on. Still difficult to tell if wire is cut as it takes patrols three hours to go out & look & then the enemy mend the wire.	
			2. Hostile artillery much more active but batteries were not shelled.	
			3. Received orders to carry out a false alarm tomorrow morning for 7 mins. Programme for 24th & 25th attached.	appx XV appx XVI appx XVI appx XVII
24			1. Alarm carried out but not much reply from enemy.	
			2. Daily programme carried out.	
			3. Two armoured cars shot with two 3 pr for 10 mins near BURNT FARM but elicited no reply.	appx XVIII
		4 pm	4 Headquarters RA moved to ROLANDERIE FARM.	
25th		4.25am	1. Bombardment commenced.	
		6am	Brigade Major sent to 8th Div HQ RA to find out if 8th Div had been successful.	
		8am	All fairly quiet in front of 23 Div	
		9am	Report of enemy reinforcements marching up from LILLE. Ordered occasional rounds to be fired at cross roads at LA VALLEE, LE BLANC COULON, MONT DE PREMESQUES	
		9.30am	Enemy guns reported to be retiring by airmen	

Instructions regarding War Diaries and Intelligence Summaries are contained in F. S. Regs., Part II. and the Staff Manual respectively. Title pages will be prepared in manuscript.

WAR DIARY
or
INTELLIGENCE SUMMARY.
(Erase heading not required.)

Army Form C. 2118.

9

Place	Date	Hour	Summary of Events and Information	Remarks and references to Appendices
ROLANDERIE FARM	Sept 25th	11am	Heard very good news of advance all along the line & communicated it to Groups.	App XIX
		3pm	B.M. sent to 8th Div HQ RA. 8th Div captured Bridoux Fort & CORNER FORT but were bombed out, so situation is much as it was except that Groups have been detailed for column sent South to meet the French.	App XX
		3.30pm	Heard that French cavalry have broken through in Champagne.	
		4pm	Issued orders for night lines & occasional fire during night on salient where wire is cut.	App XXI
		5pm	Stopped all firing - Quiet afternoon.	
	26th		1. Night quiet - Programme carried out. Ammn allowance cut down as 8th Div used more than their allowance yesterday. 2. C/103 D/103 return from 8th Div and are placed in A Group in H24 b 78 and H24 c 51 respectively & one battery which [illegible] 3. We now have 4½ batteries firing on each group. Switches both Groups.	App XXII
CROIX DU BAC	27th		1. HQ RA returned to CROIX DU BAC. and Group orders to their own HQ.	
	28th		1. 103 RA Bde remainder & C/105 returned to us and the Div Arty is re-grouped. The Howrs are kept out of the Grouping as they can fire over nearly the whole front.	App XXIII

Army Form C. 2118.

10

Instructions regarding War Diaries and Intelligence Summaries are contained in F. S. Regs., Part II. and the Staff Manual respectively. Title pages will be prepared in manuscript.

WAR DIARY
or
INTELLIGENCE SUMMARY.
(Erase heading not required.)

Place	Date	Hour	Summary of Events and Information	Remarks and references to Appendices
Sept 29			1. Nothing to record – Rain all day & nothing doing	
Croix du Bac.	30th		1. A/105 moved night 30/IX to D/105 position and was placed under Col. Loring for counter battery work.	
			2. For positions of batteries at end of month see app. XXIV	app. XXIV

Charles Mc...d
Capt
Actg Adj RA 23 Div

2353 Wt. W2544/1454 700,000 5/15 D. D. & L. A.D.S.S./Forms/C. 2118.

Confidential

App I

RA

Copy No *1*....

Ref. 1/100,000

HAZEBRUCK 5A.

23rd Division Operation Order No 1.

TILQUES.
Sept 5th 1915.

1. The Division will march to-morrow via St MARTIN au LAERT and ARQUES passing to the South of ST OMER to the area ARQUES - HAZEBROUCK. A further march will take place on the 7th Sept.
2. March Table is attached.
3. The 105th Bde R.F.A. is attached to 70th Bde Group until further orders.
4. The baggage Sections of Train will march with Brigade Groups. The remainder of Train as per March Table.
5. Refilling point - Main Road between TILQUES & ST MARTIN AU LAERT.
6. Reports to Divisional Headquarters TILQUES up to 9 a.m. after that hour to Chateau RENESCURE.

A Blair Lt. Col.
Gen. Staff 23rd Division.

App I

MARCH TABLE FOR 6TH SEPTEMBER.

Unit.	Starting Point.	Time	Billeting Area	Remarks.
D.M.T.	Church at ST MARTINS AU LAERT.	7. a.m.	RENESCURE.	
102 68th Bde Group. (under Br Gen. Serocold)	ditto.	7.8 a.m.	8.30 HAZEBROUCK.	Baggage Section of the Train will march with their Bde Groups.
103 69th Bde. Group. (under Br Gen. Derham)	ditto.	8.30 a.m.	10 – 10.30 ~~11am~~ – 11.3 WALLON CAPPEL	
H.Q. Group (less D.M.T.) (under Col. Thruston)	ditto.	9.50 a.m.	11.20 – 12noon RENESCURE.	
104 105 70th Bde Group. (under Sir D.A. Kinloch C.B. M.V.O.)	DITTO.	10.10 a.m.	CAMPAGNE 11am	
Divl. Amm Col. (Col. Drury)		11.50 a.m.		
Div. Train. (less Supply Sect.) Amm Sub Park. Div Supply Col.	Under their own arrangements.			

App II

Copy No. 4

Ref. 1/100,000

HAZEBROUCK 5A.

23rd DIVISION ORDER No. 2.

6 Sept., 1915.

1. The Division will march to-morrow via HAZEBROUCK to the area HAZEBROUCK—BAILLEUL – STEENWERCK – NEUF BERGUI (exclusive of these places). Brigade areas will be allotted to Staff Captains this evening.

2. All Artillery units will march under orders G.O.C. R.A.

3. March Table is attached.

4. Reports to Div. H.Q. up to 10 a.m., after that hour to MERRIS.

5. Refilling points at Headquarters Brigade Groups.

Issued at 3.30 p.m

A Blair Lt. Colonel,
G.S. 23rd Div.

March Table for 7th Sept

UNIT.	STARTING POINT.	HOUR.	ROUTE	REMARKS.
68th Bde Group. (less R.A. Units) (under Brigr Genl Serocold).	HAZEBROUCK ~~Station.~~	9 a.m.	BORRE-STRAZEELE BAILLEUL (excl)	1. No artillery is to use the CAMPAGNE-RENESCURE-WALLON CAPPEL-HAZEBROUCK-BORRE - STRAZEELE road until the 70th Bde Group has passed. 2. Companies of the Train will march complete with their Groups.
69th Bde Group. (less R.A. Units) (under Br Genl. Derham)	ditto	10a.m.	BORRE-STRAZEELE VIEUX BERQUIN	
H.Q. Group. (under Col Thruston)	RENESCURE	8.30 a.m	HAZEBROUCK BORRE STRAZEELE to MERRIS.	
70th Bde Group. (less R.A.) (under Br Genl. Sir D.Kinloch C.B. M.V.O.)	RENESCURE	9.10a,m.	HAZEBROUCK BORRE STRAZEELE MOOLENACHER.	

OPERATION ORDER NO.1. COPY NO. 7

app III

By Brigadier General D.Fasson, C.B.

Commanding Royal Artillery, 23rd Division.

á M.GERBEDOEN
MERRIS
7-9-15.

Reference $\frac{1}{100,000}$ HAZEBROUCK Map.

Information 1. The 23rd Divn. Arty. will be attached to 27th and 20th Division Artillery for instruction as under.

Attachment. 2. (a) To 27th Divn. Artillery

102nd F.A. Bde. (less A & D Batteries & A.C)
104th F.A. Bde. (less A & C Batteries)
105th F.A. Bde. (less C Battery and A.C)
103rd F.A. Bde. following personnel only
Brigade H.Q. Lt. Col. Henning,2nd Lt.Abbott,3 N.C.Os & men.
"A" Battery, 2 Subalterns, 12 N.C.Os and men.
"B" Battery, Major Mair, 1 Subaltern, 12 N.C.Os and men.
"C" Battery, Capt. Simpson, 1 Subaltern 12 N.C.Os and men.
"D" Battery, Capt. Stanham, 1 Subaltern, 12 N.C.Os and men.

(b) To 20th Divn. Artillery

"C" Battery, 105th Brigade. Separate instructions issued.

Os.C.To Report.3. Os.C. Brigades and Batteries attached to 27th Divn.Artillery will report themselves to Brigadier General R.A.27th Division at CROIX DU BAC at 9 a.m. tomorrow.

March 4. Ther Batteries will march to STEENWERCK, as per attached March Table, under Command of Capt.F.H.Richards, 104th F.A. Brigade, who will return after arrival at STEENWERCK.

Billeting 5. Billeting parties will report to Staff Captain R.A. at 27th Division at STEENWERCK Church at 1 p.m. tomorrow.

Ammunition.6. 104th Brigade, A.C. will supply 102nd Brigade as well as 104th Brigade.

Each Battery, 105th Brigade will take one extra wagon of Lyddite per gun from Brigade A.C.

Transfers 7. All Batteries attached to 27th Division will receive one subaltern from a Battery in 27th Division and give one in exchange.

Command. 8. Brigades and portions of Brigades remaining in present billets will be commanded as follows;-

102nd F.A. Brigade, Major Gotto
103rd F.A. Brigade, Capt. Jones-Bateman
104th F.A Brigade, Capt. Walford
105th F.A. Brigade A.C., Lt.Taylor.

Refilling Point. 9. Refilling Points will be notified later.

Chal. Brooke

Capt.
Brigade Major, R.A
23rd Division.

Copy No.1.	102nd F.A. Bde.	
... 2	103rd	...
... 3	104th	...
... 4	105th	...
... 5	S.S.O	...
... 6	23rd Divn. H.Q.	
... 7	filed	

8. 9. 15

March Table

Unit	Starting Point	Time	Route.
104th F.A. Bde (less A/104 + C/104)	STRAZEELE Railway Station	12.40 pm	VIEUX BERQUIN – LE VERRIER STEENWERCK Halt at 12.50 will be observed
105th F.A. Bde (less C/105 + A.C.)	Road junction at "B" of BERRÉ	11.45 p.m.	Route – Do – Halt at 11.50 will be omitted.
103 F.A. Bde (Personnel)	VIEUX BERQUIN Church	1.45 p.m.	Route – Do – Halt at 1.50 will be observed.
102nd F.A. Bde (less A/102 + D/102 and A.C.)	– Do –	2. p.m.	Route – Do –

Note 1. Baggage Section of Train will march with Batteries.

–do– 2. The halt at 2.50 pm will be omitted

–do– 3. If it is shorter for 102nd F.A. Brigade to march via NEUF BERQUIN it may join the Column at LE VERRIER

Copy

R.A. Divisional Headquarters.

To the Officer Commanding,

104th Brihade, R.F.A.

- - - - - - - - - - - - -

Herewith copy of March Table for tomorrow.

Orders are being delivered personally.

7-9-15.

Capt.
Brigade Major, R.A
23rd Division.

alk [V]

(1)

Confidential.

G.S.C. 2.

ALARM SIGNALS.

To.

The following Alarms Signals are circulated :-

S.O.S. To be used in the event of an attack or a mine explosion. This signal is to be followed by the number of the trench concerned, viz "S.O.S. 59". This means that trench 59 is attacked or that a mine has been exploded in it. "S.O.S. Right or Left Sector" can be similarly sent. This signal can be sent by any officer and will be answered by all available artillery fire.

GAS. To be used in the event of a gas attack. The Instructions are the same as above, viz "GAS 59" etc.

(Sgd) A. Blair.
Lt Col.
General Staff 23rd Division.

Headquarters 23rd Division.
15th September 1915.

'A' Group 'B' Group 105 FA Bde
19 FA Bde

1. For your information
2. Please note that the number of the trench will precede the signal S.O.S or Gas.

CRA

app V

B.M.

07

SECRET.

Copy......8......

Ref. 1/40,000.

H. Q. 23rd Division,
September 12th, 1915.

23rd DIVISION OPERATION ORDER NO 3.

1. The left sector of the 27th Division Area will be taken over by the 70th Bde. from the 82nd Bde. on the night 14/15 September, under orders to be issued by G. O. C. 27th Div.
The 128th Fd. Co. R. E. is attached to the 70th Bde. and will go into the billets occupied by the 17th Fd. Co. R. E. on night 14/15 September.
The 70th Fd. Ambulance will be attached to the 70th Bde. and will move to its position in the 70th Bde. Area on the night 14/15 September, under orders to be issued by A.D.M.S. 23rd Div.

2. The right sector of the 27th Division Area will be taken over by the 69th Bde. on the night of 15/16 September, under orders to be issued by G. O. C. 27th Division.
The 102nd Fd. Co. R.E. is attached to the 69th Bde. and will go into the billets occupied by the 1st Wessex Fd. Co. R. E. on night 15/16 September.
The 69th Fd. Ambulance will be attached to the 69th Bde. and will move to its position in the 69th Bde. Area on the night of 15/16 September under orders to be issued by A.D.M.S. 23rd Division.

3. The 68th Bde. will march to the 27th Divisional Reserve Area to billets N and N. W. of ERQUINGHEM - LYS on the night of 16/17 September under orders to be issued by the G.O.C. 20th Division.
The 101st Fd. Co. R.E. will be attached to 68th Bde and will march to ERQUINGHEM - LYS on the night of 15/16 September, and go into billets occupied by the 2nd Wessex Fd. Co. R. E. under orders to be issued by G.O.C. 20th Division.
The 71st Field Ambulance will be attached to the 68th Bde. and will move to its position in STEENWERCK on the night of 16/17 September, under orders to be issued by A.D.M.S. 23rd Division.

4. The G. O. C. 23rd Division takes over the 27th Divisional Area at 10 a.m. on the 16th inst.

5. The move of the Artillery 23rd Division will be arranged by the C.R.A.'s 23rd and 27th Divisions. Reliefs to be completed by 6 a.m. on the 15th inst, with the exception of the Div. Amm. Col.

6. The Train will move to the 27th Divisional Area under orders of the Officer Commanding Divisional Train.

7. The 9th S. Staffords (Pioneer Bn) will march with the 68th Bde. to billets near FORT ROMPU (H 8 C) on night 16/17 September under orders by G.O.C. 20th Division.

8. Divisional H. Q., H.Q.R.A., H.Q.R.E., the Divisional Mounted Troops, the 35th Mobile Vet. Section and the Sanitary Section will march to CROIX DU BAC starting at 8 a.m. on the 16th inst under orders of LT. COL. TILNEY.

9. The 69th and 70th Bdes. will take over all trench stores from the 27th Division including periscopes, bombs, etc.

10. All cable now laid out in the 27th Div. Area, both Divisional and Artillery, will be handed over to the 23rd Division and no paying back of cable will take place between units.

If there is any of the 10 miles of D 5 cable which was recently allotted for the Artillery of the 27th Div. not laid out it will be handed over to the 23rd Div. Artillery.

11 Acknowledge.

A.B.Blair. Lt. Col.

Issued at 3pm General Staff, 23rd Div.

To all formations and Units of Divisional Troops.

With reference to 23rd. Divisional Operation orders No. 3 of this day, the following instructions are issued:-

Billeting 1. All billeting arrangements will be made as follows:-

Infantry Brigade Groups	By the Bde Staff Captains.
All R.A. Units	By Staff Capt. R.A.
Divisional Mounted Troops Sanitary Section. 35th. Mobile Vety Section. Cyclist Company.	By Adjutant D.M.T.
Divisional Headquarters. Headquarters, R.E. Headquarters, R.A.	By the Camp Commandant.
A.S.C. Units.	By the Adjutant Train.

The 9th. South Staffords Regt. will be under the orders of the 68th. Brigade for billeting.

The above officers will arrange for time and places for billeting parties to meet them, and for guides to conduct units to their billets in the new area.

Refilling Points. 2. On the arrival of formations and units into the new area now occupied by the 27th. Division, the refilling point will be LA MENEGATE.

Until then Refilling point will be as at present.

Transport Depots. 3. The 1stLine Transport of Infantry Brigades will not remain with Battalions but will be quartered in Transport Depots. Infantry Brigade Transport Officers will report to the D.A.Q.M.G. 23rd. Division at the Headquarters 27th. Division CROIX DU BAC at 3 pm. tomorrow and receive instructions on this point.

P.T.O.

Supplies. 4. Supplies for Infantry Units of Brigades will be issued from the Refilling Point to the 1st. Line Transport Depot of the Brigade vide para. 3 and not direct to Units.

R.O. BURNE, LT. COLONEL.
A.A. & Q.M.G.

App VI Copy 6

Secret

OPERATION ORDER No. 2.

by

Brig. General D.FASSON? C.B. Commanding 23rd. Div. Artillery.

Ref. Sheet 36. MERRIS.

13/9/15.

Information 1. The left section of the 27th. Div. Area will be taken over by 70th Brigade on night of 14/15th inst. The right Section of the 27th. Div. Area will be taken over by the 69th Brigade on night of 15/16th inst. The 68th Infantry Brigade will go into Reserve at ERQUINGHEM on night of 16/17th: The G.O.C. 23rd. Div. takes over the 27th. Divn. Area at 10 a.m. on the 16th inst.

Movements 2. All Sections of Batteries and Brigade A.Cs still remaining in rest billets will be prepared to move on 14th inst. Orders for D.A.C. will be issued later.

Cable 3. All cable laid out in 27th Div. Area, both Divisional and Artillery will be handed over to the 23rd Division, and no paying back of cable between Units will take place. If there is any of the 10 miles of D 5 cable which was recently alloted for the Artillery of the 27th Division not laid out, it will be handed over to the 23rd Div. Artillery.

Refilling Point 4. For Units in 27th Division Area:-

LA MENEGATE.

For Units in Rest Billets:-

STRAZEELE West End.

Issued at.
Copy No 1, 102 FA. Bde.
2. 103 FA. Bde
3. 104 FA. Bde
4. 105 FA. Bde
5. D.A.C.
6-7-8 FILED

W. J. Smyth Lt for Capt.
Brigade Major
R.A. 23rd Division

SECRET ath VII Copy No.

OPERATION ORDER NO.3

BY

Brigadier General D. Fasson, C.B.

Commanding Royal Artillery, 23rd Division.

CROIX DE BAC
14-9-15.

Grouping.1. The R.A. 23rd Division will be grouped as follows;-

	Batteries	Zone	Inf.inZone	Remarks.
A Group (a) Lt.Col.Biddulph Commanding	102 F.A.Bde. (less C Battery)	Right Sector 23rd Division Trenches 52-58 both inclusive	69th Inf. Bde.	A/105 and B/105 may be called upon in an emergency for defensive purposes.
B Group (b) Col. Hobday Commanding	104 F?A.Bde	Left Sector 23rd Division Trenches 59-66 both inclusive	70th Inf. Bde.	C/102 may be called upom in an emergency for defensive pürposes.
attached (c) Tactically to 8th Div.	103 F.A. Bde 105 F.A. Bde (less C/105)	as ordered by G.O.C.,R.A. 8th Division		
Counter Btty.(d) attached tactically to Lt.Col.Loring's Heavy Bde.R.G.A.	C/102	as ordered by Lt.Col.Loring		

Administration. 2. All Batteries for administration and Discipline are under their own Brigade Commanders.

Communication. 3. (a) O.C. A Group will see that he has adequate telephonic communications with A/105 and B/105 either direct or through their Brigade Commanders and that arrangements for calling their fire at night are complete.

He will also see that these batteries register (if not already done) on A Group Zone as soon as possible. He will avoid clashing with any times when G.O.C.,R.A. 8th Division requires them to register for him.

(b) O.C. B Group will make all arrangements to enable him to call on C/102 when required.

(c) Os. C. Groups will ascertain the limits of battalion frontages in their Sectors and the F.O.O. sleeping at Battalion H.Q. must have telephonic communication with the battery or batteries covering the battalion.

Zones. 4. (a) Os.C. Groups will allot zones of the enemy's trenches to ~~xxx~~ their batteries, but every battery is to be registered over the whole of its arc of fire.

(b) List of new points registered during the day will be sent to H.Q.R.A. by 7 p.m. daily.

Night Lines. 5. Night lines of batteries will be laid out on their zones of the enemy's front trenches.

Reports. 6. Os.C. Groups will forward a report to H.Q.R.A. showing the zones of the batteries, the battalions covered, and their night arrangements.

They will also furnish all these particulars to the Infantry Bde. Commander of their Sectors.

Position of D.A.C.	7.	D.A.C. One Section	A.27.d.5.7
		....	A.28.c.3.9
		....	A.28.a.7.4

Capt.
Brigade Major R.A.
23rd Division.

Copy No.	1.	102 Bde.
...	2	103 Bde.
...	3	104 Bde.
...	4	105 Bde.
...	5	D.A.C.
...	6	Filed.

SECRET.

BM 1 14

App VIII

R.A. Divisional Hdqrs.

23r Division.

(2)

Headquarters

"A" Group, 23rd Division. Arty.

19th F.A. Bde.

1. The 19th F.A. Bde. are attached to "A" Group 23rd Division Artillery and will be under the command of O.C. "A" Group in all tactical matters.
2. This Brigade will remain under the command of O.C. 19th F.A. Bde. for administration and discipline.
3. O.C. "A" Group will be responsible that adequate telephonic communications is opened as soon as possible.
4. The 8th Div. may call on the 19th F.A. Bde. for offensive purposes at any time. This call will take precedence of any other work the 19th F.A. Bde may be doing at the time.
5. When the call is made the O.C. 19th F.A. Bde. will assume command of his Brigade and will command it from the present Headquarters of 103 F.A. Bde. H.17.d.3.4.
6. The O.C. 19th F.A. Bde. will place himself in communication with the 8th Division Artillery with reference to the above offensive operations, and also with O.C. 103 F.A. Bde. in order to make all necessary arrangements at the combined Headquarters of 103rd and 19th F.A. Bdes.

18-9-15.

Capt.
Brigade Major, R.A.
23rd Division.

att X

SECRET. This order is not to be taken into the trenches.

OPERATION ORDER NO. 1 Copy No. 11

BY

Brigadier General D. Fasson, C.B.

20.9.15

Commanding Royal Artillery, 23rd Division.

Ref. 1/10000 Map.sheet 36

1. Offensive operations are to be carried out by the 3rd Corps, beginning on the 25th September, as part of the operations of the First Army. The Eighth Division is going to capture the hostile trenches between the CORNER FORT N.6.d.1.6 and BRIDOUX FORT I.31.d. both inclusive.
   The further objective of the 8th Division is to be the capture of BAS MAISNIL, LE BRIDOUX and Fme HOUSSAIN with a view to bringing under effective fire the FROMELLES - RADINGHEM road and preparing the way for a subsequent advance of the whole Corps on to the AUBERS - RADINGHEM RIDGE, should such an advance be ordered.

2. The 23rd Division will co-operate by Artillery, Machine Guns, Rifle fire and Search Lights against the enemy's trenches between I.32.a.5.5 and I.21.c.5.2 and be prepared to take advantage of any success to assault the trenches on their front.

3. A timetable of operations to be carried out by the 23rd Division to assist the 8th Division is given in attached Appendix 1. (Artillery programme Appendix 2)

4. The general outline of operations will be as follows:-
   21st, 22nd, 23rd and 24th September Artillery bombardment which will continue night and day.
   25th September assault by 8th Division at daylight.

5. As the enemy is certain to employ gas shells special care will be taken by all commanding officers that gas helmets are carried by all ranks and are ~~eff~~ in efficient condition.

6. The attacking brigade of the 8th Division will mark the position of their bombers and their advanced Infantry in the German trenches by means of RED FLAGS.

7. The Artillery will be under the immediate orders of the C.R.A. but Infantry Brigadiers may call on them in case of necessity.

8. A programme of Artillery targets for each day will be issued the evening before - being arranged as far as possible so as to have fire on some part of the enemy's line during most of the day. The two principal points in front trenches which will be bombarded are salient at I.26.b.8.5. and salient at I.26.c.8.1 - and in front of both these wire will be cut - in the latter case by the 8th Division.
   The other targets will be support trenches, M.G. emplacements, cross roads, etc. Infantry Brigades are requested to inform H.Q. R.A. or their R.A. Group Commander of any suitable targets they know of.

9. During these operations the S.ec of C/104 at I.14.a.6.6., the Sec. of D/104 at I.13.c.4 6 and D/102 will come under the orders (tactically) of O.C. "A" Group.

10. Sould any alt rations in the daily programme become necessary Group Commanders will at once notify them to Infantry Brigade Commanders concerned and Headquarters R.A.

11. The amount of ammunition allowed for the operations has not yet been finally approved.
For the 21st inst the following will be the maximum expenditure -

Four batteries shooting at the two salients	30 rounds per gun H.E. 12 ... ... Shrap.
For other batteries	12 rounds per gun H.E. 50 ... ... Shrap.
C/102 Counter battery	30 rounds per gun Shrap.

Except as regards the number of rounds to be fired at the two salients, the number of rounds to be fired at each target on the programme, and any other targets which it may become necessary to engage during the day, will be fixed by Group Commanders.

12. At least one day's supply of ammunition on the above basis will be dumped at the guns and replenished each night. Should it be possible to dump more (up to 2 days supply) this will be done.

13. At the conclusion of the shooting on each target a telephonic report of the effect obtained will be sent through Group Commanders to H.Q.R.A.

14. Reports to CROIX DU BAC until 4 p.m. September 24th after which time they will be sent to ROLANDERIE FARM H.11.c.

Charles Broad
Capt.
Brigade Major, R.A.
23rd Division.

Issued at 1.30 a.m. by Motor Cyclist.

Copy No.1	A Group
... 2	B Group
... 3	23 Div.
... 4	8th Div.Arty.
... 5	50th Div. Arty
... 6	3 Corps
... 7	B-G.R.A.
... 8	B.M.R.A.
.. 9	S.C.R.A.
... 10 - 11 - 12	Filed.

APPENDIX 1.

21st September   Artillery bombardment.

22nd September   ditto

23rd September   ditto

The 69th and 70th Bdes. will send up two rockets each at 8 p.m. and the men will cheer as if they were going to attack.

24th September

Artillery bombardment.
Rifle and Machine Gun Fire from front trenches along the front of the 69th and 70th Brigades on points which have been previously bombarded.
Night firing by Machine Guns on enemy's lines of approach and where the wire has been cut.
The Search Lights are to assist the fire of the Naval Guns at 10 p.m. Their position will be arranged by the C.R.E

25th September

The 8th Division will attack the enemy at daylight.
Infantry and Machine Guns will open rapid fire on enemy's trenches and communications at an hour which will be given later and support 8th Div. attack.

SECRET 23RD DIVISIONAL ARTILLERY.

Tuesday 21st Sept. 1915.

TIME	TARGET	BATTERY SHOOTING	AMMUNITION.
9-0 a.m. to 9-45 a.m.	Parapet Salient I.26.b.8.5.	A/102	H.E.
10-10 a.m. to 11-35 a.m.	(Support Trench I.27.a	Sec. D/104 near Moat-Farm.	Shrap.
	(Brewery Support (trench I.22.c.	Do. Do.	Shrap.
	(German House	B/104	H.E.
11-55 a.m.	Salient I.26.c.8.1	D/102	H.E.
12-57 p.m. to 2-20 p.m.	Trench at LE QUESNE	B/102	Shrap.
	Salient I.26.c.8.1.	B/102	H.E.
2-50 p.m. to 3-45 p.m.	(M.G. in I.27.b.2.5	B/104	H.E.
	(Support Trench I.27.a	Sec. D/104 Nr. Moat Farm	Shrap.
	(Distillery trenches	B/104	Shrap.
4.5 p.m. to 5-30 p.m.	(Parapet I.26.b.8.5	A/102	H.E.
	(M.G. I.27 c.0.1	A/102	H.E.

NIGHT.

8 p.m. to 4 a.m.	Parapet I.26.b.8.5 40 rounds in bursts of 2.	A/102	Shrap.
8 p.m. to Midnight	Parapet I.26.c	D/102	Shrap.
Midnight to 4 a.m.	ditto. 20 rounds each in bursts of 2.	B/102	Shrap.

Appendix 2

SECRET. R.A. 23RD DIVISION.

DURING 4 DAYS BOMBARDMENT.

		SHRAP.	H.E.	
1 Battery	wire cutting I.26.b.7.5	1000		250 per gun.
1 Battery	Bombarding parapet ...		500	125 per gun
1 Battery	Bombarding I.26.c.8.1. parapet (Pt.where 8th Div. are cutting wire)		500	125 per gun
4 Batteries	Firing at Pts. in support trenches, Mr G. emplacements cross roads, etc.	3200	800	Sh.200 per gun H.E 50 per gun
1 Battery	Counter-battery	480		120 per gun

5TH DAY 5 minutes before assault of 8th Div.

3 Batteries	Bombarding parapet as above		120	10 per gun
1 Gun in parapet	Bombarding salient		50	

REMAINDER OF 5TH DAY.

7 Batteries (less 1 gun)	Firing generally as during first four days and as required by situation	1350	405	Sh.50 per gun H.E.15 per gun
1 Battery	Counter-battery	200		50 per gun

6TH DAY

7 Batteries (less 1 gun)	According to situation	1350	405	Sh. 50 per gun H.E. 15 per gun
1 Battery	Counter-battery	200		50 per gun
	Total	7780	2780	
Remainder for 4 days subsequent fighting	-----------------	Sh. 3036	H.E 804	Sh. 95 per gun H.E 25 per gun

N.B. During 5 minutes before assault on 5th day, 1 mountain gun fires into salient in I.26.c.8.1. Allotment for this and other occasions according to requirements.

REPORT ON OPERATIONS. 21st September, 1915.

app X1

1. The two parapets at I.26.b.8.5. and I.26.c.8.1 have been knocked about. The former has one hole 3 foot wide through it. The latter has several holes through it on a front of 125 yards.

2. Wire has been cut in front of the salient I.26.b.8.5. Exact details are not yet available.

3. The support trenches in I.27.a, I.22.c, and the Distillery have been thoroughly searched.

4. GERMAN HOUSE has been destroyed, likewise a suspected Machine Gun emplacement in I.27.b.2.5.

5. The enemy's gun fire has been feeble. One battery was shelled a little and the observations stations at Farm DU BIEZ and MOAT FARM were slightly shelled.

6. Before our shooting commenced this morning a farm in RUE FLEURIE was shelled, some casualties being caused to the Infantry inhabiting it.

O. Fasson

Brigadier General,
Commanding Royal Artillery,
23rd Division.

6 p.m. 21/9/15.

SECRET

23RD DIVISIONAL ARTILLERY

Programme for Wednesday 22nd September.

TIME	TARGET	BATTERY SHOOTING	AMMUNITION
~~When light is favourable 6 a.m. to 8 a.m.~~	~~Salient I.26.c.8.1~~	D/102	H.E.
9-15 to 11-35 am.	2nd Support Trench I.27.a Communication Trench, 4.5 I.27.a 1st Support Trench I.27.a	Sec. ~~B~~ D/104 (Nr. Moat Farm) B/104 Sec. D/104 (Nr. Moat Farm)	Shrap and a small proportion of H.E.
11 a.m.	Salient I.26.c.8.1	B/102	H.E.
11-50 a.m.	Salient I.26.b.7.5	A/102	H.E.
12-35 p.m. to 2-35 p.m.	Cut wire in front of Salient I.26.b.7.5	Sec.C/104 at I.14.a Sec.D/104 at I.13.c	Shrap.
3 p.m.	M.G. I.16.d.7.1	Sec.C/104 at H.12.b	H.E.
3-15 p.m. to ~~3-50 p.m.~~ 4-10 p.m.	Salient I.26.b.7.5	A/102	H.E.
3-50 p.m. to 5-10 p.m.	2nd Support trench I.27.a German House Trench running N.W. from LE QUESNE	D/104 A/104 D/104	Shrap. small proportion of H.E.
4-30 p.mto 5-10 p.m.	Support Trench in rear of Salient I.26.c.8.1	B/102	Shrap.

Guns of left Group will also register points behind enemy's lines.

NIGHT.

TIME	TARGET	BATTERY SHOOTING	AMMUNITION
8-0 p.m. to 4 a.m.	Parapet I.26.b.8.5 40 rounds in bursts of 2	A/102	Shrap.
8-0 p.m. to midnight	Parapet I.26.c	B/102	Shrap.
Midnight to 4 a.m.	ditto 20 rounds each in bursts of 2	D/102	Shrap.

SECRET.

REPORT ON OPERATIONS (3) 22nd September. 1915.

a/h XIV

1. The parapet between I.26.c.8.1 and I.26.c.9.0. 25 has been knocked out of shape.and is now a mound of earth.

2. The cutting of the wire at the salient I.26.b.8.5 has been extended. The fire was effective but grass and tress prevent the exact extent of the damage being seen.

3. The parapets during the night were not repaired. One or two working parties were dispersed by shrapnel.

4. A small work at I.27.a.8.0 erected during the night has been knocked down.

5. A suspected M.G. emplacement at I.27.a.4.6 was destroyed by 5 rounds H.E.

6. The two support trenches in I.27.a. have been knocked about and searched with shrapnel.

7. The enemy's gun fire has been slightly heavier to-day especially around BOIS GRENIER.

8. A large shell fell during the night at H.23.b.65.50 but did not burst. The hole was 12 inches in diameter and a 15 foot pole did not reach the bottom. True bearing of hole was 122° 45 '. Angle of descent 45°.

9. Infantry in right Sector trenches report having been shelled with shrapnel, a few casualties occurring. - Also about 30 shell fell in RUE FLEURIE.

P. Tasson

Brigadier General,
Commanding Royal Artillery,
23rd Division.

SECRET.

(B) (2)

app XV

R.A. Divisional Hdqtrs.
23rd Division.

Headquarters,

"A" & "B" Groups & No.2 Mountain Batty.

1. With reference to the attached papers, the programme as detailed for Sept. 25th will be carried out tomorrow morning Sept. 24th for part of the 1st and 2nd periods only, viz: 4-25 a.m to 4-32 a.m.

2. NO H.E. SHELL WILL BE USED - Shrapnel only will be used.

3. Note that the guns in the parapet will NOT fire.

CB

23-9-15.

Capt.
Brigade Major, R.A.
23rd Division.

S E C R E T.   COPY.

R.A.

G.384   23rd.

Follwoing from 3rd Corps begins. AAA From 18-10 p.m. to-night the proceedure of the Artillery rifles and machine guns will be a facsimile of the proceedure to be carried out tomorrow night AAA At 4-25 a.m tomorrow a facsimile of the assault will take place with the identical artillery programme except that the Infantry will not assault, smoke will not be discharged and guns in the parapet will not fire nor mines be exploded AAA At 4-32 a.m. all fire will cease and the normal programme taken up for the remainder of the day AAA This will enable the whole artillery programme to be practised AAA The extra shoot arranged for to-night and tomorrow night will take place.as arranged AAA ends.

23rd Div.

7-20 p.m.

- 2 -

For compliance.

for Lt. Col.

appx XVI

SECRET.

23RD DIVISIONAL ARTILLERY.

Programme for Thursday 23rd September.

TIME	TARGET	BATTERY SHOOTING	AMMUNITION.
When light is favourable 6 a.m. to 8 a.m.	Salient I.26.b.7.5	A/102	H.E.
9-15 a.m. to 11-15	1st & 2nd Support trenches I.27.a Station I.27.b	Sec.D/104(Moat Fm) B/104	Shrapnel & little H.E.
10 a.m	Support trench behind salient I.26b.7.5	C/104	do.
11-45 a.m	Salient I.26.c.8.1	B/102	H.E.
1[illegible]10 p.m	Register TROIS FETUS	A/104	Shrap.
1 p.m.	Support trenches I.26.d	B/102	Shrap.
2-15 pm to 4 pm.	Wire cutting salient I.26.b.7.5	Sec.D/104 Sec.C/104	Shrap.
2 pm. to 3-30 p.m	Repeat 9-15 a.m. to 11-15 a.m shoot.		
3 p.m	Salient I.26.c.8.1	D/102	H.E.
4-10 to 5.0 p.m.	Salient I.26.b.7.5	A/102	H.E.

Left Group will also do some registering.

NIGHT.

TIME	TARGET	BATTERY SHOOTING	AMMUNITION.
8 p.m. to 4 a.m	Parapet I.26.b.7.5 40 rounds in bursts of 2	A/102	Shrap
	Parapet parallel to above 20 rounds in bursts of 2	C/104	Shrap.
8 p.m.to midnight	Parapet I.26.c. and support trenches in rear	~~B~~ D/102	Shrap.
Midnight to 4 a.m	ditto. 20 rounds each in bursts of 2	B/102	Shrap.

(1)

SECRET.

REPORT ON OPERATIONS. 23rd September, 1915.

23RD DIVISIONAL ARTILLERY.

1. The two salients again shelled - considerable portions of the parapets are now damaged.

2. The wire in front of I.26.b.7.8 again shelled. It is difficult to find out to what extent the wire is really cut. On account of the distance apart of the English and German Trenches, it takes 2 hours for a patrol to go out and return, during which time all fire has to be stopped. An opportunity for mending the wire is thus given the enemy. So it was thought better not to send out patrols so far last night.

3. The support and communication trenches behind the first line were shelled with H.E. and searched with shrapnel.

4. The left Group has registered some more points around TRUIS FETUS and its neighbourhood.

5. Occasional bursts of shrapnel were kept up during the night on the breches in the parapet and wire.

6. The enemy's artillery has shown more activity. The ordnance used has been chiefly the Field gun and field Howitzer.

7. Various flashes have been located and made known to the heavy artillery.

8. Our front line trenches 53 - 58 were fairly heavily bombarded this morning.

9. H.18.b.2.7 was shelled this morning by 10 "Heavy" shells said to come from the direction of RADINGHEM.

10. No batteries have been shelled.

Charles Brooke Capt.

for Brigadier General
Commanding Royal Artillery,
23rd Division.

23-9-15.

akh XVII

SECRET.

23RD DIVISIONAL ARTILLERY.

Programme for Friday 24th September.

TIME	TARGET	BATTERY SHOOTING	AMMUNITION.
When light is favourable between 6 & 8 am.	Front trench & 2 support trenches on I.27.a	B & D/104	Shrap. & H.E. in proportion 3 to 1
9-10 a.m. to 10-45 a.m.	Salient & parapet either side & support trenches immediately in rear I.26.c.8.1	B/102	H.E.
10.5 a.m. to 10.35 a.m.	Reported M.G. in station & adjoining trench I.27.a	B/104	H.E.& Shrap.
11 a.m.to 12-5 p.m.	Salient I 26.b.7.5 & parapet on either side & the parallel support trench	A/102	H.E.
12-15 p.m. to 2 p.m.	Wire cutting in front & on both sides of salient I.26.b.7.5	C/104 D/104	Shrap.
12-45 p.m. to 2-30 p.m.	Cross roads at LE QUESNE the HALT and trenches between	D & A 104	Shrap.
3-5 p.m. to 4-15 p.m.	Repeat 9-10 a.m. shoot		
4-20 p.m.	Support trenches I.32.b.& d.	B/102	Shrap. & H.E. in proportion 3 to 1.
4-25 p.m. to 5 p.m.	Salient I.26.b.7.5 1st & 2nd Support trenches I.27.a	A/102 B & D/104	H.E. Shrap. & H.E. in proportion 3 to 1.

NIGHT.

TIME	TARGET	BATTERY SHOOTING	AMMUNITION.
8p.m. to 6 a.m.	Parapet & support trench & wire I.26.b.7.5 60 rounds in bursts of 2	A/102 C/104	Shrap.
8 p.m. to midnight	Parapet I.26.c.8.1 & support trenches immediately in rear 20 rounds in bursts of 2	B/102	Shrap.
Midnight to 6 a.m	ditto.	D/102	Shrap.
8 p.m. to 6 a.m.	Support trenches I.27.a 80 rounds in bursts of 2	B & D/104	Shrap.

a/h XVIII

SECRET

23RD DIVISIONAL ARTILLERY.

1st Period 4-25 a.m. to 4-30 a.m.
Amended programme for 25th Sept.
Programme issued last night will be destroyed.

BATTERY	TARGET	AMMUNITION	TOTAL FOR PERIOD
"A" GROUP B/102	Sweep hostile front parapet from I.32.a.6.5 to I.26.c.8.1	5 rds H.E. per gun	20 H.E.
Sec.D/102	Support & communication trenches in rear of above & the LOZENGE I.32.a.8.5	10 rds H.E. per gun	20 H.E.
A/102	Salient I.26.b.7.5 (two parallel trenches)	5 rds H.E. per gun	20 H.E.
Sec.C/104	Wire cutting in front of above salient on both sides.	25 rds Shrap. per gun	50 shrap.
"B" GROUP. A.B.& D/104	1st & 2nd Support trenches I.27.a Communication trench I.27.a.5.8 to I.27.c.9.9	3 rds per gun shrap. & H.E. in proportion of 3 to 1.	9 H.E. 27 shrap.
	2nd period 4-30 a.m. to 4-40 a.m.		
"A" GROUP			
Mountain Gun	Salient I.26.b.7.5	10 rds rapid for 5 mins. Then slacken. Cease fire & remove gun when 50 rds are expended.	50 shrap.
Gun in parapet D/102	Saliant I.26.c.8.1	10 rds H.E. papid. Slackening to 2 rds per min. Total period 30 mins. Search with shrap.	50 H.E. 50 Shrap.
	Remainder same as previous period, except wire cutting battery lifts on to parapet with shrapnel.	5 rds per gun shrap. & H.E. in proportion 3 to 1.	17 H.E. 53 shrap.
"B" GROUP	As in previous period	do.	15 H.E. 45 shrap
	3rd Period 4-40 a.m. 5 a.m.		
"A" GROUP. Sec. D/102	Communication trench I.32.a.8.8 to I.32.b.6.2	20 rds per gun	40 shrap
B/102	Support trench I.26.d.6.5 to I.32.b.2.2	10 rds. per gun	40 shrap
A/102	Sweeping front parapet I.32.a.5.3 to I.26.c.10.3 Occasional round H.E. to be put into parapet at I.32.a.6.7 and I.32.a.5.3	10 rds per gun	10 H.E. 30 shra[p]
Sec. C/104	Communication trench I.32.a.6.5 to I.33.a.8.10	20 rds per gun	40 shra[p]

3rd period 4-40 a.m. 5 a.m.

BATTERY	TARGET	AMMUNITION	TOTAL FOR PERIOD.
"B" GROUP. D/104	LE QUESNE cross roads and trenches in rear.	10 rds per gun	40 shrap.
A/104	HALTE & trenches near	10 rds per gun	40 shrap.
Sec.B/104	TROIS FETUS & LE GRAND MESNIL FM.	20 rds per gun	40 shrap.
Sec.B/104	Salient I.26.b.7.5	20 rds per gun	40 shrap.

---

1. Should the 23rd Division take the offensive, the attack will be delivered between I.32.a.5.3 and I.26.c.10.3.

2. The distribution of artillery fire to support this attack will be as follows.

A GROUP)
A & B/102)
Sec D/102)
Sec C/104) Bombarding front parapet and cutting wire along front to be attacked. Lifting on to support trenches and bombarding BOIS BLANCS.

B GROUP

A/104)
1 gun D/102) For defence of front of B Group

B & D/104 Left BARRAGE on salient I.26.b.7.5 and on communication trench from I.27.c.1.4 to LE QUESNE cross roads.

Sec. C/104
(Move to H.12.d.5.8) On front parapet and support trenches I.26.d.6.8 to I.26.d.8.7 (part of left Barrage)

Details to be arranged by Group Commanders and reported to H.Q.R.A. as soon as possible.

3. Orders for the above fire to commence will be issued by H.Q.R.A.and it will be divided into time periods. Batteries must be prepared to carry out the order without delay.

4. In order that some of above bombarding of parapet and cutting of wire may be done in advance the programme for 25th inst. will be added to as follows;-

4th Period

~~4th period~~ B/102 will cut wire at I.32.a.6.7 and I.32.a. 5.3. 100 rounds shrap. for each place. 2 hours to be spent on this, unless other orders are received, registration for this should take place if possible some time to-day 24th inst. as observation will probably impossible tomorrow on account of smoke.

5. Except as regards instructions given in preceding para batteries will at conclusion of 3rd period continue to fire on same targets at battery fire 2 minutes.

6. The Sec. C/104 in H.12.b will move into its new place at H.12.d.5.8 to-night, 24th inst.

7. From 5 a.m. 25th inst. the following orders will be observed as gegards wagon lines.

Horses will be exercised and watered half at a time.

All horses will be kept harnessed up day and night with slackened girths.

8. For 25th inst. Officers Commanding Groups will make such arrangements for F.O.O.'S at observing stations, in trenches, and at batalion H.Q.as to ensure that they are kept thoroughly in touch with the situation in front line. In the eventuality referred to in para. 1 F.O.O's must be pushed forward with the Infantry, and those detailed for this must be provided with wire. If possible telephones will be supplemented by visual signalling (Flags or electric lamps). Arrangements made to be reported to H.Q.R.A.

9. From 4-25 a.m. onwards on 25th inst. frequent telephonic reports are to be sent from trenches and observing stations to batteries, from batteries to Brigade H.Q, and from Brigade H.Q. to H.Q.R.A.

[signature]
Capt.
Brigade Major, R.A.
23rd Division.

24-9-15.

SECRET

23RD DIVISIONAL ARTILLERY.

appx XIX

REPORT ON OPERATIONS.

From 6 p.m. 24th Sept. to 6 p.m. 25th Sept.

1. The programme for the Bombardment and the following half hour was carried out.

2. The morning was misty and dark and little more than the outline of the hostile trenches was visible at 4-25 a.m

3. Our right flank was heavily shelled at 4-30 a.m. Our left flank has been quiet all day.

4. Observation has been more or less impossible all day.

5. Fire at 6 a.m. was reduced to 80 rounds per hour for the whole of the Divisional Artillery; at 12 noon it was further reduced to 40 rounds per hour. A few rounds all day long have been placed on the cross roads at LA VALLEE, LE BLANC COULON and MONT DE PREMESQUES.

6. Officers patrol last night reported that " the wire from I.26.b.6.7 to I.26.b.8.9 well cut; from I.26.b.8.9 to I.21.c.0.1 there were knife rests evidently blocking a gap".

7. The two armoured cars fired 200 rounds at 10 p.m. last night from the neighbourhood of Burnt Farm. The enemy did not reply.

8. The vicinity of the gun in the parapet was shelled by 4.2" and 77 mm. but it is not certain that it was spotted.

9. F.O.O's wires were cut in right section and on account of the mist communication was very difficult.

Charles Price

Capt.
Brigade Major, R.A.
23rd Division.

25-9-15.

app XX D. X 2

(B) (2)

R.A. Divisional Hdqtrs.

23rd Division.

Headquarters,

102 & 104 Brigade, R.F.A.

- - - - - - - - - - - - -

Night lines will be laid out under direction of Group Commanders to cover the front of each Group to the best advantage from a defensive point of view.

2. Group Commanders will consult with Inf. Bde. Commanders as to any stoppage of this fire while patrols are out.

3. Wires between F.O.O's at Battn. H.Q. and the covering batteries must be in working order before night time.

4. O.C. "A" Group will make sure that communication with the batteries outside his group on which he has a call are in good order.

5. Instructions as to fire during the night will be sent later.

Charles Bond

25-9-15.

Capt.
Brigade Major, R.A.
23rd Division.

afh XVI

ROYAL ARTILLERY, 23RD DIVISION.

Programme for Sept. 26th. 1915.

1. Six bursts of fire will be fired to-day on the points detailed below.
2. In each bursts fire will be opened exactly at the hour named by all guns firing. Method of fire battery fire 10 secs.
3. The TOTAL number of rounds to be fired by each GROUP in each BURST is shown below and will in no case be exceeded.
4. Infantry Brigade Commanders will be informed of the hours of firing by Group Commanders.
5. Registration will take place as follows at first opportunity.

C/103	between trenches 52-56 both inclusive	Two points which can be safely fired at.
D/103	between trenches 54-59 both inclusive	do.

Total ammunition for each Battery 8 shrapnel

PROGRAMME.

TIME	UNIT	TARGET	AMMUNITION.	
11-16 a.m.	"A" Group	Houses at N.E. end BOIS BLANCS I.32.c.4.7		4rds H.E.
		Parapet of Salient I.26.c.8.1		2rds H.E.
		Parapet of Salient I.26.b.7.5		2 rds H.E
		LE QUESNE cross roads	4 rds Sh.	
		Total for Group	4 shrap.	8 H.E.
	"B" Group	Distillery & station near	4 rds sh.	
		Trench in front LARGE FARM (I.22.a.6.0)	4 rds sh.	
		Junction of support & communication trenches I.22.d.4.4	4 rds sh.	
		Total for Group	12 rds. shrap.	
12-55 p.m.	B "A" Group	WEZ MACQUART	2 sh.	2 H.E.
		Brewery		4 H.E.
		1st Support trench I.27.a	4 sh.	
		Total for group	6 sh.	6 H.E

TIME	UNIT	TARGET	AMMUNITION.	
12-55 p.m.	A "B" Group	LA MOTTE HOUSSAIN Fme.	2 sh.	2 H.E.
		LE GRAND MAISNIL Fme.	2 sh.	2 H.E.
		Enfilade road I.27.c.8.8	4 sh.	
		Total for Group	8 sh.	4 H.E.
1-10 p.m.	B "A" Group	EST DE LA BARRIERE	4 sh.	
		Support Trench I.22.a		4 H.E.
		Station I.27.a	2 sh.	2 H.E.
		Total for Group	6 sh.	6 H.E.
	A "B" Group	1st Support trench I.32.b	2 sh.	2 H.E.
		2nd ditto	2 sh.	2 H.E.
		LE QUESNE cross roads	4 sh.	
		Total for group	8 sh.	4 H.E.
2-50 p.m.	B "A" Group	LARGE FARM	4 sh.	
		Support trenches I.21.d	4 sh.	4 H.E.
		Total for Group	8 sh.	4 H.E.
	C "B" Group	Salient I.26.b.7.5		4 H.E.
		Salient I.26.c.8.1		4 H.E.
		Front line trench between above		4 H.E.
		Total for Group		12 H.E.

3-21 p.m. Repeat 11-18 a.m. programme

4-45 p.m. Repeat 2-50 p.m. programme.

26-9-15

Capt.
Brigade Major, R.A.
23rd Division.

SECRET. **23RD DIVISIONAL ARTILLERY.** app XXII

Programme for 27th September, 1915.

1. The following will be the objectives to be fired ~~at~~ on 27th Sept.

A GROUP

Enemy's front parapet opposite trenches 52 and 53.

Support trenches in rear of above.

Trenches and houses in BOIS BLANCS.

B GROUP

Enemy's front parapet at Salient I.26.b.7.5

Support trenches in rear of above

Distillery & Station

Communication trench near LE QUESNE cross roads.

2. Group Commanders will arrange their own programmes in accordance with above.

3. A Group will fire between 7 and 9-30 and between noon and 2-30 B Group between 9-30 and noon and between 2-30 and 5 p.m.

4. The ammunition to be expended is 8 rounds per gun in proportion of 3 shrap. to 1 H.E. and as far as this allowance will permit fire should be continuous with occasional bursts.

5. The ammunition for any registration or firing other than in answer to an S.O.S. call must be taken from the allowance given in preceding paras.

6. C/102 is also restricted to 8 rounds except for any urgent call.

7. Copies of Group programmes to be forwarded to this office.

8. Acknowledge by wire.

Capt.
Brigade Major, R.A.
23rd Division.

app XXIII

SECRET. Copy No.

Operation Orders No 4

By

Brigadier General D Fasson. C.B.

Commanding Royal Artillery, 23rd Division.

27.9.15

Ref. 1/20,000 Map, Shett 36 N.W.

1. The line held by the 23rd Division is being extended, the 68th Infantry Brigade taking over trenches 50 and 51 from I.31.d.0.8 to I.31.b.9.6 BRIDOUX ROAD exclusive from the 8th Division during the night of 28/29 September.

2. The following Artillery moves will take place.

(a) On night of 27/28th the 105th Howitzer Brigade R.F.A. now attached to 8th Division will rejoin the 23rd Division "A" and "B" batteries, 105th Brigade, will remain in their present positions.
D/105 will move night of 27/28th to position formerly occupied by B/105 (I.8.a.5.5)
Night lines for above batteries tonight will be as ordered by O.C. 105th Brigade who will notify them to "A" & "B" Group Commanders.

(b) On night of 28/29th - Headquarters and "A" & "B" batteri 103rd F.A. Brigade, now attached to 8th Division and C/10 now attached to 20th Division will rejoin the 23rd Divisic Instructions regarding the grouping of the batteries of 103rd Brigade will be issued later, they will unless circumstances change remain in their present positions.
O.C. 105th Brigade will reconnoitre early tomorrow for a position for C/105 - bearing in mind that the 105th Brigade is required as far as possible to cover the whole front of the 23rd Division.

3. There will be no firing tonight except for an S.O.S. message or an urgent call from the Infantry.

Night Lines of "A" & "B" Groups will be as orders by Group Commanders.

Capt. R.A.
Brigade Major
23rd Division.

SECRET

OPERATION ORDER No.5 Copy No. 22

By 28th Sept 1915

Brigadier General B. Fasson, C.B.

Commanding Royal Artillery, 23rd Division.

Reference 1/20000 Map.

1. Para. 1 of operation orders No. 4 of 27th inst. is cancelled.

2. The following moves and groupings will take place to-night.

The Sec. of C/104 in I.14.a will join the other Section in H.12.d and the whole Battery will form part of B. Group.

A/103 will move to-night to the prepared position in H.24.c.3.7.

B/103 will move to-night to the prepared position in I.13.a.7.2.

C/105 on arrival to-night will occupy the position at I.1.d.5.2.

3. From to-night the Artillery Groups will be as follows;-

"A" GROUP under Lt.Col.Biddulph H.Q. La Rolanderie H.11.c	A) B) D)	102nd F.A. Bde.	Supporting 69th Inf. Bde. Right Sector.
	A) C) D)	103rd F.A. Bde	
"B" GROUP under Col. Hobday H.Q. I.1.c.4.5	A) B) C) D)	104th F.A. Bde.	Supporting 70th Inf. Bde. Left Sector
	B	103rd F.A. Bde.	
	C	102nd F.A. Bde. (Counter Battery)	

4. The 105th (Howitzer) Bde. (H.Q. I.1.c.1.6) will be under the direct orders of the G.O.C.,R.A. but Group Commanders can in urgent cases ask O.C. 105th Bde. direct for the assistance of his batteries.

Necessary telephonic communication to be fixed up.

5. Lt. Col. Henning R.F.A. will remain in administrative Command of his Brigade.

6. All returns and reports will be submitted through Brigade Commanders except;-

1. Report on operations of the day.
2. Daily report on enemy's artillery.
3. Daily intelligence report.
4. Daily casualty return.
5. Daily expenditure of ammunition.

which will come through Group Commanders.

7. Night lines to-night and until further orders will be arranged by Group Commanders. A list of them will be forwarded to H.Q.R.A. and any change made in them will be notified.

O.C. 105th Bde. will also forward a list of the night lines of his batteries.

8. The order for no firing to take place except in case of a hostile attack or for urgent retaliation will remain in force until further orders.

Capt.
Brigade Major, R.A.
23rd Division.

Copies No.	1 - 6	A Group
	7-12	B Group
	13	103 F.A. Bde.
	14-18	105th F.A. Bde.
	19	23rd Division
	20	No.2 Mountain Batty.
	21-22	Filed.

app XXIV

DISPOSITIONS 23rd Divisional Artillery.

RIGHT GROUP. Col. Biddulph Commanding.

A/102	I.7.d.2.1.
B/102	H.18.b.5.7.
D/102	I.19.b.3.4.
C/103	H.24.b.7.8.
D/103	H.24.c.5.1.
A/103	I.13.a.7.1.

LEFT GROUP. Col. Hobday Commanding.

A/104	I.7.b.5.5.
B/104	I.13.b.2.8.
C/104	H.12.d.4.8.
D/104	I.13.c.4.6.
C/102	I.8.c.9.3. (Counter Battery)
B/103	H.24.a.3.1.

105 F.A. Brigade. (How)

A/105	H.28.b.6.3. (Counter Battery)
B/105	H.18.d.2.4.
C/105	I.1.d.3.2.
D/105	I.8.a.6.6.

To Adjutant-General
3rd Echelon

23rd Division

121
7430

CONFIDENTIAL.

WAR DIARY

OF

General Staff Branch Headquarters 23rd. Divisional Artillery.

from October 1st. 1915 to October 31st. 1915.

Vol 3

Charles Broad
Capt.

BRIGADE MAJOR,
R.A. 23rd DIVISION.

31.10.15

Army Form C. 2118.

Instructions regarding War Diaries and Intelligence Summaries are contained in F. S. Regs., Part II. and the Staff Manual respectively. Title pages will be prepared in manuscript.

WAR DIARY
or
~~INTELLIGENCE~~ SUMMARY.
(Erase heading not required.)

HQ RA 23 DW

Place	Date 1915	Hour	Summary of Events and Information	Remarks and references to Appendices
CROIX DU BAC	Oct 1st		1. Quiet day - nothing to record.	
W. ESTAIRES	Oct 2nd		1. Quiet day. Reconnaissance for advance & retirement had not been made before the action on Sept 25th, on account of lack of time. These reconnaissances are now being made & a definite scheme worked out for both possibilities. 2. Instructions were given to all Observing Officers to watch the WEZ MACQUART - BOIS BLANCS road & neighbourhood for signs of defended localities. These exist no doubt & will be the first check to our infantry & each must be located & arrangements made for ~~cutt~~ knocking it out & cutting wire. 3. The photos help. LE MAISNIL even under looks the strongest place the photo here [illegible] does not show in the photo.	
	Oct 3 to Oct 7		1. Nothing important from an Artillery point of view has occurred. A few hostile batteries are marked down by picked up fuzes - angles of descent etc. Also by means of cross bearings endeavours are being made to mark the track of a searchlight which is supposed to travel on a motor. 2. Special night observation posts have been established in the hope of being able to spot guns by their flashes. 3. Orders have been given to thicken all hedges to hide gun flashes as the leaves fall off. 4. The [illegible] the enemy have been relieved lately & replaced by young soldiers or cavalry. Nothing heavier than a 4.2" How has been seen for several days.	

Instructions regarding War Diaries and Intelligence Summaries are contained in F. S. Regs., Part II. and the Staff Manual respectively. Title pages will be prepared in manuscript.

WAR DIARY
or
INTELLIGENCE SUMMARY.
(Erase heading not required.)

Army Form C. 2118.

2

Place	Date	Hour	Summary of Events and Information	Remarks and references to Appendices
CROIX DU BAC	8th.		Test S.O.S carried out last night. Time slow as the telephone operators are slow in getting on. The night observations are not yet satisfactory as no intersections can be got.	
			All quiet in front. The weather is misty and prevents all distant observation.	
"	9th } 10th }		Nothing to report.	
	11th		Conference held – three Brigadier Generals RA. & 3rd Corps Artillery advisor. Following points were discussed.	
			1. Retaliation. This should be done in bulk. When it is decided to retaliate some definite point should be selected and sufficient shell fired to do real damage.	
			2. In this connection it might be advisable to move a gun or two temporarily to a flank and enfilade a piece of trench.	
			3. To stop damage to ammunition it would be advisable to rub mineral jelly round the uncapped fuzes.	
			4. Arrangements should be made to send out barometer readings twice a day.	
			5. To attack the "blocks" on both sides of the infantry must be made with a gun. For this purpose a gun in the parapet is invaluable. It knocks in the hostile parapet & fills up the trench & then forms a block.	
			6. The system of cutting wire in lanes is very apt to get the infantry into trouble. It should if possible be cut all along the front of attack. Batteries cannot	

Instructions regarding War Diaries and Intelligence Summaries are contained in F. S. Regs., Part II. and the Staff Manual respectively. Title pages will be prepared in manuscript.

WAR DIARY
or
INTELLIGENCE SUMMARY.
(Erase heading not required.)

Army Form C. 2118.

3

Place	Date	Hour	Summary of Events and Information	Remarks and references to Appendices

work nearer than one battery every 100 yds a/c the difficulty of observing. The ammn required is roughly 15 rounds per yd. and it takes a 6 gun battery roughly 8 hours to cut 100 yds including rests. Possibly a mixture of H.E and shrapnel is the best ammn for the purpose. At ranges less than 2000 yds the allowance may be reduced. Guns in the parapet are no use for cutting wire as the fuze cannot be regulated under 500 yds & also they would soon be spotted & knocked out. Guns in enfilade are better for cutting wire than direct as they sweep along the front but the "line" must be very accurate.

7. Liaison officers in the attack. - One is necessary with each Bde HQ - with 4 gun batteries it is impossible to send them with Bns and also rather unnecessary. With a Brigade the RA Colonel should be the liaison officer if possible.

8. F.O.O's in the attack should not go forward until the captured trenches have been consolidated. The principle is that they should be where they get the best view. When they do go forward they must make arrangements for both wire and visual signalling and be accompanied by orderlies.

9. After the assault a barrage must be put all round the infantry. The smoke prevents the F.O.O's seeing what the enemy are doing and if

Instructions regarding War Diaries and Intelligence Summaries are contained in F. S. Regs., Part II. and the Staff Manual respectively. Title pages will be prepared in manuscript.

WAR DIARY
or
INTELLIGENCE SUMMARY.
(Erase heading not required.)

Army Form C. 2118.

4

Place	Date	Hour	Summary of Events and Information	Remarks and references to Appendices
			there is not an efficient barrage; they can cross the open.	
			10. When communication are cut, it might be useful to put single guns near F.O.O's which they can use in emergency & direct by voice control.	
			11. When wire cutting is arranged, the O.C. infantry who are to attack should accompany the RA officer to ensure that the wire is cut in the right place.	
			12. The ammn dump must not be too far back. In the late 8th Div. operation, it should have been at CROIX DU BAC. It is absolutely necessary that an officer should be in charge of the ammn in each battery. This & the question of liaison officers raises the question of 5 officers really being needed in a battery.	
			13. The distinguishing flags used by the infantry often cannot be seen a/c dust & smoke. The difficulty of spotting our infantry remains as difficult as ever.	
			14. A large previous registration by aeroplane on all hostile approaches is necessary and the 4.5" How. should be concentrated on the approaches after the assault.	

2353 Wt. W2544/1454 700,000 5/15 D. D. & L. A.D.S.S./Forms/C. 2118.

Instructions regarding War Diaries and Intelligence Summaries are contained in F. S. Regs., Part II. and the Staff Manual respectively. Title pages will be prepared in manuscript.

WAR DIARY
or
INTELLIGENCE SUMMARY.
(Erase heading not required.)

Army Form C. 2118.

5

Place	Date	Hour	Summary of Events and Information	Remarks and references to Appendices
			15. Electric signalling in a rifle barrel is a possibility & should be tried.	
			16. False observing stations are a great assistance.	
			17. S.O.S. Signal in battle should be called for by the infantry Brigadier only.	
			18. If batteries are temporarily withdrawn from action, arrangements must be made beforehand so that telephone lines are laid to the ~~that~~ new position of the men so that communication with the observing station & the Group HQ is not broken.	
CROIX DU BAC	12th – 14th		Nothing to report. Work & reconnaissance on the Reserve & Support lines. The daily reports have enabled us to mark down 5 batteries last week & 2 or 3 more this week. Log books have now been introduced into each observing station. A 5.9" battery has appeared but the location is not yet certain.	
	15th		1. Policy began of shelling WEZ MACQUART and PREMESQUES chiefly the enemy shell CHAPELLE D'ARMENTIERES to see if we can make the road safer. 2. Three batteries told off to shell 3 suspected gun positions immediately they fire in order to find out if they are really occupied gun positions.	

2353 Wt. W2544/1454 700,000 5/15 D. D. & L. A.D.S.S./Forms/C. 2118.

Instructions regarding War Diaries and Intelligence Summaries are contained in F. S. Regs., Part II. and the Staff Manual respectively. Title pages will be prepared in manuscript.

WAR DIARY
or
INTELLIGENCE SUMMARY.
(Erase heading not required.)

Army Form C. 2118.

6.

Place	Date	Hour	Summary of Events and Information	Remarks and references to Appendices
Croix du BAC	Oct. to	15 20th	1. B.G. RA. 3rd Corps informed us that a proposal was on foot to capture the GERMAN House salient. Col. Hobday was instructed to make a reconnaissance with a view to finding the best place for the wire cutting and for placing 4 guns in the parapet to batter in the parapet & also to make the "step" on either side of the infantry attack. It appears that the attack is to be in the nature of a holding attack after the manner of the 8th Div attack on Sept. 25th. The trench railway will be useful for getting the guns down to the parapet. The wire will not be easy to cut as our own salient is only 75 yds from the German one. Aeroplane registration on the communication trenches was commenced this week. Help from the 50th RA. will have to be obtained as some of the trenches can only be enfiladed from that area.	
			2. Alternative positions and alternative observation stations have been definitely selected.	
			3. All batteries have duplicated their telephone communication with usual chiefly lamps - stopped down so that it cannot be read by the enemy. Forward signalling in all cases is not fixed up.	
			4. All batteries have shelters near the battery position which can be occupied if the battery is heavily shelled and also not required to shoot. Telephone communication with the O.S. is ready.	
			5. Nine hostile batteries have been fairly definitely located by means of sound, flash & shell hole bearings - fuzes & photos etc.	

2353 Wt. W2544/1454 700,000 5/15 D. D. & L. A.D.S.S./Forms/C. 2118.

Army Form C. 2118.

7

WAR DIARY
or
INTELLIGENCE SUMMARY.
(Erase heading not required.)

Instructions regarding War Diaries and Intelligence Summaries are contained in F. S. Regs., Part II. and the Staff Manual respectively. Title pages will be prepared in manuscript.

Place	Date	Hour	Summary of Events and Information	Remarks and references to Appendices
Croix du Bac.			6. A list of hostile O.S. has been made - 20-30 of them are suspected. No doubt many are false. The policy to be followed is to confirm these and then to fire a period in the battle to knock them out.	
			7. All these suspected hostile battery positions are being established when they fire so that they may be confirmed by their fire ceasing.	
			8. A list of hostile M.G. emplacements has been prepared. They are knocked out when discovered as considerably more labour is entailed in their construction than in an O.S. and also so many alternatives are not available.	
			9. Ammunition is now plentiful. We fire 2 rounds to every German round. A fair proportion of German shell are blind - this applies chiefly to the 5.9" How - The 77 cm gun bursts regularly.	
	Oct 21st		1. The attack is to be made shortly but the point of attack has been altered to exactly the front face of hostile salient. The wire will be difficult to cut here as the trajectory will only just clear our parapet.	
			2. Reconnoitred the positions around DESPLANQUES Fme and found them much better than they look on map. They are fairly well screened.	
			3. First air report on our own positions re O/100. These should be useful.	
			4. Made arrangements to start an R.A. Signalling School. 50 men 2 N.C.O. Instructors R.A. Signalling officer and one instructor from the Signal Coy. They are all to be collected down here & stay about 3-4 weeks. Should be useful.	

2353 Wt. W2544/1454 700,000 5/15 D. D. & L. A.D.S.S./Forms/C. 2118.

Instructions regarding War Diaries and Intelligence Summaries are contained in F. S. Regs., Part II. and the Staff Manual respectively. Title pages will be prepared in manuscript.

WAR DIARY
or
INTELLIGENCE SUMMARY.
(Erase heading not required.)

Army Form C. 2118.

8.

Place	Date	Hour	Summary of Events and Information	Remarks and references to Appendices
CROIX DU BAC	Oct 22		1. Nothing to report except that point of attack has been changed back to Salient itself - chiefly on account of the difficulty of cutting the wire in the other place.	
	Oct 23		1. B.M. RA reconnoitred for places to put the guns in the parapet. Col. HOBDAY B Group. O.C. No 2 Mtn Bty - O.C. 101st Fd Coy RE accompanied reconnaissance.	

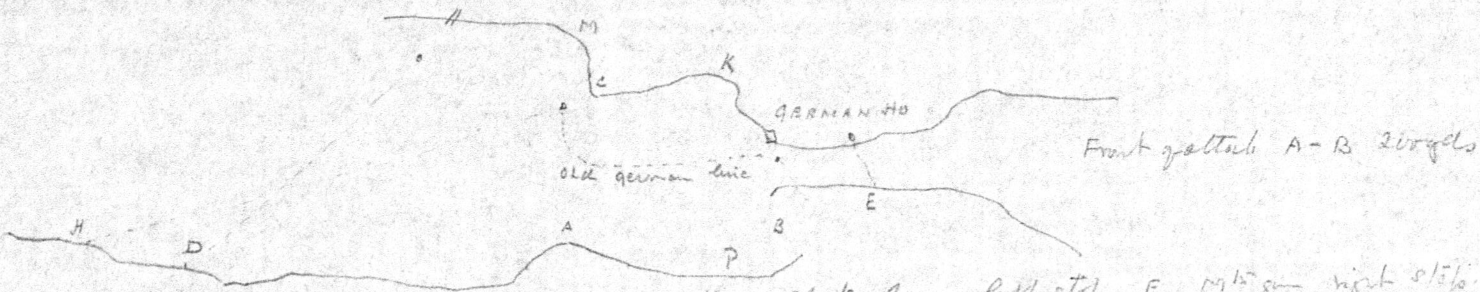

It was decided to use 4 guns viz H 18 Pr to form left stop E Mtn gun right stop. Both at points where communication trenches join front parapet. D to rake parapet C-K - B Mtn gun to rake parapet German HQ - K.
These points had all to be fixed with the aid of the aerial photos. It was impossible to see where the communication trenches joined the front parapet. The old German line on account of the points A & B being rather low completely hides the parapet C-M.
Not much really is known at present about the wire. The worst part is thought to be behind the old parapet where it is hard to see & difficult for patrols to go. The choice of 18 Pr or Mtn was decided chiefly by the difficulty of getting the respective guns down to the line trenches.

2353 Wt. W2544/1454 700,000 5/15 D. D. & L. A.D.S.S./Forms/C. 2118.

Army Form C. 2118.

9

Instructions regarding War Diaries and Intelligence Summaries are contained in F. S. Regs., Part II. and the Staff Manual respectively. Title pages will be prepared in manuscript.

WAR DIARY
or
INTELLIGENCE SUMMARY.
(Erase heading not required.)

Place	Date	Hour	Summary of Events and Information	Remarks and references to Appendices
CROIX DU BAC	Oct 24		1. Issued orders to C/103 D/102 A/104 to reconnoitre for wire cutting. The job is difficult as there are many trees, old houses near our parapet which is 10' high in places & the German wire is in places only 100 yds from our parapet. Two places at 1100 & 1500 were selected but it seems likely that they will not clear the crest at that range	
			2. The Div: Comdr decided only to have the two flank guns to cut the "stoke" one gun may be used at "P" if there is a 5 mins preliminary bombardment, but the present idea is to take the place by a surprise in the middle of the night.	
			3. Orders were issued to the above A/104 & B/104 each to find a gun & No 2 Mountain MC – three subaltern sent to confer with OC 107th Fd Coy RE. Emplacements to be begun tomorrow night.	
			4. 3rd Corps asked today for estimate of ammn required. It seems likely that we shall lose some batteries to 8th Div but 2nd Army on our left have promised some 5" How which seems a round-about way of doing it – Each man for himself.	
	Oct 25th		1. Had orders from 3rd Corps to send 2 Hows and 2 18 pdrs to 8th DW. am asking 2nd Army for loan of some 5" Hows to replace them.	
			2. Made out ammn requirements last night for two days bombardment and am told today that it is to be one days bombardment so everyone stayed up to 2 am to no purpose!	
			3. Arranged to send C/103 C/104 A/105 B/105 to 8th Div.	

2353 Wt. W2544/1454 700,000 5/15 D. D. & L. A.D.S.S./Forms/C. 2118.

Instructions regarding War Diaries and Intelligence Summaries are contained in F. S. Regs., Part II. and the Staff Manual respectively. Title pages will be prepared in manuscript.

WAR DIARY
or
INTELLIGENCE SUMMARY.
(Erase heading not required.)

Army Form C. 2118.

10

Place	Date	Hour	Summary of Events and Information	Remarks and references to Appendices
Croix du Bac.	Oct 25		4) The centre battery gun in parapet is not to be used now only the barrage guns. 5. Col. Perkins 26th Siege Coy came here this morning & arranged preliminary details for bombarding with 6" & 8" How. etc.	
	26th		1. Issued orders for registration of all points in area of attack if not already done. 2. Reconnoitred & chose two places for 50th Div. howitzers if they are given to us which seems probable 3. Received result of inspection by Flying Corps.	app IX
	Oct 27th		A/102 C/104 shelled but it is not certain that the shelling was meant for the batteries - very possibly only the cluster of farm.	
	Oct 28th		1. Date for the show fixed for about Nov 7th so that we shall be able to give the Hun a rest after our registration to quiet him down & lull any suspicion he may have. 2. Made arrangements to put another gun in the parapet in case the mountain gun in the salient should be knocked out. 3. An officer patrol - 2/Lieut JACKSON B/104 is going out tonight to find out all he can about the enemy's wire opposite the salient.	

2353 Wt. W2544/1454 700,000 5/15 D. D. & L. A.D.S.S./Forms/C. 2118.

Instructions regarding War Diaries and Intelligence Summaries are contained in F. S. Regs., Part II. and the Staff Manual respectively. Title pages will be prepared in manuscript.

WAR DIARY
or
INTELLIGENCE SUMMARY.
(Erase heading not required.)

Army Form C. 2118.

11.

Place	Date	Hour	Summary of Events and Information	Remarks and references to Appendices
Croix du Bac	Oct	29	1. Patrol last night found knife rests in front of GERMAN HOUSE but was unable to learn more as German patrols were about & the officer was alone. German wire is 140 yds from our main line ie not the salient. 2. Visited the 104 FA Bde fighting head quarters & found that they had an air line and ground line back to the main Bde HQ & one wire to each battery in group. Arranged following – each battery & lines to main HQ to be duplicated for the 1st 200 yds. Wire netting to be also held ready to run out if all lines are cut. The F HQ is only 300 yds from the deep power cable in the LILLE road so that they are going to dig a line of D5 to that. I also arranged a road for motorcycles and a place for visual signalling so hope we shall keep communication	

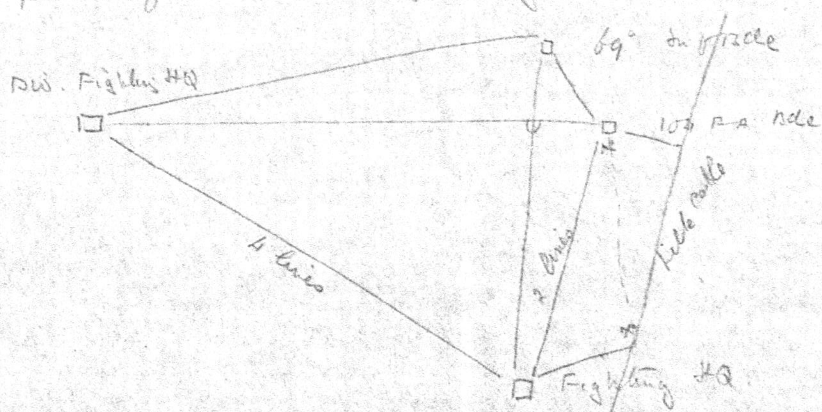

The above diagram shows the duplication of ways for getting through. In addition there are 2 lines from 104 FA Bde to each battery & each battery is joined to the next. All batteries have lamps between O.S. & battery. Some have been able to arrange forward visual to O.S.

2353 Wt. W2544/1454 700,000 5/15 D. D. & L. A.D.S.S./Forms/C. 2118.

Instructions regarding War Diaries and Intelligence Summaries are contained in F. S. Regs., Part II. and the Staff Manual respectively. Title pages will be prepared in manuscript.

WAR DIARY
or
INTELLIGENCE SUMMARY.
(Erase heading not required.)

Army Form C. 2118.

12

Place	Date	Hour	Summary of Events and Information	Remarks and references to Appendices
	Oct	29	3. Meanwhile O.P.s have been knocked about lately & will probably become untenable in the battle. 50% of these or 50 supposed are marked down so I hope we shall be able to deal with them.	
			4. Heard tonight 1500 rounds available from 5th Army. So well worth having.	
	Oct	~~29~~ 30	1. G.O.C. R.A. visited CALAIS to see wire cutting experiments.	
			2. Talked over counter battery work with adj. Loring's Bde. They say they will need help to deal with hostile observing stations as they only have two heavy batteries now.	
			3. They are going to make arrangements with next door heavies to deal with ~~hostile~~ hostile batteries Nos 6 & 10.	
			4. Several O.Ps shelled lately - a new one for the battle would be a good thing where possible	App. XI
			5. Arrangements for shooting on our own trenches if captured complete.	App. XII
	Oct	31st	1. Heard this morning that all First Army shows are postponed as 11th Corps are taking over Indian Corps front and part of 20th Div front. The postponement is only supposed to be until the re-arrangement of corps is complete.	
			Charles [illegible] Capt. Bde. Maj. R.A. 23rd Div	

2353 Wt. W2544/1454 700,000 5/15 D. D. & L. A.D.S.S./Forms/C. 2118.

S E C R E T.

R.A. Divisional Headquarters,
23rd Division.

I

Headquarters,

\- - - - - - - - - -

With reference to the attached.

1. Group Commanders will reconnoitre their areas and will prepare schemes for the withdrawal of their Batteries, a report being rendered to this office as soon as this has been done.

2. Positions will then br prepared for occupation and this work will be commenced as soon as the work on the alternative positions referred to in this office No. D.A.455 is completed.

3. This memorandum must be kept entirely secret by the Officers concerned as it is not wished that people should think that a withdrawal is contemplated under any circumstances.

18-10-15.

Capt.
Brigade Major, R.A.
23rd Division.

SECRET

R.A. Divisional Headquarters,

23rd Division.

DEFENSIVE ARRANGEMENTS.

23rd DIVISIONAL ARTILLERY.

Reference 1/20000 map, sheet 36 N.W.

1. The defences in the portion of the line occupied by the 23rd Division consist, in addition to the firing line and support trenches now held by the Infantry of

(a) The BOIS GRENIER Line running roughly along the BOIS GRENIER- Fme DESPLANQUE road.

(b) The LA VASEE line of Posts running from I.19. central along the LA VASEE - RUE ALLEE road.

(c) The L'ARMEE Line of posts running from BOIS GRENIER to GRIS POT - L'ARMEE - RUE MARLE.

2. It is not considered that a withdrawal of the Infantry from the firing line to the support trenches would necessitate any change in the present dispositions of the Artillery, but a further withdrawal to the a.b. or c. lines would require certain changes of position, and the action to be taken in this connection is indicated in the following paras.

3. The withdrawal to the BOIS GRENIER line might be of a partial nature i.e. only one Infantry Brigade might have to come back or both brigades might have to do so, it is therefore not possible to give definite instructions beforehand regarding movements of batteries, and Artillery Group Commanders will have to be guided by circumstances, but it seems evident that any Infantry withdrawal to the position of the BOIS GRENIER line in front of the following batteries,

A. Group	D/103.	D/102.	C/103
B. Group	B/103	C/102	
105th Bde.	A/105		

will necessitate their being moved further back. Suitable positions for them must therefore be selected, and for this purpose areas are allotted as follows;-

A.Group Rue de BIEZ inclusive and west of this road.

A/105 will be allotted a position by O.C. A. Group in consultation with O.C. 105th Bde.

B.Group

Between Rue des ACQUETS and L'ARMEE - Rue MARLE road both inclusive.

In the BOIS GRENIER line the junction between A and B Groups will be at I.29.a.8.1. This corresponds to the junction between the two Infantry Brigades.

4. Possible positions in the above mentioned areas are as follows:-

(1) H.16.b.2.2. Room for 12 guns. Good cover from aeroplanes. Wide field of fire, but nothing to hide flashes. Covered line of retirement. Observation station not reconnoitred.

(2) H.9.d.9.9. Room for 4 Howitzers. House spoils position for guns. Cover from aeroplane under apple trees. Observation station not reconnoitred.

(3) Under H.16.b. Under west bank of stream. Room for 3 batteries. Two positions already prepared. Ridge in front conceals guns but not the flashes. Position good. Observation station not reconnoitred.

(4) H.18.a.3.2 Under fence - fair cover - room for 4 guns. Observation station not reconnoitred.

(5) H.11.d.6.4 Position in garden - field of fire limited by house. Good cover from aeroplane.

The above positions are not necessarily recommended as being the best available, as time for reconnaissance has been limited.

5. Group Commanders should ask their Infantry Brigade Commanders to let them see their Defence Schemes.

6. A withdrawal to the BOIS GRENIER line may also possibly effect the observing stations of batteries other than those to be moved and this must be arranged for.

Capt.
Brigade Major, R.A
23rd Division.

14-10-15.

S E C R E T.

R.A. Divisional Headquarters,

23rd Division.

II

To Col. Henning, R.F.A.

Reference $\frac{1}{20,000}$ Map sheet, 36 N.W.

1. Attached is a tracing of the approximate position of the line known as the G.H.Q. 2nd line of defence.

2. It is taken from an old map handed over by the 27th Division and it is not known if it has been accurately marked in.

3. The flanks of the 23rd Division area are at road junction H.22.b.3.6 and at railway B.28.a.9.8.

4. Will you kindly reconnoitre this line and draw up a report showing:-

1. Suitable organization of defence from artillery point of view.
2. Positions for batteries, and alternative positions.
3. Approximate arcs of fire from each position.
4. Position for observing stations and alternative observation stations.
5. Positions for wagon line and ammunition columns and D.A.C.
6. Distribution of available roads for ammunition supply.
7. Amount of wire required for communication purposes.
8. Billeting accommodation available for batteries, wagon lines and columns.
9. Position of any particularly good observation points for general tactical purposes should be noted.
10. Any other points to which you think it is advisable to draw attention.
11. The report will kindly be constructed more or less as follows:-
    - (a) Short Summary.
    - (b) Part 1. General description for information of H.Q.R.A.
    - (c) Appendices - each appendix dealing in detail with each locality - position etc. so that if it should be ever necessary to occupy the line, each appendix can be detached and given to the battery etc. detailed to occupy that particular locality - position etc.

1310-15.

Capt.
Brigade Major, R.A
23rd Division.

III

S E C R E T.

Battery Positions.

23rd Divisional Artillery.

A/102	I.7.d.2.1	Under tall trees
B/102	H.18.b.5.6	In garden.
C/102	I.8.c.9½.4	In long rampart in open.
D/102	I.19.b.3.4	Under 4 willows
A/103	I.13.a.7.2	Under willows in ploughed field
B/103	H.24.a.2.1	Under trees in orchard, facing E.
C/103	H.24.b.5.8	In garden
D/103	H.24.c.5½.1	Along hedge facing S.E.
A/104	I.7.b.4½.4½.	4 mounds in open
B/104	I.13.b.1.9½	Under hedge
C/104	H.12.b.8.4	Two haystacks - 1 shed - 1 mound by Burnt Farm House.
D/104	I.13.c.3.7	One haystack and under fence
A/105	H.29.b.3.8	Along hedge
B/105	H.18.c.9.4	Mound by hedge
C/105	I.1.d.2.6	In walled garden
D/105	I.8.a.56	In garden

20-10-15.

Capt.
Brigade Major, R.A.
23rd Division.

SECRET

NIGHT LINES.

A GROUP

A/103	Trench	52
B/102	..	53
D/102	..	54
C/103	..	55
D/103	..	56
A/102	..	57-58.

B GROUP

D/104	Trench	59
B/104	Trenches	60.61.62.
B/103	..	63
A/104	..	64
C/104	..	65
C/102	..	66

105TH F.A. BDE.

A/105	Trenches	52 -54
B/105	..	55 -58
C/105	..	59 -62
D/105	..	63 -66.

2-10-16.

Capt.
Brigade Major, R.A
23rd Division.

D.A. 530

23RD DIVISIONAL ARTILLERY. Oct.1915.

ALTERNATIVE POSITIONS.

- - - - - - - - -

A. Group	H.24.c.2.3
	H.24.a.6.5
	I.19.a.2.2
	H.17.d.7.3
B. Group	I. 7.d.4.9
	I. 1.c.2.1
	I.13.c.8.3
	I.14.a.6.2
	I.24.c.3.6
105th F.A.Bde.	H.24.a.2.3
	I.1.d.4.2

Capt.
Brigade Major, R.A.
23rd Division.

VI

A L T E R N A T I V E

O B S E R V A T I O N S T A T I O N S.

UNIT	DESCRIPTION	SQUARE	REMARKS.
A GROUP			
A/102	Tree	I. 13.b.2.10	
"	House	I.19.c.9.7	
"	House	I.17.d.5.1	
"	House	I.19.b.4.1	
"	House (Sp.night)	I.8.b.4.1	
B/102	House	I.19.c.7.4	
"	House	H.18.b.2.6	
D/102	Tree	I.19.b.3.7	
"	House	I.19.c.7.4	
A/103	Trench	I.32	
"	Burnt Farm	I.20.d.3.6	
"	New Farm	I.19.c.9½.6	
C/103	House	H.30.b.6½.3	
"	New Farm	I.19.c.9½.6.	
"	House	H.30.b.7.8	
"	House	I.19.c.8.5	
D/103	Moat Farm	I.25.a.½.9	
B GROUP			
A/104	Chapelle D'Armentieres	I.9.c.3.5	
"	Lille Post	I.15.b.6.9½	
B/104	Halfway House	I.14.b.4.1	
"	Ruins	I.14.b.9.4	
"	Chapelle D'Armentieres	I.9.c.2.6½	
C/104	Fme Du Biez	I.15.b.3.5	
"	Chapelle D'Armentieres	I.9.c.4.5½	
D/104	Tree	I.14.d.6.8	
"	Brewery	H.24.d.9.5	
C/102	Lille Post	I.15.b.6.9½	
"	Cottage	I.15.d.1.7	
B/103	Moat Farm	I.25.a.1.9	
"	Chapelle D'Armentieres	I.9.c.4.5	
105th BDE.			
A/105	Convent	H.24.d.25.15	
"	Tree	H.29.b.4.1	
"	Tree	H.36.b.7.1	
B/105	Bois Grenier	H.30.b.7.3	
"	Brewery	H.30.b.5.10	
C/105	Chapelle D'Armentieres	I.8.a.8.2	
"	Tree	I.14.b.0.1	
D/105	Lille Post	I.9.d.6.0	
"	Chapelle D'Armentieres XRds	I.9.c.4½5[illegible]	
"	Chimney	I.8.a.7.1½	

VII

ESTIMATE OF AMMUNITION REQUIRED BY
23rd, DIV. ARTILLERY.

	4.5" How.		18 Pdr.	
	H.E.	SH.	H.E.	Sh.
1. Wire cutting. 1st & 2nd days.				
(a) Front of attack 200 yards.				2000.
(b) Two Feints on other parts of line, each 40 yards.				800.
2. 1st days Bombardment.				
(a) Front of attack including German House.	200.		250.	
(b) Flanks of attack.	200.		200.	
(c) Support and communication trenches, as much damage as possible is required.	500.		600.	
(d) Bombardment of parapets at two Feints.			100.	
Total 1st Day.	900.		1150.	2800
3. Night of 1st/2nd day.				
(a) To prevent repair of wire and trenches.			700	700.
4. 2nd Days Bombardment.				
(a) Repetition of 1st day.	900		1150	
(b) Extra for buildings in rear and M.G. emplacements.	150		150	
(c) Two minutes intense bombardment before the lull.	70		200	200.
5. Night 2nd/3rd day.				
(a) To prevent repair to wire and trenches.				700.

	4.5" How.		18 Pdr.	
	H.E.	Sh.	H.E.	Sh.
(b) On flanks and in rear from moment of assault for half an hour.	360		600.	600.
(c) Ditto at reduced rate till daylight.	720		1200.	1200.
(d) One 18 pdr in parapet.			200	50.
(e) One Mountain Gun in parapet 250 rounds.				
<u>Total first two days & Nights.</u>	3100.		4650.	3450.
6. <u>3rd and subsequent Days Fighting.</u>				
(a) For possible eventualities in form of counter attacks.	600.	600.	1200.	3000.
7. <u>Counter Battery allowance for 3 days.</u>				
(a) One 18 pdr Battery.			600.	600.
(b) One 4.5" How. Battery.	1200.			
8. Two 18 pdr Batteries. Possible defensive action on right section of Divisional Front.				400.
<u>GRAND TOTAL.</u>	4900	600.	6450.	7450. 10250

<u>NOTE.</u>

<u>The above estimate is based on:-</u>

(1) Two 4.5" Howitzer and seven 18 pdr Batteries for support of the attack.

(2) One 4.5" Howitzer and one 18 pdr Battery for counter battery work.

(3) Two 18 pdr batteries for feints and defensive purposes on Right Section of Divisional Front.

<u>TOTAL.</u> Three 4.5" Howitzer and ten 18 pdr batteries, as it is understood that the remainder of the 23rd Divisional Artillery will have to be loaned to another Division.

24/10/1915.

Brigadier General, R.A.
Commanding 23rd, Divn.Artillery

Secret BMS/18/7

R.A. Divisional Headquarters,
23rd Division.

VIII

Headquarters,
23rd Division.

Reference your No. S.G. 89.

I understand from Artillery Adviser 2nd Corps that he could lend two 5" Howitzer Batteries to assist this Division, also that G.O.C., R.A. 21st Division can probably help with an 18 pr. Battery. May 3rd Corps please be asked to approach the 2nd Corps on the matter and then, if approved, I can arrange details with the Officers concerned.

26-10-15.

Brigadior General,
Commanding Royal Artillery,
23rd Division.

SECRET. B.M.S. 78/6 R.A.Divisional Hdqtrs.

23rdDivision.

IX

Headquarters,

----

1. All batteries of B Group less C/104 and C/102 and also D/103, A/105, C/105 and D/105 batteries will register as many of the following points as possible if it has not already been done.

viz., 406 - 408 - 409 - 410 - 413 - 414 - 418 - 419 - 421 - 422 - 425 - 427 - 428 - 429 - 430 - 431 - 432 - 433.

2. This registration will be carried out under orders of O.C. B.Group. It is to be commenced at once (to-day) and will be spread over the next few days so as not to draw undue attention to this area.

3. A/103 should be one of the batteries to start first as it has probably most points to register.

4. Any new observation stations required for the above will have telephone wire permanently laid down to them at once.

26-10-15.

Capt.
Brigade Major, R A.
23rd Division.

IX

R.A. Divisional Headquarters,

23rd Division.

RESULT OF AN INSPECTION OF BATTERY POSITIONS

MADE TO-DAY BY THE ROYAL FLYING CORPS.

- - - - - - - - - - - - - - - - - - - -

A/102) B/102) C/102)	Good and well concealed.
D/102	Concealed except for a track behind the battery.
A/103) B/103)	Good and well concealed.
C/103	The front of the emplacements is visible. The blast from the guns has killed the grass and made a different coloured patch.
D/103	The entrances to dug-outs are visible from the rear.
A/104	Very conspicuous - probably mistaken for a dummy battery but tracks behind very conspicuous.
B/104) C/104) D/104)	Good and well concealed.
A/105	Rather conspicuous - chiefly given away by tracks leading to and from a farm near which look like an ammunition route.
B/105	Good and well concealed.
C/105	Very good - no sign of the battery.
D/105	Might be equally good but No.4 gun emplacement shows up brown earth - might be remedied by a bundle of bean stalks as the neighbourhood is all market gardens.

Above forwarded for information and necessary action.

Charles Kyrrell

26-10-15.

Capt.
Brigade Major, R.A.
23rd Division.

41

R.A. Divisional Headquarters,
23rd Division.

Headquarters,

- - - - - - - - - -

1. Two or three observation stations have been shelled the last day or two.

2. It is extremely improbable that a station which has been used daily for weeks for registration purposes should remain unknown to the enemy.

3. In order to prevent dislocation of fire during the forthcoming operations it would probably be a wise move if a new station could be occupied for the fight.

4. A good view of the battery's zone must of course be the first consideration and this consideration will prevent many battery Commanders moving, but in other cases it may be possible to have a new place ready.

5. In all cases all details of the move tothe alternative observation stations should be thought out beforehand, and all hands practised so that every man knows exactly what he has to do if the move is ordered. All these details should be known in the battery as well in case new men have to be sent up to the observation stations to replace casualties.

30-10-15.

Capt.
Brigade Major, R.A.
23rd Division.

TABLE SHOWING BATTERIES WHICH CAN BE CONCENTRATED ON EACH BRITISH TRENCH.

TRENCH	NO.	A/102	B/102	D/102	A/103	C/103	D/103	A/104	B/104	C/104	D/104	C/102	B/103	A/105	B/105	C/105	D/105
I.32	52			2	A/103			Nil. Owing to trees in front of position.						A/105	B/105	C/105	
I.26.1	53	3		D/102	A/103									A/105	B/105	C/105	
I.26.2	54	A/102	B/102	D/102	A/103	C/103	D/103						B/103	A/105	B/105	C/105	
I.26.3	55	A/102	B/102	1	A/103	C/103	D/103						B/103		B/105	C/105	
I.26.4	56	A/102	B/102		A/103	C/103	D/103				1		B/103		B/105	C/105	
I.26.5	57	3	B/102		A/103		D/103				3		B/103		B/105	C/105	
I.20.1	58	2			A/103		D/103		B/104		D/104		B/103		B/105	C/105	
I.20.2	59	2			A/103		D/103		B/104		D/104		B/103		1	C/105	2
I.21.1	60				A/103		D/103				D/104		B/103			C/105	D/105
I.21.2	61				A/103		D/103			C/104	D/104		B/103			C/105	D/105
I.21.3	62						D/103			C/104	D/104	2	B/103			C/105	D/105
I.21.4	63								B/104	C/104	3		B/103			C/105	D/105
I.15.1	64									C/104	1		B/103			C/105	D/105
I.15.2	65									C/104		C/102				C/105	D/105
I.16	66									C/104		C/102				C/105	D/105

XII

H.Q. 23rd Div:
CRA.

Vol 4

121
7678

Nov 15.

[illegible]

Army Form C. 2118.

Instructions regarding War Diaries and Intelligence Summaries are contained in F. S. Regs., Part II. and the Staff Manual respectively. Title pages will be prepared in manuscript.

WAR DIARY
or
~~INTELLIGENCE SUMMARY.~~
(Erase heading not required.)

23rd Divl Artillery. I.

Place	Date	Hour	Summary of Events and Information	Remarks and references to Appendices
Croix du Bac	Nov 1st		1. HQ & digging parties from PAYNTERS & CHAPMANS howitzer batteries 50th Div T.F. reported last night. Material etc is all ready in their positions so that they can start tomorrow. 2. Decided to place one section of A/103 in 21st Div. area in order to enfilade the wire round GERMAN HOUSE.	
	Nov 2nd		1. Wet weather hinders registration & preparation of emplacements for new batteries. 2. 2nd Lieut LYONS - armoured car sent to reconnoitre roads & positions to engage hostile searchlights. He decided to come into action in Sq I 20a and to put out a short telephone base to verify the searchlights' position by intersection. He will try tomorrow night. 3. Old 4.7 French captured battery come into action again. Most of the shell blind. 4. B.M. started work on "spotting" enemy's artillery de novo in order to see if the same results are obtained. They should be more accurate as now that the leaves are falling flashes are seen more often.	
	Nov 3rd		1. No searchlights appeared so the armoured car did nothing. 2. Enemy shelling today more up towards ERQUINGHEM which is probably our heavy guns have been spotted. No shell fell within 300 or 400 yds of them. 3. Very wet day.	

2353 Wt. W2544/1454 700,000 5/15 D. D. & L. A.D.S.S./Forms/C. 2118.

Army Form C. 2118.

Instructions regarding War Diaries and Intelligence Summaries are contained in F. S. Regs., Part II. and the Staff Manual respectively. Title pages will be prepared in manuscript.

WAR DIARY
or
~~INTELLIGENCE SUMMARY.~~

(Erase heading not required.)

2

Place	Date	Hour	Summary of Events and Information	Remarks and references to Appendices
Croix du Bac	Nov	4th-7th	Nothing particular to report. Operations are postponed a/c rearrangement of Corps as Indian Corps has been taken out. It is proposed to keep this division in front line during the winter & keep one out at a time for a month's training. Programme of proposed training was submitted.	app I.
	Nov	8th	1. Made arrangements to get wind velocity from 2nd Army balloon near STEENWERCK as our nearest is much further away. 2. The water is beginning to be a nuisance in several gun positions. Pumps are available but some have had to be evacuated. 3. The armoured car has been down several nights to shoot at searchlights but it has always been foggy. Last night was clear & the searchlights were out but the car fell into a ditch! It is fortunately under cover & will be removed by a "caterpillar" tomorrow tonight. Nothing else can move it. 4. Single guns have been taken out of batteries in several places & put in special night positions so that if they fire, the flashes which are now so visible will not give them away.	

Instructions regarding War Diaries and Intelligence Summaries are contained in F. S. Regs., Part II. and the Staff Manual respectively. Title pages will be prepared in manuscript.

WAR DIARY
or
~~INTELLIGENCE SUMMARY.~~
(Erase heading not required.)

Army Form C. 2118.

3

Place	Date	Hour	Summary of Events and Information	Remarks and references to Appendices
Croix du Bac	Nov 9th		Nothing to report.	
		10am	arranged air reconnaissance of German Ho salient. a lot of work has been done there lately and a ferro-concrete blockhouse was suspected like those put up at other places. The machine was also to engage a ~~[illegible]~~ hostile battery No 2 but it was too misty to do much.	
		11am	1. Aeroplane again went up - One howitzer battery was ranged on the new work behind the salient & two 18 Pdr. batteries fired on trenches to flanks & rear. The shooting appeared good. The airman is making his report tomorrow.	
			2. The No 2 battery was engaged & 60 rounds HE put on it. While shooting at this, the airman saw gun flashes at I 29 c 78. This battery was engaged and 40-50 4.5" HE put on it.	
			3. The wooden screen which is being erected from the Brewery to the Distillery along the road was shot at today and it appears to be much stronger than was thought. The 18 Pdr. HE does not make much impression on it so that the 4.5" will engage it tomorrow. The screen is now 2-300 yds long & must be made of sleepers with earth behind & is in fact the beginning of a breastwork.	
			4. The enemy did not reply to our fire - He was probably afraid of the aeroplane.	
			5. C/102 was heavily shot at yesterday but not damaged. D/102 was also shot at to a smaller extent.	

2353 Wt. W2544/1454 700,000 5/15 D. D. & L. A.D.S.S./Forms/C. 2118.

Army Form C. 2118.

4

Instructions regarding War Diaries and Intelligence Summaries are contained in F. S. Regs., Part II, and the Staff Manual respectively. Title pages will be prepared in manuscript.

WAR DIARY
or
INTELLIGENCE ~~SUMMARY~~.
(*Erase heading not required.*)

Place	Date	Hour	Summary of Events and Information	Remarks and references to Appendices
Croix du Bac.	Nov 12th		1. Interviewed observer today – his report attached 2. C/105 shot at Brewery screen & knocked four large holes in it – No earth or visible behind. Rain & mist all day which hindered observation. 3. The Brigade Major Capt. C.W.G. ARUND received orders to report at 3rd Corps HQ tomorrow to take up appointment as Staff Officer to Artillery Commander 3rd Corps. 2 Lieut. C.H. Hunt took over all artillery intelligence work pending arrival of new Brigade Major.	
	Nov 13th		BM handed over to Lieut. Smith.	

Charles Wood
Capt. RA

2353 Wt. W2544/1454 700,000 5/15 D. D. & L. A.D.S.S./Forms/C. 2118.

Instructions regarding War Diaries and Intelligence Summaries are contained in F. S. Regs., Part II. and the Staff Manual respectively. Title pages will be prepared in manuscript.

WAR DIARY
or
~~INTELLIGENCE SUMMARY~~.
(Erase heading not required.)

Army Form C. 2118.

5.

Place	Date	Hour	Summary of Events and Information	Remarks and references to Appendices
CROIX du BAC.	Nov 14th		Capt C. J. Clibborn from 3rd Bde RHA joined and took over the duties of Bde Major R.A.	
			Enemy's Artillery not very active during the day – Working parties could be seen engaged on the Breastwork in the vicinity of the Distillery and Brewery. Weather fine though misty and observation difficult.	
	Nov 15th		Enemy's Artillery slightly more active & one of our Artillery Observation Stations was heavily shelled and had to be vacated no casualties. Brigadier General R.A. visited all Group and Brigade Commanders during the afternoon.	
	Nov 16th		Enemy's Artillery very quiet during the day and nothing further of interest to report.	
	Nov 17th		Weather turned very wet – A great deal of movement noticed in Enemy's lines chiefly working parties and vehicles carrying material. The enemy endeavoured by means of smoke to obscure targets we fired on.	

2353 Wt. W2544/1454 700,000 5/15 D. D. & L. A.D.S.S./Forms/C. 2118.

Instructions regarding War Diaries and Intelligence Summaries are contained in F. S. Regs., Part II. and the Staff Manual respectively. Title pages will be prepared in manuscript.

WAR DIARY
or
~~INTELLIGENCE SUMMARY.~~
(Erase heading not required.)

Army Form C. 2118.

6

Place	Date	Hour	Summary of Events and Information	Remarks and references to Appendices
CROIX du BAC	Nov	18th	A frosty night later turned to light rain – The 21st Div on our left bombarded the enemy commencing at 7.30 am + The enemy replied by shelling Armentieres, La Chapelle Armentieres, Gris Pot, L'Armee etc – In all they fired about 750 to 800 rounds – but result 1 gunner wounded + one RE horse killed and 21st Div bomb school set on fire + The bombardment lasted till about 1pm when it died down.	
	Nov	19th	Weather fine a very quiet day, no artillery activity –	
	Nov	20th	A great deal of work is being done in rear of the German lines Working parties are constantly seen + A fairly quiet day –	
	Nov	21st	Our Batteries fired a good deal during the day registering the new ground we have to cover when the 8th Div are withdrawn and then 2 DIVISIONS will be holding the III Corps front the 3rd DIVISION will then be in Corps Reserve + Weather remains fine and frosty +	

Instructions regarding War Diaries and Intelligence Summaries are contained in F. S. Regs., Part II. and the Staff Manual respectively. Title pages will be prepared in manuscript.

WAR DIARY
or
~~INTELLIGENCE SUMMARY.~~
(Erase heading not required.)

Army Form C. 2118.

4/.

Place	Date	Hour	Summary of Events and Information	Remarks and references to Appendices
CROIX du BAC.	Nov 22nd		From 4.30 pm last night the 23rd D. Arty took over the defence of the line from Dead tree H 36 d 8.0 to WEZ MACQUART. This constitutes an extension of about 1200 yards of front. Weather remains fine and frosty.	
	Nov 23rd		A quiet day nothing of interest occurred.	
	Nov. 24th		Enemy's Artillery somewhat more active during the day. During the afternoon the Battery position of B/103 (Maj MAIR) was shelled with 4.2 howitzers. It was evident from the fire that the enemy were really shelling an empty gun position in rear of this Battery. Some dug outs were hit and 2 men were killed, one of whom lived till the evening. Two or three other men were buried but were unhurt.	
	Nov 25th		The Brewery Screen ~~at~~ from I 24 b to I 22 c was completed today. At present it is undoubtedly only a wooden hoarding.	
	Nov 26th		A very quiet day practically no Artillery fire in 23rd DW area.	
	Nov 24th		Enemy fired about 200 rounds. A hostile aeroplane dropped bombs weighing about 14 lbs. A good many failed to burst and 2 were picked up S of Armentieres. These were shown to the Flying Corps.	

2353 Wt. W2544/1454 700,000 5/15 D. D. & L. A.D.S.S./Forms/C. 2118.

Instructions regarding War Diaries and Intelligence Summaries are contained in F. S. Regs., Part II. and the Staff Manual respectively. Title pages will be prepared in manuscript.

WAR DIARY
or
~~INTELLIGENCE SUMMARY~~.
(Erase heading not required.)

8

Army Form C. 2118.

Place	Date	Hour	Summary of Events and Information	Remarks and references to Appendices
CROIX du Bac	Nov	28th	Artillery fire normal during the day + A German Aeroplane bomb unexploded was found, the pilot had failed to carry out the instructions and remove the 'Safety pin'.	
	Nov	29th	An offensive bombardment was carried out by 23rd Div Arty & certain 8" and 6" Siege batteries. The Distillerie at I 27 b 55 and the German front line trenches at I 26 c 81 were shelled. The Div Arty shelled certain selected points and one section cut a gap of about 20 yards in the enemy's wire at I 26 c 8.1. A hostile battery was located in O 13 b 7.0 by one of our observers, a direct hit was obtained on a gun emplacement and a 'separate explosion occurred after the shell burst. The enemy did not retaliate to any great extent. During the night one of our mountain guns shelled the wire cut during the day at uncertain intervals.	

2353 Wt. W2544/1454 700,000 5/15 D. D. & L. A.D.S.S./Forms/C. 2118.

Instructions regarding War Diaries and Intelligence Summaries are contained in F. S. Regs., Part II. and the Staff Manual respectively. Title pages will be prepared in manuscript.

Army Form C. 2118.

WAR DIARY
or
~~INTELLIGENCE SUMMARY.~~
(Erase heading not required.)

9

Place	Date	Hour	Summary of Events and Information	Remarks and references to Appendices
CROIX du BAC.	Nov 3rd		Enemy's Artillery somewhat more active than usual during the day. Two Artillery Observing Stations were hit but no material damage was done. About 12 noon a British Aeroplane was seen to be in difficulties flying low over the German lines - It eventually fell to the ground at I 22 d 9.1. An officer in leather breeches was seen moving away from the plane & A crowd of Germans collected round the plane & when this crowd amounted to 100 or so we turned our Artillery on to them & shelled them. The aeroplane was much damaged but we did not succeed in setting it on fire. C. J. Clibborn Capt RA Bde Major 23rd Div Arty	

2353 Wt. W2544/1454 700,000 5/15 D. D. & L. A.D.S.S./Forms/C. 2118.

WAR DIARY

DECEMBER

ORIGINAL.

23rd Divl Artly

—

Army Form C. 2118.

WAR DIARY
or
~~INTELLIGENCE SUMMARY.~~

(Erase heading not required.)

Instructions regarding War Diaries and Intelligence Summaries are contained in F. S. Regs., Part II. and the Staff Manual respectively. Title pages will be prepared in manuscript.

Place	Date	~~Hour~~	Summary of Events and Information	Remarks and references to Appendices
CROIX DU BAC	Nov	30th	Enemy fired 346 rounds – we fired 492. Enemy chiefly devoted their attention to LA VESEE and GRIS POT. About midday a German aeroplane fell or descended at 1 22 d 9.1, & was rapidly surrounded by about 100 Germans – Our guns shelled it & the enemy dispersed; although badly damaged, our shells failed to set the biplane on fire.	
	Dec	~~2nd~~ 1st	Enemy fired 196 rounds – we fired 225. One of our Howitzer Batteries (4.5) successfully shelled a hostile Battery at 1 36 d ½. 9½. The enemy who were firing salvos stopped firing after our second round. We continued, & there is no doubt that one hostile gun, which was in a shed, was badly damaged.	
	"	2nd	Enemy fired 189 rounds – we fired 111 rounds. The enemy shell our dam at JUNCTION of trenches 1 31.3 & 1.31.4 with 15 cm shell. A high proportion failed to burst.	
	"	3rd	Wet & misty – a very quiet day – Enemy did not fire at all.	

2353 Wt. W2544/1454 700,000 5/15 D. D. & L. A.D.S.S./Forms/C. 2118.

Instructions regarding War Diaries and Intelligence Summaries are contained in F. S. Regs., Part II. and the Staff Manual respectively. Title pages will be prepared in manuscript.

WAR DIARY

or

~~INTELLIGENCE SUMMARY.~~

(Erase heading not required.)

Army Form C. 2118.

Place	Date	~~Hour~~	Summary of Events and Information	Remarks and references to Appendices
CROIS DU BAC	Dec	4th	Enemy fired 292 rounds – About 20 Heavy H.E Shell fell between L'ARMEE and ARMENTIERES Railway Station during the afternoon.	
	"	5th	Enemy fired 212 rounds. We fired 280 rounds in retaliation & registration. We "bolted" 6 men from a suspected O.P at O 2 c 7.4. by shell fire.	
	"	6th	Enemy fired 210 rounds. We fired 530 rounds. A lane about 10 yds wide was cut in enemys wire at I.31 d. 5.6. – 150 rounds shrapnel being required. We bombarded enemys trenches in I 22 a, & trench from LARGE FARM to BREWERY, making two big gaps in parapet, & knocking wire about. An enemy battery at O 14 b 4.5 was silenced.	
	"	7th	Our guns bombarded enemy's parapet between I 26 b. 9.8 and I. 26 b. 8. 2. & the communication trenches in rear of this Section. The Howitzer fire was particularly effective. We cut wire at I 21 c 4. and I. 26 b. 8. 4½, & kept it "open" during the night.	

2353 Wt. W2544/1454 700,000 5/15 D. D. & L. A.D.S.S./Forms/C. 2118.

Army Form C. 2118.

WAR DIARY
or
~~INTELLIGENCE SUMMARY.~~
(Erase heading not required.)

Instructions regarding War Diaries and Intelligence Summaries are contained in F. S. Regs., Part II. and the Staff Manual respectively. Title pages will be prepared in manuscript.

Place	Date	Hour	Summary of Events and Information	Remarks and references to Appendices
CROIX DU BAC	Dec 8th		Our Howitzers bombarded front parapet between 126.c.8.1 and 132.a.6.6½ – & an 18 pr Battery enfiladed front trench between 132.a.6.6 and 132.a.8.8 – Two batteries blocked all cross communication trenches in rear. Results satisfactory.	
	"		Enemy shelled ARMENTIERES heavily, & put about 30 15 cm in ERQUINGHEM. They also shelled L'ARMER, WHITE CITY and BOIS GRENIER line. We retaliated firing 690 rounds.	
	" 9th		We cut wire at 116 d ½ 2, making a lane 15 yards wide, which our machine guns kept open at night. Our Howitzers breached enemys parapet at 132.a.3½.3, letting a quantity of water into their trenches. Their efforts to repair this were checked by our machine guns.	
	" 10th		Between 9 and 11-30 am enemy heavily shelled our fire & support trenches E of the line WATER FARM – DEAD COW FARM, firing about 2000 rounds. Our parapet was breached in 4 places & wire cut. We retaliated firing about 1850 rounds & were assisted by the Heavy Artillery	

Army Form C. 2118.

WAR DIARY
or
INTELLIGENCE SUMMARY.
(Erase heading not required.)

Instructions regarding War Diaries and Intelligence Summaries are contained in F. S. Regs., Part II. and the Staff Manual respectively. Title pages will be prepared in manuscript.

Place	Date	Hour	Summary of Events and Information	Remarks and references to Appendices
CROIX DU BAC	Dec	11th	We cut wire at I 21 d 1.9. One Battery enfiladed Enemy's front trenches from I 21 b 4½.4 to I 21 b 7.3. A Howitzer Battery bombarded support trench from I 21 b 7.3 to I 21 b 5.0. Another Battery cut wire at I 26 b 7.5¾. The German Artillery retaliated on CHAPELLE D'ARMENTIERES & BOIS GRENIER firing some 300 rounds.	
	"	12th	Our guns damaged enemy parapet at I 22 a 4 7. A comparatively quiet day.	
	"	13th	We fired 800 rounds. Operations consisted of a bombardment of enemy's parapets in the salient I 26 c 8.1 by 4.5" Howitzers. Meanwhile two 18 pr Batteries enfiladed communication trenches immediately in rear. All firing was by Salvos at irregular intervals. Results satisfactory.	
	"	14th	We fired 670 rounds. Wire was cut at I 32 a 3.0 making a 15 yards lane. Howitzers bombarded parapet at I 21 b 4½ 3½ and I 21 d 2.9 with good effect, whilst 18 prs shelled communication trenches.	

Instructions regarding War Diaries and Intelligence Summaries are contained in F. S. Regs., Part II. and the Staff Manual respectively. Title pages will be prepared in manuscript.

WAR DIARY

or

~~INTELLIGENCE SUMMARY.~~

(Erase heading not required.)

Army Form C. 2118.

Place	Date	~~Hour~~	Summary of Events and Information	Remarks and references to Appendices
CROIX DU BAC	Dec	15th	Enemy fired 100 rounds - Our 18 prs cut a lane 20x wide in wire at 1 32 a 7.8.	
	"	16th	Mist made observation difficult. About 2 pm enemy commenced an organized bombardment of our right Sector support trenches + vicinity of BOIS GRENIER, firing about 350 rounds with very little effect - We replied with 400 rounds on hostile trenches - + fire ceased -	
	"	17th	A very quiet day - Enemy did not fire - we fired 39 rounds against a breach in parapet at 1 22 a 3.6.	
	"	18th	Mist obscured observation all day - Very quiet -	
	"	19th	Enemy exploded a mine 30 yards in front of 21st Division's trenches at 1.11.c - + commenced a bombardment of the 21st Division trenches + those of our left Sector - They also shelled FME. DU BIEZ and CHAPELLE D'ARMENTIERES. They fired about 270 rounds. We retaliated on their communication + support trenches + also on WEZ MACQUART. We later carried out a successful bombardment of trenches about 1 32 a 3 0. Hostile wire was cut at 1 21 b 3.5.	

2353 Wt. W2544/1454 700,000 5/15 D. D. & L. A.D.S.S./Forms/C. 2118.

Army Form C. 2118.

Instructions regarding War Diaries and Intelligence Summaries are contained in F. S. Regs., Part II. and the Staff Manual respectively. Title pages will be prepared in manuscript.

WAR DIARY
or
INTELLIGENCE SUMMARY.

(Erase heading not required.)

Place	Date	Hour	Summary of Events and Information	Remarks and references to Appendices
CROIX DU BAC	Dec	20th	We cut wire at I 26 b 7.5 and I 22 a. 3.5½. & also bombarded GERMAN HOUSE. Otherwise a quiet day.	
	"	21st	A quiet day – no hostile Artillery fire. Our Howitzers obtained 12 direct hits on parapet at I 22 a b. 6½.	
	"	22nd	Enemy fired about 130 rounds mostly on our support trenches in right sector. We shelled billets at CAPINGHEM with about 200 rounds in retaliation.	
	"	23rd	Enemy fired about 1000 rounds mainly on our right sector. We retaliated heavily firing about 1500 rounds. We cut wire and bombarded parapet at I 26 c. 8.1, I 32 a. 4.¼, I 21 b. 3.5. and I 22 a 3.6½.	
	"	24th	A Howitzer Battery & an 18 pr Battery bombarded enemys trenches about I 32 a. 8¼. 8½. Howitzers & 18 prs also bombarded parapet at GERMAN HOUSE SALIENT. Howitzers also shelled GRAND MARAIS & house I 28 c 7.5. There was a good deal of retaliation by enemy & consequently by our guns also.	

Instructions regarding War Diaries and Intelligence Summaries are contained in F. S. Regs., Part II. and the Staff Manual respectively. Title pages will be prepared in manuscript.

WAR DIARY
or
~~INTELLIGENCE SUMMARY.~~
(Erase heading not required.)

Army Form C. [illegible]18.

Place	Date	Hour	Summary of Events and Information	Remarks and references to Appendices
CROIX DU BAC	Dec	25th	We cut wire at I 26 b 7.5. & bombarded parapet & support trenches in Salient I 26 b 7.5, also parapet at I 22 a 3.6½ and communication trenches leading thence to LARGE FARM. Parapet was much damaged. Several hits were obtained on SNIPERS HOUSE and LARGE FARM. Enemy shelled one of our Batteries in retaliation & although fire was accurate, no damage was done. Later our Howitzers bombarded FME DE L'EPERONNERIE damaging roof & building – whilst an 18 pr Battery searched vicinity with shrapnel. Enemy retaliated on our trenches, but ceased when we gave their trenches similar treatment.	
	"	26th	We shelled suspected billets along LE BAS HAU – MARTIN CAMP ROAD & also at RADINGHEM. Parapet at I 21 c 1.0 was also well bombarded. Enemy shelled I 26 & BOIS GRENIER.	
	"	27th	A quiet day – but Heavy Artillery was active. One of our Howitzer Batteries obtained some hits on ~~at~~ a 4.2 cm Battery at I 36 a 1.4, which was shelling CHAPELLE D'ARMENTIERES. Hostile Battery ceased firing after our 15th round.	

2353 Wt. W2544/1454 700,000 5/15 D. D. & L. A.D.S.S./Forms/C. 2118.

Army Form C. 2118.

WAR DIARY

or

~~INTELLIGENCE SUMMARY.~~

(Erase heading not required.)

Instructions regarding War Diaries and Intelligence Summaries are contained in F. S. Regs., Part II. and the Staff Manual respectively. Title pages will be prepared in manuscript.

Place	Date	Hour	Summary of Events and Information	Remarks and references to Appendices
CROIX DU BAC	Dec	28th	We cut wire at I26 c 8.2, making a lane 15 feet wide. Registration by aircraft was also carried out.	
	"	29th	Two Howitzer Batteries registered by aircraft.	
	"	30th	An exceptionally quiet day. We only fired 6 rounds.	
	"	31st	Nothing to report.	

A K Hall Capt.

BRIGADE MAJOR,
R.A. 23rd DIVISION.

2353 Wt. W2544/1454 700,000 5/15 D. D. & L. A.D.S.S./Forms/C. 2118.

C.R.A. 23rd Div.

Vol. 6

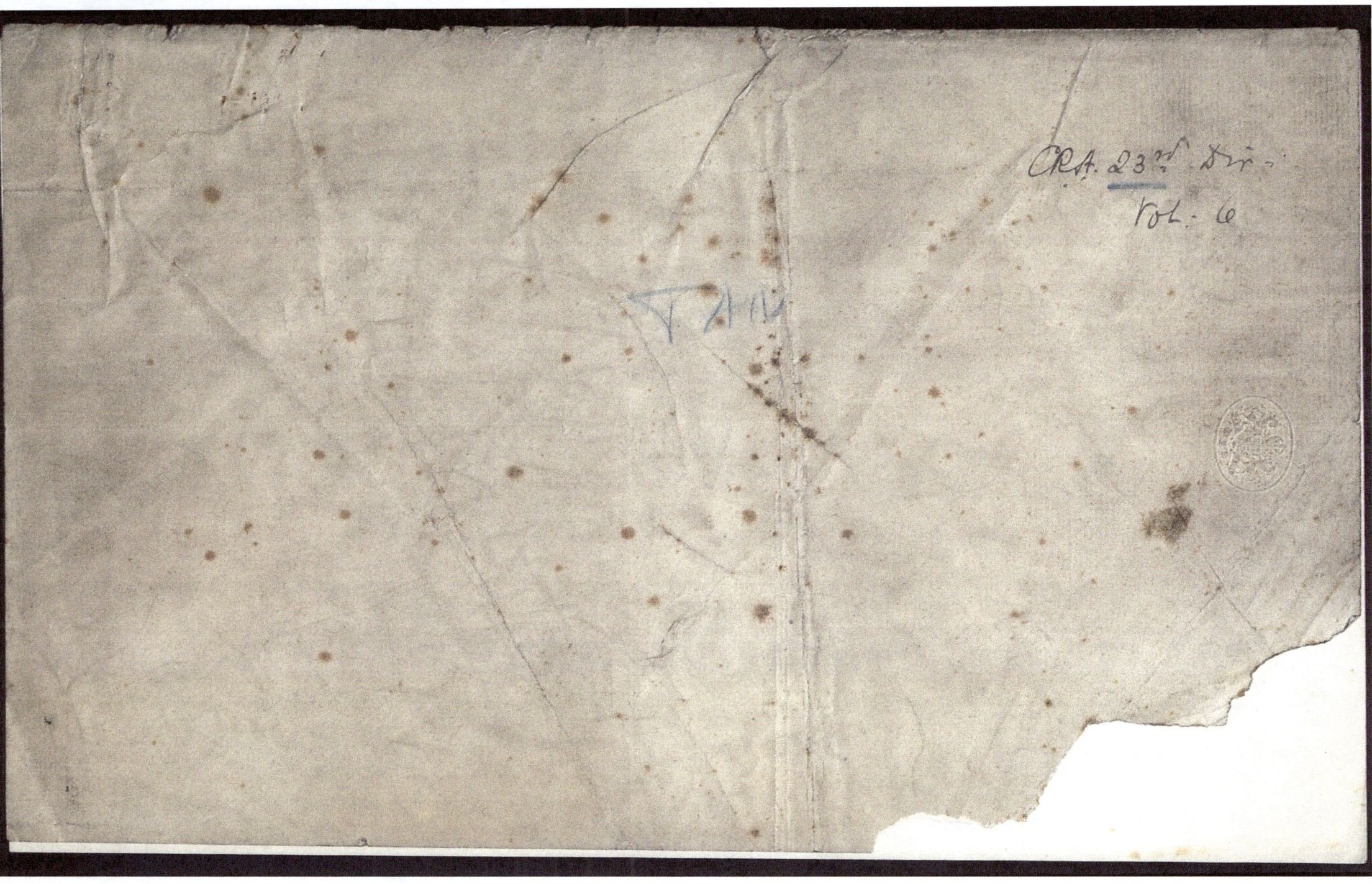

Instructions regarding War Diaries and Intelligence Summaries are contained in F. S. Regs., Part II. and the Staff Manual respectively. Title pages will be prepared in manuscript.

WAR DIARY
or
~~INTELLIGENCE SUMMARY~~.
(Erase heading not required.)

Army Form C. 2118.

Place	Date	Hour	Summary of Events and Information	Remarks and references to Appendices
CROIX DU BAC	Jan	1st 1916	At 1-30 am. two raids were carried out on the German trenches. The following preliminary bombardments had previously been carried out:-	See App. I.
			27th Dec GERMAN HOUSE + front parapet eastward from it to the road was bombarded by 25th Bde R.G.A. Parapet was breached, but was subsequently repaired by enemy on night of 29th/30th Dec.	
			28th Dec Wire was cut by 18 pr. Batteries at both points of assault, + also at I 32 a 4½. 1½ and I 22 a. 3½. 6½ as a feint.	
			31st Dec. Following buildings believed to contain machine guns were bombarded: I 16 d. 7 0, I 22 c. 6½ 9, and I 22 b. 9. 5½.	
			Actual attack. Zero time was fixed for 1.30 am night 31 Dec/1st Jan.	
			Right Attack. This attack was spotted by the enemy, who opened a brisk rifle + machine gun fire on them. Our men were ordered back + the artillery were ordered not to fire.	
			Left Attack. At 1.33 am our guns opened fire as detailed in the programme. The fire is believed to have been very	

2353 Wt. W2544/1454 700,000 5/15 D. D. & L. A.D.S.S./Forms/C. 2118.

Army Form C. 2118.

Instructions regarding War Diaries and Intelligence Summaries are contained in F. S. Regs., Part II. and the Staff Manual respectively. Title pages will be prepared in manuscript.

WAR DIARY
or
INTELLIGENCE SUMMARY.
(Erase heading not required.)

Place	Date	Hour	Summary of Events and Information	Remarks and references to Appendices
			Effective. At 2 AM the Infantry were not reported all back, so the rate of fire was reduced as arranged. At about this time the enemy opened a very heavy artillery & machine gun fire on & between our trenches. At 2.15 AM, the Infantry reported 10 men still to be accounted for, & suggested that our Artillery should cease firing. This we did, & the German fire ceased soon afterwards thus allowing these men to get back. The "2nd Period" of the programme was not carried out. Communications worked excellently & there was no hitch in the Artillery programme.	
	Jan 2nd		Enemy fired 566 rounds, & we about 1050, mostly in retaliation for his shelling our trenches. We enfiladed his parapet & support trenches between I 32 a. 3.0 and I 26 d 2.5. The light was very indifferent up to midday, & after that impossible.	

2353 Wt. W2544/1454 700,000 5/15 D. D. & L. A.D.S.S./Forms/C. 2118.

Army Form C. 2118.

WAR DIARY
or
INTELLIGENCE SUMMARY.
(Erase heading not required.)

Instructions regarding War Diaries and Intelligence Summaries are contained in F. S. Regs., Part II. and the Staff Manual respectively. Title pages will be prepared in manuscript.

Place	Date	Hour	Summary of Events and Information	Remarks and references to Appendices
	Jan	3rd	Enemy fired 270 rounds, & we about 450. PERISCOPE HOUSE, a sniping post at O.2.c.7.4 was bombarded with H.E, whilst the vicinity was swept with shrapnel at the same time. Considerable damage was observed. At request of 21st Division, a Howitzer Battery was turned on to hostile Battery at I 30 a. 2.7, which was shelling CHAPELLE D'ARMENTIERES – effect could not be observed. Registration & retaliation carried out.	
	Jan	4th	TRAMWAY HOUSE at I 28 c. 6½. 4½ was bombarded by one of our howitzer batteries, whilst an 18 pr Battery searched its surroundings with shrapnel. Six hits were obtained on the house. Two Howitzer Batteries & an 18 pr Battery also bombarded GRAND MARAIS FARM, I 28 c 2.4, with good effect; The DISTILLERIE, I 27 b. 5.5 was bombarded by Heavy Howitzers whilst an 18 pr Battery enfiladed communication trenches in the neighborhood.	

2353 Wt. W2544/1454 700,000 5/15 D. D. & L. A.D.S.S./Forms/C. 2118.

Instructions regarding War Diaries and Intelligence Summaries are contained in F. S. Regs., Part II. and the Staff Manual respectively. Title pages will be prepared in manuscript.

WAR DIARY
or
INTELLIGENCE SUMMARY.
(Erase heading not required.)

Army Form C. 2118.

Place	Date	Hour	Summary of Events and Information	Remarks and references to Appendices
	Jan	5th	Enemy fired 259 rounds, & we 269. Enemy fired about 100 rounds of 5.9 & 4.2 at one of our Battery positions D/102, an aeroplane apparently observing. The shooting was very accurate many rounds falling within a few yards of the emplacements. Only one gun was damaged & that not seriously. During the night five of our 18 pr guns at various spots fired rounds simultaneously with the 6" gun which was shelling LILLE – the idea being to make flashes at various points.	
	Jan	6th	Enemy fired 330 rounds, & we 426. Machine gun emplacements at I16d.5.5, I21c.8.3½, and I22a8.6 were shelled with 25 rounds HE each. Bursts appeared effective. Enemy shelled our support trenches, & we retaliated.	
	Jan	7th	Enemy fired 222 rounds, & we 250. Enemy shelled FME DESPLANQUES (the observing station of A/103) & knocked it down. Enemy battery position at O5c.0.8 was shelled in conjunction with the Heavy Artillery.	

Instructions regarding War Diaries and Intelligence Summaries are contained in F. S. Regs., Part II. and the Staff Manual respectively. Title pages will be prepared in manuscript.

Army Form C. 2118.

WAR DIARY

or

~~INTELLIGENCE SUMMARY.~~

(Erase heading not required.)

Place	Date	Hour	Summary of Events and Information	Remarks and references to Appendices
	Jan	9th	Enemy fired 95 rounds, & we 182 - A quiet day - Registration by aeroplane carried out.	
	Jan	10th	Enemy fired 79 rounds, & we 230 - A quiet day - Our Howitzers shelled WEZ MACQUART, TUILLERIES, FLEUR D'ECOSSE & FME de L'EPERONNERIE with good effect.	
	Jan	11th	Enemy fired 14 rounds, & we 177. Hostile Battery at I 30 a 8½.1 was engaged by a Howitzer Battery - Two pits were visible, & two direct hits were obtained on No. 3 emplacement.	
	Jan	12th	Enemy fired 131 rounds, & we 249. Our Howitzers shelled the BREWERY, I 22 d. 8½.4½, & the ESTAMINET de la BARRIERE with good effect.	
	Jan	13th	Enemy fired 43 rounds, & we 103 - Very quiet.	
	Jan	14th	Enemy fired 215 rounds, & we 740. One of our Howitzer Batteries silenced hostile battery at O 9 c. 2.2. At 12 noon the Corps Retaliation Scheme was carried out for practice - only half the full number of rounds being fired. At 4 pm, in conjunction with a smoke barrage, we	

Instructions regarding War Diaries and Intelligence Summaries are contained in F. S. Regs., Part II. and the Staff Manual respectively. Title pages will be prepared in manuscript.

WAR DIARY
or
~~INTELLIGENCE SUMMARY.~~
(Erase heading not required.)

Army Form C. 2118.

Place	Date	Hour	Summary of Events and Information	Remarks and references to Appendices
			Shelled front parapet at I22a, blowing up a large dug out & damaging parapet.	
	Jan	15th	Enemy fired 95 rounds & we 165 - One of our observing stations was shelled.	
	Jan	16th	Misty all day. Enemy fired 301 rounds - & we 453 - mostly in retaliation. Hostile Battery position at I29 a 2.8 was registered with aircraft observation.	
	Jan	17th	Enemy fired 129 rounds - & we 327 - Two machine gun emplacement & two hostile batteries were shelled.	
	Jan	18th	Enemy fired 302 rounds & we 501. Wire cutting, parapet bombardments, & hostile batteries shelled. A steel cupola in parapet at I16d 1½.7½ was badly damaged by our Howitzers.	
	Jan	19th	Enemy fired 803 rounds - & we 973 - At 8 a.m we fired 16 rounds from 4.5 Howitzers as a salvo into billets at LA VALLÉE, followed 6 minutes later by a salvo of shrapnel.	

2353 Wt. W2544/1454 700,000 5/15 D. D. & L. A.D.S.S./Forms/C. 2118.

Instructions regarding War Diaries and Intelligence Summaries are contained in F. S. Regs., Part II. and the Staff Manual respectively. Title pages will be prepared in manuscript.

WAR DIARY
or
INTELLIGENCE SUMMARY.
(Erase heading not required.)

Army Form C. 2118.

Place	Date	Hour	Summary of Events and Information	Remarks and references to Appendices
			Enemy seemed annoyed by this, for they fired persistently all day on our front, support & reserve trenches, roads, billets & supposed battery positions. Our retaliation was heavy, & we called in the 6" Howitzers to assist.	
			Enemy made accurate shooting on the billet of B/102 – putting about 100 5.9 shell into it – these were all about 100 yards beyond the battery, so no damage was done to personnel or guns.	
	Jan 20th		Enemy fired 114 rounds – we fired 268. A Howitzer Battery shelled a steel cupola in parapet at I 16 d. ½ 2. blowing away the periscope.	
	Jan 21st		Enemy fired 302 rounds – we fired 483. Effective Howitzer fire was directed on hostile Battery at O 14 a. 2 6½ – whilst an 18 pdr battery silenced another at I 29 a 6½ - 9.	

Army Form C. 2118.

Instructions regarding War Diaries and Intelligence Summaries are contained in F. S. Regs., Part II. and the Staff Manual respectively. Title pages will be prepared in manuscript.

WAR DIARY
or
INTELLIGENCE SUMMARY.
(*Erase heading not required.*)

Place	Date	Hour	Summary of Events and Information	Remarks and references to Appendices
	Jan	22nd	Enemy fired 252 rounds – we fired 522 – Wire was cut in front of GERMAN HOUSE – & a trench mortar silenced at I 32 a 6.5. The cupola located on 20th at I 16 d ½. 2 was completely wrecked by Howitzer fire.	
	Jan	23rd	Enemy fired 116 rounds – we fired 209. Registration carried out by aircraft observation.	
	Jan	24th	Very misty – Enemy fired 161 rounds – we fired 445 – Wire cutting carried out. Howitzers neutralized fire of two hostile batteries who were enfilading 21st Division trenches. Machine Gun emplacement destroyed at I 26 b. 8.7.	
	Jan	25th	Enemy fired 332 rounds – we fired 627. Wire cut & parapet breached in two places, I 16 d ½. 3 and I 21 b 5.3.	
	Jan	26th	Enemy fired 786 rounds – we fired 820. Enemy chiefly shelled Cross roads & villages, whilst we gave similar retaliation. Wire cut at I 26 b. 6½ 6½.	

Army Form C. 2118.

Instructions regarding War Diaries and Intelligence Summaries are contained in F. S. Regs., Part II. and the Staff Manual respectively. Title pages will be prepared in manuscript.

WAR DIARY
or
INTELLIGENCE SUMMARY.
(Erase heading not required.)

Place	Date	Hour	Summary of Events and Information	Remarks and references to Appendices
	Jan 27th		Enemy fired 1350 rounds; we fired 1950. Trench I 31.1 was very heavily shelled by enemy. Enemy shelled trenches again during the night. About 1320 of the rounds fired by us were in retaliation, on his trenches & villages. Two batteries were also neutralized.	
	Jan 28th		Enemy fired about 2000 rounds; we fired 3182. Enemy were scattering shell all over the area – some trenches were also heavily shelled. We retaliated chiefly on front & support trenches. A Howitzer Battery knocked out a machine gun emplacement at I 26 d. 2.5.	
	Jan 29th		Very misty – a quiet morning. Enemy fired 667 – we fired 682.	
	Jan 30th		Misty – very quiet – only a few rounds fired – nothing to report.	
	Jan 31st		Very quiet – only about 20 rounds fired – nothing to report –	

A. K. Hall.
BRIGADE MAJOR,
[illegible] 23RD DIVISION.

2353 Wt. W2544/1454 700,000 5/15 D. D. & L. A.D.S.S./Forms/C. 2118.

Routine Order No. 89. 17th January 1916.

By

Brigadier General D Fasson, C.B.

Commanding Royal Artillery, 23rd Division.

279.
POSTINGS.

Major G.M.A. Gregory and Captain J.A.French having reported their arrival on 16.1.1916 are posted to 23rd Divisional Ammunition Column.

2/Lieut. C.G. Bartleet having reported his arrival on 16.1.1916 is posted to 23rd Divisional Ammunition Column.

2/Lieut. C. Misquith, 23rd Divisional Ammunition Column is posted to 102nd Brigade with effect from 17.1.1916

No. 50037 S.S.Corpl. A Rawlinson having reported his arrival from 57 Battery is promoted Farrier Sergeant with effect from 17.1.1916 and posted to 23rd Divisional Ammunition Column.

No. 37709 S.S. Corpl. G Nunn having reported his arrival from 26th Battery, is promoted Farrier Sergeant with effect from 17.1.1916 and posted to 103rd Brigade.

W. J. Smith
Lt.
Staff Capt. R.A.
23rd Division.

Routine Order No. 98 30th January 1916.

By

Brigadier General D Fasson, C.B.

Commanding Royal Artillery, 23rd Division.

309.
PROMOTION. The vacancies for Sergeants may now be filled by suitable junior N.C.Os.

310.
SALUTING. Attention is drawn to Divn. R.O. No. 892 dated 29.1.16.
"(1) It is observed that, in some units, a considerable amount of slackness has crept in as regards saluting.

Not only are there single instances but whole groups of men are occasionally seen who take no notice of Officers.

Such want of discipline reflects seriously on the unit.

Commanding Officers, whose men are at fault, will take immediate steps to have this altered.

(2) The strictest attention of all ranks is directed to the necessity of saluting, and returning the salutes of, our Allies.

When French Officers or soldiers salute British Officers, ALL the Officers so saluted will acknowledge the compliment, irrespective of who is the senior, and in thus acknowledging the salute they will do so in the prescribed manner with the right hand, and not in a perfunctory manner.

(1st Army Routine Order No. 271 dated 27.1.16.)

311
OCCUPATION OF PASTURE LAND. Attention is drawn to Divn. R.O. No. 894 dated 29.1.16.

"Cases have occurred in which fresh pastures have been unnecessarily occupied for horse and wagon lines, and drill grounds, whilst fields in the immediate neighbourhood, which had been previously used for such purposes, were left unoccupied.

Whilst it is recognised that units are naturally reluctant to occupy fields which are deep in mud, it must be borne in mind that the continual occupation of fresh fields not only entails large expenditure in hire, but has in some cases reduced the available pasturage to such an extent that it will be most difficult for the inhabitants to find grazing for their animals during the summer.

Every effort must therefore be made to avoid taking up fresh ground, and, when fresh ground is really necessary, to occupy unsownarable land, or high lying waste ground, in preference to good pasture land."

312.
AMMUNITION Attention is drawn to 3rd. Corps. R.O. No. 381.

"Cases have recently occurred in which fuze covers issd issued with gun ammunition have not been returned to Railhead.

All Artillery Formations and Units will take steps to ensure that this is invariably done.

313.
ABSENTEES. Attention is drawn to R.O. No. 1379.
"G.R.O. Nos. 679 and 1071 are cancelled. Commanding Officers will in future transmit Absentee Reports concerning men absent in the United Kingdom, direct to the Officer i/c Records of the unit at home, who will also be informed direct of the return of any soldiers who have previously been reported absent. Reports of Absentees in this country will, as heretofore, be sent to the A.P.M. of the formation concerned.

314.
INSPECTION OF TUBE HELMETS.
Attention is drawn to G.R.O. No. 1367 dated 19.1.16. "With reference to the pamphlet C.D.S. 307 "Defensive Measures against Gas Attacks" page 4 (and "Extracts from G.R.O. Part 1., Adjutant General's Branch, page 50) under (a) Inspection of Tube Helmets, the word "fortnight" is cancelled and the following substituted "week or more frequently if a gas attack is considered imminent"

315.
INDENT FOR RATIONS. Attention is drawn to G.R.O. No. 1375. "A.B. 55 has been amended, and all units at the Front or on Lines of Communication are to demand the revised form (if not already in possession of it) from Base Stationery Depots and on receipt are to substiture it immediately for the present form, the use of which will be discontinued. The orders regarding the use of the improved forms which are printed on the back must be strictly complied with.

316.
SOLDIER'S PAY BOOKS.
Attention is drawn to R.O. No. 262 dated 19.1.1916. It has been brought to notice that a very large proportion of the soldiers pay books (Army Book 64) are incomplete. In particular the date of opening, on page 4, is neither filled in nor verified by a responsible officer. Officers Commanding Units will take steps immediately to see that this ommission is rectified. The date should be either that of the soldiers dis-embarkation, if known, and if not, that of the first payment shown in the book, and the Officer Commanding the company will verify the entry by his signature in the space provided. (G.R.O. No.1362 15.1.16.)

316.
BATHS. On Jany. 31st. Feby. 2nd and Feby. 6th Brigades will send parties of 60 men per hour to the Baths at the usual hours.

On Feby. 4th the Baths are alloted to.

8 and 10 a.m. to 25th Brigade, R.G.A.

1 p.m. and 3 p.m. to 4th Brigade, R.G.A.

W. J. Smith
Lt.
Staff Capt. R.A.
23rd Division.

[illegible] Orders No. [illegible]. [illegible] January 1916.

By

Brigadier General [illegible], C.B.

Commanding Royal Artillery, 23rd Division.

307.
POSTINGS.

The following having reported their arrival are posted to Brigades and D.A.C. as under.

6 Gunners to 102nd Brigade.

1 Driver to 103rd Brigade.

2 Drivers to 104th Brigade.

4 Drivers and 8 Gunners to 105th Brigade.

2 Drivers to D.A.C.

308
POSTING.

No. 21950 Saddler Corpl. Hull having reported his arrival is posted to 104th Brigade with effect from 28-1-16.

[illegible signature]

Lt.
Staff Capt, R.A.
23rd Division.

C.R.A. 23rd Div

Vol. 6

7

HQRA 23
Div

Army Form C. 2118.

Instructions regarding War Diaries and Intelligence Summaries are contained in F. S. Regs., Part II. and the Staff Manual respectively. Title pages will be prepared in manuscript.

WAR DIARY
or
INTELLIGENCE SUMMARY.

(*Erase heading not required.*)

Place	Date	Hour	Summary of Events and Information	Remarks and references to Appendices
CROIX DU BAC	1st Feb 1916.		Very misty – Enemy fired 13 rounds – we fired 51.	
	2nd Feb		Enemy fired 126 rounds – we fired 91. Enemy's fire was mostly on our trenches in I 31.1 and I 31.2.	
	3rd	"	Enemy fired 55 rounds – we fired 93. Registration with aircraft.	
	4th	"	Enemy fired 97 rounds – we fired 168. Good effect was observed from one of our guns sniping the road at I 36 d. 2. 5.	
	5th	"	Enemy fired 131 rounds – we fired 120 rounds – Nothing to report.	
	6th	"	Enemy fired 229 rounds – we fired 103. An 18 pdr battery breached a new canvas screen erected at I 26 d. 7. 4. – when a trench was shown to have been begun behind the screen.	
	7th	"	Enemy fired 262 rounds – we fired 253 – Most of hostile shells directed on to BOIS GRENIER line – We knocked out machine gun emplacements at I 21 c 6½ 2½ and I 27 b 2½ 9½ (in house)	

Instructions regarding War Diaries and Intelligence Summaries are contained in F. S. Regs., Part II. and the Staff Manual respectively. Title pages will be prepared in manuscript.

WAR DIARY
or
INTELLIGENCE SUMMARY.
(Erase heading not required.)

Army Form C. 2118.

Place	Date	Hour	Summary of Events and Information	Remarks and references to Appendices
CROIX DU BAC	8th Feb		Enemy fired 255 rounds - we fired 158. We engaged two machine Gun emplacements with good effect - also enfiladed enemys front line between I21b 2½.0 and I26c.8.0 -	
	9th Feb		Enemy fired 65 rounds - we fired 78 rounds - The concentrated guns of several 18 pr + Howitzer Batteries was turned on to front parapet at I26b 7.5 for practice purposes - 4 salvos being fired with good effect.	
	10th Feb		Enemy fired 291 rounds - we fired 410 - mostly in retaliation for the shelling of BOIS GRENIER - GRIS POT & our support trenches. One Section of each Battery of 102nd + 104th Bdes relieved by Sections of 34th Divisional Artillery - Sections relieved moved to Reserve area around LYNDE.	See App II
	11th Feb		Enemy fired 548 rounds - we fired 431 - Enemy shelled L'ARMEE, LA VESEE, ERQUINGHEM, BAC ST MAUR + ARMENTIERES - We retaliated on trenches + LA VALLEE, ENNETIERES + HALTE.	
	12th Feb		Enemy fired 990 rounds - we fired 1395 - Enemy fire was distributed all along our trenches, the heaviest shelling being on trenches I31.2 + I31.3. Enemy also shelled BOIS GRENIER, GRIS POT, L'ARMEE + LA VESEE - We retaliated on trenches, HALTE, LA VALLEE, RADINGHEM, CAPINGHEM, ESCOBECQUES + PREMESQUES	

2353 Wt. W2544/1454 700,000 5/15 D. D. & L. A.D.S.S./Forms/C. 2118.

Instructions regarding War Diaries and Intelligence Summaries are contained in F. S. Regs., Part II. and the Staff Manual respectively. Title pages will be prepared in manuscript.

WAR DIARY
or
INTELLIGENCE SUMMARY.
(Erase heading not required.)

Army Form C. 2118.

Place	Date	Hour	Summary of Events and Information	Remarks and references to Appendices
CROIX DU BAC February (continued).	12th		Remaining Sections of 102nd & 104th Bdes relieved by 34th Divisional Artillery - moving back to the Reserve area. 102nd Bde Amtn Column was also relieved by 175th Bde Amtn Column -	
"	13th		Enemy fired 1800 rounds - we fired 1658. Enemy shelled all our front line trenches, also BOIS GRENIER, GRIS POT, LA VESEE, L'ARMEE and RUE MARLE & BAC ST MAUR - We retaliated on trenches & villages known to contain billets.	
"	14th		A quiet day. 102nd Brigade lent to 8th Division - marched up to latter's area - This Brigade went into action on nights of 16th/17th & 17th/18th, relieving batteries of Guard's Division.	
"	15th		A quiet day - D/104 also handed over to 8th Division. 104th Bde Amtn Column relieved by 160th Bde Amtn Column -	
"	16th		An exceptionally quiet day - enemy only fired 4 rounds. One Section of each Battery of 103rd & 105th Bdes relieved by 34th Divl Artillery - & both sections of C/105 & D/105. C/105 was handed over to 8th Division - D/105 marched on 17th to Reserve area.	
"	~~17th~~		103rd Bde Amtn Column relieved by 152nd Bde Amtn Column -	
"	17th		A quiet day - New Batteries registering.	

Instructions regarding War Diaries and Intelligence Summaries are contained in F. S. Regs., Part II. and the Staff Manual respectively. Title pages will be prepared in manuscript.

WAR DIARY
or
INTELLIGENCE SUMMARY.
(Erase heading not required.)

Army Form C. 2118.

Place	Date	Hour	Summary of Events and Information	Remarks and references to Appendices
CROIX DU BAC Feb	18th		A quiet day – very misty. One Section of each Battery of 103rd Bde + A/105 + B/105 relieved by 34th Divisional Artillery, thus completing relief of all batteries. 105th Bde Amm Column also relieved – thus completing relief of all Bde Amm Columns.	
LYNDE Feb.	19th		HQ R.A relieved at 10 am by HQ RA 34th Division – HQ RA moved back to LYNDE – HQ + No 1 Section D.A.C also relieved by 34th D.A.C.	
Feb	20th		No 2 Section DAC relieved.	
Feb	21st		No 3 Section DAC relieved – entire Divisional Artillery relief completed –	
Feb	22nd		Nothing to report	
Feb	23rd		Section Training commenced.	
ESTAIRES Feb	24th		R.A HQ moved up to ESTAIRES – afternoon spent in reconnoitring possible positions E of LAVENTIE.	
Feb	25th		Reconnaissance continued.	
LYNDE	26th		R.A HQ moved back to LYNDE again.	
"	27th }		Nothing to report –	
"	28th }			

2353 Wt. W2544/1454 700,000 5/15 D. D. & L. A.D.S.S./Forms/C. 2118.

Army Form C. 2118.

Instructions regarding War Diaries and Intelligence Summaries are contained in F. S. Regs., Part II. and the Staff Manual respectively. Title pages will be prepared in manuscript.

WAR DIARY
or
INTELLIGENCE SUMMARY.

(Erase heading not required.)

Place	Date	Hour	Summary of Events and Information	Remarks and references to Appendices
PERNES. February	29th		Divisional Artillery (less 102nd Bde, C/105 + D/104) marched to PERNES area.	See App III.

Routine Order No. 101. 5th February 1916.

By

Brigadier General D Fasson, C.B.

Commanding Royal Artillery, 23rd Division.

320.
BATHS.

On Feby. 8th and 12th Brigades will send 60 men per hour at the usual times.

On Feby. 10th Divisional Troops Baths are allotted:-

8 a.m. & 10 a.m. to 4th Brigade, R.G.A.

1 p.m. & 3 p.m. to 25th Brigade. R.G.A.

321.
DEMOLITION OF UNINHABITED HOUSES.

Attention is drawn to Divisional R.O. No. 412. "General Routine Order No. 1395 dated 30th Jan. 1916 is published for information:-

1385. DEMOLITION OF UNINHABITED HOUSES.

It has been brought to the notice of the Commander-in-Chief that cases have occurred where a British Officer has authorised the demolition of an uninhabited house, which was in good condition, for the purpose of obtaining materials for repair of roads, construction of stables, horse standings, etc.
Such action is unjustifiable unless necessitated by the urgency of the military situation, and Army Commanders will issue strict orders to prevent any recurrence of acts of this nature by the troops under your command. They will take severe disciplinary action in cases of any infraction of the orders issued by them on the subject.

(a) The above order is to be read to the troops, on parade, on three successive days.
(b) Every Officer serving in the 3rd Corps Area is to be made acquainted with the above order.

Lt.
Staff Capt. R.A.
23rd Division.

Issued at 12.30 p.m.

Copy No: 1 to G.O.C. R.A. 4th Corps.
2 23rd Division (G)
3 23rd Division (Q)
4 Counter Battery Group.
5 2nd Division R.A.
6 102nd Brigade.
7 103rd Brigade.
8 104th Brigade.
9 105th Brigade.
10 23rd D. A. C.
11 & 12 Diary.

App II

8/3/6/4
Secret

ROYAL ARTILLERY, 23RD DIVISION.

1. The relief of the 23rd Divisional Artillery by the 34th Divnl: Artillery will take place between 10th and 21st February.

2. The reliefs will be by sections - (vide Table A).
Sections, of the 34th Divisional Artillery will arrive at the wagon line of the battery they relieve on the evening previous to the relief. The best temporary arrangements possible being made for their accommodation.
On the evening of the date of relief, as soon as the personnel of a Section of the 23rd Divisional Artillery has been relieved by the personnel of the 34th Divisional Artillery Section, they will proceed to the wagon line.
The 34th Divisional Artillery Sections will not come South of the BAC ST: MAUR - ERQUINGHEM Road, before 6 P.M.

3. The move of the 23rd Divisional Artillery Units to the Reserve area will be as per Table B.

4. 23rd Divisional Artillery Battery Commanders will remain in command until their second sections have been relieved.

5. O.C's "A" and "B" Groups with their own Staffs will remain in command of their Groups until 10 A.M. on 19th February. The next senior officer taking temporary command of 104th Bde: R.F.A. till Colonel Hobday rejoins it.

6. The completion of all <u>reliefs</u> (Sections, Batteries, Brigades and Groups) will be telephoned at once to Brigade and Group Headquarters and on to Headquarters R.A.

7. The 23rd Divisional Artillery, with the exception of "C" and "D" 105, will hand over their guns to the 34th Divisional Artillery and take over theirs in exchange. The former being left in their pits and the latter taken over at the wagon lines.
Guns, except for Dial Sights and Sight Clinometers, will be handed over stripped.
The interchanges of guns of "C" and D/105 with those of C/176 will be arranged between the Commanders of these Brigades.

8. All Telephone lines, Trench Stores, Maps, Photographs, Log-books etc: will be handed over to the relieving Artillery.

9. <u>All</u> periscopes in possession of Brigades and Batteries will be forwarded to Headquarters R.A. by 9 a.m. on 18th February. None are to be taken into the Reserve Area.

10. Group Commanders up to the time they hand over will keep in touch, through the Infantry Brigade Commanders with any Infantry reliefs that may be proceeding and will see that 34th Divisional Artillery Brigade Ammunition Columns as they come up get into touch with the Infantry Brigades they are to supply.

11. Instructions as to handing over of ammunition will be issued later.

12. BILLETING PARTIES.
On 9th, billeting parties of 1 Officer from 102nd and 104th Brigades and one senior N.C.O. from each Unit, will proceed to Headquarters of 160th and 175th FA Brigades respectively. The N.C.O's will take over the billets of the Units which are relieved by their Brigade in Table B.
On 15th, similar parties will proceed to Headquarters 152nd and 176th F.A. Brigades and to units which are being relieved and will take over billets.

These

12 Continued.

These N.C.O's are responsible for meeting 102nd, 103rd and 105th Brigades (less D/105) at road junction I.13.b.7.1. on day of relief and guiding the Sections to the billets.
N.C.O's of 104th Brigade and "D" Battery 105th Brigade will meet their Units at I.18.a.1.4. on day of relief.

W J Smith

Lieut:

7th February 1916. for Brigade Major R.A. 23rd Division.
R.A. S/6/4.

Copies to
102nd Bde:
103rd Bde:
104th Bde:
105th Bde:
D. A. C.
G.S. 23rd Dn:
Q. 23rd Divn:
23rd Divn: Train.
S.S.O. 23rd Divn:
R.A. 34th Divn:

TABLE "A"

Date of releif.	23rd Div: Batty.	Relieved by:-	
10th-12th Feb.			
	A.102	B.160	) One Section of each
	B.102	B.152	) Battery relieved on
	C.102	D.175	) night of 10th/11th.
	D.102	A.152	) Bty ~~Battalion~~ H.Q. and
			) remaining Section
	A.104	A.175	) night of 12th/13th.
	B.104	B.175	) H.Q. 102nd. Bde.
	C.104	C.175	) ~~night~~ of 12th/~~13th.~~
	D.104	D.160	) morning
16th-18th Feb.	A.103	A.160	) One Section of each
	B.103	C.160	) Battery relieved on
	C.103	D.152	) night of 16th/17th.
	D.103	C.152	) Bty ~~Battalion~~ H.Q. and
			) remaining Section on
	A.105	A.176	) night of 18th/19th.
	B.105	D.176	) H,Q. 103rd. 104th. &
	C.105	1 Sec. C.176	) 105th, morning of 19th
	D.105	1 Sec. C.176	)

AMMUNITION COLUMNS.

Feb. 13th.	102nd. Bde. Amm. Col.	175 ~~160th.~~ Bde. Amm. Col.
15th.	104th. " " "	160 ~~176th.~~ " " "
16th.	103rd. " " "	152nd. " " "
18th.	105th. " " "	176th. " " "

DIVISIONAL AMMINITION COLUMNS.

	23rd. D.A.C.	34th. D.A.C.
Feb. 19th.	H.Q. & No: 1 Sect:	H.Q. & No: 1 Section.
20th.	No: 2 Sect:	No: 2 Section.
21st.	No: 3 Sect:	No: 3 Section.

Ref: Sheets 36 and 36a. $^{1}/40,000$.

TABLE "B"

DATE.	UNIT.	STARTING POINT.	ROUTE.	DESTINATION.	MAPSQUARE.
11th. Feb.	1 Sect: A.102 Under	Cross Roads.	VIEUX BERQUIN - LA MOTTE	Wagon Line B.160.	B.17.d.7.1.
	1 " B.102 Senior	A.22.a.2.7.	CROSS ROADS D.24.a.1.1.-	" " B.152.	B.12.a.3.2.
	1 " C.102 Officer	8 a.m.	PA POTTE MORBECQUE -	" " D.160.	B.22.a.9.2.
	1 " D.102		CROSS ROADS C.30.b.0.7.-	" " A.152.	C.7.b.8.1.
			CROSS ROADS C.13.b.7.1.		
- do -	1 Sect: A.104 Under	C.104 Wagon line.	STEENWERK-VIEUX BERQUIN-	Wagon Line A.175.	H.4.d.1.4.
	1 " B.104 Senior	7.45 a.m.	LA MOTTE - CROSS ROADS,	" " B.175.	H.4.c.7.4.
	1 " C.104 Officer		D.24.a.1.1.- PA POTTE -	" " C.175.	H.4.d.1.5.
	1 " D.104		MORBECQUE - BOESINGHEM-	" " D.175.	H.5.c.7.1.
			CROSS ROADS I.16.a.1.4.		
			BRIDGE H.11.b.0.0.		
13th. Feb.	H.Q. 102nd. Bde.			H.Q. 160th. Bde.	B.22.a.2.7.
	A.102. less 1 Sect:)under				
	B.102. " ")senior	As above.	As above.	As above.	
	C.102. " ")officer				
	D.102. " "				
	A.104. less 1 Sect:)under				
	B.104. " ")senior	As above.	As above.	As above.	
	C.104. " ")officer				
	D.104. " "				

Ref. Sheets 36 and 36a. 1/40,000

TABLE "B" Contd.

DATE.	UNIT	STARTING POINT	ROUTE	DESTINATION	MAP SQUARE
17th Feb.	1 Sect. A.I03 under 1 " B.I03 senior 1 " C.I03 officer. 1 " D.I03	Wagon Line of A.I03 7.30 a.m.	STEENWERCK-VIEUX BERQUIN-LA MOTTE-CROSS ROADS D.24.a.1.1.-PA-POTTE-MORBECQUE-CROSS ROADS-C.20.b.0.7-CROSS ROADS C.13.b.7.1.	Wagon lines of A.160 C.160 D.152 C.152	 B.22.c.7.6 B.22.d.2.8 B.5.d.2.1 B.6.d.8.7
17th Feb.	1 Sect. A.I05 1 " B.I05 1 Sect. C.I05 1 Sect. D.I05	Wagon Line of C.I05 8 a.m.	CROSS ROADS A.22.a.2.7.-VIEUX BERQUIN-LA MOTTE-PA-POTTE-MORBECQUE-CROSS ROADS C.20.b.0.7. CROSS ROADS C.13.b.7.1. D.I05 as above to MORBECQUE-BOIS-INGHEM-CROSS ROADS I.18.a.1.4-H.11.b.9.0.	Wagon lines of A.176 B.176 (recently C.176 occupied) D.176	 B.24.c.8.1. C.25.a.9.5 C.25.a.8.6 H.11.b.1.5
19th Feb.	A.I03 less 1 Sect. B.I03 " " C.I03 " " D.I03 " "	As above	As above	As above.	
	H.Q.I05.			H.Q. 176.	B.24.a.7.3.
	A.I05 less 1 Sect. B.I05 " " C.I05 " " D.I05 " "	As above	As above	As above.	

N.B. H.Q. I03 and I04 will march under orders of O.C. these Brigades to billets of H.Q. 152 and 175 Brigades respectively B.6.d.5.5. and H.4.c.8.2.

Ref: Sheets 36 and 36a. 1/40,000

TABLE "B" 3.

DATE.	UNIT.	STARTING POINT.	ROUTE.	DESTINATION.
11th. Feb.	102nd. B.A.C.	Road Junction A.22.a.2.7. 8 a.m.	As for 102nd. Bde.	C.13.b.8.2. A.C. 160 F.A. Bde.
13th. "	104th. B.A.C.	Wagon Line A.C. 104. 8.30 a.m.	As for 104th. Bde.	H.11.a.7.5. " " 175 —do—
16th. "	103rd. B.A.C.	Wagon Line A.103. 8 a.m.	As for 103rd. Bde.	B.12.b.5.3. " " 152 —do—
18th. "	105th. B.A.C.	Lines of A.C. 105. 8 a.m.	As for 105th. Bde.	B.30.a.4.5. " " 176 —do—
19th. Feb.	H.Q. & No: 1 Sec. D.A.C.	Road Junction G.1.b.7.8. 10 a.m.	Road Junction G.1.b.7.8. DOULIEU-L.22.c.7.7.	L.22.c.7.7.
20th. "	No: 2 Sec. D.A.C.	- do -	- do -	- do -
21st. "	No: 3 Sec. D.A.C.	- do -	- do -	- do -

App III

S E C R E T.

COPY NO: 5.

OPERATION ORDER NO: 30,

by

Brig: General D.J.M.Fasson C.B.

Commanding R.A. 23rd Division.

LYNDE.

29th February, 1916.

Reference HAZEBROUCK 5 A)
and) 1/100,000
LENS 11)

1. The Divisional Artillery will march to PERNES to-day - as per attached march table.

2. N.C.O's, men and transport of R.A. H.Q's will march at the head of 103rd Brigade under command of O.C. 103rd Brigade.

3. Brigade Ammunition Columns will march with their Brigades.

4. Baggage Wagons will march at the rear of their Brigades

5. The first halt will be at 8.50 a.m. for tem minutes - subsequent halts will be arranged by the O.C. leading Brigade, who will notify arrangements to Brigades in rear by mounted orderlies.

6. All possible baggage to be carried by units.
Surplus baggage is to be dumped by 104 and 105 Brigades at their H.Q. and by R.A. H.Q. and 103rd Brigade at H.Q. R.A.
Two lorries will report at H.Q. 105th Bde: at 8 a.m. on 29th. One lorry will proceed at once to H.Q. R.A. at LYNDE and load up.
One lorry will be loaded at H.Q. 105th Bde:, proceed with loading party to STEENBECQUE STATION, unload and return at once to H.Q. 104th Bde: at WITTES.
LORRIES when loaded at LYNDE and WITTES are to proceed at once to STEENBECQUE STATION.

6 Continued. All surplus baggage is to be loaded into the trucks at STEENBECQUE STATION by 1 p.m.

A loading party of one N.C.O. and 6 men is to be detailed from each Brigade. O.C. 105th Brigade will detail an officer to be in charge of these parties.

These details are to be rationed for two days.

Transport detailed above is on no account to leave this area.

7. Billetting parties of one officer and one N.C.O. are to report at H.Q. R.A. at 7 a.m. 29th.

8. Brigades on arrival at PERNES are to be met by brigade billeting parties and conducted to their areas.

9. Acknowledge by wire.

A K Hart

Captain,

Issued at 1.40 a.m. Bde: Major R.A. 23rd Divn:

Copies to

No: 1. 103rd Bde: R.F.A.

No: 2. 104th Bde: "

No: 3. 105th Bde: "

No: 4 D. A. C.

5 & 6 Filed.

M A R C H   T A B L E .

UNIT.	STARTING POINT	HOUR.	ROUTE.	DESTINATION.
104th Bde:	Level Crossing over railway on WITTES - AIRE Road.	8.0 a.m.	WITTES - AIRE - ST: HILAIRE - FERFAY - PERNES.	PERNES.
105th Bde:	Road junction ½ mile N.W. of the W in WITTES.	8.0 a.m.	- do -	- do -
R.A. H.Q's and 103rd Bde:	Cross Roads ½ mile W. of B in BLARINGHEM.	8.0 a.m.	- do -	- do -
23rd Divn: Am: Col:	Road junction S.W. of the 1st N in NEUF BERQUIN.	10.0 a.m.	MERVILLE - ST: VENANT - LILLERS - BRUAY - PERNES.	- do -

NOTE. Hour of start is for head of Brigade.

CRA 23 Div
Vol 8

WAR DIARY

for

March

Instructions regarding War Diaries and Intelligence Summaries are contained in F. S. Regs., Part II. and the Staff Manual respectively. Title pages will be prepared in manuscript.

WAR DIARY
or
INTELLIGENCE SUMMARY.
(Erase heading not required.)

Army Form C. 2118.

Place	Date	Hour	Summary of Events and Information	Remarks and references to Appendices
PERNES	March 1st		Verbal instructions received to the effect that 23rd Division is to take over part of the line from IXth French Corps from about the SOUCHEZ RIVER to the BOYEAU D'ERSATZ – Exact frontage nor date of relief not yet known. C.R.A interviewed C.R.A. IVth Corps in the morning + in afternoon interviewed Genl. PELLERIN, G.O.C. Artillery, French IXth Corps.	
"	"	2nd	C.R.A again saw C.R.A IVth Corps in morning + then proceeded to Headquarters French Divisional Artillery at CHATEAU DE LA HAIE – reconnoitring some of the positions in the neighborhood of ABLAIN-St NAZAIRE	
"	"	3rd	C.R.A reconnoitred ground around CARENCY – Decided on 3 groups to be composed as follows:– 'A' Group Lt. COLONEL W. A. NICHOLSON (105th Bde R.F.A) A/104. B/104. C/104. 1 How Battery of 105th Bde.	

Instructions regarding War Diaries and Intelligence Summaries are contained in F. S. Regs., Part II. and the Staff Manual respectively. Title Pages will be prepared in manuscript.

WAR DIARY
or
INTELLIGENCE SUMMARY
(Erase heading not required.)

Army Form C. 2118

Place	Date	Hour	Summary of Events and Information	Remarks and references to Appendices
PERNES	March 3rd (continued).		"B" Group. Lt Colonel P. W. B. HENNING (103rd Bde RFA) A/103 B/103 C/103 1 How Battery of 105th Bde. "C" Group. Lt Colonel H. BIDDULPH (102nd Bde R.F.A). A/102 B/102 C/102 1 How Battery of 105th Bde. RESERVE GROUP. Colonel E. A. P. HOBDAY (104th Bde RFA). D/102 D/103 D/104. C/105 (HOW). The Commanders of A, B, & C Groups were sent up this morning & attached to corresponding French Groups.	

1875 Wt. W593/826 1,000,000 4/15 J.B.C. & A. A.D.S.S./Forms/C. 2118.

Instructions regarding War Diaries and Intelligence Summaries are contained in F. S. Regs., Part II. and the Staff Manual respectively. Title Pages will be prepared in manuscript.

WAR DIARY
or
INTELLIGENCE SUMMARY
(Erase heading not required.)

Army Form C. 2118

Place	Date	Hour	Summary of Events and Information	Remarks and references to Appendices
PERNES	4th	March	Heavy Snowstorm. Battery Commanders of A, B & C Groups were sent up to be attached to French Batteries. G.O.C. R.A carried out further reconnaissance - Orders issued for the relief.	See App. IV
"	5th	"	Further reconnaissance. Relief commenced.	See App V
"	6th	"	Further reconnaissance. Orders issued for completion of relief on night of 7th/8th March	See App VI
"	7th	"	Further reconnaissance.	
CHATEAU DE LA HAIE	8th	"	R.A HQs moved to CHATEAU DE LA HAIE - G.O.C, R.A relieved French Artillery Commander at 10 a.m. A fairly quiet day on account of snow. C/103 shelled by 5.9s without damage	
"	9th	"	A quiet day - our trenches S of the SOUCHEZ River were shelled during afternoon.	
"	10th	"	Flashes of a hostile Battery located. Enemy active with aerial torpedoes during afternoon	

1875 Wt. W593/826 1,000,000 4/15 J.B.C. & A. A.D.S.S./Forms/C. 2118.

Instructions regarding War Diaries and Intelligence Summaries are contained in F. S. Regs., Part II. and the Staff Manual respectively. Title Pages will be prepared in manuscript.

WAR DIARY
or
INTELLIGENCE SUMMARY
(Erase heading not required.)

Army Form C. 2118

Place	Date	Hour	Summary of Events and Information	Remarks and references to Appendices
CHATEAU DE LA HAIE.	11th March		Very misty. Some aerial torpedoes fired into our trenches.	
	12th	"	Observing Stations heavily shelled on LORETTE spur all day – Aerial torpedoes fired at our support trenches. A German aeroplane came down near MESNIL BOUCHE – occupants being captured.	
	13th	"	Orders issued for Reserve Group to relieve 5th London Brigade in 2nd Division Area – to enable 47th Division to relieve 23rd Division – 23rd Division to subsequently relieve 2nd Division. LORETTE spur + support trenches shelled with 5.9 shell. Light bad for observation.	See App VII
	14th	"	Our trenches fairly heavily shelled – we retaliated. SOUCHEZ, CARENCY, ABLAIN ST NAZAIRE, and NOTRE DAME DE LORETTE spur were all shelled. One of our wagon lines was shelled without damage.	
	15th	"	Enemy again active with aerial torpedoes. Two of our Batteries in CARENCY were shelled with 100 5.9s without damage except 5 men wounded. One of our O.Ps was destroyed by a direct hit of a 5.9.	

1875 Wt. W593/826 1,000,000 4/15 J.B.C. & A. A.D.S.S./Forms/C. 2118.

Instructions regarding War Diaries and Intelligence Summaries are contained in F. S. Regs., Part II. and the Staff Manual respectively. Title Pages will be prepared in manuscript.

WAR DIARY
or
INTELLIGENCE SUMMARY
(Erase heading not required.)

Army Form C. 2118

Place	Date	Hour	Summary of Events and Information	Remarks and references to Appendices
CHATEAU DE LA HAIE	16th	March	Again fairly heavy shelling of our trenches by aerial torpedoes + 5.9, necessitating some retaliation by us. We engaged a 77 mm Battery located at S4c 7 8. Orders issued for our relief by 47th (LONDON) Division.	See App. VIII
"	17th	"	Observing Stations on LORETTE again shelled. Aerial torpedoes fired into our trenches. We shelled working parties about S9a + S.3.a Relief commenced.	
	18th	"	New Sections registering. Enemy shelled CARENCY + ABLAIN. We shelled two suspected Trench Mortar positions with Howitzers.	
	19th	"	A quiet day. Relief continued. During the night the Germans fired 5 green rockets in succession. This being our S.O.S signal, fire was opened, but fortunately stopped before much ammunition had been wasted.	

1875 Wt. W593/826 1,000,000 4/15 J.B.C. & A. A.D.S.S./Forms/C. 2118.

Army Form C. 2118

Instructions regarding War Diaries and Intelligence Summaries are contained in F. S. Regs., Part II. and the Staff Manual respectively. Title Pages will be prepared in manuscript.

WAR DIARY
or
INTELLIGENCE SUMMARY
(Erase heading not required.)

Place	Date	Hour	Summary of Events and Information	Remarks and references to Appendices
BRUAY	20th	March	G.O.C. R.A handed over command to G.O.C. R.A. 47th Division & RA HQ moved to BRUAY.	
"	21st	"	Nothing to report – orders issued for relief of 2nd Divisional Artillery.	See App IX
	22nd	"	One Section per Battery relieved Sections 2nd Divisional Artillery. Also Brigade Ammunition Columns.	
	23rd	"	Remaining Sections relieved Sections 2nd Divisional Artillery.	
BOYEFFLES	24th	"	R.A. H.Q relieved R.A. H.Q. 2nd Division. Registration carried out.	
"	25th	"	Neighborhood of M7b heavily shelled with 5.9. Trenches of SOUCHEZ Sector were twice shelled fairly heavily.	
"	26th	"	CALONNE shelled in retaliation for a small scheme carried out by us.	
"	27th	"	A fair amount of shelling by the enemy, mostly around CALONNE & the NOTRE DAME DE LORETTE heights.	

1875 Wt. W593/826 1,000,000 4/15 J.B.C. & A. A.D.S.S./Forms/C. 2118.

Instructions regarding War Diaries and Intelligence Summaries are contained in F. S. Regs., Part II. and the Staff Manual respectively. Title Pages will be prepared in manuscript.

WAR DIARY
or
INTELLIGENCE SUMMARY
(Erase heading not required.)

Army Form C. 2118

Place	Date	Hour	Summary of Events and Information	Remarks and references to Appendices
BOYEFFLES	28th	March	CALONNE & neighborhood shelled - Right Battalion of ANGRES Sector fairly heavily shelled.	
"	29th	"	Enemy's artillery fairly active all over our zone. Our action limited to necessary retaliation.	
"	30th	"	Light good & German artillery very active - AIX NOULETTE was shelled three times - & LORETTE was steadily bombarded with about 150 5.9 shell. We engaged a hostile Battery at M28 b 8.3	
"	31st	"	Enemy's artillery very active - He shelled the mine at FOSSE 10 with some 45 8.2 Howitzer shell, doing some damage. One of our Observing Stations completely destroyed by 5.9. Some intermittent shelling throughout the night.	

A. K. Hay.
BRIGADE MAJOR,
R.A. 23rd DIVISION.

1875 Wt. W593/826 1,000,000 4/15 J.B.C. & A. A.D.S.S./Forms/C. 2118.

app IV

S E C R E T.

S/3/14.

Urgent

O.C. 102nd Brigade R.F.A.
O.C. 103rd Brigade R.F.A.
O.C. 104th Brigade R.F.A.
O.C. 105th Brigade R.F.A.

1. The Battery Commanders , their servants, and one telephonist per Battery of the following units will proceed by road, mounted, to the French Artillery Headquarters at CHATEAU DE LA HAIE tomorrow, 4th March - to reach the Chateau by 11.0 a.m.

One G.S. Wagon per Brigade will convey the Officer's kits and three days rations and forage for the whole party

A/102	A/103	A/104	
B/102	B/103	B/104	B/105
C/102	C/103	C/104.	

On arrival they will be conducted to the French Batteries which they will ultimately relieve, and they will be accomodated there.

2. One Section of each of the above Batteries will be ready to move up on the 5th March and relieve one Section of the French Batteries on the night of the 5th/6th March. The other Section will probably move up on the 6th, and relieve the remaining French Section on the night of 6th/7th March.

Further orders will however be issued later about the reliefs.

3. The O.C. B/105 will take over the vacant position about X.9.b.5.1.

A.K. Hay
Captain,

3rd March, 1916. Brigade Major R.A. 23rd Division.

NOTES ON THE FRENCH POSITIONS.

FRONTAGES.	1.	The frontage held is from the SOUCHEZ RIVER to point S.15.a.5.1. To cover this front the French have eight 75 m.m. Batteries. These are divided into 3 groups, as below :-	
		No: 1 Group. -	3 Batteries from SOUCHEZ RIVER to S.9.a.2.2. (about).
		No: 2 Group. -	3 Batteries from S.9.a.2.2. to S.9.c.2.2. (about).
		No: 3 Group. -	2 Batteries from S.9.c.2.2. to the cross roads at S.15.a.5.1.
RELIEFS.	2.	The above Groups will be taken over by us as follows :-	
		No: 1 Group.	3 Batteries 102nd Brigade and (temporarily) 1 Howitzer Battery, under command of Colonel BIDDULPH.
		No: 2 Group.	3 Batteries 103rd Brigade and (temporarily) 1 Howitzer Battery, under command of Colonel HENNING.
		No: 3 Group.	3 Batteries 104th Brigade, the third Battery occupying a vacant position about X.10.a.5.8. and (temporarily) 1 Howitzer Battery, under the command of Colonel NICHOLSON.
GROUP HEADQUARTERS.	3.	No: 1 Group.	About X.2.b.5.5. (in the BOIS DE BOUVIGNY).
		No: 2 Group. No: 3 Group.	At the MOULIN TOPART at X.8.d.3.0.
BATTERY POSITIONS. (Approximate).	4.	No: 1 Group.	One Battery at R.28.c.4.2. One Battery at X.3.a.4.1. One Battery at X.15.d.9.1.
		No: 2 Group.	One Battery at X.15.a.3.0. One Battery at X.15.d.10.3. One Battery at X.16.c.6.0.
		No: 3 Group.	One Battery at X.4.c.5.4. One Battery at vacant position about X.10.a.5.8. One Battery just N.E. of CARENCY.

Colonel NICHOLSON will select the positions for the 3 Howitzer Batteries - one of which will be in the road at about X.9.b.5.1. in a vacant French position

NAMES OF FRENCH GROUP COMMANDERS. 5. No: 1 Group. Commandant BOURGEOIS.

No: 2 Group. Commandant BOUDET.

No: 3 Group. Commandant LAZARE.

OBSERVING STATIONS. 6. Group Commanders will ascertain the O.P's for their Groups.

Sd) A.K.HAY, Captain,

2.3.16. Brigade Major R.A. 23rd Division.

(2)

O.C. 102nd Brigade R.F.A.
O.C. 103rd Brigade R.F.A.
O.C. 104th Brigade R.F.A.
O.C. 105th Brigade R.F.A.

Republished for information of Battery Commanders concerned.

A. K. Hay.

Captain,

3.3.16. Brigade Major R.A. 23rd Division.

App V

S E C R E T.

COPY NO: 22

S/3/16.

OPERATION ORDER NO: 31.

BY

Brigadier General D.J.M.Fasson C.B.

Commanding R.A. 23rd Division.

PERNES.

Reference Sheet 36 B. 1/40,000. 4th March, 1916.

MARCH. 1. One complete Section, plus Battery Staff, of each of the undermentioned Batteries will march to the Forward Area on 5th March, and relieve one Section of the French Batteries in action, as soon after dark on the evening of 5th March as possible.

A/102	A/103	A/104
B/102	B/103	B/104
C/102	C/103	C/104

March Table is attached.

WAGON LINES. 2. Battery Commanders (at present in the forward area) will arrange to meet their sections on arrival at GAUCHIN LEGAL and conduct them to the wagon line at present occupied by the French Battery they are relieving. The best arrangements possible must be made for the night and until such time as the French evacuate their wagon lines. If accommodation at the gun line is scanty Battery Staffs should be accommodated at the wagon lines during the night of 5th/6th.

RELIEFS. 3. Arrangements for the conduct of the reliefs on the night of 5th/6th March must be made by the Group and Battery Commanders concerned in agreement with their French opposites. Group and Battery Commanders must understand that for the present they will be under the command of Colonel DAROQUE, the French C.R.A. to whom report should be sent as soon as each relief is completed. Sections will register front trenches they cover the day after they go into action.

AMMUNITION. ~~One hundred and seventy six rounds per~~ gun will be at once dumped at the gun line. This amount will be increased to 200 rounds later – when Ammunition Columns arrive.

The percentage ordered for 18 Pr: Batteries by the IVth Corps is 70% Shrapnel and 30% H.E. This proportion will gradually be reached by bat batteries drawing H.E. to replace Shrapnel expended until adjusted as above.

5.

RATIONS. 5. Sections marching to forward area on 5th inst: will take one Supply wagon. These wagons will pick up rations and forage for the

(THIS PARA IS CONTINUED ON THE NEXT PAGE).

6th inst. at PERNES refilling point on their way through under arrangements of each Brigade.

Guides must be left at GAUCHIN LEGAL to direct them to their wagon lines on arrival.

Rations and forage for the 7th for the whole Battery will be drawn by the advanced Section in the forward area at a time and place to be notified later.

TRANSPORT 6. Sections marching on the 6th inst will take their own baggage wagons only.

Sections marching on the 5th inst. will take one G.S. Wagon each for the extra baggage of the whole Battery.

No other transport will be allowed.

The G.S. Wagons for the 5th instant will be detailed by O.C. 23rd Divn. Amm. Column to report at each Brigade H.Q. on the evening of 4th inst. complete with drivers and horses rationed up to and including the 6th instant.

The O.C. 23rd D.A.C. will dump the ammunition of these nine wagons for the purpose. They will be returned to the D.A.C. on the 6th instant by Group Commanders.

RESERVE GROUP 7 The Officers acting at present as Commanders of 102nd and 103rd Brigades in the back area will cease to command them at 9 a.m. on 6th inst., when Colonel E.A.P. HOBDAY assumes command of the "Reserve Group" comprising D/102, D/103 and D/104.

He will issue at once the necessary orders for the moves of D/102 and D/103 into vacated billets at FLORINGHEM at 9 a.m. 6th. March.

OTHER MOVES 8. Orders for the moves of Sections and Brigade Ammunition Columns on 6th instant will be issued later.

Orders regarding the 105th (Howitzer) Brigade and 23rd D.A.C. will also be issued, but both units should be prepared to move on 7th inst.

R.A., H.Qs. move to the CHATEAU DE LA HAIE on 7th inst.

BRIGADE HEADQUARTERS 9. Brigade Headquarters of 102nd, 103rd and 105th Brigades will march to the forward area on 6th instant - and relieve the French Group Headquarters when the Battery reliefs are completed on the night of 6th/7th inst.

The Headquarters of 104th Brigade will remain with Colonel HOBDAY in the "Reserve Group".

The Headquarters of 105th Brigade will be with Colonel NICHOLSON in his new Group.

NAMING OF GROUPS. 10 Groups will be known as follows:-

NAME.	COMMANDING OFFICER	STAFF
"A" Group	Colonel NICHOLSON (Temporarily Major Walford)	105th H.Q.
"B" Group	Colonel HENNING	103rd. H.Q.
"C" Group	Colonel BIDDULPH	102nd. H.Q.
"Reserve"	Colonel HOBDAY	104th. H.Q.

The Battalions in the trenches are known by the same letter as the Group covering them - viz "A", "B", and "C" from right to left in the trenches.

Major Grose will remain in command of 105th Brigade until such time as they are divided amongst the Groups, using his own Battery Staff to assist him in administration after the departure of 105th Brigade Staff on 6th instant.

11. Acknowledge.

Captain.
Brigade Major, R.A. 23rd Divn.

Issued at 7 p.m.

Copies to:-

No. 1. O.C. 102nd Bde.

No. 2. O.C. 103rd Bde.

No. 3. O.C. 104th Bde.

No. 4. O.C. 105th Bde.

No. 5. O.C. A/102 (In forward area)

No. 6. O.C. B/102 (" " ")

No. 7. O.C. C/102 (" " ")

No. 8. O.C. A/103 (" " ")

No. 9. O.C. B/103 (" " ")

No. 10. O.C. C/103 (" " ")

No. 11. O.C. A/104 (" " ")

No. 12 O.C. B/104 (" " ")

No. 13. O.C. C/104 (" " ")

No. 14. O.C. A Group " " ")

No. 15 O.C. B Group" " ")

No. 16 O.C. C Group " " ")

No. 17 & 18 23rd Division.

No. 19. Staff Captain R.A.

No. 20. 23rd D.A.C.

No. 21 and 22 DIARY.

MARCH TABLE.

UNIT.	STARTING POINT.	HOUR OF START.	ROUTE.	DESTINATION.
104th Bde:	Road Junction at H.12.d.5.3.	8 A.M.	Cross roads H.18.b.8.8. - Cross roads I.10.c.4.½. - cross roads I.23.a.5.8. - DIVION - HOUDAIN - cross roads P.10.a.10.9. - REBREUVE - cross roads P.13.d.5.7. - GAUCHIN LEGAL.	Wagon Line of French Battery Each Section to be met at GAUCHIN LEGAL under arrangements of Battery Commanders, and conducted to wagon line.
102nd Bde:	Junction of three roads at E.10.d.7.9.	8 A.M.		
103rd Bde:	Cross roads at H.9.d.8.7.	8. A.M.		

A D D E N D A.

Since writing these orders the following alterations have had to be made owing to the French requirements.

1. The first Section per Battery will march on the 5th March, as ordered in para. 1. - but only one gun will go into action on night of 5th/6th - the other gun on night of 6th/7th.

2. The remaining Section per Battery will march on the 7th instead of 6th, both these guns going into action night of 7th/8th, thus completing the relief. Rations and forage for 7th will therefore only be drawn for one Section in forward area (see para 5).

3. O.C. "A" Group will however put a whole Section into his vacant position on the night of 5th/6th.

4. Colonel HOBDAY will assume command of Reserve Group on 7th March instead of 6th (see para 7).

App VI

S E C R E T.

S/3/16/2

COPY NO: 23.....

OPERATION ORDER NO: 32

By

Brig: General D.J.M.Fasson C.B.

Commanding R.A. 23rd Division.

PERNES.

Reference Sheet 36 B. 1/40,000. 6th March, 1916.

MARCH. 1. The remaining Section of each of the undermentioned Batteries will march to their wagon line in forward area on 7th March, and relieve the remaining Section of the French Batteries in action after Midnight on the night 7th/8th March.

UNIT.	WAGON LINE.	BATTERY POSITION.
A/102	R.26.a.5.7.	R.34.a.7.9.
B/102	Q.14.a.9.6.	X.3.a.5.3.
C/102	P.30.c.6.5.	X.16.c.1.1.
A/103	Q.35.a.2.7.	X.16.c.3.7.
B/103	P.30.a.5.3.	X.18.d.8.0.
C/103	P.30.a.2.8.	X.14.b.9.3.
A/104	ESTREE CAUCHIE	X.15.d.10.5.
B/104	- do -	X.4.c.5.5.
C/104	- do -	X.10.a.5.8.

NOTE. All above map squares are approximate.

The Brigade Headquarters of 102nd Brigade, 103rd Bde: and 105th Bde: will march with their Sections, 105th Bde: H.Q. marching with 104th Bde: Sections. Group Commanders will arrange to have their Brigade H.Q's met on the road and conducted to their billets for the night.

The Bde: Ammunition Columns of 102nd, 103rd & 104th Bdes: will accompany their own Brigades. The first two named will billet at GAUCHIN LEGAL - the last at ESTREE CAUCHIE. Billeting parties will meet the Staff Captain R.A. at GAUCHIN LEGAL at 10.30 a.m.

A March Table for the above is attached (A)

AMMUNITION 2. One hundred and seventy six rounds will be at once dumped at each gun (18 Pr: Q.F.) This is to be increased to 200 rounds per gun on 8th inst: Another 100 rounds per gun will be maintained at the wagon line, seventy six per gun in the Brigade Ammunition Columns, and two rounds per gun in the Divisional Ammunition Column.

Brigade Ammunition Columns will on arrival immediately send a mounted orderly to remain with Infantry Brigade Ammunition Reserves.

102nd to 68th Brigade.
103rd to 69th Brigade.
104th to 24th (Brigade
(Pioneers.

OTHER MOVES. 3. The following units will march to the destinations shown on 8th inst: Billeting arrangements will be communicated to them separately.

March Table is attached (B).

RESERVE GROUP. to BARAFFLE and OLHAIN.
(D/102, D/103, D/104 & C/105).

105th (How) BDE: (less H.Q. and C/105) to CAUCOURT.

23RD DIVISIONAL AMMUNITION COLUMN to CAUCOURT.

RESERVE GROUP. 4. C/105 is posted to the Reserve Group with effect from 9 a.m. 7th instant. This Group will now be composed as under.

O.C. Colonel E.A.P. HOBDAY.

H.Q. 104th Brigade.

D/102, D/103, D/104 and C/105.

SUPPLIES. 5. Advanced Sections of "A" "B" and "C" Batteries of 102, 103 and 104 Brigades will draw rations in the forward area for the whole Battery for consumption on the 8th inst: H.Q. 102, 103, 105 and Bde: Ammunitio Columns 102, 103 and 104 will draw rations at PERNES on the 7th for consumption on 8th. Supply wagons will be marched to GAUCHIN LEGAL under Brigade arrangements and there met by a guide of the unit.

81ST SIEGE BATTERY. 6. Will be prepared to march to the forward area on 7th inst: further orders will be sent separately.

7. ACKNOWLEDGE.

Issued at 8.30 p.m. A.K. Hay. Captain,
Bde: Major R.A. 23rd Divn:

Copies to :-

No: 1. O.C. 102nd Bde:
No: 2. O.C. 103rd Bde:
No: 3. O.C. 104th Bde:
No: 4. O.C. 105th Bde:
No: 5. O.C. A/102 (In forward area).
No: 6. O.C. B/102 - do -
No: 7. O.C. C/102 - do -
No: 8. O.C. A/103 - do -
No: 9. O.C. B/103 - do -
No: 10 O.C. C/103 - do -
No: 11 O.C. A/104 - do -
No: 12. O.C. B/104 - do -
No: 14 O.C. "A" Group - do -
No: 15 O.C. "B" Group - do -
No: 13 O.C. "C" Group - do -
No: 17 & 18 23rd Division.
No: 19. Staff Captain R.A.
No: 20. 81st Siege Battery.
No: 21. 23rd D.A.C.
No: 22 and 23 DIARY.

M A R C H   T A B L E .   (A)

UNIT.	STARTING POINT.	HOUR OF START.	ROUTE=
104th Brigade.	Road Junction at H.12.d.5.3.	10.30 a.m.	Cross roads H.18.b.8.8. - Cross roads I.10.c.4.½. - Cross roads I.23.a.5.8. - DIVION - HOUDAIN -
102nd Brigade	Junction of three roads at H.10.d.7.9.	10.30 a.m.	Cross roads P.10.a.10.9. - REBREUVE - cross roads
103rd Brigade	Cross roads at H.8.d.8.7.	10.30 a.m.	P.16.d.5.7. - GAUCHIE LEGAL.

M A R C H   T A B L E . (B)

UNIT.	STARTING POINT.	HOUR.	ROUTE.	DESTINATION.
105th Bde: (less C/105)	Road Junction H.22.b.8.5. (FAUX)	10.0 a.m.	PERNES - BOURS - DIEVAL - LA COMTE - CAUCOURT.	CAUCOURT.
23rd D. A. C.	Cross Roads H.13.a.3.5.	9.0 a.m.	VALHUON - LA THIEULOYE - MAGNICOURT - CAUCOURT.	CAUCOURT.
RESERVE GROUP.	Cross roads C.23.a.5.1.	9.30 a.m.	DIVION - HOUDAIN.	BARAFFLE - OLHAIN.

App VII

S E C R E T. COPY NO: ..11..

S/3/22.

OPERATION ORDER NO:, 33

by

Brig. General D.J.M.Fasson C.B.

Comnd.: R.A. 23rd Division.

Reference Sheets 36 b S.E. & 36 c S.W. 12th March, 1916.

I. The Reserve Group will relieve the following batteries now in the 2nd Division front.

23rd Division.		2nd Division	Battery	Wagon Line
D/102	relieves	13th LONDON	X.28.b.4.5.	Q.II.a.5.7.
D/103	"	14th LONDON	R.27.d.8.I.	Q.II.a.5.6.
D/104	"	12th LONDON	R.II.c.7.I.	R.13.b.2.4.
C/105	"	22nd LONDON	M.8.a.5.9.	NOEUX les MINES.

2. The above reliefs will be carried out under the orders of Major Hartland-Mahon, Comndg: Reserve Group.
The first Sections will go into position night 14th/15th March. The second sections night of 15th/16th March, from which date the above units of 23rd Divisional Artillery come under the orders of the G.O.C. R.A. 2nd Division.

3. Major Hartland-Mahon and Reserve Group Battery Commanders (except O.C. D/102) will proceed mounted to H.Q. 2nd Divisional Artillery at BOYEFFLES at 10 a.m. 13th instant for reconnaissance purposes, returning to FREVILLERS in the evening.
O.C. D/102 will proceed direct to the position of 13th LONDON Battery.

4. Guns will be handed over by the LONDON Batteries in the pits - stripped, but No: 7 Dial Sights will not be exchanged.

5. 18 pounder Batteries will maintain 200 rounds per gun at the Battery position, and 100 rounds per gun in the wagon line. 4.5 Howitzer Batteries - 150 rounds per gun at the Battery and 50 per gun in wagon line.

6. Major Hartland-Mahon will arrange for the 103rd Brigade Ammunition Column to relieve the 5th LONDON B. A. C. (at Q.4.b.9.3) on 15th instant.
From the 15th inclusive, 103rd Brigade Ammunition Column will supply both "B" and "C" Groups - and will also supply S.A.A. to 68th Infy: Bde: **as well as to 69th Inf: Brigade.**

7. Orders will be issued later re Brigade Staff 104th Brigade.

8. The following are the arrangements for transport and supply of Reserve Group :-
The Supply Wagon will march with the first section, the baggage wagon with the second section.
An extra G.S. Wagon per Battery will be furnished by the 23rd D.A.C. on the evening of 13th March, to Reserve Group H.Q. at FREVILLERS. These wagons will march with the first Sections on 14th inst: and will be returned to the D.A.C. on the 15th instant.
Rations for the first section are to be drawn before marching. Advanced Sections will draw rations for the whole Battery on 15th at Refilling Point. Q. 21 - 22.
After the 15th inst: units of the Reserve Group will continue to draw from this same Refilling Point until further orders.
102nd Brigade Ammunition Column will draw rations on 15th at the above Refilling Point.

9. ACKNOWLEDGE.

A. K. Hall.
Captain,
Brigade Major R.A. 23rd Divn:

Issued at 7.30 p.m.

Copies to :-

No: I. 23rd Division.
No: 2. 23rd Division (Q)
No: 3. 2nd Divisional Artillery.
No: 4. "A" Group.
No: 5. "B" Group.
No: 6. "C" Group.
No: 7. Reserve Group.
No: 8. 23rd D.A.C.
No: 9. Staff Captain R.A.

Nos: IO and II. Diary.

App VIII.

S E C R E T.

S/3/23/3

OPERATION ORDER NO: 34

by

Brigadier General D.J.M.Fasson C.B.

Commanding R. A 23rd Division.

COPY NO: 12.

Reference Sheet 36 B, I/40,000.

16th March, 1916.

RELIEFS. I. The 23rd Divisional Artillery will be relieved in CARENCY Sector by the 47th Divisional Artillery, on the nights of 17th/18th and 19th/20th March one section per Battery being relieved on each night.

Reliefs are not to commence before 6 p.m. on the nights indicated.

Headquarters of Groups will not hand over command to incoming Group Commanders till 10 a.m. 20th March at which hour the G.O.C. R.A. 47th Division will take over command from G.O.C. R.A. 23rd Division.

The 23rd Divisional Artillery units will march to the Reserve Area under the Senior Officer of each Brigade as shown in Table "A" (attached), units of 47th Divisional Artillery "doubling up" at wagon lines for night of relief.

GUNS. 2. Guns will be handed over to relieving units in the position, except No: 7 Dial Sights, which will be retained by 23rd Divisional Artillery. Guns of 47th Divisional Artillery, less dial sights, will be taken over at wagon lines.

WIRE. 3. All wire will be left down, and no wire is to be taken over from 47th Division units.

MAPS. 4. All copies of the following maps will be handed over -

Secret Map I/10,000 (One per Group).
36 B, S.E. I/20,000.
36 C, S.W. I/20,000.

Also all air photos (R.A. H.Q. only), registers, log books, tracings etc:

AMMUNITION. 5. Two hundred rounds per gun will be handed over by I8 pounder Batteries, and I50 by Howitzer Batteries at the guns; and they will take over 76 per gun (I8 Pr) and 58 per gun (Howitzers) at the wagon line from 47th Divisional Artillery Batteries.

The remaining I24 rounds per gun (I8 Pr) and 44 per gun (Howitzer) will be taken over by the 23rd D.A.C. from the 47th D.A.C. I05th B.A.C. will take over the balance of 48 rounds per gun from its relieving B.A.C.

SUPPLIES. 6. Rations for I9th will be drawn by all units at Q.22 on I8th instant.

On I9th, units in Reserve Area will draw at BRUAY, remainder at Q. 22.

On 20th, advanced Sections will draw at BRUAY for remainder of their Batteries, and the Brigade H.Q.

TRANSPORT. 7. The 23rd D.A.C. will furnish one G.S. Wagon per Battery for transport of surplus baggage on the I8th instant. O's C. Brigades will inform the O.C. 23rd D.A.C. when and where these wagons are to report.

They will be returned to D.A.C. on the I9th instant by units concerned.

BILLETING PARTIES. 8. Each Brigade will send one Officer per Brigade and an N.C.O. per Battery to the Reserve Area on I7th instant to arrange the billeting of their units as per Table "A". The D.A.C. will send a billeting party on the I9th inst:

9. Table "B" (attached) gives present distribution of 47th Divisional Artillery Units in billots.

10. ACKNOWLEDGE.

A. K. Hay

Captain,

16th March, 1916. Brigade Major R.A. 23rd Division.

Issued at 7.30 p.m.

Copies to :-

No: 1. to 23rd Division.
No: 2. to 23rd Division (Q).
No: 3. to 47th Division.
No: 4. to 47th Divisional Artillery.
No: 5. to 2nd Divisional Artillery.
No: 6. to O.C. "A" Group R.F.A.
No: 7. to O.C. "B" Group R.F.A.
No: 8. to O.C. "C" Group R.F.A.
No: 9. to O.C. 105th Brigade R.F.A.
No: 10. to O.C. 23rd Divisional Amn: Column.
Nos: 11 & 12 to Diary.

T A B L E " A ".

Unit of 23rd D.A.	Relieved by	Time	Date	Billets in Reserve Area	Route to Billets	Date of March	Hour of Start	Remarkss.
H.Q. IO2 Bde: A/IO2 B/IO2 C/IO2	H.Q. 7th London Bde 7th London Bde:	IO am. 6 pm.	20th I7th/I8th and I9th/20th	CAMBLAIN-CHATELAIN (I.I5) (less A/IC2) (a)	GAUCHIN-LEGAL - RANCHICOURT - HOUDAIN-DIVION - CAMBLAIN CHATELAIN	I8th 20th		(a) A/IO2 on relief by Battery of 7th London Bde: will relieve D/IO3 in 2nd Division at R.27.d.7.2. Section by Section, on the same nights. D/IO3 will march into billets to be indicated by 2nd Divl: Amn: Coln: at BARLIN. D/IO3 will have guns in action, and will take over guns of 7th London Bde: from A/IO2 at the latter's wagon line (R.26.a.9.4) D/IO3 will draw rations from Q.22.
H.Q. IO3 Bde: A/IO3 B/IO3 C/IO3 B.A.C./IO3	H.Q. 6th London Bde 6th London Bde: B.A.C. 6th London	IO am 6 p.m. Noon	20th I7th/I8 and I9th/20 I9th	DIEVAL (O.7)	CAUCOURT - FREVILLERS - DIEVAL.	I8th and 20th B.A.C. on I9th	As ordered by O.C.'s C. Brigades and D. A. C.	
O.C. "A" (b) Group A/IO4 B/IO4 C/IO4 B.A.C/IO4	O.C. 5th Lon: Bde: 5th London Bde B.A.C/5th Lon: Bde:	IO am 6 pm. Noon	20th I7th/I8th and I9th/20th I9th	LA THIEULOYE (N.30)	ESTREE CAUCHIE - FREVILLERS - MAGNICOURT - LA THIEULOYE.	I8th and 20th B.A.C. on I9th		
H.Q. IO5 (b) Bde: A/IO5 B/IO5 D/IO5 B.A.C/IO5	H.Q. 5th Lon: Bde: B/I76 22 Lon By 2I Lon By 8th London B.A.C.	IO am. 6 pm Noon	20th I7th/I8th and I9th/20th I9th	CALONNE - RICOUART and (I.II) two Batteries in CAMBLAIN-CHATELAIN.	CAUCOURT - HERMIN RANCHICOURT - HOUDAIN - CALONNE-RICOUART.	I8th and 20th B.A.C. on I9th		(b) O.C. "A" Group has IO5th Bde: H.Q. Staff with him - NOT the IO4th Bde: H.Q. which is in Reserve.
23rd D.A.C.	47th D.A.C.	IO am.	20th	BRUAY (J.IO.c)	Shortest Route	20th		

TABLE "B".

UNIT.	BILLETS.
6th LONDON BRIGADE.	
H. Q.	O.8.b.2.7.
15th London Battery	O.14.a.5.8.
16th " "	O.7.b.4.5.
17th " "	O.8.c.6.9.
B. A. C.	O.8.c.7.5.
7th LONDON BRIGADE.	
H. Q.	I.9.c.9.2.
18th London Battery	I.15.b.3.7.
19th " "	I.9.c.9.5.
20th " "	I.9.c.5.3.
B. A. C.	I.15.b.1.5.
8th LONDON BRIGADE.	
H. Q.	I.11.a.1.8.
21st London Battery	I.4.b.0.9.
B/176	I.16.d.8.4.
B. A. C.	I.23.a.8.8.
47th Divisional Ammunition Column.	
H. Q.	J.10.d.1.1.

NOTE.

The 5th London Brigade and 22nd London Battery are not in the Reserve Area, but at FREVILLERS. Its billets there will not be taken over by 104th Brigade, who will find billets as per Table "A".

App IX

S E C R E T.
S/3/25.

COPY NO: 12.

OPERATION ORDER NO: 35.

by

Brigadier General D.J.M.Fasson C.B.

Reference :- 36 B - 1/40,000.

21st March, 1916.

RELIEFS. 1. R.A. 23rd Division will relieve R.A. 2nd Division. Reliefs will be carried out after dark by Sections, as per attached Table. Battery Commanders and a few telephonists will accompany their first Sections, and must check registration on front trenches on 23rd instant. Other details to be arranged between Group Commanders concerned. (See S/3/24/3).

GUNS. 2. Guns will be taken over and handed over stripped.

MAPS. 3. R.A. 23rd Division will take over all maps except 1/40,000. Maps for Batteries who do not relieve 2nd Division Batteries, will be issued by R.A. Headquarters 23rd Division. Registers, log books, and air photos will be taken over.

AMMUNITION. 4. (a) All ammunition of 2nd Division Batteries at the gun pits will be taken over, even if more than 200 rounds a gun, and 2nd Division Batteries will take over at wagon lines from 23rd Division whatever they require to enable them to march out with full wagons.

(b) Brigade Ammunition Columns supply their own Batteries and also the Batteries of 2nd Division which own Brigade is relieving, as per attached Table, with effect from noon 22nd instant until all 2nd Division are out. They will ascertain position of Infantry Brigade Ammunition Reserve before 12 noon 22nd instant, and will supply S.A.A. from 12 noon 22nd instant.

HOWITZER BRIGADE. 5. Lieut: Colonel W.A.NICHOLSON will retain administrative control of the Howitzer Batteries, whilst they are under the command of Group Commanders for all tactical purposes.

SUPPLIES. 6. First Sections and Brigade Ammunition Columns will refill at BRUAY on 22nd instant.
All R.A. units will refill at BARLIN STATION on 23rd instant. Hour will be notified later.

TRANSPORT. 7. Supply wagons will accompany first Sections, baggage wagons second Sections.
O.C. 23rd D. A. C. will detail 1 G.S. Wagon per Battery to report to Headquarters of each Brigade on evening of 21st instant. These wagons will transport surplus baggage on 22nd instant, and will be returned to D.A.C. on 23rd instant.

BILLETING PARTIES. 8. Representatives of each Battery will proceed to the wagon lines in new area on the morning of 22nd instant.

R.A. H.Q. 9. R.A. Headquarters will close at BRUAY at 10 a.m. 24th instant, and reopen at BOYEFFLES (R.13.a.10.8) at the same hour.

10. ACKNOWLEDGE.

C. H. Hunt 2/Lt.
~~Captain,~~
pp Brigade Major R.A. 23rd Division.

TABLE OF RELIEFS. (1).

Unit of R.A. 23rd Divn:	Relieves	Map Square	Wagon Line	Dates of Relief	REMARKS.
R.A. 102nd Bde:	44th ~~41st~~ Brigade	R.21.b.8.8.	-	10 a.m. 24th	
A/102	-	R.27.d.8.2.	Q.11.a.5.6.	Completed.	
B/102	New Position	R.22.b.7.1.	~~R.13.a.6.4.~~ K34a	22/23 & 23/24	Takes over 2 guns of 17th Battery and 2 of 9th Battery. Wagon line is at present occupied by D/113.
C/102	9th Bty:	R.22.b.8.4.	Q.5.c.5.5.	22/23 & 23/24	
D/102	-	X.28.b.3.5.	Q.11.a.5.7.	Completed.	
B.A.C. 102	-	Q.4.b.9.9.	-	Completed.	Supplies S.A.A. to 68th Infantry Bde:
R.A. 103rd Bde:	36th Bde:	R.10.b.9.1.	-	10 a.m. 24th.	
A/103	71st Bty	R.22.b.4.8.	Q.5.c.7.3.	22/23 & 23/24	
B/103	48th Bty:	R.17.b.3.3.	R.2.c.4.9.	- " -	
C/103	~~15th~~ 71st Bty:	M.7.b.4.7	Q.11.b.6.4.	- " -	15th & 71st Batteries have 12 guns in actio[n] in line. ~~4 guns of 71st will remain in present position for Counter Battery work - thus leaving 8 guns to be relieved.~~ The 4 centre pits will be left empty
D/103	~~71st~~ 15th Bty:	M.7.b.~~5.7~~ 5.8	Q.11.b.6.4. ~~R.34.a.~~	- " -	
B.A.C. 103	B.A.C. 36th	Q.11.a.5.2.	-	Noon 22nd	Supplies S.A.A. to 69th Infantry Bde:
R.A. 104th Bde:	34th Bde:	R.5.b.10.10.	-	10 a.m. 24th.	
A/104	70th Bty:	M.1.b.3.9.	R.13.a.6.4.	22/23 & 23/24	
B/104	50th Bty:	R.5.d.5.8.	Q.5.a.5.2.	- " -	
C/104	16th Bty:	R.6.a.5.0.	Q.5.d.1.6.	- " -	
D/104	-	R.11.c.7.1.	R.13.b.2.4.	Completed.	
B.A.C. 104	B.A.C. 34th	K.31.d.5.1.	-	Noon 22nd	Supplies S.A.A. to 24th Infy: Bde: and Pioneers.

TABLE OF RELIEFS. (2)

Unit of R.A. 23rd Divn:	Relieves	Map Square	Wagon Line	Dates of Relief	REMARKS.
H.Q. 105th Bde:	~~44th~~ 41st Bde:	Q.5. 2 3 1	-	10 a.m. 24th	
A/105	56th Bty:	R.28.c.7.3.	K.31.d.4.1.	22/23 & 23/24	
(x) B/105	New Position	~~R.27.d.4.7.~~ M 1 d. 1 4	Q.5.c.6.4.	22/23rd Wagon line	B.A.C. 41st Bde: at present occupying thi wagon line must vacate it at 12 noon ~~[illegible]~~ 22nd instant.
* C/105 (Counter Bty)	~~New Postn:~~	M 8 a 5. 9 ~~M.1.d.~~	Noeux LES MINES	Completed ~~[illegible]~~	~~47th Bty: leave their guns to [illegible]/105 and take over guns of C/105 at Hitter's present position in [illegible] [illegible]/105 will take over guns of D/105.~~
D/105	47th Bty:	R.11.b.4.7.	Q 5 d 3. 4 ~~[illegible]~~	22/23 & 23/24	
B.A.C. 105	B.A.C. 44th	Q.5.b.9.3.	-	Noon 22nd	Supplies all 4.5 Howitzer Batteries.
23rd D.A.C.	2nd D.A.C.	(K.27.c. (K.33.b.	-	Noon 24th	
R.A. H.Q.	R.A. H.Q. 2nd Divn:	R.13.a.10.5.	-	10 a.m. 24th	

(x) B/105 will now be in Centre (ANGRES) Group - instead of the Right (SOUCHEZ) Group . The position at M.1.d.1.4. is now being made by C/105 and will be ready by night of 23rd at latest.

*C/105 remains where it is, and acts as Counter-Battery when under orders of 4th Corps Counter-Battery Group.

Instructions regarding War Diaries and Intelligence Summaries are contained in F. S. Regs., Part II. and the Staff Manual respectively. Title Pages will be prepared in manuscript.

WAR DIARY

or

~~INTELLIGENCE SUMMARY~~

(Erase heading not required.)

Army Form C. 2118

DW 23 RA Vol 4

Place	Date	Hour	Summary of Events and Information	Remarks and references to Appendices
BOYEFFLES	1st April		During the morning enemy shelled FOSSE.4 with 8" Howitzer, doing some damage. CALONNE, AIX-NOULETTE, and SIEGE.11, were all shelled in the morning. The position of C/103 was shelled in the afternoon & again in the evening, one gun being slightly damaged. The SOUCHEZ Sector was also shelled, & between 9 and 11 pm the CALONNE Sector trenches were heavily shelled. We did a little work for the Counter-Battery Group - otherwise action confined to retaliation.	
	2nd	"	Enemy active against the SOUCHEZ Sector all day with aerial torpedoes & heavy shell. He also fired about 100 rounds of 8" and 5.9" into R5a, apparently looking for an A-A Battery, which was not there. Except for a false gas alarm, our artillery action was retaliation only.	
	3rd	"	A quiet day - on account of haze.	
	4th	"	Another very quiet day - hazy and misty.	
	5th	"	SOUCHEZ Sector trenches heavily shelled in the morning. An attempt was made during night of 4th/5th by the 68th Infantry Brigade to blow in	

Instructions regarding War Diaries and Intelligence Summaries are contained in F. S. Regs., Part II. and the Staff Manual respectively. Title Pages will be prepared in manuscript.

WAR DIARY
or
INTELLIGENCE SUMMARY
(Erase heading not required.)

Army Form C. 2118

Place	Date	Hour	Summary of Events and Information	Remarks and references to Appendices
			an enemy sap in M 20 B. We put a barrage round the working party, but the enterprise was a failure because the "torpedo" employed refused to go off.	
BOYEFFLES	6th April		SOUCHEZ Sector was again heavily shelled at intervals throughout the day. We engaged two batteries, & also knocked out a machine gun emplacement.	
	7th	"	SOUCHEZ Sector shelled during morning with Trench Mortars & guns. We cut wire at three points opposite the CALONNE front.	
	8th	"	CALONNE was heavily shelled in the morning & afternoon – also Observing Stations on NOTRE DAME DE LORETTE. We continued the wire cutting opposite CALONNE front.	
	9th	"	Enemy fairly quiet – Some shelling of SOUCHEZ Sector, and CALONNE – The wire cutting opposite CALONNE was continued by us.	
	10th	"	At 4.20 am four Batteries of CALONNE group fired salvos to catch enemy at "Stand to". In the afternoon a bombardment & feint attack was carried out on the CALONNE Sector –	See App. X

Army Form C. 2118

Instructions regarding War Diaries and Intelligence Summaries are contained in F. S. Regs., Part II. and the Staff Manual respectively. Title Pages will be prepared in manuscript.

WAR DIARY
or
~~INTELLIGENCE SUMMARY~~

(Erase heading not required.)

Place	Date	Hour	Summary of Events and Information	Remarks and references to Appendices
BOYEFFLES	11th April		A very quiet day.	
	12th April		Bad light – very quiet – Beyond some shelling of the CALONNE front with 4.2 and trench mortars, nothing of importance occurred.	
	13th	"	The CALONNE sector was shelled at intervals throughout the day. Observing Stations on NOTRE DAME DE LORETTE were also shelled.	
	14th	"	Enemy fairly active all along our front, although no very heavy shelling took place. A false Gas alarm at 11-45 pm.	
	15th	"	CALONNE shelled throughout the morning. The majority of the mines in the back area were shelled with heavy guns by the enemy. In the afternoon trench mortars were active against ANGRES Sector. Later BOUVIGNY – BOYEFFLES was heavily shelled. We shelled LENS, LIEVIN and CITÉ DE CAUMONT in retaliation.	
	16th	"	Enemy active all along our front. We did some counter-battery work. An 18pr gun "sniped" the roads in LIEVIN throughout the day. We retaliated heavily	

1875 Wt. W593/826 1,000,000 4/15 J.B.C. & A. A.D.S.S./Forms/C. 2118.

Instructions regarding War Diaries and Intelligence Summaries are contained in F. S. Regs., Part II. and the Staff Manual respectively. Title Pages will be prepared in manuscript.

WAR DIARY
or
~~INTELLIGENCE SUMMARY~~
(Erase heading not required.)

Army Form C. 2118

Place	Date	Hour	Summary of Events and Information	Remarks and references to Appendices
			for the shelling of our trenches in the SOUCHEZ Sector.	
BOYEFFLES	17th	April	Enemy again active - specially against SOUCHEZ Sector. We dispersed several working parties effectually -	
"	18th	"	Misty - a quiet day - We dispersed two working parties.	
"	19th	"	Very quiet - nothing of importance	
LE VIELFORT	20th	"	R.A. 23rd Division relieved by R.A. 2nd Division, and marched back into rest billets about BRUAY.	See App XI
"	21st 22nd 23rd	"	Holidays - except for cleaning up.	
"	24th 25th 26th 27th 28th 29th	"	Section Training.	
"	30th	"	Sunday - A holiday.	

A. K. Hay
BRIGADE MAJOR,
R.A. 23rd DIVISION.

1875 Wt. W593/826 1,000,000 4/15 J.B.C. & A. A.D.S.S./Forms/C. 2118.

App X.

SECRET

Copy No: 17.

S/1/22.

OPERATION ORDER NO: 36,

by

Lt: Colonel W.A.NICHOLSON R.F.A.

C.R.A. 23rd Division.

Reference Secret 1/10,000)
Trench Map.)

OBJECT. 1. A "feint" will be made by the 68th Infantry Brigade on a date to be notified later. The objects of this operation are

(a) To kill Germans.

(b) To cause material damage.

(c) To combine with other operations on our right.

Our Infantry will not actually attack.

AMMUNITION. 2. A proportion of the ammunition allotted will be kept in hand to deal with possible retaliation by the enemy. The following figures are approximate only :-

NATURE OF AMMUNITION	To be expended in the operation	Kept in hand for retaliation	TOTAL.
18 Pr: Shrapnel	1200	300	1500
H. E.	800	700	1500
4.5 How: H. E.	300	100	400
6" How: H.E.	100	50	150
9.2" How: H. E.	50	10	60

OPERATION. 3. The "feint" will consist of three Artillery phases :-

(a) Wire Cutting.
(b) Preliminary Slow Bombardment.
(c) Final intense Bombardment.

In the first bombardment as much material damage as possible will be done. In the final bombardment the chief object is to kill Germans.

ALLOCATION OF ARTILLERY.

4. (a) For purposes of the operation, one Section (18 Prs) of 1st Division, about G.27.d, will be lent to the CALONNE Group.

(b) A/102 is placed under orders of ANGRES Group.

(c) One 18 Pr: gun of 1st Division in CALONNE will be lent to CALONNE Group for wire-cutting only.

(d) The 49th Siege Battery will be under direct orders of G.O.C. R.A. 23rd Division.

(e) The Counter-Battery Group are being asked to co-operate with 9.2 inch Howitzers.

(f) The SOUCHEZ Group will participate only so far as retaliation may become necessary on their Sector.

(g) Co-operation of medium Trench Mortars will be arranged by the R.A. Staff Officer for Trench Mortars after consultation with the G.O.C. 68th Infantry Brigade. They will cut wire at selected points, and also participate in the bombardments.

WIRE CUTTING.

5. Wire will be cut by the CALONNE Group at three places, to be selected by O.C. Group.

About M.15.b. (By 1st Division gun in CALONNE.

About M.15.d.

About M.20.b. or M.21.a.

Wire cutting will commence on the afternoon of the day preceeding the operation, 100 rounds shrapnel and 10 H.E. being allowed for each place.
On the morning of the operation this will be continued, the lanes being further cleared and widened by another 50 Shrapnel and 5 H.E. at each point. All wire cutting to be finished by 12 noon on the day of operation. The infantry machine guns will keep the lanes open during preceeding night.

SLOW BOMBARDMENT.

6. (a) Actually there will be no interval between the termination of the preliminary slow bombardment and the commencement of the final intense bombardment, but, for purposes of definition, the slow bombardment will commence at minus 3 hours from "zero" time and end at minus one minute from "zero" - a total of 2 hours and 59 minutes continuous, deliberate bombardment. At one minute before "zero" the bombardment will become intense (see para 7).

(b) The frontage of the slow bombardment will be from M.20.b.2.¾. to M.9.d.8.0.

(c) This will be subdivided as follows:-

ANGRES GROUP (including A/102). :- M.20.b.2.¾. to M.21.a.8½.8.

CALONNE GROUP :- M.21.a.8½.8. to M.9.d.8.0. (including Section 1st Division).

(d) Objectives for 18 Prs: will be front trenches, support and communication trenches.

B/105 will bombard CITE DES CORNAILLES.

D/105 " " trench junctions selected by Group Commander.

(e) Ammunition for this bombardment is allotted as follows:-

	18 Pr: SH:	18 Pr: H. E.	4.5" How: H.E.
Each Group (including attached units).	100	250	100.

The shrapnel will be allotted mostly to enfilade guns.

(f) Rates of fire of 18 Prs: and Howitzers will be regulated to evenly cover the 2 hours and 59 minutes.

(g) The 49th Siege Battery (6 inch Hows) will bombard the double row of houses and trenches running from about M.16.c.6.9. to M.22.a.7.8½. Sixty rounds will be evenly distributed over the period of bombardment.

(h) The 4th Corps Counter-Battery Group will be asked to fire 40 rounds 9.2 Howitzer at PUITS No: 16 during this period.

FINAL BOMBARDMENT.

7.(a) At one minute before "zero" the frontage of bombardment will be reduced, its Northern limit being the railway at M.15.b.6.2¼. Guns of the CALONNE Group previously firing North of this point will be switched South of the railway at precisely one minute before zero. The Southern boundary of ANGRES Group and the dividing point between Groups remains unchanged.

(b) All 18 Prs: and 4.5 Howitzers will fire on front parapet for one minute, i.e. till "zero" time, 18 Prs: Section Fire 15 seconds; Howitzers, Section Fire 30 seconds.

(c) At "zero" hour, every Infantry company in front trench will dischrage a red rocket. At this signal all 18 Prs: and 4.5 Howitzers will immediately "lift" their fire on to the second support line, which runs roughly through M.15.c.9.0. - M.15.d.8.2. - M.21.b.2.3. - M.21.c.2.7½. At the same moment the Infantry will light smoke candles all along the front of bombardment. Fire will be maintained on this line from "zero" to 0.5 minutes, at Section Fire 20 seconds for 18 pounders, and Section Fire 40 seconds for Howitzers.

(d) At 0.5 minutes every company in front line will fire a green rocket. At this signal all 18 Prs: and 4.5 Howitzers will drop their fire back on to the front line and fire for one minute at Section Fire 10 seconds, Howitzers at Section Fire 20 seconds. Operations end at 0.6, when all guns get back on to their normal zones and stand by.

(e) The allotment of ammunition to each Group for the period from one minute before "zero" to 0.6 is

18 Pr: Shrapnel	275.
" H.E.	130.
4.5 Howitzer	50.

Should the number of guns employed by Groups necessitate alteration in above rates of fire, they will alter the rates of fire proportionally, but the above expenditure is not to be exceeded. Shrapnel should be fired by all 18 Prs: during the final minute, 0.5 to 0.6.

(f) During this bombardment the 49th Siege Battery will fire 40 rounds into the double row of houses from M.22.a.8.4. to M.22.c.0.9½.

(g) The 4th Corps Counter-Battery Group will be asked to put 10 rounds 9.2 inch Howitzer into CITE DE ROLLENCOURT during the same period.

<u>RETALIATION.</u> 8. For purposes of possible retaliation <u>after</u> the operation, the ammunition shown in column 2 of Para 2 is normally allotted in the proportion of one third to each Group. Group Commanders will exercise a strict supervision on this expenditure, it being limited to what is strictly necessary, and R.A. Headquarters being kept informed of expenditure. It is hoped that any German retaliation may finish before evening, and it is undesirable to provoke retaliation. Calls for retaliation by the Heavy Howitzers must be made through R.A. Headquarters.

<u>ORDERS.</u> 9. Group Commanders will submit their operation orders with time tables, to this office by 4 p.m. 5th April.

<u>ZERO HOUR.</u> 10- Zero hour and arrangements for synchronizing watches will be issued later.

11. ACKNOWLEDGE.

A. K. Hay.

Captain,

3rd April, 1916. Brigade Major R.A. 23rd Divn:

Issued at 7.15 p.m.

Copies to :-

No: 1 GO.C. R.A. 4th Corps.

2 to 4 23rd Division.

5 G.O.C. 68th Infantry Brigade.

6. G.O.C. 69th Infantry Brigade.

7. G.O.C. 24th Infantry Brigade.

8 4th Corps, Counter-Battery Group.

9 G.O.C. R.A. 1st Division.

10 G.O.C. R.A. 47th Division.

11 SOUCHEZ GROUP.

12 ANGRES GROUP.

13 CALONNE GROUP.

14 O.C. 49th Siege Battery.

15 R.A. Trench Mortar Officer.

16 & 17 Diary.

SECRET. S/1/22/2.

URGENT.

ADDENDA TO R.A. 23RD DIVISION OPERATION ORDER NO: 36

OF 3RD APRIL, 1916.

1. Paragraph 2. of the above order is now cancelled.
The ammunition to be actually expended in the operation, apart from any subsequent retaliation is as follows:-

18 Pr: Shrapnel	1500	rounds.
-"- H.E.	2000	"
4.5 How: H.E.	600	"
6" How: H.E.	150	"
9.2 inch How: H.E.	60	"

2. The above necessitates the following re-allotments.

Para 6 (e). Will now read:-

	18 Pr: SH:	18 Pr: H.E.	4.5 How: H.E.
Each Group (including attached units)	150	600	250

Para 7 (e). Will now read:-

	18 Pr: SH:	18 Pr: H.E.	4.5 How: H.E.
Each Group (including attached units)	375	375	50

The extra 100 rounds 18 Pr: Shrapnel here provided should be devoted to the last minute 0.5 to 0.6, or if it cannot all be got off in the minute, guns should fire as fast as possible till it is expended, prolonging the time if necessary.

The additional 245 rounds of H.E. should be put into the period from minus one minute up to zero - and the balance which cannot be got off in this minute should be spread over the period zero to 0.5.

Para 6 (g). The 49th Siege Battery will fire 110 rounds in this bombardment.

Para 6 (h). The 4th Corps Counter-Battery Group will be asked to fire 50 rounds of 9.2" Howitzer in this period.

3. Group Commanders will immediately on receipt revise their rates of fire in accordance with the above instructions.

4. As regards retaliation, there is sufficient ammunition in hand over and above the amount mentioned in para 1. of this minute to cope with the situation. Groups, including SOUCHEZ Group, may therefore reckon on the following expenditure for retaliation purposes.

18 Pr: Shrapnel	100 rounds.
-"- H.E.	300 "
4.5 How: H.E.	50 "

There is however no desire to prolong the strafe after 0.6, therefore retaliation should be judiciously applied.

5. On receipt of these instructions Group Commanders will arrange to "dump" to-night the following ammunition for those batteries which are taking part in the operations. (This includes A/102 - but not the Section 1st Division).

18 Pr: Shrapnel	50 rounds per gun.
-"- H.E.	50 " " "
4.5" How: H.E.	50 " " "

The 49th Siege Battery will arrange for a total of 250 rounds to be available at the battery.

6. ACKNOWLEDGE.

A. K. Hay

Captain,

7th April, 1916. Brigade Major R.A. 23rd Division.

Issued at 4.30 p.m.

App XI

COPY NO: 16

OPERATION ORDER NO: 37.

BY

Br: General D.J.M.Fasson C.B.

Commanding R.A. 23rd Division.

Reference Sheet 36 B, 1/40,000. 17th April, 1916.

RELIEFS. 1. R.A. 23rd Division will be relieved by R.A. 2nd Division on the night of 19/20th April, as per attached Table. On completion of reliefs each Battery will march into billets in the Reserve Area on the same night.
Battery Reliefs will be completed by 10 p.m. on 19th.
D.A.C. at noon on 20th.
Headquarters R.A. and Group Headquarters will hand over command at 10 a.m. on 20th.

GUNS. 2. All guns will be handed over to 2nd Division stripped at gun positions. The 71st Battery will bring up and hand over to C/103 four guns which will be put into latters new position at R.12.a.6.3.
23rd Division Units will take over stripped guns of 2nd Division, which will be handed over parked at the places shown in the Table.
Each Brigade will send a Q.M.S. or senior N.C.O. and a suitable guard of N.C.O's and men with the Billetting Officer on morning of 19th to take over these guns. Where these guns are not at present parked at the billets to be occupied by the Brigade, gun limbers must be detached to pick up the guns on the night 19th/20th.

COMMUNICATIONS 3. Telephone lines will be handed over as they stand.

MAPS, ETC: 4. All maps (except 1/40,000), photographs, log books, registers, etc, will be handed over.

AMMUNITION. 5. Instructions regarding handing over of ammunition are being issued separately.

BILLETTING PARTIES. 6. One Officer of each Brigade and one Senior N.C.O. per unit will proceed to the billetting area early on 19th.

DETACHED UNITS. 7. C/103 and C/105 will remain in action as Counter-Batteries. One Subsection (4 wagons) of 103rd and 105th Brigade Ammunition Columns will be attached to those Batteries from noon 19th instant.

A detachment (7 wagons) of 23rd D.A.C. will similarly be attached to 2nd D.A.C. from noon 20th instant.

REFILLING. 8. Units will refill at BRUAY STATION on 20th, except detached units, who will draw at BARLIN till further orders.

TRANSPORT. 9. The draught horses of the Train will join units on 18th or 19th. They will be returned to the Train at LA CAUCHIETTE (I.13.d) on 20th instant.

O.C. 23rd D.A.C. will detail one G.S. Wagon to report at each Battery wagon line (less C/103 and C/105) at 9 a.m. on 19th, and one wagon to 105/B.A.C. Men and horses to be rationed by D.A.C. for 20th. These wagons will be returned to D.A.C. at BRUAY by 2 p.m. on 20th.

TRENCH MORTARS. 10. Orders regarding the relief of Trench Mortar Batteries and their move to billets at FOSSE DE LA CLARENCE will be issued by the Divisional Trench Mortar Officer.

11. ACKNOWLEDGE.

A.K. Hay. Captain,

Brigade Major R.A. 23rd Division.

Issued at 6.30 p.m.

Copies to:-

No: 1.	R.A. 4th Corps.
2.	23rd Division.
3.	23rd Division (Q).
4.	R.A. 2nd Division.
5.	102nd Brigade R.F.A.
6.	103rd " "
7.	104th " "
8.	105th " "
9.	23rd Divisional Ammunition Column.
10.	4th Corps Heavy Artillery.
11.	C/103.
12.	C/105.
13.	Staff Captain R.A.
14.	Divisional Trench Mortar Officer.
15 & 16.	Diary.

TABLE OF RELIEFS.

Unit	Relieved by	Date	Moves to Billets at	Route for march.	Takes over guns parked at	Remarks.
H.Q. R.A.	H.Q. R.A. 2nd Division.	10 a.m. 20th.	LE VIELFORT (J.26.a.8.5)	Direct.	-	
102nd Bde:	41st Bde:	19th/20th	CAMBLAIN CHATELAIN and CALONNE RICOUART.	HAILLICOURT - BRUAY	CAMBLAIN CHATELAIN (16 guns).	
103rd Bde: (less C/103)	38th Bde:	19th/20th	DIEVAL.	BARLIN - MAISNIL LES RUITZ - HOUDAIN.	DIEVAL. (10 guns).	Less 2 guns at present on loan to 47th D.A.C.
104th Bde:	34th Bde:	19th/20th	LA THIEULOYE.	RANCHICOURT - LA COMTE	DIVION. (14 guns) CAMBLAIN CHATELAIN (2 guns).	
105th Bde: (less C/105)	47th Bty: 58th Bty:	19th/20th	DIVION.	RUITZ - BRUAY STATION (J.16.d.7.5)	FOSSE DE LA CLARENCE (8 guns)	2 guns with I.O.M. at OURTON. 2 guns on loan to 47th D.A.C.
23rd D.A.C.	2nd D.A.C.	Noon 20th	BRUAY.	Direct.	-	

Routine Order No: 153.   4th April, 1916.

By

Lieut: Colonel W.A.Nicholson.

Commanding Royal Artillery, 23rd Division.

---

390 Postings. No: 41402, Gr Galvin, and No: 23254, Dr Adams, are posted from D/104 Bde. R.F.A. to A/105 Bde. R.F.A. and attached to H.Q. R.A. 23rd Div'n for duty from 4.4.1916.

Dr George Clayton, A/105 Bde. R.F.A. attached H.Q.R.A. is posted to A/104 Bde. R.F.A. from 4.4.1916.

The following having reported their arrival are posted to Brigades as under :-

10 Gunners to 102nd Brigade.
10 - do - to 103rd "
10 - do - to 104th "
10 - do - to 105th "
2 a/Bdrs to D.A.C.
1 Telephonist to 104th Brigade.
2 Drivers to 102nd Brigade.
2 - do - to 103rd "
3 - do - to 104th "
2 - do - to 105th "

391 BRICKS. Bricks will be drawn between 9 a.m. and 1 p.m. each day from stack at R.13.a.3.5. on authority from C.R.E. 23rd Div:

W. J. Smith.

Lieut:

Staff Captain R.A. 23rd Division

NOTICE.

A horse belonging to B/103 Bde. R.F.A. and bearing the following description, is missing :-

No: 39. Blue roan mare, 16 hands, 39 marked near side of neck, white stockings hind legs.

4

AKH

Routine Order No. 137.   5th April 1916,

By

Lt. Colonel W.A. Nicholson,

Commanding Royal Artillery, 23rd Division.

392
PROMOTIONS & POSTINGS.

No. 35253 Acting B.S.M. Acres 104th Brigade is confirmed in the rank of B.S.M. with effect from 17th January 1916 and is posted to 102nd Brigade R.F.A. with effect from 5-4-16.

No. 22569 Acting B.S.M. Morris is confirmed in the rank of B.S.M. with effect from 18th January 1916 and is posted to 23rd D.A.C.

393
APPOINTMENTS

32889 B.S.M. Griffiths 102nd Brigade R.F.A. is appointed Acting R.S.M. 104th Brigade with effect from 5-4-16.

No. 8592 B.Q.M.S. Bromley 105th Brigadenis appointed Acting B.S.M. and is posted to 105th Brigade R.F.A. withbeffect from 5-4-16.

No. 5311 Sergt G Turner, 20th A.A. Battery is appointed Acting B.Q.M.S. and is posted to 105th Brigade R.F.A. with effect from 5-4-16.

The temporary appointment of No. 18211 B.S.M. Fox A. as Acting R.S.M. 104th Brigade R.F.A. terminates with effect from 5-4-16.

W. J. Smith.
Lt.
Staff Capt R.A.
23rd Division.

N O T I C E

File

Routine Order No. 138.   6th April 1916

By

Lieut. Colonel W.A. Nicholson,

Commanding Royal Artillery, 23rd Division.

394.
DETACHMENT.   2DLieut. C.G. BARTLEET, 23rd D.A.C. is detached for duty to Z/23 Trench Mortar Battery and will join on 7-4-16.

W. J. Smith

Lt.
Staff Capt R.A.
23rd Division.

Routine Order No. 139.   12th April 1916.

By

Brigadier General D Fasson, C.B.

Commanding Royal Artillery, 23rd Division.

395
DISCIPLINE.   Attention is drawn to Corps R.O. No. 889 of 10-4-16.

The following has been received from Headquarters, First Army, dated the 9th instant.
"When passing through the village of PERNES yesterday afternoon in an open motor car, the General Officer Commanding passed a large body of N.C.O's and Privates of the...Battalion......
The Car was driving at the slowest pace possible, yet not a single soldier of this party paid any Military Respect - in fact, even when the car stopped and an Aide-de-Camp was sent to ascertain the name of the Regiment, the men still displayed a reluctance to conduct themselves as self-respecting soldiers.

The G.O.C. regards this as the worst case in respect to unsoldierlike, ill-disciplined conduct that he has yet experienced, and he directs that Lieut. General Sir H. Wilson will see to it that episodes of such unedyfying nature do not occur in the future"

In future, all cars carrying flags will be saluted.

This Order will be read out on three successive parades of all units.

396
ANTI-GAS GOGGLES. Attention is drawn to Divn. R.O. No. 1216.
3. All goggles in possession of the troops should be examined and indents should be submitted to Ordnance Officers concerned for Spicer goggles to replace others of inferior types, which on replacement should be returned to Ordnance Officers for despatch to the Base.

397
FOOT GEAR   Attention is drawn to Divn, R.O. No. 1218 of 12-4-16.

All F.S. Boots, shoepacks, thigh gum boots, short gum boots and Soles inner for gum-boots will be collected by units ready for return to Base on 1st May.

Lumbermans boots may be retained until worn out. No gum boots either thigh or short are to be destroyed, they are all to be sent to the Base whatever their condition.

398

399

FIELD GENERAL COURT MARTIAL.

A Field General Court Martial composed as under will assemble at H.Q. 103rd Brigade at 10 a.m. Thursday the 13-4-16 for the purpose of trying No. 41443 Driver William Glencross, C/103 Brigade R.F.A. and such other persons as may be brought before them.

President.

Major W.M. Shaw, A/105th Brigade R.F.A.

Members

Captain A Hobert, B/102nd Brigade R.F.A.

Lieut. P.N. Ellis, C/104th Brigade R.F.A.

The accused will be warned and all witnesses required to attend.

The proceedings will be forwarded to Staff Captain R.A. marked "Confidential".

O J Smith.

Lt.
Staff Capt R.A.
23rd Division.

BM
J.M.a
Ly 4

Routine Order No. 142. 17th April 1916 88

AKTZ

By

Brigadier General D Fasson, C.B.

Commanding Royal Artillery, 23rd Division.

402
CORRESPONDENCE WITH STRANGERS. Attention is drawn to G.R.O. No. 1503.
All ranks are forbidden:-

(i) To insert advertisements, or to have letters inserted, in any publication, inviting strangers to communicate with them.

(ii) To answer the advertisements of strangers who offer to write to the troops.

(iii) To advertise or to have letters inserted in any publication asking for gifts or loans of articles of personal equipment for themselves and for gifts of clothing and necessaries and medical comforts for the use of the troops.

When acknowledging gifts received the greatest care must be taken to avoid giving information of military value.

It has come to knowledge that hostile agents (especially females) are making use of the means indicated above to collect information of value to the enemy, and that in corresponding with them officers and men are playing into the hands of the enemy spy system.

This order is to be published in orders issued by all formations and units and is to be promulgated to all troops now serving in this country and to all troops who may arrive in this country in the future.

403
PROMOTIONS - WARRANT OFFICERS, Class 1. Attention is drawn to G.R.O. No.1505

1. The second paragraph of G.R.O. No. 906, dated 10th June,1915, relating to the promotion of Warrant Officers, Class 1, is cancelled, and the following substituted-

Vacancies among Warrant Officers, Class 1, due to similar circumstances, may be filled as follows:-

(a) Death)Substantive promotion
(b) Discharge from the Service.)allowed immediately.
(c) Prisoner of War) Acting promotion allowed immediately,
(d) Missing) followed after 3 months by substantive promotion.
(e)Sent home sick or wounded) Acting promotion allowed after an
(f)Sent home inefficient) of one month. No substantive promotion.

2. The authority to make substantive promotions under (a),(b), (c) and (d) above is subject to the reservation that such promotion is permissible in the particular circumstances of the case for the individual concerned. The extra numbers required for the expansion of the Army should in general be appointed to the acting rank only, unless the individual selected for the appointment is serving for the duration of the war only, in which case he may be given the substantive rank, if such is allowed by the Authorized War Establishment.

3. Regular non-commissioned officers serving on a normal peace engagement posted to New Army units are not eligible for substantimo promotion to Warrant Officers, Class 1., in those units. Promotion to the rank of Acting Warrant Officer, Class 1., in the Territorial Force is governed by A.C.1. number 342 of 1916.

4. If in any case prior to the 31st December 1915, a vacancy in categories (c) or (f) was filled by substantive promotion under the authority of 2-?? letter No. 121/4575 (A.G.1) of 8th April, 1915, the promotion will be allowed to stand. (Authority - W.O. Letter No. 121/4575 (A.G.1), dated 1?th March 1916)

404
~~144~~
ARTILLERY, TELEPHONE EQUIPMENT. Attention is drawn to G.R.O. No. 1511. The issue of the following equipment for each Artillery Brigade and Battery is approved:-

	Per Battery	R. A. Bde H.Q.
Solution rubber, 3 oz. tubes	8	8
Tape rubber pure (½ lb. tins) tins	1	1

Indents should be submitted to Ordnance Officers concerned

That portion of G.R.O. No. 744 relating to these articles is cancelled.

405
~~145~~
MEDIUM TRENCH MORTAR BATTERY - VERY PISTOLS Attention is drawn to G.R.O. No. 1512.

In continuation of G.R.O. No. 1263 approval is given for the issue of pistols, signal (1-inch) to Medium Trench Mortar Batteries on a scale of 2 per Battery.

Indents should be sent to Ordnance Officers concerned, but supply will not be made until issues already authorised to other units have been completed.

W. G. Smith
Lt.
Staff Capt R.A.
23rd Division.

Routine Order No: 143. 18th April, 1916.

By

Brigadier General D.J.Fasson, C.B.,

Commanding Royal Artillery, 23rd Division.

406.
AMMUNITION BOXES.

First Army Routine Order No: 349 dated 16th April, 1916, is republished :-

"Attention is directed to General Routine Order 1109:

"All ammunition packages, except grenade boxes, are urgently required at the Base and every endeavour must be made to collect and despatch them to Railhead."

407.
PAINTING OF VEHICLES.

The Painting of all vehicles is to be proceeded with as expeditiously as possible.

408.
POSTING 2/Lt. W.P. Pakenham-Walsh having reported his arrival is posted to 105th Brigade R.F.A. with effect from 18-4-16.

409
PROMOTION Shoeing Smith Cuncliffe J, 23rd D.A.C. is promoted Shoeing-Smith Corporal with effect from 18-4-16 and posted to 23rd D.A.C.

410
COURT OF ENQUIRY A Board of Officers composed as under will assemble at 105th Brigade R.F.A. Headquarters at 10 a.m. Wednesday 19th inst, for the purpose of enquiring into and reporting upon the circumstances under which a G.S. wagon on charge of C/105 Brigade R.F.A. became lost. O.C. C/105 will arrange for all witnesses to be present. Proceedings to be forwarded to Staff Captain R.A. 23rd Division.

President.

Captain C.D.W. Archer, 23rd D.A.C.

Members

Lieut J Abbey, C/103rd Bde R.F.A.
Lieut T.J. Craig, A/104th Bde R.F.A.

W. J. Smith.
Lt.
Staff Capt R.A.
23rd Division.

Instructions regarding War Diaries and Intelligence Summaries are contained in F. S. Regs., Part II. and the Staff Manual respectively. Title Pages will be prepared in manuscript.

WAR DIARY
or
~~INTELLIGENCE SUMMARY~~
~~(Erase heading not required.)~~

Army Form C. 2118

CRA 23 Div

Vol. 10

Place	Date	Hour	Summary of Events and Information	Remarks and references to Appendices
LE VIELFORT	1st	May	Battery Training commenced.	
"	2nd, 3rd, 4th, 5th, 6th, 7th, 8th, 9th, 10th, 11th, 12th		Battery Training of all Batteries – Nothing else to report.	
	13th	"	Relief of 2nd Divl. Artillery commenced	See App. XII
	14th	"	Reliefs continued	
BOYEFFLES	15th	"	R A HQ 23rd Division relieved R.A. HQ 2nd Division. CALONNE rather heavily shelled.	
"	16th	"	Enemy slightly shelled positions of D 103 and D 104 – In former case two men wounded, in latter a gun knocked out & 3 casualties. Our Batteries were busy registering.	

1875 Wt. W593/826 1,000,000 4/15 J.B.C. & A. A.D.S.S./Forms/C. 2118.

Army Form C. 2118

Instructions regarding War Diaries and Intelligence Summaries are contained in F. S. Regs., Part II. and the Staff Manual respectively. Title Pages will be prepared in manuscript.

WAR DIARY
or
~~INTELLIGENCE SUMMARY~~
(Erase heading not required.)

Place	Date	Hour	Summary of Events and Information	Remarks and references to Appendices
BOYEFFLES	17th May		Reorganization of Ammunition Columns carried out. All four Bde Ammn Columns abolished. D.A.C reorganized into an "A" Echelon of 3 Sections, and a "B" Echelon of 1 Section. Surplus personnel + transport sent to CALAIS Base.	
"	18th May		Orders issued for the reorganization of the Divisional Artillery into four mixed Brigades, each of three 18pr Batteries + one How Battery – to take effect from midday 19th May – Thus:–	
			102nd Bde: A/102 as before; B/102 as before; C/102 as before; D/102 (How) late A/105.	
			103rd Bde: A 103 as before; B 103 as before; C 103 as before; D 103 (How) late B/105	
			104th Bde: A 104 as before; B 104 as before; C 104 as before; D 104 (How) late C/105.	
			105th Bde: A 105 late D 102; B 105 late D 103; C 105 late D 104; D 105 (How) as before	
"	19th May		Nothing to report.	

1875 Wt. W593/826 1,000,000 4/15 J.B.C. & A. A.D.S.S./Forms/C. 2118.

Army Form C. 2118

Instructions regarding War Diaries and Intelligence Summaries are contained in F. S. Regs., Part II. and the Staff Manual respectively. Title Pages will be prepared in manuscript.

WAR DIARY
or
INTELLIGENCE SUMMARY
(Erase heading not required.)

Place	Date	Hour	Summary of Events and Information	Remarks and references to Appendices
BOYEFFLES	20th	May	The enemy artillery shelled our observation stations and positions suspected of containing our heavy artillery.	
	21st	May	There was a continuous shelling during the morning of battery positions with heavy artillery. In the early afternoon battery positions near Bully Grenay were shelled with lachrymatory shell. This shell was also used against our ~~positions~~ observations stations on Lorette Spur. About 3.30 p.m. we opened barrage fire on the enemy trenches opposite the Souchez sector in response to a gas S.O.S. Call. This was afterwards cancelled it having arisen from the	

1875 Wt. W593/826 1,000,000 4/15 J.B.C. & A. A.D.S.S./Forms/C. 2118.

Instructions regarding War Diaries and Intelligence Summaries are contained in F. S. Regs., Part II. and the Staff Manual respectively. Title Pages will be prepared in manuscript.

WAR DIARY
or
INTELLIGENCE SUMMARY
(Erase heading not required.)

Army Form C. 2118

Place	Date	Hour	Summary of Events and Information	Remarks and references to Appendices
BOYEFFLES	21st May		quantity of gas given off from the employment of a large number of gas shell on the 47th Division front, to the south.	
			About 4.30 pm in response to call of the 47th Division 18 Pr batteries of our right sector barraged the left sector of the 47th Division and 4.5" Howitzer and 6" Howitzer batteries bombarded sensitive points in the enemy front lines.	
	21st May		At 7 pm on the evening 21st May one 18 Pr battery one section 18 Prs and one 4.5 How battery were ordered into position already prepared to reinforce our left sector.	
	22nd May		At 2 am orders were issued for a 4.5" How battery of 23rd Division, at that moment in reserve, to reinforce 2nd Divisional Artillery at CAUCOURT in rear of 47th Div. Two eighteen pounder batteries ~~taken~~ in reserve were ordered	

1875 Wt. W593/826 1,000,000 4/15 J.B.C. & A. A.D.S.S./Forms/C. 2118.

Army Form C. 2118

WAR DIARY
or
INTELLIGENCE SUMMARY
(Erase heading not required.)

Instructions regarding War Diaries and Intelligence Summaries are contained in F. S. Regs., Part II. and the Staff Manual respectively. Title Pages will be prepared in manuscript.

Place	Date	Hour	Summary of Events and Information	Remarks and references to Appendices
BOYEFFLES	22nd May		to move into wagon lines in the 23rd Division Area the same afternoon.	
			The barrage fire was continued, in the form of bursts of fire during the whole of the 22nd May.	
			The enemy during the day continued to shell suspected battery positions, and also shelled BULLY GRENAY and AIX NOULETTE.	
			Arrangements were made to increase the strength of the bombardment to cover the counter attack of the 47th Division	See Appx XIII
			The attack having been cancelled the barrage was continued at a steady rate.	See Appx XIV XIVa.
			AIX NOULETTE was very heavily shelled that evening and in all two eighteen pounder guns were put out of action. Casualties were small but a battery commander was killed.	

1875 Wt. W593/826 1,000,000 4/15 J.B.C. & A. A.D.S.S./Forms/C. 2118.

Instructions regarding War Diaries and Intelligence Summaries are contained in F. S. Regs., Part II. and the Staff Manual respectively. Title Pages will be prepared in manuscript.

WAR DIARY
or
INTELLIGENCE SUMMARY
(Erase heading not required.)

Army Form C. 2118

Place	Date	Hour	Summary of Events and Information	Remarks and references to Appendices
BOYEFFLES	22nd May		During the night the two eighteen pounder batteries began preparation of positions and one gun was put in position in each battery	
	23rd May		During the day the barrage was continued and orders were issued in connection with the attack of the 47 Division at 8.25 pm that evening	Appx XV XVa XVI
			The enemy shelled our battery positions throughout the day and again bombarded the villages of BULLY GRENAY and AIX NOULETTE. By 8.15 pm there was a complete cessation of shelling of the 23rd Divisional Area. The observers of RA 23rd Division were able, from flash of rifles and position from which lights were thrown up, to estimate the progress	

1875 Wt. W593/826 1,000,000 4/15 J.B.C. & A. A.D.S.S./Forms/C. 2118.

Instructions regarding War Diaries and Intelligence Summaries are contained in F. S. Regs., Part II. and the Staff Manual respectively. Title Pages will be prepared in manuscript.

WAR DIARY
or
INTELLIGENCE SUMMARY
(Erase heading not required.)

Army Form C. 2118

Place	Date	Hour	Summary of Events and Information	Remarks and references to Appendices
BOYEFFLES	23rd	May	of the 47th Division attack. The progress of the attack not having been successful the rate of our fire was slackened on request from that division. Later it was again increased when the enemy were found to have been driven from	
"	24th	May	parts of the line attacked. By 3 am. 24th May the fire of our guns had been slackened and finally ordered to cease at the request of the 47th Division.	
"	25th	"	LORETTE, AIX-NOULETTE, SAINS-EN-GOHELLE and BOYEFFLES were all shelled. Our action confined to registration.	
"	26th	"	AIX-NOULETTE and Battery positions in neighborhood were heavily shelled. We engaged one German Battery with 4·5 Howitzers.	

1875 Wt. W593/826 1,000,000 4/15 J.B.C. & A. A.D.S.S./Forms/C. 2118.

Instructions regarding War Diaries and Intelligence Summaries are contained in F. S. Regs., Part II. and the Staff Manual respectively. Title Pages will be prepared in manuscript.

WAR DIARY
or
INTELLIGENCE SUMMARY
(Erase heading not required.)

Army Form C. 2118

Place	Date	Hour	Summary of Events and Information	Remarks and references to Appendices
BOYEFFLES	27th May.		Enemy continued shelling our Batteries.	
"	28th	"	We received an S.O.S at about 10-30pm from 1st Division, & fired about 200 rounds on CALONNE front. Engaged 4 different Batteries during the day - getting a direct hit on one gun.	
"	29th	"	German artillery very active shelling Batteries all day long with heavy shell (5.9 and 8.2 inch). We shelled a supposed ammunition depot with 6 inch Hows -	
"	30th	"	Enemy very quiet.	
"	31st	"	We co-operated with 4th Corps Heavy Artillery in engaging 20 different batteries with one-round salvos. Enemy fairly active - He put a few lachrymatory gas shell into one Battery (C 105).	

A K Hay
BRIGADE MAJOR,
R.A. 23rd DIVISION.

1875 Wt. W593/826 1,000,000 4/15 J.B.C. & A. A.D.S.S./Forms/C. 2118.

Appendix XII

S E C R E T.

S/3/31.

COPY No: 18.

R.A. 23rd Division Order No: 38.

Reference Sheet 36 B S.E. 2. 1/10,000. 10th May, 1916.

RELIEFS. 1. R.A. 23rd Division will relieve R.A. 2nd Division in the SOUCHEZ and ANGRES Sectors on the 13th/14th and 14th/15th May, reliefs being carried out by Sections as per attached Table. Battery Commanders will accompany first Sections.
Headquarters R.A. and Group Headquarters will take over commands at 10 a.m. on 15th May.

COUNTER - BATTERIES. 2. C/103 and C/105 will be relieved by 71st and 47th Batteries respectively, as shown in the Table.
C/103 and C/105 will march back to Reserve billets at LA THIEULOYE, immediately they are relieved, and come under command of O.C. 104th Brigade.

GUNS. 3. All guns taken over from 2nd Division in gun pits, and all guns left parked at CAMBLAIN CHATELAIN, DIEVAL, LA THIEULOYE, and DIVION will be stripped.
Guns for handing over will be all parked together at the above villages at a spot to be selected by O.C. 102nd, 103rd, 104th and 105th Brigades respectively, by 12 noon 14th May, by which time representatives of 2nd Division and C/103 and C/105 will have arrived to take them over.
The total guns to be handed over at each place are as follows:-

CAMBLAIN CHATELAIN	16	18 Prs: to 2nd Division.
DIVION	4	Hows: to 2nd Division.
DIEVAL	14	18 Prs: to 2nd Division.
LA THIEULOYE	4	18 Prs: to C/103.
- do -	4	Hows: to C/105.

MAPS, ETC. 4. Units will take over from 2nd Division all maps (except 1/40,000), photographs, log books, registers, etc.

COMMUNICATIONS 5. Telephone lines will be taken over as they stand.

ATTACHMENT. 6. The Orderly Officer and 4 trained telephonists of H.Q. 104th Brigade will be attached to H.Q. 102nd Brigade with effect from 10 a.m. 15th May.

TRENCH MORTARS. 7. Orders are issued separately by the Divisional Trench Mortar Officer.

AMMUNITION. 8. Units will take over all ammunition in the pits of the batteries they relieve. They will hand over ammunition in the wagon lines to fill up the unit relieved to its authorised proportion.

TRANSPORT 9.

TRANSPORT. 9. O.C. 23rd D.A.C. will send one G.S. Wagon to each Battery of 102nd Brigade, "A", "B" and D/103, and "B", "C" and D/104th Brigade, and "A", "B", "D" and B.A.C. 105th Brigade on 12th instant.
These drivers and horses will be rationed for two days in advance by the D.A.C. and will be returned to the D.A.C. by 14th instant.
Drivers & horses of Baggage Wagons will join units from the Train on 12th instant.

SUPPLIES. 10.(a) All Units except H.Q. R.A. H.Q. Brigades, C/102, 1 Section B/104, A/104, and B.A.C. 104, draw rations in forward area on 14th May, at a place to be notified later.

(b) H.Q. R.A., H.Q. Brigades, A/104, and B.A.C. 104 draw in Reserve Area on that date.

(c) C/102 and 1 Section B/104 draw in 17th Corps area on 14th and future dates.

(d) On and from 15th May H.Q. 104, C/103, C/105 and B.A.C. 104 draw in Reserve Area; all other units in forward area.

BILLETTING 11. A billetting officer from each Brigade with an N.C.O. from each unit will proceed to the forward area on the morning of 13th May.
He will arrange to take over billets from the units which are now in occupation and will inform the Town Major what billets are being taken over.

12. ACKNOWLEDGE.

A.K. Hall

Captain,

Brigade Major R.A. 23rd Division.

Issued at 1.30 p.m.
By Despatch Rider.

Copy No: 1 to G.O.C. R.A. 4th Corps.
2 23rd Division (G).
3 23rd Division (Q).
4 G.O.C. R.A. 2nd Division.
5 G.O.C. R.A. Heavy Artillery, 4th Corps.
6. 102nd Brigade R.F.A.
7 103rd Brigade R.F.A.
8 104th Brigade R.F.A.
9 105th Brigade R.F.A.
10 23rd D.A.C.
11 C/103.)
12 C/105.)
13 24th Siege Battery.) c/o R.A. 2nd Dn:
14 49th Siege Battery.)
15 Staff Captain R.A.
16 Divisional Trench Mortar Officer.
17 R.A. Signal Officer.
18 & 19 Diary.

TABLE OF RELIEFS.

UNIT	GUN POSITION	RELIEVES	HOUR & DATE	WAGON LINE	ACTION TO BE TAKEN WITH PRESENT GUNS.	REMARKS.
R.A. 23rd Divn:	BOYEFFLES	R.A. 2nd Divn:	10 am. 15th May	NIL	NIL	
SOUCHEZ GROUP.						
H.Q. 102nd Bde:	R.21.b.8.7½.	H.Q. 41st Bde:	10 am. 15th May	NIL	NIL	
"A" 102	R.27.d.7½.2.	2 guns 9th Bty: 2 guns 17th Bty:	13th May and 14th May.	R.13.b.2.4. (Formerly B/102)	Parks 4 guns at CAMBLAIN CHATELAIN	Same position.
"B" 102	R.22.a.8.4.	4 guns 9th Bty:	- do -	Q.11.b.6.4. (Relieves C/103)	- do -	Same position.
"C" 102 and 1 Sectn: B/104	X.28.b.4.5.	6 guns 16th Bty:	- do -	W. of ST: ELOI (Relieves 16th By)	- do -	Old position of D/102
"D" 102	R.22.b.3.8.	4 guns 17th Bty:	- do -	Q.5.d.1.6. (Formerly C/104)	- do -	Old position of B/103
"C" 104	R.34.d.9.6.	NIL.	14th May.	K.34.a.6.4. (Formerly B.A.C. 104)	Takes guns with it.	New position. Will remain at wagon line till position is ready.
"A" 105 How:	R.28.c.4.5.	4 guns 47th Bty:	13th May and 14th May.	Q.5.b.9.3. (Same as before)	PARKS 4 HOWS: AT DIVION.	Same position.
"D" 105 How:	R.22.c.8½.5.	NIL	13th May.	K.35.d.8.3. (Old Yeomanry Lines)	Takes guns with it.	New position. Will remain at wagon line till position is ready.
B.A.C. 102	NIL	B.A.C. 41st Bde:	12 noon 14th May	Q.11.a.5.2. (Same as before)	NIL	Supplies SOUCHEZ Infy Bde: always. Will supply C/104 & Sectn: B/104 in addition.

TABLE OF RELIEFS (continued).

ANGRES GROUP.

UNIT	GUN Position	RELIEVES	HOUR AND DATE	WAGON LINE	ACTION TO BE TAKEN WITH PRESENT GUNS.	REMARKS.
H.Q. 103rd Bde:	R.10.b.9½.2.	H.Q. 36th Bde:	10 am. 15th May	NIL	NIL	
"A" 103	R.17.b.2.9.	4 guns 48th By:	13th May and 14th May.	R.1.d.9.7. (Same as before)	Parks 4 guns at DIEVAL.	Same position.
"B" 103	M.7.b.1.5.	4 guns 71st By:	- do -	Q.5.c.7.3. (Same as before)	- do -	Position originally occupied by C/103 - in centre of row of houses.
"D" 104 9 D/103	R.11.c.8.2.	2 guns 15th By: 2 guns 71st By: at present at R.10.d.6.6.	After dark 13th and 14th May.	K.31.d.4.1.	Parks 4 guns at LA THIEULOYE.	Same position but fires on ANGRES Sector. Will transfer guns by night from R.10.d.6.6. to R.11.c.8.2.
"B" 105 How:	M.1.d.1.3.	2 guns 47th By: 2 guns 56th By:	13th May and 14th May.	Q.5.c.8.4. (Same as before)	Parks 4 guns at LA THIEULOYE.	Same position.
B.A.C. 103	NIL	B.A.C. 36th Bde	12 noon 14th May.	Q.5.c.5.5. (Same as before)	NIL	Supplies ANGRES Infty: Brigade always. Supplies D/104 in addition

TABLE OF RELIEFS (Continued).

RESTING BRIGADE.

UNIT	GUN POSITION	RELIEVES	HOUR AND DATE	WAGON LINE	ACTION TO BE TAKEN WITH PRESENT GUNS	REMARKS.
H.Q. 104th Bde:	LA THIEULOYE	NIL	NIL	NIL	NIL	
"A" 104	LA THIEULOYE	NIL	NIL	NIL	Retains its guns	Divisional Training Battery.
"B" 104 less	Not yet selected	NIL	14th May	1 Sec: with C/102 1 Section at K.34.a.6.4.	Takes 2 guns and parks 2 at DIEVAL	Will remain at wagon line till a position has been found for them.
"C" 103	LA THIEULOYE	Relieved by 71st Battery	13th/14th & 14th/15	NIL	Takes over 4 guns at LA THIEULOYE.	In rest under O.C. 104th Brigade.
"C" 105 How:	LA THIEULOYE	Relieved by 47th Battery	15th/16th	NIL	Takes over 4 Hows: at LA THIEULOYE.	In rest under O.C. 104th Brigade.
B.A.C. 104	NIL	NIL	NIL	LA THIEULOYE	NIL	Supplies Infantry Brigade in Reserve always.

OTHER UNITS.

UNIT	GUN POSITION	RELIEVES	HOUR AND DATE	WAGON LINE	ACTION TO BE TAKEN WITH PRESENT GUNS	REMARKS.
H.Q. 105th Bde:	K.27.c.	H.Q. 44th Brigade	14th May	NIL	NIL	Administrative control of Howitzer Brigade.
B.A.C. 105 How:	NIL	B.A.C. 44th Bde:	12 noon 14th May	K.31.d.4.1. (Same as before)	NIL	Supplies all How: Batts: 23rd Divn: and 4 Hows: of 56th Bty: at present in CALONNE Group.
23rd D. A.C.	NIL	2nd D.A.C.	12 noon 15th May	K.27.c.7.2. (Same as before)	NIL	Supplies all B.A.C's of 23rd Divn: and also B.A.C. of 34th Bde: at present in CALONNE Group.

SECRET.

S/3/31/2.

G.O.C. R.A. IVth Corps.
23rd Division (G)
23rd Division (Q)
G.O.C. R.A. 2nd Division.
G.O.C. R.A. Hy: Arty: IVth Corps.
102nd Brigade R.F.A.
103rd Brigade R.F.A.
104th Brigade R.F.A.
105th Brigade R.F.A.
23rd D.A.C.
C/103.
C/105.
24th Siege Bty:
49th Siege Bty:

In certain copies of Table of Reliefs issued under this office No: S/3/31/ (Secret) of today's date, under "ANGRES GROUP". the following relief was omitted.
"UNIT. "D" 103. GUN POSITION M.7.b.4.7. RELIEVES 4 guns
"15th Battery. HOUR AND DATE 13th May and 14th May.
"WAGON LINE. Q.11.b.C.4. (Same as before). ACTION TO BE
"TAKEN WITH PRESENT GUNS. Parks 4 guns at DIEVAL. REMARKS
"Same position."

A. K. Hay.
Captain,

10th May, 1916.

Brigade Major R.A. 23rd Division.

Appendix XII.

SECRET.

S/3/31.

COPY No: 19

R.A. 23rd Division Order No: 38.

Reference Sheet 36 B S.E. 2. 1/10,000. 10th May, 1916.

RELIEFS. 1. R.A. 23rd Division will relieve R.A. 2nd Division in the SOUCHEZ and ANGRES Sectors on the 13th/14th and 14th/15th May, reliefs being carried out by Sections as per attached Table. Battery Commanders will accompany first Sections.
Headquarters R.A. and Group Headquarters will take over commands at 10 a.m. on 15th May.

COUNTER - BATTERIES. 2. C/103 and C/105 will be relieved by 71st and 47th Batteries respectively, as shown in the Table.
C/103 and C/105 will march back to Reserve billets at LA THIEULOYE, immediately they are relieved, and come under command of O.C. 104th Brigade.

GUNS. 3. All guns taken over from 2nd Division in gun pits, and all guns left parked at CAMBLAIN CHATELAIN, DIEVAL, LA THIEULOYE, and DIVION will be stripped.
Guns for handing over will be all parked together at the above villages at a spot to be selected by O.C. 102nd, 103rd, 104th and 105th Brigades respectively, by 12 noon 14th May, by which time representatives of 2nd Division and C/103 and C/105 will have arrived to take them over.
The total guns to be handed over at each place are as follows:-

CAMBLAIN CHATELAIN	16	18 Prs: to 2nd Division.
DIVION	4	Hows: to 2nd Division.
DIEVAL	14	18 Prs: to 2nd Division.
LA THIEULOYE	4	18 Prs: to C/103.
- do -	4	Hows: to C/105.

MAPS, ETC. 4. Units will take over from 2nd Division all maps (except 1/40,000), photographs, log books, registers, etc.

COMMUNICATIONS 5. Telephone lines will be taken over as they stand.

ATTACHMENT. 6. The Orderly Officer and 4 trained telephonists of H.Q. 104th Brigade will be attached to H.Q. 102nd Brigade with effect from 10 a.m. 15th May.

TRENCH MORTARS. 7. Orders are issued separately by the Divisional Trench Mortar Officer.

AMMUNITION. 8. Units will take over all ammunition in the pits of the batteries they relieve. They will hand over ammunition in the wagon lines to fill up the unit relieved to its authorised proportion.

TRANSPORT 9.

TRANSPORT. 9. O.C. 23rd D.A.C. will send one G.S. Wagon to each Battery of 102nd Brigade, "A", "B" and D/103, and "B", "C" and D/104th Brigade, and "A", "B","D" and B.A.C. 105th Brigade on 12th instant.
These drivers and horses will be rationed for two days in advance by the D.A.C. and will be returned to the D.A.C. by 14th instant.
Drivers & horses of Baggage Wagons will join units from the Train on 12th instant.

SUPPLIES. 10.(a) All Units except H.Q. R.A. H.Q. Brigades, C/102, 1 Section B/104, A/104, and B.A.C. 104, draw rations in forward area on 14th May, at a place to be notified later.

(b) H.Q. R.A., H.Q. Brigades, A/104, and B.A.C. 104 draw in Reserve Area on that date. at OURTON on 13th & 14th

(c) C/102 and 1 Section B/104 draw in 17th Corps area on 14th and future dates.

(d) On and from 15th May H.Q. 104, C/103, C/105 and B.A.C. 104 draw in Reserve Area; all other units in forward area.

DAC draw at Barlin on & from 13th

BILLETTING 11. A billetting officer from each Brigade with an N.C.O. from each unit will proceed to the forward area on the morning of 13th May.
He will arrange to take over billets from the units which are now in occupation and will inform the Town Major what billets are being taken over.

12. ACKNOWLEDGE.

BAC of 102 103 & 105 drawing for their HQs on 14th must find out which Groups are feeding their HQ, ~~and~~ where dumps are.
102 HQ Group
103 69th "
105 HQ Group

A.K. Hall

Captain,

Brigade Major R.A. 23rd Division.

Issued at 1.30 p.m.
By Despatch Rider.

Copy No: 1 to G.O.C. R.A. 4th Corps.
2 23rd Division (G).
3 23rd Division (Q).
4 G.O.C. R.A. 2nd Division.
5 G.O.C. R.A. Heavy Artillery, 4th Corps.
6. 102nd Brigade R.F.A.
7 103rd Brigade R.F.A.
8 104th Brigade R.F.A.
9 105th Brigade R.F.A.
10 23rd D.A.C.
11 C/103. } c/o R.A. 2nd Dn:
12 C/105. }
13 24th Siege Battery. }
14 49th Siege Battery. }
15 Staff Captain R.A.
16 Divisional Trench Mortar Officer.
17 R.A. Signal Officer.
18 & 19 Diary.

TABLE OF RELIEFS.

UNIT	GUN ₱ POSITION	RELIEVES	HOUR AND DATE	WAGON LINE	ACTION TO BE TAKEN WITH PRESENT GUNS	REMARKS.
R.A. 23rd Divn:	BOYEFFLES	R.A. 2nd Divn:	10 am. 15th May	NIL	NIL	
SOUCHEZ GROUP.						
H.Q. 102nd Bde:	R.21.b.8.7½.	H.Q. 41st Bde:	10 am. 15th May	NIL	NIL	
"A" 102	R.27.d.7½.2.	2 guns 9th Bty: 2 guns 17th By:	13th May and 14th May.	R.13.b.2.4. (Formerly B/102)	Parks 4 guns at CAMBLAIN CHATELAIN	Same position.
"B" 102	R.22.a.8.4.	4 guns 9th Bty:	- do -	(Relieves C/103) Q.11.b.6.4.	- do -	Same position.
"C" 102 and 1 Sectn: B/104	X.28.b.4.5.	6 guns 16th By:	- do -	W. of ST: ELOI (Relieves 16th By)	- do -	Old position of D/102
"D" 102	R.22.b.3.8.	4 guns 17th Bty:	- do -	(Formerly C/104) Q.5.d.1.6.	- do -	Old position of B/103
"C" 104	R.34.d.9.6.	NIL	14th May	K.34.a.6.4. (Formerly B.A.C. 104)	Takes guns with it≠	New position. Will remain at wagon line till position is ready.
"A" 105 How:	R.28.c.4.5.	4 guns 47th Bty:	13th May and 14th May.	Q.5.b.9.3. (Same as before)	Parks 4 Hows: at DIVION.	Same position.
"D" 105 How:	R.22.c.8½.5.	NIL	13th May.	K.35.d.8.3. (Old Yeomanry Lines)	Takes guns with it.	New position. Will remain at wagon line till position is ready.
B.A.C. 102	NIL	B.A.C. 41st Bde:	12 noon 14th May.	Q.11.a.5.2. (Same as before)	NIL	Supplies SOUCHEZ Inf Bde: always. Will supply C/104 & Secn: B/104 in addition.

TABLE OF RELIEFS (continued).

ANGRES GROUP.

UNIT	GUN POSITION	RELIEVES	HOUR AND DATE	WAGON LINE	ACTION TO BE TAKEN WITH PRESENT GUNS.	REMARKS.
H.Q. 103rd Bde:	R.10.b.9½.2.	H.Q. 36th Bde:	10 am. 15th May	NIL	NIL	
"A" 103	R.17.b.2.9.	4 guns 48th By:	13th May and 14th May.	R.1.d.9.7. (Same as before)	Parks 4 guns at DIEVAL.	Same position.
"B" 103	M.7.b.1.5.	4 guns 71st By:	- do -	Q.5.c.7.3. (Same as before)	- do -	Position originally occupied by C/103 - in centre of row of houses.
"D" 103	M.7.b.4.7.	4 guns 15th By:	- do -	Q.11.b.6.4. (Same as before)	- do -	Same position.
"D" 104	R.11.c.8.2.	2 guns 15th By: 2 guns 71st By: at present at R.10.d.6.6.	After dark 13th and 14th May.	K.31.d.4.1.	Parks 4 guns at LA THIEULOYE.	Same position but fires on ANGRES Sector. Will transfer guns by night from R.10.d.6.6. to R.11.c.8.2.
"B" 105 How:	M.1.d.1.3.	2 guns 47th By: 2 guns 56th By:	13th May and 14th May.	Q.5.c.8.4. (Same as before)	Parks 4 guns at LA THIEULOYE.	Same position.
B.A.C. 103	NIL	B.A.C. 36th Bde	12 noon 14th May.	Q.5.c.5.5. (Same as before)	NIL	Supplies ANGRES Infty: Brigade always. Supplies D/104 in addition.

TABLE OF RELIEFS (continued).

RESTING BRIGADE.

UNIT	GUN POSITION	RELIEVES	HOUR AND DATE	WAGON LINE	ACTION TO BE TAKEN WITH PRESENT GUNS	REMARKS.
H.Q. 104th Bde:	LA THIEULOYE	NIL	NIL	NIL	NIL	
"A" 104	LA THIEULOYE	NIL	NIL	NIL	Retains its guns	Divisional Training Bty:
"B" 104 less 1 Section.	Not yet selected	NIL	14th May	1 Sec: with C/102 1 Section at K.34.a.6.4.	Takes 2 guns and parks 2 at DIEVAL	Will remain at wagon line till a position has been found for them.
"C" 103	LA THIEULOYE	Relieved by 71st Battery	13th/14th & 14th/15th	NIL	Takes over 4 guns at LA THIEULOYE.	In rest under O.C. 104th Brigade.
"C" 105 How:	LA THIEULOYE	Relieved by 47th Bty:	15th/16th	NIL	Takes over 4 Hows: at LA THIEULOYE.	In rest under O.C. 104th Brigade.
B.A.C. 104	NIL	NIL	NIL	LA THIEULOYE	NIL	Supplies Infantry Bde; in Reserve always.

OTHER UNITS.

UNIT	GUN POSITION	RELIEVES	HOUR AND DATE	WAGON LINE	ACTION TO BE TAKEN WITH PRESENT GUNS	REMARKS.
H.Q. 105th Bde:	K.27.c.	H.Q. 44th Brigade	14th May	NIL	NIL	Administrative control of Howitzer Brigade.
B.A.C. 105 How:	NIL	B.A.C. 44th Bde:	12 noon 14th May	K.31.d.4.1. (Same as before)	NIL	Supplies all How: Batts: 23rd Divn: and 4 Hows: of 56th Bty: at present in CALONNE Group.
23rd D. A. C.	NIL	2nd D. A. C.	12 noon 15th May	K.27.c.7.2. (Same as before)	NIL	Supplies all B.A.C's of 23rd Divn: and also B.A.C. of 34th Bde: at present in CALONNE Group.

Routine Order No. 153. 1st May 1916

By

Brigadier General D Fasson, C.B.

Commanding Royal Artillery, 23rd Division.

478
ILLICIT TRAFFIC IN DRINK Attention is drawn to R.O.No. 359 of 28/4/16.

"Carrying away liquor by N.C.Os and men from Estaminets is strictly prohibited.

The purchase, or gratuitous acceptance, of spirits by N.C.Os and men is forbidden.

479
CABLE DRUMS AND REELS Attention is drawn to R.O.No. 364 of 28/4/16.

The issue pf cable is hampered for want of Drums and Reels.

All empty Drums and Reels, not required for reeling up, must be returned to Divisional Ordnance Officers with Corps Troops for despatch to Railhead.

Ordnance Officers will keep a record of the number of these articles issued and returned by units with a view to checking expenditure.

Lt.
Staff Capt R.A.
23rd Division.

Routine Order No: 160.

By

Brigadier General D.J.M.Fasson C.B.

Commanding Royal Artillery, 23rd Division.

492. FIELD GENERAL COURT MARTIAL.

A Field General Court Martial composed as under will assemble at Headquarters 104th Brigade R.F.A. at 10 a.m. on ~~[illegible]~~, 17th May, 1916, for the trial of No: 55231 Driver James Lafferty, B/104th Brigade R.F.A. and such other persons as may be brought before them.

Wednesday

President.

Major J.Grose, C/105th Brigade R.F.A.

Members.

Captain W.A.J.Simpsom, C/103rd Brigade R.F.A.
Lieutenant A.Window, 23rd Divn: Ammunition Col:

Waiting Member.

Lieutemant F.J.Coulter, B/104th Brigade R.F.A.

The accused will be warned . and all witnesses warned to attend.
Proceedings to be forwarded to Staff Captain R.A. marked "Confidential"s.

493. TRENCH MORTAR BATTERIES) A.F.B.158.

G.R.O. No: 1568 dated 14th May, is republished:-
"Heavy Medium and Light Trench Mortar Batteries will render A.F.B. 158 on the last day of each month to the Deputy Adjutant General, A.G's Office at the Base. Any casualties that may affect Officers of Trench Mortar Batteries during the month will be at once reported to the above mentioned Officer".

494. STEEL HELMETS.

Until a full issue is available, all steel helmets received will be given to Officers, N.C.O's and men whose work takes them into forward lines.

[illegible signature]

Captain,

15th May, 1916. Staff Captain R.A. 23rd Division.

Routine Order No: 161.

By

Brigadier General D.J.M.Fasson C.B.

Commanding Royal Artillery, 23rd Division.

17th May, 1916.

495. FIELD GENERAL COURT MARTIAL.

A Field General Court Martial, composed as under, will assemble at Headquarters 103rd Brigade R.F.A. at 10 a.m. on Friday, 19th May 1916, for the trial of No: 45413 Driver Walter Barton, D/103rd Bde: R.F.A. and No: 41294 Driver James McBeth, B/103rd Brigade R.F.A. and such other persons as may be brought before them.

President.

Major G.Badham-Thornhill, D/105th Bde: R.F.A.

Members.

Captain F.H.Richards, C/104th Bde: R.F.A.
2/Lieut: W.S.Judge, D/102nd Brigade R.F.A.

Waiting Member.

2/Lieut: G.R.Robertson A/103rd Brigade R.F.A.

The accused will be warned and all witnesses required to attend.

Proceedings to be forwarded to Staff Captain R.A. marked "Confidential".

W. J. Smith

Captain,

Staff Captain R.A. 23rd Division.

N O T I C E.

LOST. B.S.A. push bicycle was taken from outside Orderly Room, 23rd Division Tunnelling Coy:, FOSSE 5, BARLIN, about 9.30 p.m 14th May. No: 12 painted white on rear mud guard.
If in possession of any R.A. Unit it is to be returned to 23rd Division Tunnelling Coy: at once.

Routine Order No.162. 19th May, 1916.

By

Brigadier-General D.J.M.Fasson, C.B.

Commanding Royal Artillery, 23rd Division.

496. DIVINE SERVICE.

Divine Service on Sunday May 21st will be held as follows :-

Church of England.

In Hersin Cinema.
7.30 a.m. Holy Communion.
9.0 a.m. Holy Communion.
9.45 a.m. Service for R.A.
6.30 p.m. Evening Service.

Sains en Gohelle.
7.30 a.m. Holy Communion in Recreation Room.
6.0 p.m. Evening Service in School behind Mairie.

Boyeffles.
10.0 a.m. Service in the open.

497. BAGS, TOOL, SHOEMAKERS, FILLED.

First Army Routine Order No.103 para. 377 dated 14th May, 1916, is republished :-

"Issue of Bags, Tool, Shoemakers, Filled, is approved on the scale "of :-
"2 extra per Infantry Battalion, 1 per Battery of Artillery, "where not already authorised, or in possession, provided that they are "only demanded when there are men qualified to use them.
""Indents should be submitted to Ordnance Officers concerned."

498. FORAGE.

First Army Routine Order No.378 d/- 14th May, 1916 is republished:-

"In order to supplement the 10 lbs hay, per animal arriving on the daily Supply Train, the following amounts of green forage may be purchased locally ;
For Light Draught Horses 4 lbs per diem.
For Heavy Draught Horses 6 lbs per diem.
In the case of Heavy Draught Horses the balance of the hay ration as authorised under G.R.O.1399 may be made up by the issue of Straw as at present.
NOTE:- 2 lbs. Green Forage equals 1 lb. Hay."

W. J. Smith

Captain,

Staff Captain, R.A. 23rd Division.

Routine Order No.163. 21st May, 1916.

By

Brigadier-General D.J.M.Fasson, C.B.

Commanding Royal Artillery, 23rd Division.

499. GUN SPARES.

No Gun Spares are to be returned to ORDNANCE under any circumstances.

500. COMBINED LEAVE AND TICKET WARRANTS.

23rd Divnl. Routine Order No.1312 d/- 18th May, 1916, is republished :-

"With reference to the Combined Leave and Ticket Warrants both portions of the form i.e. the ticket portion and the leave portion are to be filled in with the station of destination."

Units are reminded that in forwarding applications for leave of Officers and O.Rs. the station of destination must always be included.

W. J. Smith.

Captain,

Staff Captain, R.A. 23rd Division.

Routine Order No. 168. 28th May, 1916.

By

Brigadier-General D.J.M.Fasson, C.B.

Commanding Royal Artillery, 23rd Division.

505. FIELD GENERAL COURT MARTIAL.

A Field General Court Martial, composed as under, will assemble at Headquarters 103rd Brigade, R.F.A. at 10 a.m. on Tuesday, 30th May 1916, for the trial of No. 38303 Driver Arthur Price, B/103rd Brigade, R.F.A. and such other persons as may be brought before them.

President.

Major W.M.Shaw, D/102nd Bde. R.F.A.

Members.

Captain F.J.Richards, C/105th Bde. R.F.A.
2/Lieut. E.L.Bowley, A/104th Bde. R.F.A.

Waiting Member.

2/Lieut. J.Palmer, 23rd D.A.C.

The accused will be warned and all witnesses required to attend.

Proceedings to be forwarded to Staff Captain, R.A. marked "Confidential".

W.J.Smith.

Captain,

Staff Captain, R.A. 23rd Division.

Routine Order No: 169 30th May, 1916.

By

Brigadier General D.J.M.Fasson, C.B.

Commanding Royal Artillery, 23rd Division.

---

506. COMMAND. Lt-Colonel W.A.Nicholson will take over temporary command of 23rd Div: Amm: Column in addition to his other duties.

507 MANURE. Units are to have manure conveyed daily to the nearest manure dump or are to incinerate it.

There is to be no accumulation of manure in horse - lines.

508 DISCIPLINE, The G.O.C., R.A. has noticed a large number of men without Cap Badges.

Steps are to be taken AT ONCE to remedy this.

W. J. Smith,
Captain,
Staff Captain, R.A., 23rd Division.

AR

Appx XIII

SECRET.

IVTH CORPS ORDER NO. 109.

(Reference Trench Map 1/10,000, Edition 7.A., Sheets 36.B.S.E.4 and 36.C.S.W.3.)

1. The 47th Division with the assistance of the 25th Division, will retake the line of resistance in the "P" BERTHONVAL and CARENCY Sections by a night attack to-night.

The line to be retaken runs from S.21.d.6.4. through S.21.b.4.3 - S.15.C.9.1½ to S.15.a.1.7.

The 47th Division will also consolidate the line which runs roughly from S.21.b.1.4½ - S.15.c.4½.3 toS.15.c.0.7 (shewn on the map as dotted trenches).

2. The 99th Infantry Brigade has been placed at the disposal of the 47th Division for the attack and a battalion of the 6th Infantry Brigade will be held in readiness to occupy the MAISTRE line and SWITCH on the TOPART Ridge.

3. The troops will be assembled for the attack under cover of darkness.

The assault will take place after the rising of the moon, the exact time to be fixed by the 47th Division and communicated to the 25th Division.

4. The dividing line between the 25th and 47th Divisions is CENTRAL AVENUE inclusive to 47th Division.

5. The G.O.C., R.A., IVth Corps will arrange that all guns of the 23rd Division that now bear on the 47th Division front and all guns of the 2nd Division for which positions can be found, as well as the whole of the IVth Corps Heavy Artillery are placed under the orders of the 47th Division.

The artillery of the 1st and XVIIth Corps will assist.

6. Till the moment of assault the line captured and held by the Germans together with their old front line, communication trenches, and lines of approach will be kept under steady fire, with occasional bursts of intense fire.

The enemy will be prevented from consolidating at all costs.

7. Two Sections and Headquarters 226th and 1 other Field Company R.E. 2nd Division will be moved to VILLERS AU BOIS as soon as possible by motor transport, and come under 47th Division.

8. As soon as the 99th Infantry Brigade pass to the assault the 140th Infantry Brigade will be withdrawn.

9. All infantry working parties under the C.E., IVth Corps will return to their units.

10. Please acknowledge.

Sd. H. de PREE,
Brigadier General,
General Staff, IVth Corps.

22nd May, 1916.

SECRET.
******

Copy No. 6

47th (LONDON) DIVISION OPERATION ORDER No.63.
****

22nd May 1916.

(Reference Map - 1/10,000 Secret Map, GIVENCHY, Edition 7.A).

1. The present position as regards front line is shown on attached tracing.

The 99th Inf.Brigade, 2nd Division, all available Artillery of 2nd Division which can be got into position, any Artillery of 23rd Division which can bear on our front, and IVth Corps Heavy Artillery, have been placed under the orders of G.O.C. 47th Division.

The 226th Field Company and one other Field Company of the 2nd Division are coming up and will come under the orders of G.O.C. 47th Division on arrival at VILLERS AU BOIS.

The 6th Inf.Brigade, 2nd Division, is now arriving at MAISNIL BOUCHE and GOUY SERVINS.

2. The G.O.C. intends to regain and consolidate the lines, shown in red on tracing, as far South as CENTRAL AVENUE after dark tonight.

The 25th Division are attacking at the same time to regain and consolidate the lines South of CENTRAL AVENUE.

3. The attack will be carried out as follows :-

(a). On the Right -
99th Inf.Bde. - Commander - Lt.Col.BARKER, 22nd R.Fus., with Right flank on CENTRAL AVENUE (inclusive) and Left flank on LANDWEHR AVENUE and GRANBY AVENUE (exclusive).

(b). On the Left -
142nd Inf.Bde.- Commander - Br.Gen.LEWIS, C.M.G. with Right flank on LANDWEHR AVENUE and GRANBY AVENUE (inclusive) and Left flank on UHLAN ALLEY (inclusive).

(c) 99th Inf.Bde. will relieve 140th Inf.Bde. within limits mentioned in (a) and on CABARET ROUGE SPUR South of ERSATZ.

142nd Inf.Bde. will relieve 140th and 141st Inf.Bdes. within limits mentioned in (b); but will not relieve 141st Inf.Bde. on CABARET ROUGE SPUR North of ERSATZ.

CENTRAL AVENUE is allotted to 99th Inf.Bde., CABARET ROAD to 142nd Inf.Bde.

The 22nd and 23rd Battalions, London Regt. will come under the command of G.O.C. 142nd Inf.Bde. from receipt of this order.

TOPART SPUR will be held by the 4 Permanent Machine Guns only; but a battalion of 6th Inf.Bde. is held in readiness to occupy the Spur if required.

All Machine Guns of 140th and 141st Inf.Bde. Machine Gun Companies now in action will remain in action and come under orders of G.O.C. the Section in which they are located.

4. The C.R.A. will arrange to keep the captured trenches, and original enemy front line behind them, under continuous heavy artillery fire with intense bursts at varying intervals from all natures of guns which can be brought to bear throughout the day and up to the moment of assault in order to completely isolate the Germans in the captured trenches.

At

At the hour (1-30 a.m.) fixed for assault, the barrage will be lifted to line shown in Green on tracing, but without any change of rate of fire until 1-35 a.m. when the rate will be increased.

The C.R.A. will detail a senior Liaison Officer to Headquarters 99th, 142nd, and 141st Inf.Bdes.

5. The 226th Fd.Co.R.E. is allotted to the 99th Inf.Bde. and the 2/3rd Lon.Fd.Co.R.E. and 1 Company 4th R.W.Fus., both under command of O.C. 4th R.W.Fus., to the 142nd Inf.Bde. to assist in consolidation.

The Companies will move into position under the orders of the G.O.C. Brigade to which allotted. The C.R.E. is arranging for to dump Tools and Entrenching materials at CABARET ROUGE as soon after dark as possible. G.O.C. Assaulting Brigades will arrange to equip their consolidating and working parties at this dump on the way up. He will also be responsible for keeping communication trenches cleared of falls.

6. (a). The attack will be over the open and will be launched at 1-30 a.m. 23rd May.

Dress - Fighting Order , 300 rounds S.A.A. per man. Rations for 23rd on the man.

(b). Inf.Bde. Commanders are responsible that the present line held by the Division is so held continuously at all costs.

(c). Trenches on West slope of ZOUAVE VALLEY and the ALHAMBRA and COLISEUM will be garrisoned.

(d). Dug-out and trench accommodation is allotted -

To 99th Inf.Bde. In ZOUAVE VALLEY between BOYAU CENTRAL and LANDWEHR AVENUE and GRANBY AVENUE.
At CABARET ROUGE - South of CABARET ROAD.
LIGNE BAJOLLE.) LIGNE MAISTRE.) South of CABARET ROAD.

To 142ndInf.Bde. In ZOUAVE VALLEY between LANDWEHR AVENUE and GRANBY AVENUE and UHLAN ALLEY.
LIGNE BAJOLLE.) LIGNE MAISTRE.) North of CABARET ROAD.
Point "G" - X.23.a.50.20.

(e). 140th Inf.Bde. will be withdrawn to CAMBLAIN L'ABBE and Wood thereabouts.

141st Inf.Bde. troops relieved to VILLERS AU BOIS.

(f). 99th Inf.Bde. will take over Advanced Headquarters of 140th, and 142nd Inf.Bde. will share Headquarters of 141st Inf.Bde., both at CABARET ROUGE.

(g). Stokes Mortars of 140/1 and 140/2 L.M.Batteries will be handed over to 142nd Inf.Bde.

(h). 99th and 142nd Inf.Bdes. will be in position for attack by 12-30 a.m. 23rd May.

7.

7. Watches will be synchronised at Brigade Headquarters VILLERS AU BOIS at 5 p.m. by Divisional Staff Officer.

8. Divisional Headquarters will remain at Chateau DE LA HAIE.

B Burnett Hitchcock

Lt. Colonel,
General Staff,
47th (London) Division.

Issued at

Copy No. 1. Op. Order File.
2. War Diary.
3. A.A.&.Q.M.G. . (No tracing).
4. General Staff.
5. 2nd Div.Arty.
6. 23rd Div.Arty.
7. 25th Div.Arty.
8. 47th Div.Arty.
9. to 14. 47th Div.Engrs. (3 copies only of tracing).
15. 140th Inf.Bde.
16. 141st Inf.Bde.
17. 142nd Inf.Bde.
18. 99th Inf.Bde.
19. 6th Inf.Bde.
20. 47th Div.Sigs. . (No tracing).
21. 4th R.W.Fus.
22. 47th Div.Train. . ,,
23. 47th Div.Med. . ,,
24. 4th Corps.
25. 2nd Divn.
26. 23rd Divn.
27. 25th Divn.
28. 4th Corps H.Arty.
29. XVIIth Corps H.Arty.

Cpy No 6
23rd D A

Identification Trace for use with Artillery Maps.

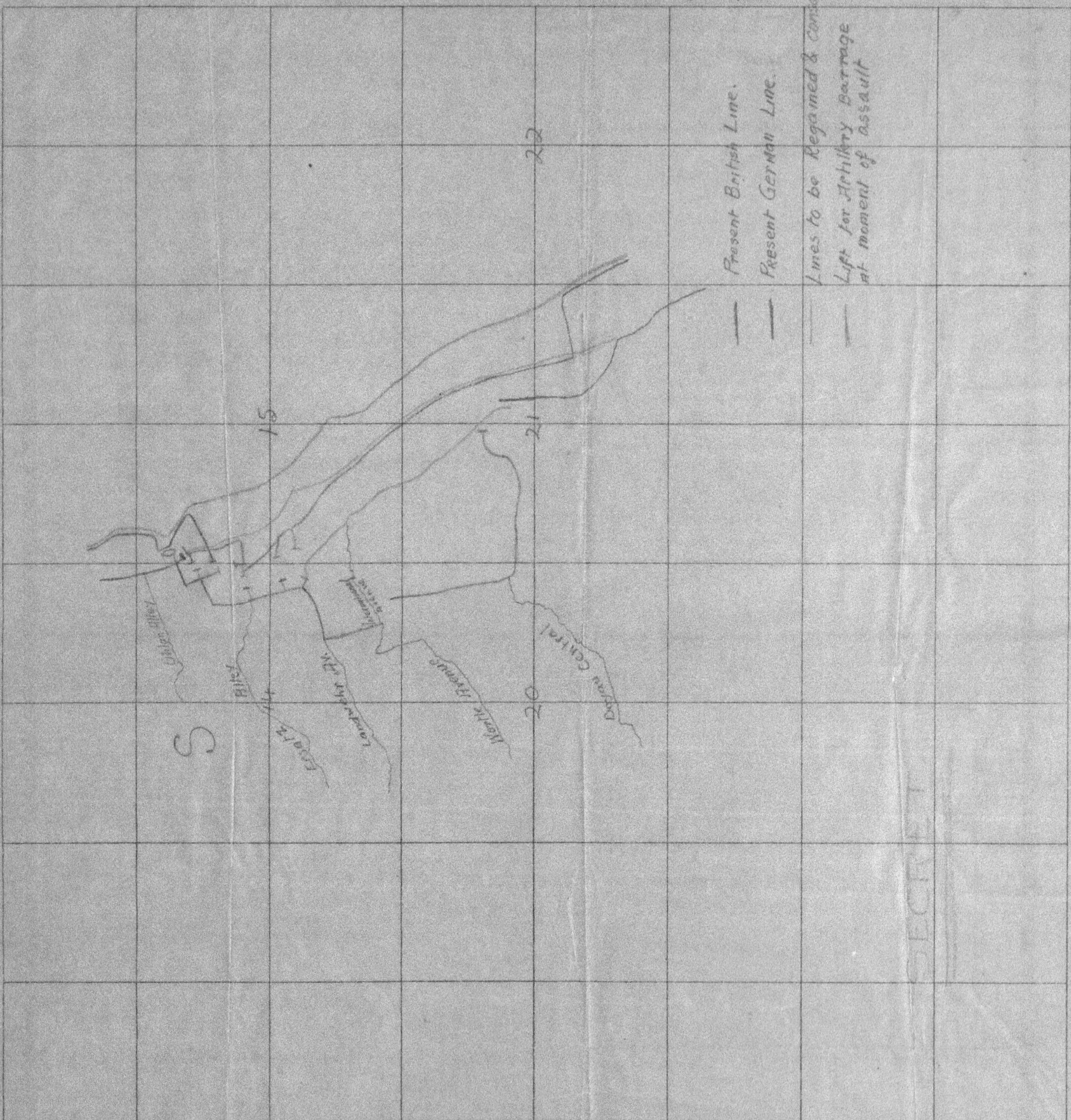

NOTE.—(1). These traces are intended to facilitate the communication of information as to the position of targets, which have been located on a squared map.

(2). The squares on this trace are 1,000 yards in length on the 1/20,000 scale, and 2,000 yards in length on the 1/40,000 scale.

(3). The squares on the trace are fitted to the squares of the map showing the targets, which are then drawn on the trace. Sufficient letters and numbers must also be added to enable the recipient to place the trace in the correct position on his own map. A little detail may also be traced, but this is not essential. The name and scale of the map to which the trace refers must be always given. The trace can be used for either the 1/20,000 or 1/40,000 scale.

G.S.G.S. 3023

Tracing taken from Sheet Givenchy

of the 1:10000 map of

Signature

Date 22/5/16

S E C R E T.

COPY No. 10

47th Divisional Artillery Operation Order [illegible]

Reference Map 1/10,000
GIVENCHY.

22nd May 1916.

1. The artillery of the 2nd and 47th Divisions will be distributed as follows:-

LEFT GROUP under Lt.Col. [illegible], including the [illegible] Brigade R.F.A., 2nd Division.

RIGHT GROUP under Lt.Col. [illegible] D.S.O., including the 34th Brigade R.F.A. 2nd Division.

BERTHONVAL GROUP under Lt.Col.PEAL, including the 41st Bde.R.F.A. (2nd Divn.

Zones will be as follows:-

LEFT GROUP from [illegible] to [illegible].
RIGHT GROUP from [illegible] to [illegible].
BERTHONVAL GROUP from [illegible] to [illegible].

2. The 2nd D.A. Batteries will in every case barrage the old German front line. 47th D.A. Batteries will barrage present German front line within the above limits.

3. Fire will be carried out as previously ordered until 8.0 p.m. by all the above Groups.

At 8.0 p.m. the whole barrage will lift for two minutes to the green line as shown on attached tracing.

Fire will then be brought back on to the original lines and continued until 8.45 p.m. when fire will again be brought to bear on the green line for two minutes. On completion of this fire will again be brought back on to the original line and will continue there until 9.[illegible] p.m. when the range will be gradually lengthened up to the green line and will remain there.

4. Group Commanders will use their discretion as to placing the fire of their 4.5" Howitzers Batteries when the opposing lines are close together.

5. The 23rd and 25th D.A. are assisting in front of the flanks of our line.

The Ist, IVth and XVIIth Corps Heavy Artilleries are also forming a barrage behind.

6. Watches will be synchronised by Group Cmdrs.

R. [illegible] Brigade Major for
Brigadier General Comdg.,
47th Divnl. Arty.

22/5/16.

Issued to:-

Copy No.1 Right Group.
2 Left Group.
3 Berthonval Group.
4 61st Siege Battery.
5 47th Division.
6 IVth Corps Arty.
7 Ist Corps Heavy Arty.
8 IVth Corps Heavy Arty.
9 XVIIth Corps Heavy Arty.
10 23rd Divnl. Artillery.
11 25th Divnl. Artillery.
12 File.

Appx XIVa

SECRET. Copy No. 2.

lVth CORPS ORDER NO. 110.

22nd May, 1916.

1. On account of a considerable addition to the Heavy Artillery of the lVth Corps, made by G.O.C. First Army, and in order to give more time to consolidate the ground won during darkness, the attack ordered in lVth Corps Order No. 109 will be put off till dusk to-morrow evening.

2. The 140th Infantry Brigade will be relieved to-night. All troops intended for the assault will also be got up to-night to the position from which the assault will be delivered. With the above exceptions the plans will remain the same.

3. The artillery will keep up a continuous fire as already directed. This fire will be specially heavy during the hours of darkness in order to prevent the enemy relieving or consolidating.

4. Please acknowledge.

Signed H. de PREE,
Brigadier General,
General Staff, lVth Corps.

Copy No. 1 to 2nd Division.
2 to 23rd Division.
3 to 25th Division.
4 to 47th Division.
5 to G.O.C., R.A., lVth Corps.
6 to G.O.C., Heavy Artillery, lVth Corps.
7 to First Army.
8 to 1st Corps.
9 to XVllth Corps.
10 to A.D. of S., lVth Corps.
11 to "Q" lVth Corps.
12 to A.D.M.S., lVth Corps.
13 to C.E., lVth Corps.
14 to No. 18 Squadron R.F.C.
15 to A.P.M., lVth Corps.
16 to File.
17 to War Diary.

To C.R.A. SECRET
S.G.44/48.

For your information.

[signature]
Major,
General Staff, 23rd Division.

Appx XIV

SECRET

23rd Div Artz.

G.W. 360 22nd May 1916.

Reference Operation Order No.63.

The attack is postponed until night 23/24th hour will be circulated later AAA Reliefs will take place as ordered but no more troops than are required to garrison the line are to be moved up AAA Consolidation of present line will be vigorously carried on AAA Artillery fire will be carried on throughout the night and tomorrow AAA 99th 141st and 142nd Inf Bdes will report dispositions AAA Addressed all recipients of 47th Div Operation Order No. 63.

47th DIV

7.15 p.m.

B. Burnett Hitchcock

General Staff,
47th (London) Division.

Appx XVa

S E C R E T. COPY NO. 7

47th. Divisional Artillery Operation Order No. 21.

Reference map 1/10,000
Sheet GIVENCHY Va. 23rd. May 1916.

Reference 47th. D.A. Operation Order No. 20 dated 22/5/16 - postponed:-

1. Redistribution of Zones will be as follows:-

(a) LEFT GROUP ZONE.

From an East and West line running through S.15.a.0.3.
to " " " " " " " S.15.c.0.3.

(b) RIGHT GROUP ZONE.

From an East and West line running through S.9.c.2.3.
to " " " " " " " S.15. central

(c) BERTHONVAL GROUP ZONE.

From an East and West line running through S.15.c.0.3.
to " " " " " " " S.21.a.0.3.

2. The Infantry attack will be launched at 8.35 p.m. today 23rd. May.

3. The following time-table of fire will be carried out:-

7.0 p.m. Increase to 100 rounds per Battery per hour.
7.15 p.m. Intense burst - section fire 30 seconds.
7.20 p.m. Lift to Green Line.
7.25 p.m. Return to old line - reduce rate to 100 rounds per hour.
8.10 p.m. Batteries will commence lifting gun by gun to Green Line.
8.35 p.m. All guns will be on the Green Line.
8.30 p.m. Intense fire - section fire 30 seconds until further orders.

Batteries of 2nd. D.A. will co-operate commencing at 8.30 p.m. and will fire on the old German front line.

4. The 81st. Siege Battery will continue on present targets at a slow rate of fire and will increase slightly at 8.30 p.m.

5. Watches will be synchronised by Group Headquarters.

6. This order ~~will~~ is to ~~be~~ be circulated in writing and is not to be referred to by telephone or wire.

R. Cavanagh
Brigade Major,
47th. Divnl. Arty.

23/5/16.

Issued to:-

Copy No.
1. Right Group.
2. Left Group
3. Berthonval Gp.
4. 81st.Siege By.
5. 47th.Div.
6. 4th. Corps Arty.
7. 23rd. D.A.
8. 25th. D.A.
9. 1st.Corps H.A.
10. 4th.Corps H.A.
11. 17th.Corps H.A.

Appx XV

SECRET.   Copy No. 6

47th (LONDON) DIVISION OPERATION ORDER No. 64.

23rd May 1916.

(Reference Map - 1/10,000 Secret Map GIVENCHY, Edn. 7a)

Reference Operation Order No. 63 and G.W.360 dated 22nd May 1916.

1. The attack as ordered in the above mentioned Operation Order and postponed will now be launched at 8.25 p.m. 23rd May.

2. At this hour the field artillery barrage will lift and become intensive at 8.30 p.m.
Heavy artillery will lift backwards from the objective gradually commencing at 7.30 p.m.
Rations for 24th will be carried on the man.

3. This order will be circulated in writing only and will NOT be referred to by telephone or by wire.

4. Watches will be synchronised by telephone from Divisional Headquarters between 4 p.m. and 5 p.m.

5. Acknowledge receipt in writing by bearer.

B. Burnett Hitchcock

Lt. Colonel,
General Staff,
47th (London) Division.

Issued at 12.30 p.m.

Copy No. 1	Operation Order File.	
2	War Diary.	
3	A.A. & Q.M.G.	
4	General Staff.	
5	2nd Div. Arty.	
6	23rd Div. Arty.	
7	25th Div. Arty.	
8	47th Div. Arty.	
9 to 14	47th Div. Engrs.	
15	140th Inf. Bde.	
16 & 17	Adv 141st Inf. Bde.	Sent in duplicate by separate messengers.
18 & 19	" 142nd Inf. Bde.	
20 & 21	" 99th Inf. Bde.	
22	47th Div. Sigs.	
23	4th Bn. R. W. F.	
24	47th Div. Train.	
25	47th Div. Meds.	
26	4th Corps.	
27	2nd Division.	
28	23rd Division.	
29	25th Division.	
30	4th Corps Heavy Artillery.	
31	XVII Corps Heavy Artillery.	

S E C R E T.

Appx XVI

Copy No: 8....

S/1/24.

23RD DIVISIONAL ARTILLERY ORDER NO 39.

Reference Map 1/10,000 Secret Map GIVENCHY. 23rd May, 1916

1. The R.A. 23rd Division will co-operate with the R.A. of 47th Division during night of 23rd - 24th May.

2. The attached/gives table the allotment of tasks to the batteries of the R.A. 23rd Division.

3. Three 18 - Pdr: batterieswill barrage a portion of the enemy front opposite the 47th Division and a battery of 6" Howitzers and a battery of 4.5" Howitzers will bombard sensitive points in the enemy line.

4. The assault will be delivered at 8.25 p.m. 23rd May.

5. Watches will be synchronised between 5 p.m. and 6 p.m. from Divisional Headquarters R.A. 23rd Division.

6. This order will be circulated in writing only and will NOT be referred to by telephone or by wire.

7. Acknowledge receipt by bearer.

W J Arnott

Issued at 4.45 p.m. Captain,

23rd May, 1916. a/Brigade Major R.A. 23rd Division.

Copy No: 1 to G.S. 23rd Division.
2 to R.A. 47th Division.
3 to R.A. IVth Corps.
4 to 24th Siege Bty: R.G.A. (23rd D.A.)
5.to SOUCHEZ Group. (23rd D.A.)
6. File.
7 M.G., R.A., 1st Army.
8)
9) File.
10)

R.A. 23rd DIVISION - TABLE OF TASKS.

DATE	TIME	UNIT	GUNS	TARGET	RATE OF FIRE	REMARKS.
23rd May	Now until 8.30 p.m.	3 18 Pr: Batts: of SOUCHEZ Group	4 18 Prs 4 18 Prs 4 18 Prs	SOUCHEZ River to S.9.a.1.0. S.9.a.1.0. to S.9.c.3.0. S.9.c.3.0. to S.15.a.6½.2.	13 Salvoes per Battery per hour.	Irregular bursts of fire along the enemy front line trenches.
		One 4.5 How: Bty SOUCHEZ Group.	4 4.5 Hows:	S.15.b.6.7½. S.15.a.9½.2½. S.15.a.9½.7½.	10 Salvoes per hour	
	Now until 7.30 p.m.	24th Siege Bty: R.G.A.	4 6" Hows:	S.15.a.10.8. (a) S.15.c.9.0. (b)	Section Fire 4 minutes.	One gun on point (a) 3 guns on point (b)
	7.30 p.m. until 8.15 p.m.	24th Siege Bty: R.G.A.	4 6" Hows:	S.15.a.10.8. (a) S.15.c.9.0. (b)	Section Fire 4 minutes.	The guns on point (b) move back on to S.15.d.5.6.
	8.15 p.m. until 8.30 p.m.	24th Siege Bty: R.G.A.	4 6" Hows:	S.15.a.10.8. (a) S.15.d.5.6. (b)	Section Fire 4 minutes	One gun on point (a) 3 guns on point (b)
	8.30 p.m. until further orders	3 18 Pr: Batts: of SOUCHEZ Group	4 18 Prs 4 18 Prs 4 18 Prs	SOUCHEZ River to S.15.a.6½.2.	Section Fire 1 minute 15 seconds.	Continuous barrage of enemy front line trenches.
	- do -	~~[illegible]~~ One 4.5 How: Battery.	4 4.5 Hows:	Points S.15.b.6.7½. " S.15.a.9½.2½. " S.15.a.9½.7½.	Section Fire 1 minute 30 seconds.	
	- do -	One 6" How: Battery.	4 6" Hows:	Points S.15.a.10.8. " S.15.d.5.6.	Section Fire 2 minutes.	

All other batteries R.A. 23rd Division (less counter batteries) on night lines covering 23rd DIVISION FRONT.

Instructions regarding War Diaries and Intelligence Summaries are contained in F. S. Regs., Part II. and the Staff Manual respectively. Title Pages will be prepared in manuscript.

WAR DIARY
~~or~~
~~INTELLIGENCE SUMMARY~~
~~(Erase heading not required.)~~

C.R.A. 23rd Div
Vol 11

Army Form C. 2118

Place	Date	Hour	Summary of Events and Information	Remarks and references to Appendices
BOYEFFLES	1st	JUNE	The 2nd Division (on our right) carried out an attack at 8-30pm on part of the line lost at the VIMY RIDGE, preceeded by a heavy bombardment. The whole of the 23rd Divisional Artillery took part in the action, our rôle being entirely Counter-Battery work. The enemy replied on most of our Batteries, in some cases heavily.	See App XVII
"	2nd	"	A quiet day. Enemy shelled & brought down one of our observation balloons.	
"	3rd	"	At one am. we bombarded enemys front line trench from M 32 d to to S 2 b for a few minutes, and then lifted the fire back to form a barrage round the portion of the trenches entered by our raid. The raiding party successfully entered, shot & bayonetted 12 Germans and bombed 5 dug-outs, and then withdrew. Our fire was maintained till all our men were back. Commencing at about 8-30 am the Germans shelled our SOUCHEZ Sector trenches, culminating in a heavy bombardment about 7-30pm, probably in retaliation for the raid.	
"	4th	"	Some shelling of SOUCHEZ Sector and NOTRE DAME DE LORETTE. Batteries were mostly registering trenches of their adjacent Groups.	

1875 Wt. W593/826 1,000,000 4/15 J.B.C. & A. A.D.S.S./Forms/C. 2118.

Instructions regarding War Diaries and Intelligence Summaries are contained in F. S. Regs., Part II. and the Staff Manual respectively. Title Pages will be prepared in manuscript.

WAR DIARY

or

~~INTELLIGENCE SUMMARY~~

~~*(Erase heading not required.)*~~

Army Form C. 2118

Place	Date	Hour	Summary of Events and Information	Remarks and references to Appendices
BOYEFFLES	5th	JUNE	SOUCHEZ Sector shelled by enemy.	
"	6th	"	Enemy active against ANGRES and SOUCHEZ Sectors, especially with trench mortars. Our Howitzers shelled spots where Trench Mortars were suspected. We sniped movement in LIEVIN – engaged a battery at M22c.3.7, and also retaliated for the shelling of our trenches.	
"	7th	"	Constant shelling of our SOUCHEZ Sector by guns and trench mortars all day. Our Howitzers again shelled likely places for trench mortars. We also retaliated on German trenches.	
"	8th	"	Again constant and heavy shelling of SOUCHEZ sector – trench mortars being particularly active. A heavy minenwerfer was located firing, and stopped by six hits on the parapet of his emplacement by one of our Howitzers.	
"	9th	"	A quieter day. We dispersed some working parties – registered with aeroplane – practised some aeroplane "GF" shoots, and retaliated for trench mortars fired into ANGRES Sector.	

1875 Wt. W593/826 1,000,000 4/15 J.B.C. & A. A.D.S.S./Forms/C. 2118.

Army Form C. 2118

WAR DIARY
or
~~INTELLIGENCE~~ SUMMARY
(Erase heading not required.)

Instructions regarding War Diaries and Intelligence Summaries are contained in F. S. Regs., Part II. and the Staff Manual respectively. Title Pages will be prepared in manuscript.

Place	Date	Hour	Summary of Events and Information	Remarks and references to Appendices
BOYEFFLES	10th	June	Enemy persistently shelled our SOUCHEZ and ANGRES trenches with Trench mortars + howitzers. We retaliated with 4.5 Hows, 18 prs and Trench mortars, and on two occasions called on the 8" Howitzers to assist.	
"	11th	"	Left company ANGRES. I. fairly heavily shelled. We retaliated. A test shoot carried out with Howitzers to ascertain difference between N.C.T and Ballistite charges.	
"	12th	"	Orders for our relief by 47th Divisional Artillery issued. Slight trench mortar activity on SOUCHEZ Sector	App XVIII
"	13th	"	A very quiet day.	
"	14th	"	No hostile action. One section per Battery relieved by 47th Divisional Artillery. Trench Mortar Batteries relieved.	app XIX
"	15th	"	No action – very quiet day. One Section per Battery relieved by 47th Div Arty – thus completing reliefs. Our 3 Trench Mortar Batteries (X/23, Y/23 + Z/23) sent by motor bus to 8th Corps at MARIEUX on orders from 23rd Division.	

1875 Wt. W593/826 1,000,000 4/15 J.B.C. & A. A.D.S.S./Forms/C. 2118.

Army Form C. 2118

Instructions regarding War Diaries and Intelligence Summaries are contained in F. S. Regs., Part II. and the Staff Manual respectively. Title Pages will be prepared in manuscript.

WAR DIARY
or
INTELLIGENCE SUMMARY
(Erase heading not required.)

Place	Date	Hour	Summary of Events and Information	Remarks and references to Appendices
CLARQUES CHATEAU	16th	June	We were relieved this morning by H.Q. R.A. 47th Division, & moved back to CLARQUES – The Division is in G.H.Q. reserve from 6 pm to-day.	
"	17th 18th	June June	Nothing to report.	
"	19th	June	Divisional Field day – practising attack by passing thro' another Division – No 18 Squadron R.F.C. cooperated.	
"	20th	"	Orders to send advance parties by rail on 21st June to AILLY-SUR-SOMME. Brigades practise getting guns across trenches.	
"	21st	"	Staff Captain & advance parties left as above.	
"	22nd	"	Divisional Artillery Field day (moving warfare)	
"	23rd	"	Orders received for entrainment of 23rd Div Artillery on 25th June by standard programme of entrainment to LONGUEAU.	
"	24th	"	Nothing to report.	
"	25th	"	23rd Divisional Artillery entrained at AIRE, BERGUETTE, and LILLERS for LONGUEAU.	

1875 Wt. W593/826 1,000,000 4/15 J.B.C. & A. A.D.S.S./Forms/C. 2118.

Instructions regarding War Diaries and Intelligence Summaries are contained in F. S. Regs., Part II. and the Staff Manual respectively. Title Pages will be prepared in manuscript.

WAR DIARY
or
INTELLIGENCE SUMMARY
(Erase heading not required.)

Army Form C. 2118

Place	Date	Hour	Summary of Events and Information	Remarks and references to Appendices
BELLOY SUR SOMME	26th	June	Having detrained at LONGUEAU, 23rd Divisional Artillery went into billets as follows:- HQ R.A. BELLOY. 102nd Bde } 103rd " } BELLOY. 104th " } 105th " } LA CHAUSSÉE 23rd D.A.C. ARGOEUVES. Orders received that the Division is in G.H.Q. Reserve - & forms part of Second Corps.	
"	27th	"	Reconnaissance of front around ALBERT and FRICOURT.	
"	28th	"	-Ditto-	
"	29th	"	-Ditto-	
ALLONVILLE	30th	"	23rd Divisional Artillery marched into close billets as follows:- All Brigades CARDONNETTE 23rd DAC } HQ.RA } ALLONVILLE.	

G. K. Hall Major R.A.
Brigade Major 23rd Division

1875 Wt. W593/826 1,000,000 4/15 J.B.C. & A. A.D.S.S./Forms/C. 2118.

App XVIII

SECRET.

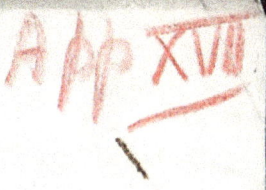

23rd Divisional Artillery Special Operation Report.

1. OUR ARTILLERY.

The 23rd Divisional Artillery and the 24th Siege Battery were employed in Counter-Battery work. Batteries opened fire at 4.5 p.m. engaging the following Batteries with one Section each, commencing at the rate of Section Fire 5 minutes:-

236	522	537	578
259	523	539	600
511	525	547	608
521	535	569	

All these Batteries had been registered during the morning. As soon as any of them were observed active by our observers or the R.F.C. a quick burst of fire was poured into them. Subsequently the following additional Batteries were located firing and engaged by the Sections held in reserve, with bursts of fire, or a slow rate, according to their activity at the moment:-

237	521	540	601
253	532	574	602
505	527	598	613

At 8.30 p.m. every gun increased its rate to Section Fire 15 seconds, and at 8.45 p.m. a burst of ten rounds Gun Fire was poured in by all Batteries, subsequently being maintained at Section Fire 15 seconds till 9.15 p.m. when it was reduced to Section Fire 30 seconds. This rate was maintained till 10.15 p.m. when it was further reduced to Section Fire one minute. At 10.45 p.m. all Batteries were ordered to stop firing, the only subsequent action being at 12.15 a.m. when Battery No: 601 had to be engaged again. Practically all the Batteries fired at were confirmed as "active" by reports of the R.F.C.

2. At about 7 p.m. the enemy in the ANGRES Sector were reported to be standing to, so some salvos of shrapnel were fired on their trenches in the hope of causing casualties.

3. HOSTILE ACTION.

The German Artillery opened fire almost at once. In the ANGRES Sector his fire was chiefly directed on BULLY - GRENAY and our Field and Heavy Batteries. In the SOUCHEZ Sector the neighbourhood of R.22.a, R.22.b, R.28.c, R.33.a. and R.33.c. all caught it fairly heavily from 4.2 and 77 m/m. With the exception of the demolition of some houses in BULLY, the damage was insignificant. Communications were in some cases cut - notably with BULLY-GRENAY.

4. EXPENDITURE OF AMMUNITION.

	Shrapnel.	H.E.
18 Pounders.	2442	1456
4.5 Hows:	-	1567
6 inch Hows:	-	279

A. K. Hay.
Captain,

2nd June, 1916. Brigade Major R.A. 23rd Division.

App. XVIII

S E C R E T.   COPY NO: ..19...

S/3/41.   R.A. 23rd Division Order No: 42.

Reference Map HAZEBROUCK 5 A, 1/100,000.   12th June 1916.

1. RELIEF.

The 23rd Divisional Artillery will be relieved by the 47th Divisional Artillery on the nights of 14/15th, and 15/16th by Sections.
Details as per attached Table.

2. GUNS.

Guns will be handed over in the pits, stripped of sights and stores.
Guns of 47th Division will be taken over similarly at Wagon Lines.

3. WIRE.

All Wire laid down will be handed over as it stands.
No wire will be taken over from 47th Division.

4. MAPS.

The following will be handed over:-

(a) Log-books.
(b) Registers.
(c) Aeroplane photographs.
(d) Panoramas.
(e) Blue prints of trenches.
(f) SECRET Trench Maps.
(g) All tracings of the Sector. All other maps will be retained. Receipts will be obtained for the above, and a duplicate copy forwarded to this office.

5. AMMUNITION.

Each Section will march out full, filling up the previous night, if necessary, from the Dump at the guns.
The balance of the Dump at the guns will be handed over, and a receipt obtained.
An officer will be responsible for the handing over.
The D. A. C. will march full.

6. KENT BATTERY.

The 1/4th KENT Battery will remain in action and will come under command of the Left Group, 47th Divisional Artillery, on their taking over the Group.

7. TRENCH MORTARS.

The personnel of all Batteries will be relieved on the 15th June. All guns will be handed over in the Line to the 47th Divisional Artillery.
Eight two inch guns will be taken over at the Reserve Billet from the 47th Divisional Artillery on the 14th June.
No guns will be taken over in place of the French Guns.

8. MARCH.

After its relief, the personnel of each Section will proceed to its wagon line.
The Sections will march under Brigade arrangements on the following morning to the Half way billets shown in attached Table, starting not later than 6 a.m.
On the next morning, Sections will march to their final destination, which will therefore be reached by the first Sections on 16th, and by the second Sections on 17th June.

9. BILLETING.

An officer from each Brigade Headquarters, with a suitable billeting party will meet the Staff Captain R.A. at the cross roads in DIVION (J.19.c.0.9) at 11 a.m. on 14th June.

10. TRANSPORT.

No extra transport is available. Baggage wagons of Train will join units on 14th instant.

11. SUPPLIES.

Refilling on 15th: All Batteries and 104th and 105th H.Q's in Halfway Area. Advanced Sections draw and dump rations for rear Sections. H.Q's 102nd and 103rd, and D.A.C. as at present.

Refilling on 16th: All Batteries, and 104th and 105th H.Q's at final area. H.Q's 102nd and 103rd and D.A.C., at Halfway Area.

Exact points to be notified later.

12. RESERVE POSITIONS.

Groups will hand over lists of alternative and reserve positions and O.P's, and reports of work done on same.

13. R.A. HEADQUARTERS.

R.A. Headquarters will close at BOYEFFLES at 10 a.m. 16th June and reopen at CLARQUES CHATEAU the same day. Brigades will send mounted orderlies on arrival on 16th, who must bring map position of their respective Headquarters.

16. ACKNOWLEDGE.

A. K. Hay.

Captain,

Brigade Major R.A. 23rd Division.

TABLE OF RELIEFS.

(Vide HAZEBROUCK 5 A, 1/100,000)

UNIT	RELIEVED BY	DATES	HALF-WAY BILLETS.	FINAL DESTINATION.	REMARKS.
H.Q. R.A.	H.Q. 47th R.A.	10 a.m. 16th June.	-	CLARQUES CHATEAU.	
H.Q. 102	H.Q. 233th Bde:	10 a.m. 16th June.	CAMBLAIN-CHATELAIN	UPEN D'AVAL.	
A/102	C/236	14/15th June 15/16th "	- do -	WESTREHEM	
B/102	1 Section A/236	14th/15th	- d*	- do -	Takes 2 guns out on 14th/15th.
C/102	D/235	14th/15 June 15th/16th	- do -	NIELLES	The attached Section of B/104 will take its guns out on 15th/16th.
D/102	D/236	- do -	- do -	- do -	
H.Q. 103	H.Q. 235th Bde:	10 a.m. 16th June	DIVION	CLARQUES.	
A/103	C/238	14/15 June 15/16 "	- do -	- do -	
B/103	C/235	- do -	- do -	- do -	
C/103	34th Batty:	- do -	- do -	- do -	
D/103	D/238	- do -	- do -	- do -	

P.T.O.

H.Q. 104	H.Q. 237	15th June	CALONNE-RICOUART	THEROUANNE	
A/104	B/238	14th/15th June 15th/16th "	CALONNE-RICOUART and	- do -	
B/104 Section at R.34.d.	1 Section A/236	14th/15th	FOSSE CLARENCE - do -	- do -	The Section at X.28.d.4.8. is not being taken over by 47th Division, & will take its guns out on 15/16th
C/104	B/237	14th/15th 15th/16th	- do -	- do -	
D/104	D/235	- do -	- do -	- do -	
H.Q. 105	H.Q. 238	15th June	DIVION	HAMETZ	
A/105	A/237	14th/15th June 15th/16th "	- do -	- do -	
B/105	B/235	- do -	- do -	- do -	
C/105	A/235	- do -	- do -	- do -	
D/105	No one	15th/16th	- do -	- do -	Is not being taken over by 47th Division. Will take all its guns out on 15th/16th.
H.Q. D.A.C.	H.Q. 47th D.A.C.	12 noon 16th	SAINS-LES-PERNES and TANGRY.	ROQUETOIRE	
No: 1 Sectn:	47th D.A.C.	- do -	- do -	- do -	
No: 2 Sectn:	- do -	- do -	- do -	- do -	
No: 3 Sectn:	- do -	- do -	- do -	- do -	
No: 4 Sectn:	- do -	- do -	- do -	ECQUES	
Trench Mortar Batteries	47th T.M.B.	15th	-	ROQUETOIRE	1 Motor Lorry per Battery will pick up personnel and material at cross roads R.3.c.2.6. at 9 a.m. 16 June.

Issued at 10 a.m.

Copies to :-

No: 1. G.O.C. R.A. IVth Corps.
2. 23rd Division.
3. 23rd Division (Q).
4. G.O.C. R.A. 47th Division.
5. G.O.C. R.A. 2nd Division.
6. G.O.C. R.A. 1st Division.
7. G.O.C. Heavy Artillery, IVth Corps.
8. 102nd Brigade R.F.A.
9. 103rd Brigade R.F.A.
10. 104th Brigade R.F.A.
11. 105th Brigade R.F.A.
12. 23rd D. A. C.
13. A/104.
14. C/103.
15. D/104.
16. Staff Captain R.A.
17. Divisional Trench Mortar Officer.
18. No: 18 Squadron R.F.C.
19 & 20. Diary.

S E C R E T.

S/3/41-2.

ADDENDA TO R.A. 23RD DIVISION ORDER NO: 22.

1. B/102 will be relieved by four guns of C/237 - one Section each night.

2. The Section of B/104 at X.28.d.4.8. will be relieved by a Section of A/236. This relief will take place on the night of 15th/16th.

3. D/105 will be relieved by the 4th KENT Battery at R.28.c.7.6. by Sections on the nights of 14th/15th and 15th/16th June.

A. K. Hay.

Captain,

12th June, 1916. Brigade Major R.A. 23rd Division.

App XIX

S E C R E T

and

U R G E N T.

Copy

S/3/61-S.

R.A. Headquarters,

23rd Division.

O.C. X/23 T.M.Battery.
O.C. Y/23 T.M.Battery.
O.C. Z/23 T.M.Battery.

1. You will be relieved to-morrow, 14th June, at 2 p.m. by Personnel of the 47th Division, handing over your Guns to them in the Trenches.

2. You will take over Guns of 47th Division at the Billets in PETIT SAINS.

3. At 8 a.m., 15th June, Motor Buses will be at the Cross Roads in R.3.c.2.5. to convey your Battery with your Guns via ST POL and DOULLENS to the Headquarters 8th Corps at MARIEUX, where you will receive further orders.

4. You will take two days rations with you.

5. The O.C. Battery will report here at 5 p.m. on 14th June for any further instructions.

6. ACKNOWLEDGE RECEIPT BY BEARER.

10.30 p.m.

13th June, 1916.

A.K.Hay,

Captain,

Brigade Major, R.A., 23rd Division

Office Copy

Routine Order No. 170.   1st June, 1916.

By

Brigadier-General D.J.M.Fasson, C.B.

Commanding Royal Artillery, 23rd Division.

509. SALUTING.

First Army Routine Order No. 389 d/- 28th May, 1916, is republished :-

"It is again necessary to draw attention to slackness in regard to SALUTING :-

1. Not only are there single instances of slackness, but whole groups of men are occasionally seen who take no notice of Officers.

Such want of discipline reflects seriously on the unit.

Commanding Officers, whose men are at fault, will take immediate steps to have this altered.

2. The strictest attention of all ranks is directed to the necessity of saluting, and returning the salutes of, our Allies.

When French Officers or soldiers salute British Officers, ALL the Officers so saluted will acknowledge the compliment, irrespective of who is senior, and in thus acknowledging the salute they will do so in the prescribed manner with the right hand and not in a prefunctory manner.

3. When Non-Commissioned Officers or men, not under arms, meet an Officer or Officers, all of the former should salute smartly, with the hand farthest away from the Officers whom they are passing.

In this connection, it has been ascertained that, in some Units, Non-Commissioned Officers and men have been wrongly taught that it is only the senior who should salute in such cases. This is to be at once corrected. There is no foundation in the King's Regulations, or anywhere else, for such a practice.

It is when men are working as a fatigue party, standing at ease, or when sitting or standing about that the senior calls them to attention and is the only one to salute.

These instructions are to be made known to all new Formations on joining the First Army"

The above First Army Routine Order will be republished in regimental and battery orders.

510. GAS HELMETS.

All ranks will invariably wear their gas helmets. Any case of neglect of these orders is to be severely dealt with.

To be republished in Brigade and Battery Orders and to be read out on 3 parades.

511. LEAVE.

Attention is once again called to Div, Routine Order, reference Station of destination must always be included in submitting applications for Leave of Officers and O.Rs.

Applications for Leave - Officers - must be submitted to Headquarters R.A., 8 days in advance.

512. COMMUNICATIONS.

It has come to notice that recently in some cases the recognised system, which has been establis hed in this Divisional Artillery for a long time in connection with communications between batteries and battalions has been changed i.e. as regards what F.O.Os are to be at Battalion H.Q. and for what periods; the provision of R.A. telephonists at Battalion H.Q. by day and night and their duties while there.

It is to be clearly understood that the Orders which have been issued from time to time by the G.O.C., R.A. in this connection are to be strictly adhered to, unless sanction to the contrary has been received from H.Q. R.A. 23rd Division.

It is no excuse that Groups or Batteries which have been relieved had other arrangements.

The G.O.C.,R.A. considers that it reflects very badly on all concerned that changes as indicated above, have taken place without the knowledge of those who are responsible.

The G.O.C.,R.A. has noticed with regret that the changes that have been made, tend generally, to less thorough work by the R.A. towards ensuring the best possible co-operation between Infantry and Artillery. This is contrary to the spirit which he hoped animated all ranks of the 23rd Divn. Artillery.

W. J. Smith.
Captain,

Staff Captain, R.A. 23rd Division.

LOST from Wagon line at Fosse 7 on 27-5-16, Bay Mare 15 Hands - White stockings both hind - Starvand blaze - No.59 on Near fore. Information to O.C. A/104.

Routine Order No. 171.   2nd June, 1916.

BY

Brigadier-General D.J.M.Fasson, C.B.

Commanding Royal Artillery, 23rd Division.

513. WATER TANKS.

All Units in possession of water tanks will forward lists of same, stating capacity, to reach H.Q.R.A. 23rd Division not later than 3rd June.

514. DIVINE SERVICE.

Divine Service will be held on Sunday, June 4th, 1916, as follows :-

For Roman Catholics in and around Aix-Noulette.

Mass in the Chapel at the Farm next to the Ambulance Station at 11 a.m.

Mass at the Wood of Noulette in the Military Recreation Room at 9.30 a.m.

W.J. Smith.

Captain,

Staff Captain, R.A. 23rd Division.

8178

Routine Order No. 172. 3rd June, 1916.

By

Brigadier-General D.J.M.Fasson, C.B.

Commanding Royal Artillery, 23rd Division.

515. DISCHARGES.

G.R.O. No.1593 d/- 30/5/16 is republished :-

The New Military Service Act, 1916, having now received Royal Assent, no soldier of regular army or Territorial Force will be allowed during continuance of present war to be discharged on completion of his engagement unless when the time for discharge occurs he has served a period of 12 years or more together with the extra year for which he is liable under Section 87 of the Army Act and has also attained the age of 41 years. Army Orders 49, 79, and 86, of 1916, are cancelled. Particulars will shortly be communicated of bounties payable to men required under Section 2 of New Military Service Act to continue in Service beyond the extra year for which they are liable under Army Act.

Authority War Office telegram No.20497 dated 27th May,1916.

516. DENTAL TREATMENT, OFFICERS ON LEAVE.

G.R.O. No.1596 d/- 30/5/16 is republished :-

It has been brought to notice that a considerable number of Officers while on short leave from the Expeditionary Force apply to the War Office for an extension of leave on the grounds that they require urgent dental treatment.

Facilities exist in France whereby officers are able to receive urgent Dental Treatment and applications for extension of leave for this purpose are not to be submitted.

517. DISPOSAL OF DOCUMENTS FOR PURPOSES OF RECORD, &c.

G.R.O. No.1597 d/- 30/5/16 is republished :-

With reference to Field Service Regulations, Section 129, para 2, the following procedure will be adopted in future. Papers required by units in the Field, for local reference, will be filed, and marked "K" (Keep). This file will be periodically reviewed, and any papers in it that are no longer required with the unit will, either be destroyed, or sent to Home Records for safe custody.

Other papers which may be of historical interest will be sent by units (not formations) in the Field direct to the Officer i/c Records for safe custody, and will be marked "R".

In despatching documents and records the following instructions will be observed :-

All papers etc., will be packed in parcels or envelopes weighing not more than 10 lbs. and will be sent by post. They are not to be packed in boxes, and sent by train through A.M.F.O. When the documents are of a secret nature the parcel or envelope must be registered.

Each parcel or envelope must contain a list of its contents, and the designation of the unit by which it is forwarded.

G.R.O. 1245, dated 6th November, 1915, is cancelled.

518. BOUNDS TIME AT WHICH TROOPS MUST BE IN BILLETS.

G.R.O. No.1599 d/, 30/5/16 is republished :-

With reference to G.R.O. 1247 of 6th Nov. 1915, the hour by which all Warrant Officers, non-commissioned officers, and men, except those on duty and others with special passes, must be in their billets, is exyended to 9 p.m. nightly from the 1st June 1916, until further orders.

519. WAR DIARIES.

G.R.O. No. 1598 d/- 30/5/16/ is republished :-

1. The reports required under King's Regulations paras. 1930 and 1932 will not be required during the continuance of the Campaign

2. War Diaries which are kept by General or an Army H.Q. and which contain any matter of a specially secret nature will be sent under cover addressed to the D.S.D. at the War Office and not the D.A.G., 3rd Echelon.

3. All other War Diaries will be dealt with as follows :-

(a) The original will be sent to the D.A.G. 3rd Echelon on the last day of each month unless otherwise ordered.

(b) The duplicate copy will be sent to the Officer in Charge of Records of the Unit concerned for safe custody, as a secret document and for preservation to be returned at the end of the War to the O.C. the Unit. The duplicate copy of a War Diary of a staff or formation not affiliated to any record office at home will be forwarded to the D.A.G. 3rd Echelon and marked duplicate copy. If required for a reference a C.O. may retain the duplicate copy for a period of 3 months before sending it away for custody.

4. Each Diary will be enclosed in two covers, the inner one marked "Secret".

A covering letter from the O.C. Unit signed by him will accompany the Diary.

G.R.O. 543, 1097, 1125, 1212 and 1389 are cancelled.

520. EAR DRUM PROTECTORS FOR ARTILLERY.

G.R.O. No. 1604 d/- 30/5/16 is republished :-

Approval is given for the issue of ear drum protectors on a scale of 6 pairs per gun of all natures of artillery.

Indents should be submitted for the number required and issue will be made as supplies become available.

521. HANDLING OF AMMUNITION.

G.R.O. No. 1605 d/- 30/5/16 is republished :-

The attention of all concerned is drawn to the necessity of careful handling in the case of boxed complete rounds of ammunition and cases contained filled fuzes. Any such package which has sustained a fall in loading or unloading should be placed on one side as unfit for issue.

Such packages should be marked "Damaged in Loading" and, after an examination by an Inspecting Ordnance Officer to ensure that they are fit to travel, should be returned to the ammunition Base for transmission to England.

522. PROMOTIONS, TRANSFERS & POSTINGS.

No.20632 B.Q.M.S. Jamieson, G. is promoted B.S.M. with effect from 1.6.16 and posted to 103rd Brigade, R.F.A.

No.57202 Sergt. Whatling, A. is promoted B.Q.M.S. and posted to 103rd Brigade, R.F.A. with effect from 4.6.16.

No.56221 Sergt. Young, J. is transferred from D/102nd Brigade, R.F.A. to A/105th Brigade, R.F.A.

A. K. Hay

Captain,

Staff Captain, R.A. 23rd Division.

Routine Order No. 173.

4th June, 1916.

By

Brigadier-General D.J.M.Fasson, C.B.

Commanding Royal Artillery, 23rd Division.

523. FIELD GENERAL COURT MARTIAL.

A Field General Court Martial, composed as under, will assemble at Headquarters, 104th Brigade, R.F.A. at 10 a.m. on Tuesday, 6th June, 1916, for the trial of No.96598 Driver William McDonald, D/104th Brigade, R.F.A. and such other persons as may be brought before them.

President.

Major H.S.Stanham, B/105th Brigade, R.F.A.

Members.

Capt. G.D.Tidmarsh, D/105th Bde. R.F.A.
2/Lt. W.W.McKeown, A/103rd Bde. R.F.A.

Waiting Member.

2/Lt. E.J.Jackson, B/104th Bde, R.F.A.

The accused will be warned and all witnesses required to attend.

Proceedings to be forwarded to Staff Captain, R.A. marked "Confidential".

524. POSTINGS.

6 Gunners and 1 R.A. Fitter having reported their arrival are posted to 105th Brigade, R.F.A.

No.L29537 a/Bdr. G. Stephenson, R.A. having reported his arrival is posted to H.Q.R.A. 23rd Division and attached to D/102nd Brigade, R.F.A. with effect from 1st June, 1916.

W. J. Smith.

Captain,

Staff Captain, R.A. 23rd Division.

Routine Order No 174.   5th June, 1916.

By

Brigadier-General D.J.M.Fasson, C.B.

Commanding Royal Artillery, 23rd Division.

525. POSTINGS, OFFICERS.

Captain H.F.Willcocks, R.F.A. having reported his arrival from 56th Battery, R.F.A. is posted to 105th Brigade, R.F.A. with effect from 3rd June, 1916.

526. ADVANCES OF CASH - OFFICERS.

Attention is drawn to G.R.O. 1600 d/- 30th May, 1916, which should be republished in Brigade, Battalion &c orders :-

"With reference to G.R.O. No. 1493, Regimental Officers requiring renewals of the advance book will apply through their Commanding Officer, who will state the circumstances which necessitates the renewal.

The application will be accompanied by the counterfoils of the old book, which will be returned to the officer after the necessary particulars have been extracted. If a book is lost a report is to be made at once to the Field Cashier of the Formation.

No fresh book will be issued in these cases until 21 days have elapsed.

With reference to G.R.O. 1326, the number of times that an officer can draw advances in any one month will not exceed three, nor will the total of any one drawing, exceed 125 francs".

W. J. Smith.

Captain,

Staff Captain, R.A. 23rd Division.

Office Copy

Routine Order No. 175. 6th June, 1916.

By

Brigadier-General D.J.M.Fasson, C.B.

Commanding Royal Artillery, 23rd Division.

527. POSTINGS.

The following having reported their arrival are posted to Brigades and D.A.C. as under with effect from 5.6.16. -

1	Farrier Sergt.	to	103rd Bde. R.F.A.
1	Corpl. S.S.	-	104th Bde. R.F.A.
2	Shoeing smiths	-	104th Bde. R.F.A.
2	Gunners	-	103rd Bde. R.F.A.
3	Gunners	-	105th Bde. R.F.A.
5	Drivers	-	104th Bde. R.F.A.
5	Telephonists	-	103rd Bde. R.F.A.
2	do	-	102nd Brigade, R.F.A.
2	do	-	104th Bde, R.F.A.
2	do	-	105th Bde. R.F.A.
1	Water Duty Gunner to each Brigade and D.A.C.		

W. J. Smith.

Captain,

Staff Captain, R.A. 23rd Division.

Routine After Order No. 176. 6th June, 1916.

By

Brigadier-General D.J.M.Fasson, C.B.

Commanding Royal Artillery, 23rd Division.

528. **FIELD GENERAL COURT MARTIAL.**

Reference Routine Order No. 173 para 523 d/- 4th June,1916 The Field General Court Martial convened by this order will re-assemble at Headquarters, 104th Brigade, R.F.A. at 2 p.m. tomorrow 7th instant for the trial of No.96598 Driver William McDonald, D/104th Brigade, R.F.A.

All witnesses will be required to attend.

W. Smith.

Captain,

Staff Captain, R.A, 23rd Division.

Routine Order No: 176.   7th June, 1916.

By

Brigadier General D.J.M.Fasson, C.B.

Commanding Royal Artillery, 23rd Division.

528
GAS HELMETS.

The order that all Personnel in Gun Positions must invariably carry Gas Helmets is not being obeyed.

Cases of neglect of this order will in future be severely dealt with.

To be read out on parade.

W. J. Smith
Captain,
Staff Captain, R.A., 23rd Division.

ROutine Order No: 177 8th June 1916

By

Brigdier General D.J.M.Fasson, C.B.

Commanding Royal Artillery, 23rd Division.

529. FIELD GENERAL COURTS MARTIAL.

A Field General Courts Martial, composed as under, will assemble at Headquarters, 23rd Divisional Ammunition Column at 10 a.m. on Monday, 12th June 1916 for the trial of No44180 Driver Harold Hodgson, No 1 Section, 23rd Divisional Ammunition Column, and No34333 Driver Edward Stenbridge No1 Section 23rd Divisional Ammunition Column. and such other persons as may be brought before them.

President.

Major R.G.Peiniger B/104th Brigade R.F.A.

Members

Captain. A.Hobert B/102nd Brigade R.F.A.
Lieut A.Andrews C/105th Brigade R.F.A.

Waiting Member

Lieut W.W.Caithness B/103 Brigade R.F.A.

The accused will be warned and all witnesses required to attend.

Proceedings to be forwarded to Staff Captain, R.A. marked "Confidential"

W. J. Smith.

Captain,

Staff Captain, R.A. 23rd Division.

Routine Order No: 178. 9th June, 1916.

By

Brigadier General D.J.M.Fasson, C.B.

Commanding Royal Artillery, 23rd Division.

530. FIELD GENERAL COURTS MARTIAL.

Reference Routine Order No: 529, dated 8.6.16.

Major C.A.N.Hume-Spry, C/102nd Brigade R.F.A. will be President of the F.G.C.M. convened by above quoted Order, in place of Major R.G.Peiniger B/104th Brigade R.F.A.

531. Postings.

Captain A.G.Courage, R.A., 2nd. Division, reported his arrival on the 8th May and is posted to Command No: 3 Section 23rd Div: Amm: Column.

Captain J.A.French, R.F.A. is appointed supernumerary for duty with 23rd Div: Amm: Column.

Captain,

Staff Captain, R.A., 23rd Div'n.

N O T I C E.

Church Parade, Sunday 11th May.

Roman Catholics in and around AIX NOULETTE.

Mass 11 a.m. at AIX NOULETTE in the Chapel at Farm next to Ambulance.

Routine Order No: 179.   10th June, 1918.

By

Brigadier General D.J.M.Fasson, C.B.

Commanding Royal Artillery, 23rd Division.

532. HONOURS AND AWARDS.

The G.O.C., R.A. has the greatest pleasure in publishing the following extracts from First Army memo No: 21/436/AMS dated 8.6.18.

"The General Officer Commanding-in-Chief has, under authority granted by His Majesty the King, awarded decorations as stated to the undernamed :-

MILITARY CROSS.

2/Lieut: L.S.CAMPBELL,   A/105 Brigade R.F.A.

MILITARY MEDAL.

No: 56877, Bombr. A.PEACOCK,   A/105 Brigade R.F.A.

W. J. Smith.

Captain,

Staff Captain, R.A., 23rd Div'n.

N O T I C E .

LOST. Dark Brown Gelding, age about 9 years, Height 15-1, white coronet off hind, "A" branded and 29 clipped on near hind quarter, with set of saddlery complete. Last seen at Cross Roads SAINS-EN-GOHELLE, R.7.a.10.7. Please forward any information regarding same to O.C. B/102 Brigade R.F.A.

Office Copy

Routine Order No: 180.

12th June, 1918.

By

Brigadier General D.J.M.Fasson, C.B.

Commanding Royal Artillery, 23rd Division.

533. SUPPLY WAGONS.

Battery Supply Wagons after delivery of Rations on 14th will proceed to LA CAUCHIETTE DIVION.

534. TELEPHONE EQUIPMENT - ROYAL ARTILLERY UNITS.

General Routine Order/No: 1326 is republished :-

The following scales of telephone equipment are approved for

(a) Horse and Field Artillery.
(b) Heavy and Siege Artillery.

Any Telephone equipment in excess of these scales will be handed over to Ordnance Officers concerned for return to the Base.
These scales are the sole authority for the issue of telephone equipment to the Artillery Units specified and issues will not be authorised under Mobilization Store Tables (Army Form G.1098.) until these tables have been revised to agree with the scale.
General Routine Orders 350, 660, 696, 774, that part of 892 referring to Royal Artillery and Divisional Amm'n Columns, 932, 995, 1023, 1363, 1434, and 1511 are cancelled.

	Scale (a) Horse and Field Arty:	
	Bde. Hd. Qtrs.	Battery.
Section 28.		
Batteries inert "O" 6 cell.		
Cable electric D.1 (⅛ or 1/6th mile lengths) miles.	3 6	5
Cable electric D.3, miles ...	6	-
Cells electric inert 'S' ...	16	12
" " " 'S' Spare	16	12
Galvanometer detector Q. & I.	1	-
" " " case	1	-
Tape I.R. (½-lb tins) tins ...	1	1
Tape insulating commercial pattern, lbs.	4	4
Solution I.R. tubes ...	8	8
Wire electric S.11. yards ...	40	12
" " enamelled, No: 25, miles	4	4

P.T.O.

	Scale (a) Horse and Field Arty:	
	Bde. Hd. Qtrs.	Battery.
Section 29.		
Bar carrying drum telephone wagon.	1	-
Barrows drum universal ...	-	-
Belts waist reel cable No: 2	2	4
- do - Sockets spare	-	1
Boxes, spare cell, large ...	1	-
" " " small ...	-	1
Buckets reel cable No: 2	2	5
Cases telephone hand 'A'	-	-
Cases pin earth small ...	-	4
Climbers pole, pairs ...	-	-
Couplers cable (spare) ...	2	2
Cords telephone 'A' ...	-	-
Cords telephone field ...	-	1
Drum cable wagon telephone	6	-
" " " " spare	1	-
Guards hand telegraph equipment, prs.	2	-
Guys telegraph pole	6	-
Hammers R.E. telehraph sledge	1	-
Hocks clamp cable	4	8
Implements inserting cable	1	-
Jumpers	1	-
Ladders field telegraph	1	-
Pins earth	9	6
Pickets guy telegraph light	10	-
Pipes earth	-	-
Pipe hose I.R. ½" yards	6	-
" " I.R. ¼" special yards	30	-
Pliers sidecutting 5" pairs	14	9
Poles telegraph wood 17-ft.	4	-
Pouches telephone equipment	-	3
Reels cable No: 1	-	4
Bars carrying reel cable No: 1	-	2
Reels cable No: 2	2	8
" " " spindles	2	5
" " " " rivets spare	-	6
" " " " springs	-	1
" " No: 3	4	4
Reels cable No: 3 spindles	2	2
Sticks crook, long	1	-
" " short	1	-
Screens telephones	3	2
Exchange Artillery Telephone 12-lines	1	-
Telephones hand 'A' (Spare)	-	-
" " 'A' (earpieces spare.	-	-
Telephones microphone capsule	3	2
Telephone sets portable D.Mark III	8	6
Telephones portable C.Mark II	-	-
Telegraph sets vibrating R.A.	-	-
Tools electricians sets	1	-
Screwdrivers electricians	2	2
Apparatus laying out cable R.A. sets	-	2
Switchboard metallic circuit, 10-line cordless	-	-
Section 9		
Cloth emery No: F Sheets	12	12
Section 21		
Wagons telephone	1	-

P.T.O

534 (Con'd)

Carried as a Reserve by DIVISIONAL AMMUNITION COLUMNS.

Cable electric D.3, miles	6 per Column.
Wire steel hard, enamelled	12 per Column.

D. A. Smith.

Captain,

Staff Captain, R.A., 23rd Division.

ROUTINE ORDER No181 15th June 1916

By

Brigadier General D.J.M.Fasson, C.B.

Commanding Royal Artillery, 23rd Division.

535. **FIELD GENERAL COURTS MARTIAL.**

A Field General Courts Martial, composed as under, will assemble at Headquarters, 104th Brigade R.F.A.at THEROUANNE at 10-0a on Monday the 19th June, 1916 for the trail of No 29073 Driver Thoma Evans, No 1 Section, 23rd Div Amm Col, and No 46096 Gunner Thomas McLaughton, C/104th Brigade R.F.A. and such other persons as may be brought before them.

President

Major W.M.Shaw,	D/102 Brigade R.F.A.
Members	
Captain W.H.Powell	B/103rd Brigade R.F.A.
2/Lieut W.V.Bucknell	A/105th Brigade R.F.A.
Waiting Member,	
Lieut C.N.Ellis	C/104th Brigade R.F.A.

The accused will be warned and all witnesses required to attend, Proceedings to be forwarded to Staff Captain, R.A. marked "Confidential"

536. FURLOUGH

Men re-engaging for duration of War after 25th May 1916 are not entitled to the months furlough.
(IV) Corps Wire A/961 D/- 12-6-16,)

537. Postings.

The following having reported their arrival are posted as under:-

3 Howitzer Gunners to 102nd Brigade R.F.A.
2 " " to 103rd Brigade R.F.A.
2 " " to 104th Brigade R.F.A.
2 Gunners to 103rd Bde R.F.A.
3 " to 104th Bde R.F.A.
One Water Duty Gunner to each Brigade and D.A.C.
1 Driver to 102nd Brigade R.F.A.
4 " to 103rd Brigade R.F.A.
3 to 104th Brigade R.F.A.
1 Bomdr for C/103rd Brigade
1 Wheeler for 104th Brigade

538. Lieut C.H.Hawkins will remain with D.A.C. until further orders.

539. COMMAND.

Lt-Colonel W.A.Nicholson ceased to Command 23rd D.A.C. with effect from 15/6/16.

W.J.Smith.
Captain,
Staff Captain, R.A., 23rd Division.

ROUTINE ORDER No 182 17th June,1916

By

Brigadier General D.J.M.Fasson, C.B.
Commanding Royal Artillery, 23rd Division.

546
MARCH DISCIPLINE

Units will march uniformly cloaked or uncloaked.
When halted on the march, Officers, N.C.O's. and men will dismount.

Vehicles are, if possible, to be washed on the day of arrival in billets. When this is not possible they must be washed early next morning.

W. J. Smith
Captain,
Staff Captain, R.A.,23rd Division.

87

Routine Order No: 183. 18th June, 1916.

By

Brigadier General D.J.M.Fasson, C.B.

Commanding Royal Artillery, 23rd Division.

541.
ORDNANCE STORES.

Units must clear stores at once from Dump at ENQUINEGATTE.

542.
ORDNANCE WORKSHOP.

The nearest shop is No: 17 on ISBERGES - ST: VENANT Road.

543.
GAS HELMETS - DATING OF AND REPLACEMENT OF "P" HELMETS BY "P.H." HELMETS.

Attention is called to G.R.O. No: 399 of the 14th inst:

(1) The date on which Helmets are issued to N.C.O's. and men should be clearly and distinctly marked on each helmet, and NOT on the satchel. In course of time the chemicals on the helmets may cause this date to become bleached, and when this is found to be the case on any inspection of helmets, orders are to be given for re-marking.

(2) All "P" helmets should have been replaced long ago by "P.H" helmets, but it has come to notice that, in some cases, there are still a number of "P" helmets remaining with Units.

All Units in possession of any "P" helmets are to at once take steps to have them replaced.

544.
VEHICLES.

First Army R.O. No: 393 d/- 8th June, 1916 is republished:-

"Attention is directed to G.R.O's. 981 and 1417, which are republished for information":-

"During the hot weather the spokes and felloes of wheels "are liable to shrink, with the result that the tyres get loose and "the wheels become unserviceable.

"A simple method of preventing shrinkage consists in winding "round the spokes, close up to the nave, a rope made of plaited straw "or hay, which should be kept wetted. The rope is passed in and out "through the spokes, half-a-dozen or so turns being generally used, "and the coils secured in position by tying".

"Units, which have not already done so, are to carry out "these instructions forthwith.

"It must be borne in mind, however, that the above precautions "become useless unless the straw, or other plaiting, is regularly and "systematically kept wetted when the weather is dry".

"This applies to all G.S. Wagons and other vehicles with "2nd class wheels.

W. J. Smith.
Captain,

Staff Captain, R.A., 23rd Division.

Routine Order No: 184. 20th June, 1916.

By

Brigadier General D.J.M.Fasson, C.B.

Commanding Royal Artillery, 23rd Division.

545.
FIELD GENERAL COURT MARTIAL.

A Field General Court Martial composed as under, will assemble at Headquarters 104th Brigade R.F.A. at 10 a.m. on Thursday, 22nd June, 1916, for the trial of No: 38436 Driver Arthur Walker, D/104th Brigade R.F.A., and such other persons as may be brought before them.

PRESIDENT.

Major G. Badham-Thornhill, D/103rd Bde. R.F.A.

MEMBERS.

Capt: G.W. Dalgleish, 23rd Div: Ammn Column.
2/Lt: J.C. Misquith, A/102nd Bde. R.F.A.

WAITING MEMBER.

2/Lt: H. Hall, D/104th Bde. R.F.A.

The accused will be warned and all witnesses required to attend.

Proceedings to be forwarded to Staff Captain, R.A., marked "Confidential".

546.
FIRES IN BILLETS AND CANTONMENTS.

G.R.O's Nos: 1295 and 1436 dated 9th December, 1915 and 3rd March, 1916 respectively, are republished :-

"1295. - Wholesale destruction of property has been caused by fires in barns, outbuildings, etc., due to neglect of the most ordinary precautions on the part of the troops occupying them.

Striking matches, kindling fires, smoking, or the use of naked lights in or near buildings where straw, hay, etc., are stored is strictly forbidden. Commanding Officers will take steps to ensure that this order is made known to every man under their Command.

In this connection General Routine Order No: 630 is republished :-

/ LANTERNS, TENTS, FOLDING.

P. T. O.

82

546. (Cont'd.)
FIRES IN BILLETS AND CANTONMENTS.

LANTERNS, TENTS, FOLDING.

'During the winter months the scale of Lanterns, tent, folding, on charge of Units may, with the approval of the General Officer Commanding the formation, be increased to a number not exceeding double the establishment laid down in their respective Mobilization Store Tables.

In the case of Units for whom no establishment is laid down, issues will be made in accordance with the number approved by the General Officer Commanding the formation to which the Unit is allotted'."

"1436. - With reference to General Routine Order No: 1373, dated 19th January, 1916, attention is drawn to the serious danger incurred by the indiscriminate erection of extemporised fire places in or near barns or other buildings occupied by the troops in the vicinity of thatched roofs.

The O.C. Unit is held responsible that no such structure should be built or erected in billets occupied by his Unit in a manner to obviously constitute a source of danger from fire.

Where a Unit occupies a billet already provided with such a structure erected by troops previously in occupation, the O.C. Unit will arrange for its use as a fire-place to be made impossible, unless all necessary steps are first taken to obviate danger from fire.

Attention is directed to King's Regulations, paras, 1029 to 1031."

The above G.R.O's are to be read out on parade to every Unit in the Division at least once a month and O.C. Units will be held responsible that every Officer and man under his Command are aquainted with these orders.

(A.G's. memo No: B/1650 dated 16.6.16.)

W. J. Smith.

Captain,

Staff Captain, R.A. 23rd Division.

07

Routine Order No: 185. 21st June, 1916.

By

Brigadier General D.J.M. Fasson, C.B.,

Commanding Royal Artillery, 23rd Division.

547.
FIELD GENERAL COURT MARTIAL.

A Field General Court Martial composed as under, will assemble at Headquarters 104th. Brigade R.F.A. at 10 a.m. on Friday, 23rd June 1916, for the trial of No: 41087, Bombardier Thomas Brunt, B/105th Brigade R.F.A., No: 29255, Driver Hugh Jones, A/104th Brigade R.F.A., No: 56560, Shoeing-Smith Thomas McNamara, No: 1 Section, 23rd Div'l Amm: Column, R.F.A., No: 56676, Shoeing-Smith Edwin Poulteney, No: 1 Section 23rd Divisional Ammunition Column R.F.A., and such other persons as may be brought before them.

PRESIDENT.

Major C.A.N. Hume-Spry, C/102nd Brigade R.F.A.

MEMBERS.

Capt: W.A.J. Simpson, C/103rd Brigade R.F.A.
Lieut W.A. Polglaze, B/103rd Brigade R.F.A.

WAITING MEMBER.

2/Lt: W.G.C. Lovell, B/104th Brigade R.F.A.

The accused will be warned and all witnesses required to attend.

Proceedings to be forwarded to Staff Captain, R.A., marked "Confidential."

548.
POSTINGS.

The following having reported their arrival, are posted, with effect from 20th June, 1916, as follows :-

2 Gunners, R.F.A. to 102nd Brigade R.F.A.

1 Saddler, R.F.A. to 102nd Brigade R.F.A.

2 Drivers, R.F.A. to 104th Brigade R.F.A.

A. K. Hay
Captain,
for Staff Captain, R.A., 23rd Division.

Routine Order No. 186.

22nd June 1916

By

Brigadier General D.J.M.Fasson, C.B.,

Commanding Royal Artillery, 23rd Division.

549. Promotion.

Lieut R.S.P.Wolls is to wear the badges of the rank of Captain whilst in command of A/102nd Brigade R.F.A. to date from 29th April 1916.

G. J Pritchard Lt-RF
for Captain.
Staff Captain R.A., 23rd Divn

Routine Orders No. 187 — 27th June, 1916

By

Brigadier General D.J.M.Fasson, C.B.,

Commanding Royal Artillery, 23rd Division.

550, **FIELD GENERAL COURT MARTIAL**

A Field General Court Martial composed as under will assemble at Headquarters 23rd Divisional Ammunition Column at 10 a.m. tomorrow 28th June, 1916 for the trial of No 41296 Driver Robert Wilkie No 1 Section 23rd Divisional Ammunition Column and such other persons as may be brought before them.

President	
Major R.G.Paiger	B/104th Brigade
Members	
Captain G.D.Tidmarsh	D/105th Brigade
2/Lieut J.H.Abbott	C/103rd Brigade
Waiting Member	
2/Lieut F.G.Squire	23rd D.A.C.

The accused will be warned and all witnesses required to attend.

Proceedings to be forwarded to Staff Captain, R.A., marked "Confidential".

51 Postings

The following having reported their arrival are posted as under,

1 Telephonist to 102nd Brigade R.F.A.

1 Telephonist to 103rd Brigade R.F.A.

[illegible]

[illegible]

Routine Order No: 188.   28th June, 1916.

By

Brigadier General D.J.M. Fasson, C.B.,

Commanding Royal Artillery, 23rd Division.

552.
FIELD GENERAL COURT MARTIAL.

A Field General Court Martial composed as under, will assemble at Headquarters 104th Brigade R.F.A., at 10 a.m. on Thursday, 29th June, 1916, for the trial of No: 40696, Gunner William George Kyle, B/104 Brigade R.F.A., No: 84131, Gunner Malcolm Tait, B/104 Brigade R.F.A., No: 40680, Driver James Tancy, No: 2 Sect: 23rd Div: Amm: Column, No: 56112, Gunner Michael John Knafsey, No: 2 Sect: 23rd Div: Amm: Col: No: 49290, Driver Frederick George Hawkins, D/104 Bde. R.F.A, and such other persons as may be brought before them.

PRESIDENT.

Major W.M. Shaw, D/102nd Brigade R.F.A.

MEMBERS.

Captain H.F. Willcocks, A/105th Bde. R.F.A.
Lieut: F. Fox, D/103rd Brigade R.F.A.

WAITING MEMBER.

Lieut: W.H. Borwick, C/104th Brigade R.F.A.

The accused will be warned and all witnesses required to attend.

Proceedings to be forwarded to Staff Captain, R.A., marked " Confidential ".

553.
CORPS ORDNANCE WORKSHOP.

Attention is directed to D.R.O. No: 1496, dated 27th inst

The Corps Ordnance Workshop (Light) is situated at VILLERS-BOCAGE.

W J Sawett.

Captain,

Staff Captain, R.A., 23rd Division.

NOTICE.

LOST from Station at LONGEAU on night of 25th/26th inst: a bicycle No: B.5075 with two Officers' Waterproofs. If found, please return to H.Q.,R.A. 23rd Division.

WAR DIARY

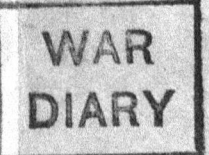

23rd Divisional Artillery

C. R. A.

23rd DIVISION.

J U L Y 1 9 1 6

Appendices :-

Artillery Orders.
Barrage Tables.
Artillery Routine Orders.

Instructions regarding War Diaries and Intelligence Summaries are contained in F. S. Regs., Part II. and the Staff Manual respectively. Title Pages will be prepared in manuscript.

WAR DIARY
or
INTELLIGENCE SUMMARY
(Erase heading not required.)

23

July

Army Form C. 2118

C.R.A. 23 Div

Vol 12

Place	Date	Hour	Summary of Events and Information	Remarks and references to Appendices
ALLONVILLE	1st July		R.A.H.Q. ordered to join Divisional HQ at VAUX and marched there at midday. At 10pm 23rd Divisional Artillery marched into bivouacs as follows:- R.A.H.Q at BAIZIEUX- 102nd Bde, 103rd Bde, 23rd D.A.C. } at BEAUCOURT. 106th Bde, 105th Bde } at ST GRATIEN-	App XIX
BAIZIEUX.	2nd	"	Nothing to report. From midnight we cease to be G.H.Q reserve, and are attached to IIIrd Corps.	
	3rd	"	Orders received that 23rd Divisional Artillery will gradually relieve 34th Divisional Artillery- Our Infantry relieved 34th Division Infantry-	
	4th	"	Arrangements made for relieving 34th Divisional Artillery by Sections on 5th and 7th.	
	5th	"	Orders for above relief cancelled – Fresh orders that 23rd Divisional Artillery will go into action near FRICOURT at once – Both 23rd and 34th Divisional Artilleries will therefore be in support of 23rd Division Infantry – both Artilleries being under command	

1875 Wt. W593/826 1,000,000 4/15 J.B.C. & A. A.D.S.S./Forms/C. 2118.

Instructions regarding War Diaries and Intelligence Summaries are contained in F. S. Regs., Part II. and the Staff Manual respectively. Title Pages will be prepared in manuscript.

WAR DIARY
or
INTELLIGENCE SUMMARY
(Erase heading not required.)

Army Form C. 2118

Place	Date	Hour	Summary of Events and Information	Remarks and references to Appendices
	5th (Continued).		of G.O.C. RA 23rd Division – Reconnaissances carried out at once, and all 4 Brigades moved into action in the open in squares F2a, b and F3.c (just N of FRICOURT) – 102nd, 103rd, 104th and 105th being the order of Brigades from East to West. All wagon lines + D.A.C in squares E10a and c. HQ. R.A moved to the MOULIN VIVIER (E16a)	
MOULIN VIVIER	6th July		All batteries reported in action by daylight – Registration carried out on the ~~...~~ country in the vicinity of CONTALMAISON. Orders issued to all Brigades for the attack on the CONTALMAISON – BAILIFF WOOD position tomorrow.	See App ~~XX~~
	7th July		The Artillery Programme was carried out as in App: XX At 3 p.m. the 24th Infantry Bde retired from CONTALMAISON which was then shelled by our Artillery. The 24th Infantry Bde having established themselves in a line through X.16.d.4.1., X22.b.6.8. and 0.8. and the 68th Infantry Bde to the West of	

1875 Wt. W593/826 1,000,000 4/15 J.B.C. & A. A.D.S.S./Forms/C. 2118.

Instructions regarding War Diaries and Intelligence Summaries are contained in F. S. Regs., Part II. and the Staff Manual respectively. Title Pages will be prepared in manuscript.

WAR DIARY
or
INTELLIGENCE SUMMARY
(Erase heading not required.)

Army Form C. 2118

Place	Date	Hour	Summary of Events and Information	Remarks and references to Appendices
	7th (continued)		CONTALMAISON on a line through X.15.b.9.1. to X16.c.3.0. eastward to X.5.d.5.1. A barrage of fire was kept up during the night 7th/8th to the west of and through the village of CONTALMAISON.	
	8th July		During the day the 68th Infantry Bde: advanced slowly in the trenches and through BAILIFF WOOD west of CONTALMAISON and 24th Infantry Bde: attempted unsuccessfully to obtain a hold on the southern portion of CONTALMAISON. Artillery action was limited to keeping up curtain fire in advance of Infantry positions.	
	9th July		At 5 AM it was reported that the enemy were present in large numbers in CONTALMAISON. Fire was brought on to the village and then lifted back to the original barrage.	
			During the evening the 68th Infantry Bde cleared BAILIFF WOOD and made progress in the trench to the north of it	
	10th July		During the day parties of enemy were engaged to N.E. of CONTALMAISON.	

1875 Wt. W593/826 1,000,000 4/15 J.B.C. & A. A.D.S.S./Forms/C. 2118.

Instructions regarding War Diaries and Intelligence Summaries are contained in F. S. Regs., Part II. and the Staff Manual respectively. Title Pages will be prepared in manuscript.

WAR DIARY
or
INTELLIGENCE SUMMARY
(Erase heading not required.)

Army Form C. 2118

Place	Date	Hour	Summary of Events and Information	Remarks and references to Appendices
	10th	(continued)	Orders issued to all Brigades for the attack of 69' Infantry Bde on CONTALMAISON at 5 pm	See App XXI
			The rapidity of the advance of the Infantry caused modification of time of lifts but at no time was the advance retarded. The enemy leaving the the village for the open were effectively engaged.	
			During the night a barrage was kept up on the north of the divisional front.	
			During the night 10th/11th 68th Infantry Bde was relieved by the 1st Division.	
	11th July		On the morning of the 11th a counter attack from the N.E of CONTALMAISON came under well observed fire and broke down entirely. The enemy 2nd Line was registered and possible posts in advance of his 2nd Line were subjected to bursts of fire	
			During the afternoon of the 11th 104' and 105th Brigades were moved forward to positions due north of FRICOURT about X.7. a. and c.	
			On night of 11th/12th 69' Infantry Bde was relieved by 1st Brigade 1st Division	

1875 Wt. W593/826 1,000,000 4/15 J.B.C. & A. A.D.S.S./Forms/C. 2118.

Instructions regarding War Diaries and Intelligence Summaries are contained in F. S. Regs., Part II. and the Staff Manual respectively. Title Pages will be prepared in manuscript.

WAR DIARY
or
INTELLIGENCE SUMMARY
(Erase heading not required.)

Army Form C. 2118

Place	Date	Hour	Summary of Events and Information	Remarks and references to Appendices
	11th	(continued)	During the night of 11th/12th the line was completely linked up with the Division on our right to MAMETZ WOOD, and posts were established in THE CUTTING north of CONTALMAISON.	
			Artillery barrage was continued.	
	12th	July	Registration of the German 2nd Line and the ground round POZIERES was continued.	
			Barrages kept up to assist in establishment of a line of strong points in PEARL WOOD, CONTALMAISON VILLA, PEARL ALLEY and BLACK WATCH ALLEY.	
	13th	July	Orders issued for bombardment of 2nd Line on 14th instant.	
			Barrage fire maintained to assist strong points being reached by night for establishment of machine guns.	
	14th	July	Bombardment of second line system and roads and communication trenches in rear just north of BAZENTIN-LE-PETIT WOOD	See App XXII
			Three batteries were pushed forward to assist in wire cutting previous to forthcoming operations.	
			The 25th Brigade R.F.A., 1st Division was placed at the disposal of the 1st Division under the orders of C R A 23rd Division. Two Batteries were	

1875 Wt. W593/826 1,000,000 4/15 J.B.C. & A. A.D.S.S./Forms/C. 2118.

Instructions regarding War Diaries and Intelligence Summaries are contained in F. S. Regs., Part II. and the Staff Manual respectively. Title Pages will be prepared in manuscript.

WAR DIARY
or
INTELLIGENCE SUMMARY
(Erase heading not required.)

Army Form C. 2118

Place	Date	Hour	Summary of Events and Information	Remarks and references to Appendices
	14th		(continued) ordered into positions to enfilade the enemy 2nd Line and one into a wire cutting position.	
	15th	July	Orders issued for bombardment of enemy 2nd Line to facilitate the attack of the 1st Division on the trench system from the direction of BAZENTIN-LE-PETIT WOOD. A second bombardment was carried out during the afternoon the first attack having failed. This attack was also unsuccessful. A night barrage was kept up on this system and on the trenches in rear	See App. XXIII
	16th	July	Orders were issued for two batteries to proceed to take up position for cutting the wire opposite the front of the 1st Division on the enemy 2nd Line.	
			At daylight batteries commenced to cut the wire of both front and support line trenches opposite the 1st Division front.	
			Two batteries of 25th Brigade registered the enemy 2nd line system.	
			102nd Brigade R.F.A. and D/25 moved forward into positions between MAMETZ WOOD and BAZENTIN.	

1875 Wt. W593/826 1,000,000 4/15 J.B.C. & A. A.D.S.S./Forms/C. 2118.

Instructions regarding War Diaries and Intelligence Summaries are contained in F. S. Regs., Part II. and the Staff Manual respectively. Title Pages will be prepared in manuscript.

WAR DIARY
or
INTELLIGENCE SUMMARY

(Erase heading not required.)

Army Form C. 2118

Place	Date	Hour	Summary of Events and Information	Remarks and references to Appendices
MOULIN VIVIER	16th July (Continued)		~~Night~~ The 3rd Brigade supported by 23rd Divisional Artillery launched a successful night attack at midnight against German second system from BAZENTIN-LE-PETIT WOOD to about X 5 central.	See App XXIV
	17th	"	104th Brigade moved forward to about X 23 central – Bad light prevented much registration of the "switch line" beyond in X6a + S.D. Attack on POZIERES by 34th Division at 8 pm failed, resulting in a postponement of our attack on 2nd line up to the BAPAUME road.	
	18th	"	All Batteries registering "switch line". Germans developed a very heavy shell fire against our positions, particularly near BAZENTIN-LE-PETIT WOOD – As it appeared a counter-attack might be impending we barraged the "switch" line from 4 to 6.30 pm, when things quietened down. A night barrage was maintained all night	

1875 Wt. W593/826 1,000,000 4/15 J.B.C. & A. A.D.S.S./Forms/C. 2118.

Instructions regarding War Diaries and Intelligence Summaries are contained in F. S. Regs., Part II. and the Staff Manual respectively. Title Pages will be prepared in manuscript.

WAR DIARY
or
INTELLIGENCE SUMMARY
(Erase heading not required.)

Army Form C. 2118

Place	Date	Hour	Summary of Events and Information	Remarks and references to Appendices
MOULIN VIVIER	19th	July	Wire cutting along Switch line + MUNSTER ALLEY commenced. 105th Brigade moved forward one gun per Battery to position in the road just S.E of ACID DROP COPSE - at X23 a and b.	
	20th	"	Wire cutting continued - remainder of 105th Brigade moved up.	
	21st	"	Wire cutting continued. Heavy shelling by enemy.	
	22nd	"	Orders issued for attack on Switch line and MUNSTER ALLEY early tomorrow morning. Preliminary bombardment by our 4.5 Howitzers took place this evening.	See App XXV.
	23rd	"	Zero hour was 12.30 am this morning. The artillery programme was carried out as per orders. The attack failed, + subsequently at 6-0 am we re-established a slow barrage all along Switch line + MUNSTER ALLEY, which was maintained all day. Up till midnight no change in our situation, which is exactly similar to that on 22nd, with exception of an infantry post at S2 c 1.7.	

1875 Wt. W593/826 1,000,000 4/15 J.B.C. & A. A.D.S.S./Forms/C. 2118.

Instructions regarding War Diaries and Intelligence Summaries are contained in F. S. Regs., Part II. and the Staff Manual respectively. Title Pages will be prepared in manuscript.

WAR DIARY
or
INTELLIGENCE SUMMARY
(Erase heading not required.)

Army Form C. 2118

Place	Date	Hour	Summary of Events and Information	Remarks and references to Appendices
MOULIN VIVIER	24th July		Heavy shelling by enemy all day. Towards evening a Counter-attack appears to have been attempted from HIGH WOOD. We opened a heavy barrage on switch line at 9pm, which prevented any hostile advance on our front. Orders issued for attack on MUNSTER ALLEY at 2am 25th inst.	See App XXVI.
"	25th July		Attack failed completely as far as 1st Division were concerned. Some progress was however made by 1st Australian Division on our left in POZIERES & O.G.1. and O.G.2. A heavy counter attack was made by the Germans about 8-30 am near the WINDMILL in R35c9.3 We put a strong barrage of two Brigades across the main road – & the attack broke down under the combined fire of our Guns & the Australian Artillery –	

1875 Wt. W593/826 1,000,000 4/15 J.B.C. & A. A.D.S.S./Forms/C. 2118.

Instructions regarding War Diaries and Intelligence Summaries are contained in F. S. Regs., Part II. and the Staff Manual respectively. Title Pages will be prepared in manuscript.

WAR DIARY
or
INTELLIGENCE SUMMARY
(Erase heading not required.)

Army Form C. 2118

Place	Date	Hour	Summary of Events and Information	Remarks and references to Appendices
ALBERT	26th July		At noon the 1st Division was relieved by the 23rd Division. The artillery supporting the 23rd Division remained unchanged, consisting of R.A 23rd Division and one R.F.A. Brigde each from the 1st and 34th Divisions. HQ of the Division and Divisional Artillery opened at noon at ALBERT. During the day 26th and night of 26th-27th some progress was made in bombing up the southwest end of MUNSTER ALLEY. Orders were issued for a bombardment of the SWITCH LINE on the morning of 27th in order to create a diversion during the attack of 13th and 15th Corps on LONGUEVAL and DELVILLE WOOD.	Appx XXVII
	27th July		The orders for the bombardment were carried out. 13th and 15th Corps were reported to have attacked successfully. Bombing in MUNSTER ALLEY continued and fire to assist this was directed on its North Eastern end. Notice of an attack on O.G.1 and O.G.2 North East of POZIERES was received from the 2nd ANZAC DIVISION. Our fire confined to night barrage.	

1875 Wt. W593/826 1,000,000 4/15 J.B.C. & A. A.D.S.S./Forms/C. 2118.

Instructions regarding War Diaries and Intelligence Summaries are contained in F. S. Regs., Part II. and the Staff Manual respectively. Title Pages will be prepared in manuscript.

WAR DIARY
or
INTELLIGENCE SUMMARY
(Erase heading not required.)

Army Form C. 2118

Place	Date	Hour	Summary of Events and Information	Remarks and references to Appendices
ALBERT.	28th July		The attack of the 2nd Anzac Division met with little success and an advance by our Infantry up MUNSTER ALLEY was driven back to the original point. From 1 – 2.30 pm. the N.E. end of MUNSTER ALLEY at its junction with the SWITCH LINE was bombarded with 4.5 How and heavy howitzers.	
"	29th	July	A feint bombardment of switch line & MUNSTER ALLEY carried out at 3pm – Divisional & RA HQs moved to camp to W 27 c. central at 8 pm.	
W27c. 5.5	30th	"	Another feint bombardment carried out early this morning – The real attack by 19th Division on the intermediate line took place at 6-10pm – We bombarded dangerous parts of the switch line which could threaten left flank of 19th Division from 6-9pm to 7-10pm.	
W27c. 5.5	31st	"	Registration of the new trench – otherwise nothing to report – Personnel of C 103 brought out for a rest.	

A. K. Hay
Major
Bde Major RA
23rd Division.

1875 Wt. W593/826 1,000,000 4/15 J.B.C. & A. A.D.S.S./Forms/C. 2118.

App XIX

S E C R E T.

COPY NO: ...

S/12/12/15.

R.A. ORDER NO: 44.

Reference AMIENS Sheet 1/100,000.

1st July, 1916.

1. The 23rd Divisional Artillery will march tonight as follows:-

103rd Brigade) Under the command of Col: Henning to
102nd Brigade) BEAUCOURT.

105th Brigade) Under the command of Colonel Nicholson
104th Brigade) to ST: GRATIEN.

23rd D.A.C.) Under command of Major Buchanan
35 Mobile Sec: (Vety) to BEAUCOURT.

b2. Starting Point is the cross roads ¾ mile North of the B in BOIS DE MAI.

3. Heads of Columns will pass this point as follows:-

103rd Bde: at 10 p.m.
102nd Bde: at 10.15 p.m.
105th Bde: at 10.30 p.m.
104th Bde: at 10.45 p.m.
D.A.C. and Vety: Section at 11 p.m.

4. All units will march via the Main AMIENS - BEAUCOURT Road.

5. On arrival at destinations all units will go into bivouac - reporting their arrival to Headquarters R.A.

6. Headquarters R.A. will be at BAIZIEUX.

A.K. [signature]
Major,
Brigade Major R.A. 23rd Divn:

Issued at 8.15 p.m.

Copies to:-

No: 1 102nd Bde:
2 103rd Bde:
3 104th Bde:
4 105th Bde:
5 and 6 D.A.C.
7 and 8 Filed.
9 23rd Division.

Col. Hunt

Historical Section (Military Branch),
Committee of Imperial Defence,
Audit House,
Victoria Embankment,

30th [illegible]

App XX.

S E C R E T.

S/1/36.

COPY NO: 34

R.A. 23RD DIVISION ORDER NO: 46.

Reference LA BOISSELLE 1/5000 (Southern Sheet)

6th July, 1916.

1. The 23rd Divisional Artillery will co-operate in the attack on 7th July. One copy of 23rd Division Operation Order No: 52 is issued herewith to each Brigade.

2. The Artillery Programme is given in Tables A, B, and C, attached.

3. The O's C. 102nd and 103rd Brigades will each arrange to fire 50 THERMITE (incendiary) shell into CONTALMAISON village at 8.30 A.M. 7th July - from their Howitzer Batteries.

4. For purposes of Liason and F.O.O. work only, Brigades will be grouped as follows:-

RIGHT GROUP. 102nd and 103rd Brigades under command of Lieut: Colonel P.W.B.HENNING.

LEFT GROUP. 104th and 105th Brigades under command of Lieut: Colonel W.A.NICHOLSON.

The Right Group will have one Liaison Officer with 24th Infantry Brigade H.Q. and one F.O.O. with each of the front line Battalions of this Brigade.
The Left Group will have the same with 68th Infantry Brigade.
These Liaison Officers and F.O.O's will have telephone communications with their Group H.Q., and, if possible, visual signalling will also be established.
The above Officers will be at their places by 8 a.m.
H.Q. 24th Infantry Brigade will be F.2.b.7.9.
H.Q. 68th " " " " X.26.c.central.

5. Demands for ammunition will be made to the H.Q. D.A.C. which will be at E.10. central.

Issued at 5 p.m.

A.K. Hay
Major,
Brigade Major R.A. 23rd Division.

Copy No: 1 to R.A. IIIrd Corps.
2 23rd Division.
3 34th Divnl: Artillery.
4 19th Divnl: Artillery.
5. 17th Divnl: Artillery.
6 to 10. 102nd Bde: R.F.A.
11 to 15. 103rd " "
16 to 20 104th Bde: R.F.A
21 to 25 105th " "
26 to 30 23rd D. A. C.
31 Staff Capt: R.A.
32 R.A. Sig: Officer
33 & 34 Diary.
35 File.

T A B L E A.

BOMBARDMENT FROM 7.20 A.M. to 8 A.M.

UNIT		RATE OF FIRE	NATURE OF AMMUNITION	REMARKS.
102nd Bde:	That part of CONTALMAISON Village which is South of an imaginary line drawn E. and W. through the Church.	3 rounds per gun and How: per minute	H.E.	
103rd Bde:	That part of CONTALMAISON Village which is North of an imaginary line drawn E. and W. through the Church.	3 rounds per gun and How: per minute	H.E.	
104th Bde:	Search trench from X.16.b.2.3. to X.16.d.4.1.	3 rounds per gun and How: per minute	H.E.	
105th Bde:	Trench from X.16.a.1.0. to X.16.c.5.9. and the front edge of BAILIFF WOOD.	3 rounds per gun and How: per minute	H.E.	* 18 Pr: Batteries will divide front up equally between them. The Howitzers will sweep the whole front allotted to the Brigade, but at least one Section of Howitzers must be on front edge of BAILIFF WOOD.

TABLE B.

~~BOMBARDMENT~~ FROM 8 A.M. to 9.30 A.M.

UNIT	OBJECTIVES	RATES OF ~~FIRE~~	NATURE OF AMMUNITION.	REMARKS.
102nd Bde:	Trench from THE CUTTING to X.16.b.8½.4½.	8 A.M. to 8.30 A.M. Guns 2 rounds per minute per gun. Hows: 1 round per minute per How: 8.30 A.M. to 9 a.m. Guns and Hows: 1 round per minute per gun. 9.0 A.M. to 9.30 A.M. Guns 2 rounds per minute per gun, Hows: 1 round per minute per How:	Guns: Shrapnel - Hows: H.E.	This lift is to be gradual. The Battery shooting at the most Southern end of CONTALMAISON will lift at 8 a.m. - the next battery at 8.3 a.m. the next at 8 .6 a.m. and so on at intervals of three minutes.
103rd Bde:	Trench from X.16.b.8½.4½ to 7.2 to 4.2 to X.16.b.2.5.			This lift is to be gradual, and will be carried out in a similar manner to that of 102nd Brigade (see above).
104th Bde:	One 18 Pr: Bty: and one How: Bty:- CONTALMAISON WOOD and trench just in front of it. Two 18 Pr: Batts:- Trench from X.16.b.2.5. to road fork at X.16.a.7.4.			This lift is to be gradual, and carried out on the same system as that of 102nd & 103rd Bdes: The first Battery to lift should be turned on to the trench X.16.b.2.5. - X.16.a.7.4., the next Battery on to CONTALMAISON WOOD, and so on at 3 minute intervals.
105th Bde:	Trench running from road fork at X.16.a.7.4. to X.16.a.1.8.			The whole Brigade will make this lift at 8 a.m.

T A B L E C.

FROM 9.30 A.M. ONWARDS.

UNIT	OBJECTIVES	RATE OF FIRE	NATURE OF AMMUNITION	REMARKS.
102nd Bde:	Trench running from X.11.c.1.6. through X.13.b.4.9. to X.10.d.2.2.	One round per gun and How: every two minutes to begin with, and subsequently regulated according to circumstances.	GUNS : SHRAPNEL HOWS: H. E.	
103rd Bde:	Trench running from X.16.b.4.9. through X.16.b.2.7. to X.16.b.1.8.			
104th Bde:	Trench from X.16.a.9.9. to X.10.c.6.3., and also CONTALMAISON WOOD.			
105th Bde:	Search trench from X.10.c.6.3. to X.10.c.6.9.			

app XXI.

SECRET & URGENT.

S/1/60-2.

102nd Bde:	23rd Division	For information.
103rd Bde:	69th Brigade	
104th Bde:	34th D. A.	
105th Bde:		

1. The 69th Infantry Brigade, supported by 23rd and 34th Divisional Artilleries, and Heavy Artillery, will attack CONTALMAISON to-day at 4.30 p.m. The attacking infantry will move from about X.15.b. and d. due East on to CONTALMAISON.

2. For purposes of the operation, 23rd Divisional Artillery Brigades will be under the direct orders of the G.O.C. R.A., and will not be grouped.

3. Captain Britten (H.Q. R.A. Staff) will be liason officer at 69th Brigade Advanced H.Q's at SCOTS REDOUBT, and will be in direct communication with G.O.C. R.A.

O.C. 102nd and 104th Bdes: will each detail a F.O.O. with telephones, etc, who will accompany the Right and Left Battalions in the attack. They will be in communication with Captain Britten.

4. The Artillery Programme is as per attached Tables.

5. ACKNOWLEDGE.

A. K. Hay.
Major,
Brigade Major R.A. 23rd Divn:

10th July, 1916.

BARRAGE "A".

4 p. m. to 4.30 p.m.

UNIT	OBJECTIVE	RATE OF FIRE	AMMN:	REMARKS.
102nd Bde: (less D/102)	THE CUTTING (A.17.a.5.5.) and Trench and road for 50 yards on either side of it.	1 round per gun per minute	SH:	Seven guns of this Brigade being out of action, only five are available.
103rd Bde: and A/105	Trench X.16.d.2.4. to X.16.d.2.9.	1 round per gun per minute. round per How: per $1\frac{1}{2}$ minutes.	Guns SH: Hows: H.E.	Hows: will bombard about Point 24. Rates of fire of Guns and Hows: will be increased by half from 4.20 to 4.30 p.m.
104th Bde: (less D/104) and B/105.	Trench X.16.d.2.9. to X.16.b.2.5.	Ditto (less Hows:)	SH:	Ditto (less Hows:)
	HOUSES in CONTALMAISON as follows:-			
D/102	D/102 houses between X.16.b.2.3. and 4.2.	1 round per How: per $1\frac{1}{2}$ minutes	H.E.	
D/104	D/104 houses between X.16.b.4.2. and 7.2. and one gun on the CHATEAU.			
D/105	D/105 houses around X.16.b.8.6. and 8.4.			
C/105	Bombard point X.16.b.2.5.	1 round per gun per $1\frac{1}{2}$ minutes	H.E.	Increase rate to $1\frac{1}{?}$ round per gun per minute from 4.20 to 4.30 p.m.

BARRAGE "B"

4.30 to 5 p.m.

UNIT	OBJECTIVE	RATE OF FIRE	AMMN:	REMARKS.
(less D/102) 102nd Bde:	SAME AS FOR BARRAGE "A".			
103rd Bde: and A/105	Same as for Barrage "A".	4.30 p.m. to 4.45 p.m. 18 Prs: 1 round per gun per minute. Hows: 1 round per gun per 2 minutes. 4.45 p.m. to 5.p.m. 18 Prs: 1½ rds: per gun per minute. Hows: 1 rd: per gun per 1½ mins	Guns SH: Hows: H.E.	During this period our Infantry will advance through BAILIFF WOOD and N. and S. of it.
104th Bde: (less D/104) and B/105	Same as for Barrage "A".		SH:	
D/102 D/104 D/105	Same as for Barrage "A".		H. E.	
C/105	Same as for Barrage "A".		H. E.	

BARRAGE "C"

5 p.m. to 5.30 p.m.

UNIT	OBJECTIVE	RATE OF FIRE	AMN:	REMARKS.
102nd Bde: (less D/102)	SAME AS FOR BARRAGE "A".			
103rd Bde: and A/105	X.16.d.3.3. to X.16.b.0.5.	5 p.m. to 5.5.p.m. 18 Prs: 1½ rds: per gun per minute. Hows: 1 round per how: per 1 minute. 5.5 p.m. to 5.25 p.m. 18 Prs: 1 rd: per gun per minute. Hows: 1 round per How: per 2 minutes. 5.25 p.m. to 5.30 p.m. to 5.5. pm Same as for 5	Guns SH: Hows: H.E.	Hows: about the Church.
104th Bde: (less D/104) and B/105	X.16.b.0.5. through X.16.b.4.2. to X.16.b.4.5.		SH:	Infantry now enter and search main trench X.16.b.2.5. to X.16.d.2.4.
D/102 D/104 D/105	Same as for Barrage "A" except no shooting W. of line X.16.d.3.3. to X.16.b.4.5.		H.E.	
C/105	Scatter shrapnel around the CHATEAU.		SH:	

BARRAGE "D"

5-30 p.m. to 6-30 p.m.

UNIT.	OBJECTIVE	RATE OF FIRE.	AMM'N.	REMARKS.
102nd Bde.	SAME AS FOR BARRAGE "A" WITH ADDITION OF D/102.			
103rd Bde. (less D/103) and A/105.	X.17.a.0.7. to X.17a.0.0.	5-30 to 5-35 p.m. Guns: 1½ rounds per gun per min: Hows: I round per How: per minute. 5-35 to 6-15 p.m. Guns: I round per Gun per minute. Hows: I round per How: per 2 mins: 6-15 to 6-30 p.m. Same as 5-30 to 5-35 p.m.	S H	Infantry now enter village up to first road.
104th Bde. (less D/104) and B/105.	X.17.a.0.0. to X.17.a.0.5.		S H	
D/103.	THE CUTTING.		H.E.	
D/104. D/105 C/105.	PEARL ALLEY from X.17.d.0.5. to X.17.a.9.3.		Hows: H.E. Guns: S H.	

B A R R A G E "E".

6.30 p.m. to 7 p.m.

UNIT	OBJECTIVE	RATE OF FIRE	AMN:	REMARKS
102nd Bde:	THE CUTTING and along road for 100 x to N. E.	6.30 to 6.35 p.m. Guns 1 round per gun per minute. Hows: 1 round per How: per 1½ minutes. 6.35 to 6.55 p.m. Guns 1 round per gun per 1½ minutes. Hows: 1 round per How: per 2 minutes. 6.55 to 7 p.m. Same as 6.30 to 6.35 pm.	Guns SH: Hows: H.E.	Hows: on THE CUTTING.
103rd Bde: (less D/103) and A/105	X.17.c.5.6. to X.17.a.0.5.		SH:	Infantry now enter and search up to line of THE CHATEAU.
104th Bde: (less D/104) and B/105	X.17.a.0.5. to THE CUTTING.		H.E.	
D/103 D/104 D105 C/105	PEARL ALLEY from X.17.d.0.5. to X.17.a.9.3.		Hows: H.E. Guns SH:	

BARRAGE "F".

7 P. M. ONWARDS.

UNIT	OBJECTIVE	RATE OF FIRE	AMMN:	REMARKS.
102nd Bde; (loss D/102)	PEARL ALLEY from X.17.d.0.5. to X.17.b.1.0.	One round per gun per 5 minutes to commence with.	Half H. E. Half SH:	Infantry are consolidating the Village.
103rd Bde: (less D/103)	X.17.b.1.0. through X.17.a.9.3. to X.17.a.7.7.			
104th Bde: (less D/104)	X.17.a.7.7. to X.17.a.0.7.			
105th Bde: (loss D/105)	X.17.a.0.7. to X.16.d.2.7.			

NOTE. Infantry will show flares at 6 p.m.

App XXII

SECRET.

S/1/61.

COPY NO: 10.......

R.A. 23rd DIVISION ORDER NO: 47.

Reference (Sheet 57 D, S.E. 4 1/10,000.
(Rough Tracing of Air Photo.

13th July, 1916.

1. The 13th and 15th Corps are attacking the second line between LONGUEVAL and BAZENTIN LE PETIT WOOD on 14th July.
After the assault the 1st Brigade, 1st Division will link up with the left of the 21st Division at the S.W. corner of BAZENTIN LE PETIT WOOD.
Machine guns are being placed by 1st Brigade in shell holes between LOWER WOOD and German Trench at S.7.d.3.0. and also in LOWER WOOD, before zero hour.
The 1st Brigade are seizing CONTALMAISON VILLA to-night. The N.W. corner of MAMETZ WOOD, PEARL WOOD, X.11.d.7.0. and X.11.c.4.7. are other advanced posts occupied by us.

2. The 23rd Divisional Artillery will bombard the enemy's second system of trenches between the road at X.12.c.8.6.a and the road at X.12.a.1.6. in accordance with the attached Table, commencing at 3 a.m. on 14th July. Care is to be exercised that there is no firing S.E. of the road X.12.c.8.6. to S.7.b.4.5. after zero hour.

3. The 13th and 15th Corps Infantry will use green flares for communicating with aeroplanes. The 1st Division Infantry will not show any flares.

4. Zero hour will be notified later. Units will obtain Signal time at 10.15 p.m. to-night.

5. ACKNOWLEDGE.

A.K. Hay

Issued at 6.45 p.m.

Major,
Brigade Major R.A. 23rd Division.

Copies to:-

No: 1 R.A. IIIrd Corps.
2 1st Division.
3 102nd Brigade R.F.A.
4 103rd " "
5 104th Brigade R.F.A.
6 105th " "
7 21st Divisional Artillery.
8 34th " "
9 27th H.A. Group.
10 Diary.

T A B L E.

To commence at 3.0 a.m. 14th July.

UNIT.	OBJECTIVES.	RATE.	REMARKS.
102nd Bde: R.F.A.	(a) Front Trench X.12.c.8.6. to X.12.c.7.7. (Junction of track with front trench. (b) Support trench S.7.d.1.9½. to X.12.a.8.2. (Both those points are junctions of roads with the trench). (c) Search road S.7.d.1.9½. to S.7.c.5.2½. (d) MIDDLE WOOD (1Section Hows: and 1 Section 18 Prs).	3 a.m. to 3.20 a.m. 1 rd per gun per 3 mins: with 1 SH: to 3 H.E. 3.20 to 3.30 a.m. 2 rds per gun per minute with SH: 3.30 to 4.0 a.m. 1 rd: per gun per minute) " SH: 4.0 to 4.30 a.m. 1 rd: per gun per 2 mins) 4.30 to 5.0 a.m. 1 rd: per gun per 3 mins) 2 SH: 5.0 to 6.30 a.m. 1 rd: per gun per 4 mins) to 1 H.E.	
103rd Bde: R.F.A.	(a) Front Trench X.12.c.7.7. to X.12.a.3.1. (b) VILLA WOOD (1 Howitzer and 1 18 Pr: gun).		(a) Especially the small salient.
104th Bde: R.F.A.	(a) Front Trench X.12.a.3.1. to X.12.a.1.6. (b) Communication Trench X.12.a.3.4. to X.12.a.5.6. (c) Search road X.12.a.3.8. as far as the tracks shown on sketch.		
105th Bde: R.F.A.	(a) Support trench X.12.a.8.2. to X.12.a.3.8. (b) Search communication trench from X.12.a.6.4½. for 200 yards to the East.		One Battery to engage target (b)

NOTE. From 3.20 to 3.30 a.m. Hows: will fire 1 rd per gun per minute.
" 3.30 to 4.0 a.m. " " " 1 rd per gun per 2 minutes.
Other rates as for 18 Prs:

ROUGH TRACING
(Not to Scale)
OF AIR PHOTO

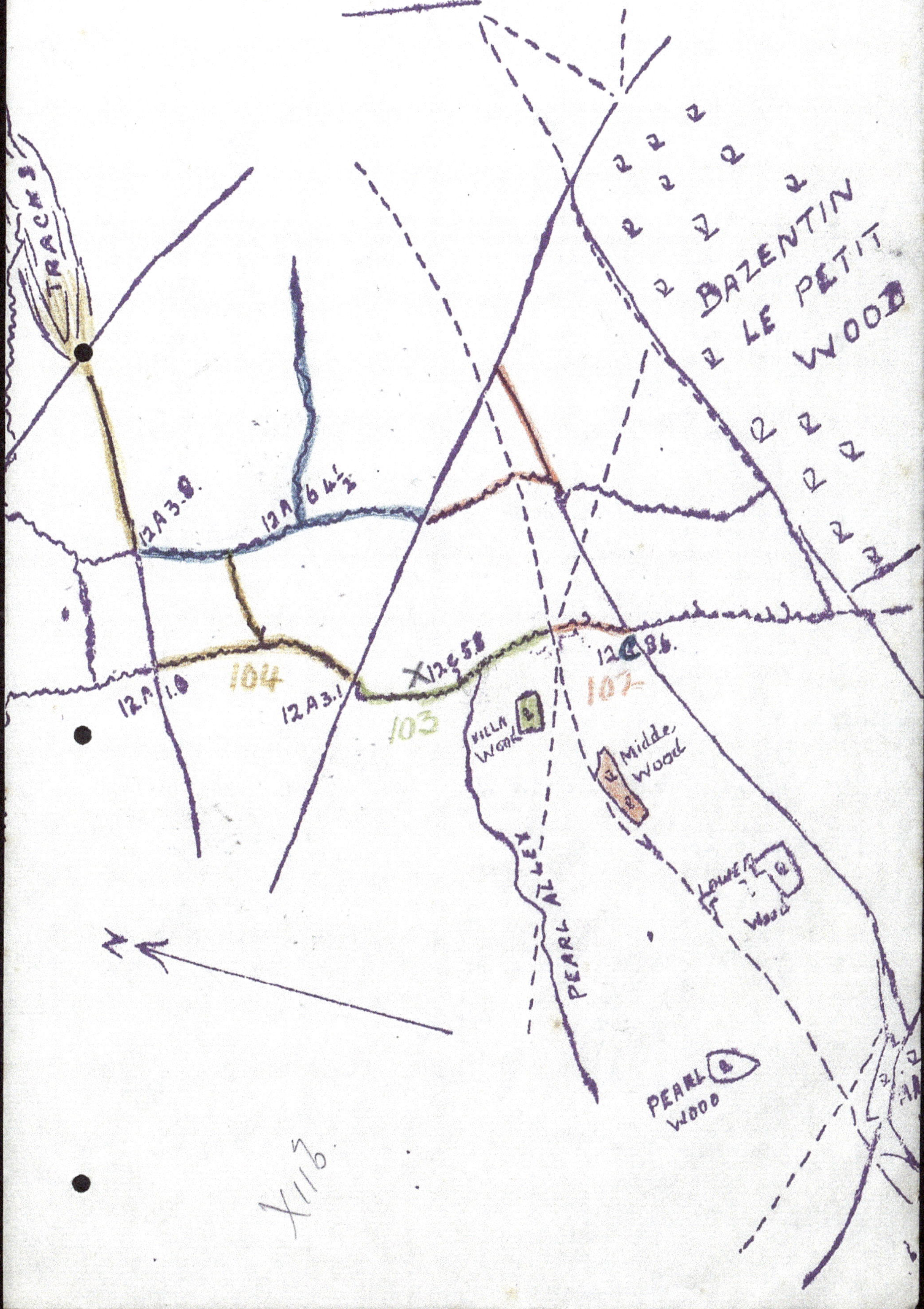

app XXIII

SECRET

S/1/62.

COPY NO: ...12...

R.A. 23rd Division Order No: 48.

Reference Sheet 57 D, S.E. 4. 1/10,000. 14th July, 1913.

1. 3rd Brigade (1st Division) are attacking German front and Support Lines between X.12.c.5.7. and X.5.b.3.1. on 15th July at 9 a.m.
The attack will be made from the Western edge of the BAZENTIN-LE-PETIT WOOD working up in a N.W. direction behind the trenches.

2. The present situation in these trenches is reported to be that two Companies Loyal North Lancs: hold from the BAZENTIN-LE-PETIT WOOD, 250 yards of front line and 500 yards of Support Line.

3. Our infantry will constantly light red flares to indicate their positions.

4. Wire cutting will be carried out at four places before 8.30 a.m. by Batteries already detailed for the work.

5. The 23rd Divisional Artillery and the 26th Brigade R.F.A. (25th) assisted by the 3rd Corps Heavy Artillery, will bombard the enemy's positions as per attached Table.

6. Units will obtain Signal Time at 7 a.m. 15th July.

7. ACKNOWLEDGE.

A.K. Hay

Major,

Issued at 12.30 a.m. 15.7.16. Bde: Major R.A. 23rd Division.

Copies to:-

No: 1	R.A. IIIrd Corps.
2 & 3	1st Division.
4	R.A. 21st Division.
5	R.A. 19th Division.
6	3rd Corps Heavy Artillery.
7	102nd Brigade R.F.A.
8	103rd " "
9	104th " "
10	105th " "
11 & 12	Diary.
13	25 Bde "

TABLE OF BOMBARDMENT.

UNIT.	8.55 a.m. to 9 a.m.	9 a.m. to 9.20 a.m.	9.20 a.m. to 9.40 a.m.	9.40 a.m. to 10 a.m.
102nd Bde:	Front Trench X.12.a.1.3. to X.5.d.8.0.	Front Trench X.5.d.8.0. to X.5.d.4.5.	Front Trench X.5.d.4.5. -X.5.b.1½.0.	Front Trench X.5.b.1½.0 -X.5.a.8½.6.
103rd Bde:	Front Trench X.5.d.8.0. to X.5.d.4.5.	Front Trench X.5.d.4.5. to X.5.b.1½.0.	Front Trench X.5.b.1½.0. to X.5.a.8½.6.	Front Trench X.5.a.8½.6 to R.35.c.6.0.
104th Bde:	Support Trench X.12.a.4.7. to X.6.c.2.2.	S.Trench X.6.c.2.2. to X.5.d.7.8.	S. Trench X.5.d.7.8. to X.5.b.4.1.	S.Trench X.5.b.4.1. to X.5.b.2.6.
105th Bde:	S. Trench X.6.c.2.2. to X.5.d.7.8.	S. Trench X.5.d.7.8. to X.5.b.4.1.	S. Trench X.5.b.4.1. to X.5.b.2.6.	S. Trench X.5.b.2.6. to R.35.c.9.0.
25th Bde: R.F.A. (a) Wire cutting guns	Com: Trench X.11.b.9½.7½. to X.12.a.2.9½.	Road X.5.d.4½.4½. to X.5.d.7.8½.	Line X.5.b.1½.0. to X.5.b.4.1.	Road X.5.a.8½.5. to X.5.b.2.5½.
(b) Enfilade guns.	Front Trench X.12.a.1.6. to X.5.d.4.5.	Front Trench X.5.d.8.0. to X.5.b.1½.0.	Front Trench X.5.d.4.5. to X.5.a.8½.6.	Front Trench X.5.b. 1½.0. to R.35.c.6.0.
Rate of Fire	18 Prs: 2 rds per gun per minute. Hows: 1 rd per gun per minute.	18 Prs: 1 rd per gun per minute. How: 1 rd per gun per 1½ minute.	As for 9 to 9.20 a.m.	As for 9 to 9.20 a.m.

UNIT.	10 a.m. to ~~10.30~~ 11 a.m.	~~10.30~~ 11 a.m. onwards.
102nd Bde:	Front Trench X.5.a.8½.5. to X.5.a.8.9½.	Do not shoot.
103rd Bde:	Front Trench X.5.a.8.9½. to R.35.c.4.3.	Do not shoot.
104th Bde:	Support Tronch X.5.b.2.5¼. to R.35.c.8½.1.	Support trench R.35.c.7.4. R.35.c.4.7.
105th Bde:	Support Tronch R.35.c.8½.1. -R.35.c.6.5.	Support Tronch R.35.c.4.7. to R.35.c.0.9.
25th Bde: (a) Wire cutting guns	Road X.5.a.6½.9½. to R.35.c.6.1.	Do not shoot.
(b) Enfilade guns.	Front Tronch X.5.a.8½.5. to R.35.c.4.3.	Support Trench R.35.c.7.4. to R.35.c.0.9.
Rate of Firo	As for 9 to 9.20 a.m. 1 rd per gun per 2 mins	1 rd per gun por 5 minutos.

App XXIV

COPY NO: 31.

SECRET.

S/1/63.

R.A. 23rd Division Order No: 49.

Reference (OVILLERS 1/10,000.
(LONGUEVAL 1/10,000.

16th July, 1916.

1. The 1st Division are attacking the German second line with its support trench, and the two communication trenches leading N.E. from it, from PEARL ALLEY to X.5.d. inclusive. The attack will be a frontal one.

2. Zero hour will be midnight 16th/17th July, at which hour the Infantry will assault.
Signal time will be communicated to Brigades at 7 p.m.

3. When our Infantry have captured the objective, they will show red flares.
Observers from each Brigade will watch for these.

4. Artillery Programme is as per attached Tables.

5. ACKNOWLEDGE.

A.K. Hay

Major,

Brigade Major R.A. 23rd Divisi[on]

Issued at 9 p.m.

Copies to :-

Nos: 1 and 2	1st Division.
3	R.A. 3rd Corps.
4	R.A. 34th Division.
5 to 9	102nd Bde: R.F.A.
10 to 14	103rd Bde: R.F.A.
15 to 19	104th Bde: R.F.A.
20 to 24	105th Bde: R.F.A.
25 to 29	25th Bde. R.F.A.
30 & 31	DIARY.

L E F T   F L A N K   B A R R A G E.

UNIT	OBJECTIVE	TIME	RATE	OBJECTIVE	TIME	RATE.
D/104	Trench Junction X.5.d.2½.9½.	11.50 p.m. to 12.15 a.m.	18 Prs: and French 4 rds: per gun per minute. Hows: 2 rds: per gun per minute.	Trench Junction X.5.a.8½.8.	12.15 a.m. to 12.50 a.m.	Graduall y slow down to 18 Prs: 1 rd: per gun per minute. Hows: 1 round per gun per 2 minutes.
E/105	Trench Junction X.5.b.5.1.			Trench Junction X.5.b.0.8½.		
1 How: Bty: 34th D.A.	Trench Junction X.5.d.3½.7½.			Trench Junction X.5.b.1.8½.		
2 18 Pr: Batts: 34th D.A.	Trench X.5.c.1.3. to X.5.c.10.8.			Same objective i.e. Trench X.5.c.1.3. to X.5.c.10.8.		
2 French 75 Batts:	Communication Trench X.5.b.5.1. to X.5.b.10.5.			Support Trench) From points 100 x N. of Railway for another 100 x to N.		
1 French 75 Bty:	Communication Trench X.5.b.2.1. to X.5.b.4½.1½.			Communication Trench X.5.b.1.8½. to R.35.d.5.2½.		

N. B. The Southern limit of the Left Flank Barrage is a line drawn parallel to and 200 yards North of Track running through X.5.d.central.

FRONT LINE BARRAGE.

UNIT	FIRST OBJECTIVE	TIME	RATE	LIFT ON TO "SWITCH" LINE (See Tracing)	TIME	RATE.
104 Bde: (less D/104)	Front Trench from PEARL ALLEY (X.12.c.5.8.) to Trench Junction X.11.b.9½.7.	11.50 p.m. to midnight.	3 rounds per gun per minute, increasing to four rounds a gun per minute for last 5 minutes.	Trench from Railway in S.2.a. to S.1.b.0.1.	Midnight to 12.50 a.m.	3 rds: per gun per minute till 12.15 a.m. then slow down to 1 rd: per gun per minute. (a)
105th Bde: less D/105	Front Trench from Trench Junction X.11.b.9½.7. to X.5.d.3.5.			Trench from S.1.b.0.1. to X.6.a.5.7.		
115 th Bty: R.F.A.	Enfilade Front Trench X.12.c.5.8. to X.11.b.9½.7.			Trench S.2.a.0.0. to S.1.d.5.8.		
113 Bty: R.F.A.	Enfilade Front Trench from X.11.b.9½.7. to X.5.d.3.5.			Trench S.1.d.5.8. to S.1.b.1.0.		

(a) Special attention to be paid to point X.12.c.3.9. One gun to be laid on it

SUPPORT LINE BARRAGE.

UNIT	FIRST OBJECTIVE	TIME	RATE	LIFT ON TO "SWITCH" LINE (See tracing)	TIME	RATE	SECOND LIFT
103rd Bde: less D/103	Support Trench from X.12.a.8.2. X.5.b.2.8.	11.50 P.M. to 12.5 A. M.	18 Prs: 3 rounds per gun per minute increasing to 4 rounds for last 5 minutes. Hows: 2 rounds per gun per minute.	Trench S.1.b.10.0. to X.6.a.4.7.	12.5 a.m. to 12.50 a.m.	18 Prs: 3 rounder per gun per minute till 12.15 am. then reduced to 1 round per gun per minute Hows: 1 round till 12.15 a.m. then 1 per gun per 2 minutes.	NIL.
A/102	Enfilade Support Trench X.12.a.8.2 to X.6.c.0.6.			Trench in X.6.a.			NIL.
B/102	Enfilade Support Trench X.6.c.0.8. to X.5.b.2.8.			Trench in S.1.d			NIL.
C/102	Enfilade Commtn: Trench from X.6.c.3.3. for 300 yards to N.E.			Trench in S.2.a.			NIL. (Orders are being sent by O.C. 103rd Bdo:).
114th Bty:	Enfilade Commtn: trench from X.12.a.6.5. for 300 yards to N.E.			Trench in S.1.d.			NIL.
D/102	Communication Trench from X.6.c.3.3. for 50 yards to N.E.			Communication trench from about X.6.c.8.5. to its N. Eastern end.	12.5 a.m. to 12.20 a.m.		From 12.20 to 12.50 am. switch to trench X.5.b.9.5. to X.6.a.2.8.
D/103	Communication trench from X.12.a.6.5. for 50 yards to N.E.			Communication trench from about X.7.b.3.9. to its N. Eastern end.			From 12.20 to 12.50 a.m. switch to trench X.6.a.2.5. to X.6.a.3.8.

app XXV

SECRET.

S/1/69.

COPY NO: 39....

R.A. 23rd Division Order No: 50.

Reference (LONGUEVAL) (OVILLERS) 1/10,000 (Tracings issued of switch line)

22nd July, 1916.

1. The 1st Division are attacking the switch line on 23rd July, from the road in S.2.a.5.3. up to the junction of MUNSTER ALLEY at X.6.a.4½.7. and also MUNSTER ALLEY itself.
The dividing line between the 1st Brigade on the right and 2nd Brigade on the left is the CONTALMAISON - MARTINPUICH road inclusive to 2nd Brigade.
A simultaneous attack will be made by 1st Australian Division on our left against O.G.1, O.G.2 and POZIERES Trench and by 19th Division against switch line on our Right.

2. Zero hour will be communicated later. Signal time will be given to units at 9 p.m. Watches of all Officers must be exactly set.

3. Infantry will show flares at 5 a.m. and 7 a.m. Special Artillery Observers will be on the watch to report position of flares.

4. Artillery Programme is as per attached Tables.

5. ACKNOWLEDGE.

A.K. Hay
Major,
Brigade Major R.A. 23rd Division.

Issued at 2.45 p.m.

Copies to:-

Copy Nos 1 & 2 to	1st Division.
3	R.A. 3rd Corps.
4	1st Divisional Artillery.
5	1st Australian Artillery.
6	Liaison Officer, 1st Brigade.
7	Liaison Officer, 2nd Brigade.
8 - 12	102nd Brigade R.F.A.
13 - 17	103rd " "
18 - 22	104th " "
23 - 27	105th " "
28 - 32	25th " "
33 - 37	175th Brigade R.F.A.
38	Staff Captain R.A.
39 & 40	Diary.

P R E L I M I N A R Y   F I R E.

HOUR ON 22ND JULY	UNIT	OBJECTIVES	RATE	REMARKS.
4 p.m. to 6 p.m.	D/102 D/103 D104 D/105 D/175	Switch line, 1st Brigade Ft: " " 1st Bde: Front " " " " " Switch line, 2nd Bde: Front " " " " "	1 round per gun per 5 minutes	Deliberate bombardment of saps, strong points and machine guns, which will be communicated verbally to units concerned. Fire to be carefully observed.
6 p.m. to 6.30 p.m.	D/102 D/103 D/104 D/105 D/175	MUNSTER ALLEY.	1 round per gun per minute.	Exact points will be communicated verbally to units concerned.
6.30 p.m. to 12 midnight	D/102 D/103 D/104 D/105 D/175	Switch Line, 1st Bde: Front " " " " " " " " " " Switch Line 2nd " " " " " " "	1 round per gun per 5 minutes.	Exact points will be communicated verbally to units concerned.
From 10.30 pm. to 10.45 pm.	102 Bde: (less D/102) 105 Bde: (less D/105) 25th Bde: 103 Bde: (less D/103)	Switch Line S.2.a.5.3. to S.1.d.8.9. Switch Line S.1.d.8.9. to S.1.d.3.9. Switch Line S.1.d.3.9. to X.6.a.7.3. Switch Line X.6.a.7.3. to X.6.a.1.9. and also MUNSTER ALLEY.	1 round per gun per 4 minutes.	Fire to be on and just in front of the German wire, the object being to drive in any enemy wiring parties and patrols.

BOMBARDMENT.

HOUR 23RD JULY	UNIT	OBJECTIVES	RATE	PROJECTILE	REMARKS.
Minus 5 minutes to Zero	103rd Bde: including C/102	Switch Line from road at S.2.a.5.3. to S.1.d.8½.9.	18 Prs: Six rounds per gun per minute. Hows: Two rounds per gun per minute.	18 Prs: S H R A P N E L. Hows: H. E.	
	175th Bde:	Switch Line from S.1.d.8½.9. to road at S.1.d.3.8.			
	25th Bde:	Switch line from road at S.1.d.3.8. to junction of MUNSTER ALLEY at X.6.a.5.5.			
	102nd Bde:	Switch Line from junction of MUNSTER ALLEY at X.6.a.5.5. to a point X.6.a.3.7. exactly 150 yards N.W. of MUNSTER ALLEY Junc:			
	D/104	Switch Line from road at S.1.d.3.8. to junction of MUNSTER ALLEY at X.6.a.5.5.			
	1 18 Pr: Bty: of 104th Bde:	Switch line from point X.6.a.3.7. exactly 150 yards N.W. of MUNSTER ALLEY to a point 150 yards N. of the POZIERES Railway.			
Minus four minutes to Zero	104th Bde: (less 1 18 Pr: Bty; & D/104)	MUNSTER ALLEY from its junction with Switch Line to X.6.a.2.4.			
	105th Bde:	MUNSTER ALLEY from X.6.a.2.4. to its junction with O.G.2. (Hows: to be on junctions of MUNSTER ALLEY with Switch Line and O.G.2.).			

F I R S T   L I F T.

HOUR 23RD JULY	UNIT	OBJECTIVES	RATE	PROJECTILE	REMARKS
ZERO TO 0.5.	103rd Bde: (including C/102) (less D/103) 175th Bde: (less D/175) 25th Bde: 102nd Bde: (less D/102).	Lift 200 yards to North or North East of Switch Line - Where Batteries are firing in partial enfilade this will necessitate change of direction.	18 Prs: (Except 1 Bty: 104th Bde:) 4 rounds per gun per minute. Hows: Two round per gun per minute.	-18-PRS: SHRAPNEL. HOWS: H. E.	
	1 18 Pr: Bty: of 104th Bde:	Do not lift. Remain on switch line from X.6.a.3.7. to 150 yards N. of the POZIERES Railway. Maintain rate of 6 rounds per gun per minute.			Care to be taken by the 18 Pr: Bty: of 104th Bde: and D/105 that they do not shoot South of the point X.6.a.3.7.
	104th Bde: (less 1 18 Pr: Bty: & D/104) 105th Bde: (less D/105)	18 Prs: lift to the POZIERES railway, between Switch Line and O.G.2, dividing point between the two Brigades being X.5.b.8.8. D/105 will lift to Switch Line between point X.6.a.3.7. and 150 yards N. of POZIERES Railway.			
	D102 D/103 D/104 D/175	O.G.2. from a point X.5.b.3.3. to the POZIERES - BAPAUME road. Detail in remarks column.			D/102 X.5.b.3.3. to road X.5.b.2.6. D/103 X.5.b.2.6. to X.5.b.0.8. D/104 X.5.b.0.8. to main road. D/175 Junction of main road with O.G.2

SECOND LIFT.

HOUR 23RD JULY	UNIT	OBJECTIVES	RATE	PROJECTILE	REMARKS.
0 . 35. TO 0 . 5	103rd Bde: including C/102 (less D/103)	Point M.32.c.7.2. to road at M.32.c.0.3.	18 Prs: Two rounds per gun per minute. Hows: One round per gun per minute.	18 PRS: HALF SHRAPNEL, HALF H.E. HOWS: H. E.	
	175th Bde: (less D/175)	Road at M.32.c.0.3. to railway at M.31.d.5.4.			
	25th Bde:	Railway at M.31.d.5.4. along railway to R.36.c.7.2.			
	102nd Bde: (less D/102)	R.36.c.7.2. to R.36.c.0.0.			
	1 18 Pr: Bty: of 104th Bde: and D/105.	No lift - remain on last target.			
	104th Bde: (less 1 18 Pr: Bty: & D/104).	R.36.c.0.0. to R.35.d.6.2.			
	105th Bde: (less D/105)	R.35.d.6.2. to WINDMILL at R.35.c.9.3.			
	D/103	O.G.2. from X.5.b.2.6. to X.5.b.0.8.			
	D/104	O.G.2. from X.5.b.0.8. to WINDMILL at R.35.c.9.3.			
	D/102 D/175	Houses and road about S.W. corner of MARTINPUICH noar M.32.c.5.9.			

FINAL BARRAGE.

HOUR 23RD JULY	UNIT	OBJECTIVES	RATE	PROJECTILE	REMARKS.
0.35 till further orders	103rd Bde: including C/102 (less D/103)	Point M.32.a.7.5. to railway at M.32.c.0.5.	18 Prs: 1 round per gun per minute, reducing to 1 round per gun per two minutes after 20 minutes. Hows: 1 round per gun per 4 minutes.	18 PRS: HALF SHRAPNEL, HALF H.E. HOWS: H. E.	
	175th Bde: (less D/175)	Railway at M.32.c.0.5. to railway at M.31.d.0.3.			
	25th Bde:	Railway at M.31.d.0.3. to point R.36.c.0.0.			
	105th Bde: (less D/105)	Point R.36.c.0.0. to WINDMILL at R.35.c.9.3.			
	104th Bde: (less D/104)	Main road from R.35.d.9.9. to M.25.d.9.7.			NOTE. All three 18 Pr: Batteries.
	D/102	Railway M.32.a.6.6. to M.32.a.4.4.			
	D/175	Railway M.32.a.4.4. to M.32.c.0.7.			
	D/103 D/104 D/105	STOP FIRING.			

appxxvi

SECRET.

B/1/70.

COPY NO: 41

R.A. 23rd Division Order No: 51.

25th July, 1916.

Reference (OVILLERS) (LONGUEVAL) 1/10,000 (Tracings.

1. Simultaneous attacks are being made on 25th July as follows:-

(a) 1st Australian Division against O.G.1. and O.G.2. from the West, from X.5.b.2.0. up to and including the BAPAUME road.

(b) 3rd Brigade, 1st Division, against MUNSTER ALLEY up to point X.6.a.2.4. inclusive.

As soon as this objective has been gained, strong posts will be constructed in MUNSTER ALLEY at its junction with O.G.2. with point X.6.a.2½.4½.

2. Zero hour will be communicated later.

3. Signal time will be given to units between 8 and 9 p.m. to-night. All watches must be carefully set.

4. Artillery Programme as per attached Tables.

5. ACKNOWLEDGE.

A.K. Hay

Major,

Issued at 6.30 p.m. Brigade Major R.A. 23rd Division.

Copies No: 1 & 2 to 1st Division.

3	R.A. IIIrd Corps.
4	1st Divisional Artillery.
5	34th Divisional Artillery.
6	1st Australian Artillery.
7	Liaison Officer 1st Brigade.
8	Liaison Officer 3rd Brigade.
9 to 13	102nd Brigade R.F.A.
14 to 18	103rd " "
19 to 23	104th " "
24 to 28	105th " "
29 to 33	25th " "
34 to 38	175th " "
39	Staff Captain R.A.
40 & 41	Diary.

BOMBARDMENT.

HOUR	UNIT	OBJECTIVES	RATE	PROJECTILE	REMARKS.
Minus two minutes till zero.	D/102	MUNSTER ALLEY X.5.b.4.1. to X.5.b.7.3. - especially Junc:	18 Prs: Six rounds per gun per minute. -Hows:- Two rounds per gun per minute.	18 PRS: SHRAPNEL HOWS: H. E.	
	D/103	MUNSTER ALLEY X.5.b.7.3. to X.6.a.0.4.			
	D/104	MUNSTER ALLEY X.6.a.0.4. to X.6.a.3½.5.			
	104th Bde: less D/104	MUNSTER ALLEY from O.G.2. to X.6.a.3½.5. especially Junc: with O.G.2. and East end of communication trench just N.W. of X.5.b.4.1.			
	105th Bde: less 1 Batty;	MUNSTER ALLEY from X.6.a.3½.5. to Switch Line, and 75 yards of Switch Line either side of junction with Switch also old gun positions just East.			Howitzers on junction of MUNSTER ALLEY and Switch Line.
	103rd Bde: plus C/102 & 1 Battery 105th Bde: - less D/103	Railway in X.5.b. from O.G.2. to the Switch Line.			
	Two French 75 m/m Batteries.	Railway in X.5.b. from O.G.2 to Switch Line - especially junction with O.G.2.			
	175th Bde:	Trench X.5.a.7.7. - X.5.b.0.8. - R.35.d.5.3. (1 Battery). Main road from O.G.2. to R.35.d.6.6. (2 Batteries (1 How: Battery)			

P. T. O.

BOMBARDMENT. (continued).

Minus two minutes till zero.	102nd Bde: (less C/102) (less D/102)	O.G.2. from MUNSTER ALLEY to X.5.b.0.8.	18 Prs: Six rounds per gun per minute Hows: Two rounds per gun per minute.	18 Prs: SHRAPNEL. HOWS: H.E.	
	39th Bde:	Switch Line from S.1.d.1.9. to 50 yards N.W. of MUNSTER ALLEY - Hows: on junction with MUNSTER ALLEY.			
	25th Bde:	Switch Line from 50 x S.E. of MUNSTER ALLEY to 450 x N.W. of railway in X.6.a.			

L I F T.

HOUR.	UNIT	OBJECTIVES.	RATE.	PROJECTILE.	REMARKS.
Zero to 0.25.	105th Bde: (less 1 Batty:	No lift - remain on same target.	0 to 0.5 18 Prs: 6 rounds per gun per minute. HOWS: 2 rounds per gun per minute. 0.5 to 0.25 18 Prs: 1 round per gun per minute. HOWS: 1 round per gun per 2 minutes.	18 PRS: SHRAPNEL. HOWS: H. E.	
	103rd Bde: plus C/102 & 1 Bty: 105th Bde:	Railway in X.5.b. from point 150 yards N.E. of junction with O.G.2. to Juno: with Switch Line.			Including D/103.
	D/102	Junction of railway with Switch Line at X.6.a.1.9.			
	175th Bde:	Trench from R.35.d.2.0. to R.35.d.5.3. (1 Battery). Main road from point 150 yards N.E. of junction with O.G.2. to point R.35.d.6.6. (2 Batteries Howitzers about the Windmill.			
	D/104	Old Battery positions about X.6.a.2.9. -5.9.-8.6.-6.6.			
	102nd Bde: (less C/102) (Less D/102)	Trench R.35.d.2.0. to R.35.d.5.3. (1 Battery). Main road from point 150 yards N.E. of junction with O.G.2. to point R.35.d.6.6. (1 Battery).			
	39th Bde:	No lift - remain on same target.			
	25th Bde:	No lift - remain on same target.			
	104th Bde: (less D/104)	Railway in X.5.b. from point 150 yards N.E. of junction with O.G.2. to Juno: with Switch Line. Trench R.35.d.2.0. to R.35.d.5.3. Trench R.35.c.7.4. to R.35.d.4.6.			One Battery on each.
	Two French 75 m/m Batteries.	Area about the Windmill.			

P. T. O.

FINAL BARRAGE.

HOUR	UNIT	OBJECTIVES	RATE	PROJECTILES	REMARKS.
0.25 till daylight - or longer if situation demands.	105th Bde: (loss D/105)	Switch Line S.2.a.5.3. to S.2.a.0.0.	18 Prs: 1 round per gun per minute for first 10 minutes then slowing down gradually to 1 round per gun per 5 minutes. Hows: 1 round per gun per 5 minutes.	18 PRS: HALF SHRAPNEL - HALF H.E. HOWS: H. E.	
	175th Bde: (less D/175)	Switch Line S.2.a.0.0. to S.1.d.1.9.			
	39th Bde:	Switch Line from S.1.d.1.9. to 50 x N.W. of MUNSTER ALLEY. Hows: on Junc: with MUNSTER ALLEY.			
	25th Bde:	Switch Line from 50 x S.E. of MUNSTER ALLEY to 450 x N.W. of railway.			
	104th Bde: (less D/104)	R.35.d. central to R.36.c.0.0.			
	102nd Bde: (less D/102) (less C/102)	Switch Line S.1.d.1.9. to X.6.a.6.6.			
	103rd Bde: D/102 D/104 D/105 D/175 French Batts:	STOP FIRING.			

app XXVII

S E C R E T.

S/1/72.

COPY NO: 10

R.A. Order No: 52.

Reference LONGUEVAL) 1.10,000 Map. OVILLERS)

23th July, 1916.

1. The 13th and 15th Corps are attacking near LONGUEVAL and DEVILLE WOOD to-morrow, 27th instant. In order to create a diversion, the following Artillery programme will be carried out on 23rd Division front, by 102nd, 104th and 25th Brigades.

<u>6.10 to 6.40 a.m.</u>

102nd, 104th and 25th Brigades will open on their night barrage on the switch line at 1 round per gun per minute, increasing to 3 rounds per gun per minute for the last 5 minutes.

<u>6.45 to 7.10 a.m.</u>

All guns of the above Brigades will fire a salvo at 6.45 a.m. and then continue at 1 round per gun per 3 minutes till 7.5 a.m. then at 3 rounds per gun till 7.10 a.m.

<u>At 7.10 a.m.</u>

All above Brigades lift to outskirts of MARTINPUICH. If MARTINPUICH is out of range, batteries which cannot reach it will search communication trenches and roads leading to MARTINPUICH, commencing 300 yards behind switch line. Rate 1 round per gun per minute.

<u>At 7.40 a.m.</u> all drop back on to the switch line again, firing a salvo at 7.40, then continuing at 3 rounds per gun per minute.

<u>At 7.45 a.m.</u> Lift as at 7.10 a.m. and fire at 1 round per gun per 3 minutes till 8 a.m.

<u>8.0 a.m.</u> Cease Fire.

2. Howitzers will participate in above. 18 Prs: ½ H.E. ½ Shrapnel throughout.

3. All units concerned will obtain signal time from R.A. Signal Office at 5.0 a.m.

4. ACKNOWLEDGE BY WIRE.

A.K. Hall

Major,

Brigade Major R.A. 23rd Division

Issued at 11.15 p.m.

Copy No: 1 to 23rd Division.
2 102nd Bde: R.F.A.
3 104th Bde: R.F.A.
4 25th Bde: R.F.A.
5 103rd Bde: R.F.A.
6 105th Bde: R.F.A.
7 175th Bde: R.F.A.
8 R.A. 3rd Corps.
(5–8: For information only.)
9 & 10 Diary.

Routine Order No: 189. 2nd July, 1916.

By

Brigadier General D.J.M. Fasson, C.B.

Commanding Royal Artillery, 23rd Division.

554.
FIELD GENERAL COURT MARTIAL.

A Field General Court Martial composed as under, will assemble at Headquarters, 102nd Brigade R.F.A., at 10 a.m. on Monday, 3rd July, 1916, for the trial of :- No: 68656 Corporal-Fitter WILLIAM CARTWRIGHT, D/102nd Brigade R.F.A., No: 46095, Gunner JAMES KANE, B/105th Brigade R.F.A., No: 50546, Driver JOHN HEXTALL, Hd: Qtrs: 103rd Brigade R.F.A., and such other persons as may be brought them.

PRESIDENT.

Major J.C. Walford, D.S.O., A/104th Bde. R.F.A.

MEMBERS.

Captain J.A. French, 23rd Div: Amm: Column.
2/Lieut: G.H. Hawkins, 23rd Div: Amm: Column.

WAITING MEMBER.

2/Lieut: L.A. Austen-Leigh, C/102nd Bde. R.F.A.

The accused will be warned and all witnesses required to attend.

Proceedings to be forwarded to Staff Captain, R.A., marked "Confidential".

555.
POSTINGS.

The following Officers are posted with effect from 30/6/16, from 23rd Div: Amm: Column to 103rd Brigade R.F.A.:-

2/Lieut: C. Glosson.
2/Lieut: A.E.G. Knight.

No: 50155, B.S.M. A.E. Alexander, 23rd D.A.C. is posted to B/102nd Brigade R.F.A. with effect from 2/7/16.

556 TRANSFERS.

No: 67430, Sergeant C. Atkins, 23rd Div: Amm: - Column is transferred to C/102nd Brigade R.F.A. with effect from 2/7/16.

No: 49195, Corporal R. Rodway, C/102nd Brigade R.F.A. is transferred to 23rd Div: Amm: Column with effect from 2/7/16.

W. J. Smith

Captain,

Staff Captain, R.A., 23rd Division.

Routine Order No: 190. 3rd July, 1916.

By

Brigadier General D.J.M. Fasson, C.B.,

Commanding Royal Artillery, 23rd Division.

557.
CONDEMNED GUNS.

Attention is directed to G.R.O. No: 1654, dated 30th June, 1016.

" When a Gun or Howitzer is reported as condemned for wear the number of equivalent full charges fired should be stated.

Batteries of Artillery will therefore arrange to keep the necessary records, and will transfer such records to other Batteries if and when the guns change hands."

558.
BADGES AND TITLES - Abnormal Issues.

Attention is directed to Fourth Army R.O. No: 160 dated 1st inst:

" It having been brought to notice that the issue of badges and titles in some formations continue to be abnormally heavy, the following extract from General Routine Orders No: 55 is re-published for information :-

'The practice of soldiers disposing of their regimental badges is strictly prohibited'".

W. J. Frend

Captain,

Staff Captain, R.A., 23rd Division.

Office Copy

Routine Order No: 191.

6th July, 1916.

By

Brigadier General D.J.H. Fasson, C.B.,

Commanding Royal Artillery, 23rd Division.

559
POSTINGS.

The following Officers having reported their arrival, are posted as under with effect from 6/6/16.

Lieut: Philipson, J.T. R.F.A. to 102 Brigade.
2/Lieut: Rutledge, J.W. to 103 Brigade.
2/Lieut: Delamain, F.G. R.F.A. to 104 Brigade.
2/Lieut: Hendry, P. to 23rd Div: Amm: Column.
2/Lieut: Mills, W.R.G. to 23rd Div: Amm: Col:
2/Lieut: Cranshaw, W. to 23rd Div: Amm: Column.

560.
TRAFFIC.

Traffic on the road ALBERT - VIVIER MILL must not be impeded by horses watering or in any other way.

561.
ADVANCED DRESSING STATIONS.

Advanced Dressing Stations at BECOURT WOOD and LOZENGE WOOD X.27.b.
Each Brigade will form a Regimental Aid Post in the gun line.

W. J. Smith
Captain,

Staff Captain, R.A., 23rd Division.

Routine Order No: 192.

10th July, 1916.

By

Brigadier General D.J.M. Fasson, C.B.,

Commanding Royal Artillery, 23rd Division.

562.
TRANSFER.

Lieut: W.R.Young, R.F.A., 19th Divisional Arty, is transferred to 23rd Divisional Artillery for temp'y - Command of B/105th Brigade R.F.A. with effect from 10/7/16.

563.
POSTINGS.

The following Officers are posted from 23rd D.A.C. to 104th Brigade R.F.A., with effect from 8/7/16.

2/Lieut: J.H. Hutchinson.
2/Lieut: M.D. Mackenzie.

W. J. Smuts.

Captain,

Staff Captain, R.A., 23rd Division.

N O T I C E .

LOST. from MEAULTE, Bay mare, height 15 hands, Age 8 years, Bty. No: 51.
White Stockings both hind. Star & Blaze.
Information required by O.C. A/104 Bde. R.F.A.

File

<u>Routine Order No. 193</u> <u>13th July 1916</u>

By

Brigadier General D.J.M. Fasson, C.B.

<u>Commanding Royal Artillery, 23rd Division.</u>

564
POSTINGS. The following Officers having reported their arrival are posted as under with effect from 13/7/16.

2/Lt. L.A.DENT to 23rd D.A.C.

Lt. J. ABBEY to 103rd Brigade R.F.A.

Lt. R.L.JOHNSON to 103rd Brigade R.F.A.

565
POSTINGS The following having reported their arrival are posted to Brigades as under with effect from 13/7/16.

1 Fitter to 102nd Brigade R.F.A.

1 Gunner to 103rd Brigade R.F.A.

1 Shoeing Smith to 102nd Brigade R.F.A.

1 Shoeing Smith to 103rd Brigade R.F.A.

566
BOMBS Bombs are not to be thrown into the river ANCRE.

W J Smith.
Capt.
Staff Capt R.A.
23rd Division.

After Orders. 13th July 1916

By

Brigadier General D.J.M. Fasson,

Commanding Royal Artillery, 23rd Division.

FIELD GENERAL COURT MARTIAL.

A Field General Court Martial will assemble at Headquarters, 23rd Divisional Ammunition Column at 10.30 a.m. Friday the 14th July 1916 for the purpose of trying No. 45340 Gunner (Acting Fitter) Robert Thomas Morlry, A/105 Brigade R.F.A.

President.

Major M.G. Buchannan, 23rd D.A.C.

Members.

Captain C.D.W. Archer, 23rd D.A.C.

Lieut. C.E. Skinner, D/104 Brigade R.F.A.

Waiting Member.

Lieut. J.T.Fletcher, D/102 Brigade R.F.A.

The accused to be warned and all witnesses required to attend.

The Proceedings to be forwarded to Staff Captain R.A. 23rd Division marked "Confidential".

W. J. Smith.

Captain.

Staff Captain, R.A. 23rd Division.

Routine Order No. 194 15th July 1916

By

Brigadier General D.J.M. Fasson, C.B.

Commanding Royal Artillery, 23rd Division.

537
DISCIPLINE

No. 49290 Driver F. G. HAWKINS, "D" Battery, 104th Brigade R.F.A, was tried by Field General Court Martial and found guilty of, "When on Active Service Drunkenness" and "When on Active Service using threatening language to his superior officer" and was sentenced to 1 years imprisonment with Hard Labour. This sentence was put into operation.

W. J. Smith.
Capt.
Staff Captain, R.A. 23rd Division.

Routine Order No. 195. 17th July 1916

By

Brigadier General D.J.M.Fasson, C.B.
Commanding Royal Artillery, 23rd Division.

568
FIELD GENERAL COURT MARTIAL.

A Field General Court Martial composed as under will assemble at Headquarters, 23rd D.A.C., at 10 a.m. Tuesday, July 18th 1916. for the purpose of trying No. 72635 Gunner James Baker, 8.M Trench Mortar Battery, and No. 5483 Driver Joseph Taylor, 23rd D.A.C.

President

Major J. Grose, D/104th Brigade R.F.A.

Members

Captain A. Window, 23rd D.A.C.

Lieut. W.P. Hickman, B/102 Brigade R.F.A.

Waiting Member

2/Lieut. D.W.S. Hacker, 23rd D.A.C.

The accused to be warned and all witnesses required to attend.

The Proceedings to be forwarded to Staff Captain R.A., 23rd Division marked "Confidential".

Captain.
Staff Captain, R.A. 23rd Division.

Routine Order No. 196 20th July 1916

By

Brigadier General D.J.M. Fasson, C.B.

Commanding Royal Artillery, 23rd Division.

569
DISCIPLINE. No. 45540 Gunner (Acting Fitter) R.T. Thorley, A/105th Brigade R.F.A. was tried by Field General Court Martial and found guilty of "Absenting himself without leave" and was sentenced to 1 years imprisonment with Hard Labour.

570
LED HORSES. Attention is drawn to Divn. R.O. No. 1557 of 19/7/16. All led horses are to be kept off the roads and are to move on the fields alongside. Where necessary extra bridges should be made across trenches with this object.

Damage is being done to roads and congestion caused especially in the neighbourhood of watering places by mounted troops and led horses moving on the roads.

To be read onnthree parades.

(Auth: III Corps Telegram No. A/110 d/- 18-7-16)

571
POSTINGS. The following Officers having reported their arrival are posted as under with effect from 20-7-16.

Lieut. G. Fenton to 103rd Brigade R.F.A.
2/Lt. V. Smith to 102nd Brigade R.F.A.
2/Lt. H.S. Johnson to 104th Brigade R.F.A.
2/Lt. N.J. Watson to 105th Brigade R.F.A.
2/Lt. G.L. Patterson to 23rd D.A.C.

2/Lt. W. Cranshaw is postedfrom the D.A.C. to 104th Brigade R.F.A.

572
Postings. The following having reported their arrival are posted to Brigades with effect from 20-7-16.

2 Drivers to 103rd Bde R.F.A.
2 Drivers to 104th Bde R.F.A.
2 Drivers to 105th Bde R.F.A.
3 Gunners to 105th Bde R.F.A.
2 Telephonists to 104th Bde R.F.A.
1 Saddlers to 102nd Bde R.F.A.
1 Saddler to 104th Bde R.F.A.
1 Corporal to 103rd Bde R.F.A.

W. J. Smith
Capt.
Staff Captain, R.A. 23rd Division.

N O T I C E

LOST from H.Q. 103rd Bde R.F.A. on 18-7-16 Bay Gelding 16 hands [illegible] old faint star, one white stock [illegible] marked 99 on rear hind hoof.

Routine Order No. 197 21st July 1916

By

Brigadier General D Fasson, C.B.

Commanding Royal Artillery, 23rd Division.

573
POSTINGS. The following having reported their arrival are posted to Brigades as under with effect from 21/7/1916.

5	Telephonists	to	102nd	Brigade
5	"	"	103rd	"
5	"	"	104th	"
5	"	"	105th	"

D. F. Smith.

Captain.
Staff Captain, R.A. 23rd Division.

Routine Order No. 198 — 23rd July 1916

By

Brigadier General D.J.M. Fasson, C.B.

Commanding Royal Artillery, 23rd Division.

The B.G.R.A. 29th Division wishes to express his appreciation of the excellent work done for the 29th Division by the Officers, N.C.O's and Men of the Trench Mortar Batteries X/23 and Y/23 during the time these batteries were attached to the 29th D.A.

The shooting of these batteries during the bombardment in June was of the greatest assistance, and the untiring energy and zeal of all ranks deserves the highest praise.

He trusts that you will very kindly communicate these temarks to the batteries concerned.

W. J. Smith.

Captain.
Staff Captain, R.A. 23rd Division.

Routine Order No. 199 27th July 1916

By

Brigadier General D. Fasson C.B.

Commanding Royal Artillery, 23rd Division.

574
HONOURS AND REWARDS. Attention is drawn to Divn. R.O. No. 1576.

"The G.O.C. has very great pleasure in publishing the following extract from III Corps Memo. No. OR3/503/A3/16 dated 26-7-1916.

"The Corps Commander has awarded the MILITARY MEDAL to the following:-

102nd Brigade R.F.A.

No. 50951 Sergt. J. Middleton (Died of Wounds)
56854 Bombr. J.E. Russell.
38264 Gunner A.E. Guest.

575
AMMUNITION REFILLING POINTS. Attention is drawn to Corps R.O. No. 120 dated 25/7/16.

A Guard, furnished by the Formation concerned, will be mounted at all Ammunition Refilling Points.

W. J. Smith.

Captain.
Staff Captain, R.A. 23rd Division.

Office Copy

Routine Order No. 200 28th July 1916

By

Brigadier General D.J.M. Fasson C.B.

Commanding Royal Artillery, 23rd Division.

576
COMMAND Major B.G. Buchanan assumed command of 23rd D.A.C. with effect from 23/6/1916.

577
TRANSFER 2/Lieut. P. Hendry, 23rd D.A.C. is posted to 102nd Brigade R.F.A. with effect from 27/7/16.

578
APPOINTMENT. No. 50308 B.Q.M.S. Morton T, 102nd Bde is appointed a/B.S.M. and posted to 103rd F.A. Brigade with effect from 27/7/16.

No. 57202 B.Q.M.S. Whatling H, 103rd Bde is appointed a/B.S.M. and posted to 103rd F.A. Brigade with effect from 27/7/16.

No. 49834 Sergt. Mitchell A, 23rd D.A.C. is appointed a/B.Q.M.S. and posted to 103rd F.A. Brigade with effect from 27/7/16.

No. 14590 Sergt. Coldwell R.A, 102nd Bde is appointed a/B.Q.M.S. and posted to 102nd F.A. Brigade with effect from 27/7/16.

W. J. Smith.
Captain.
Staff Captain, R.A. 23rd Division.

N O T I C E

LOST. An Officers Mess Cart (with no axle) Taken from about F.8.a.5.8. Any information to be communicated to O.C. B/105th Brigade R.F.A.

Routine Order No. 201 29th July 1916

By

Brigadier General D Fasson, C.B.

Commanding Royal Artillery, 23rd Division.

579
TRANSFER. Lieut. H Cornwell, 23rd D.A.C. is posted to 203rd Brigade R.F.A. with effect from 29-7-16.

2/Lieut. W.R.G.Mills, 23rd D.A.C. is posted to 105th Brigade R.F.A. with effect from 29-7-16.

580
POSTINGS. The following officers having reported their arrival are posted as under with effect from 29-7-16.

2/Lieut. L.G. Lock to 104th Bde R.F.A.
2/Lieut. L.L. Kellie to 23rd D.A.Cw
2/Lieutz R.F. Crux to 23rd D.A.C.
2/Lieut. H.K.F. Fairchild to 102nd Bde R.F.A.
2/Lieut. N. Goring to 23rd D.A.C.
2/Lieut W.H. Dean to 23rd D.A.C.

581
POSTINGS. The following having reported their arrival are posted as under with effect from 29-7-16.

1 B.S.M. to 103rd Bde R.F.A.
1 Bombr. to 104th Bde R.F.A.
1 Shoeing Smith to 103rd Bde R.F.A.
3 Gunners to 103rd Bde R.F.A.
2 Gunners to 104th Bde R.F.A.
3 Gunners to 105th Bde R.F.A.

582.
APPOINTMENT. No. 57202 B.Q.M.S. Whatling H, 103rd Brigade ceases to hold the appointment of a/B.S.M. with effect from 29-7-16.

No. 14590 Sergt. Coldwell R.A. ceases to hold the appointment of a/B.Q.M.S. with effect from 29-7-16.

Captain.
Staff Captain, R.A. 23rd Division.

Routine Order No. 202 31st July 1916

By

Brigadier General D Fasson, C.B.

Commanding Royal Artillery, 23rd Division.

583
POSTINGS. The following postings are made with effect from 31/7/16.

From Base	2 Corporals	to	102nd F.A. Bde.	
" "	2 "	"	103rd "	"
" "	1 "	"	105th "	"

From 102nd F.A. Bde 3 Bombardiers to 105th F.A. Bde on promotion to Corporal.

1 F.Q.M.Sergeant from 103rd F.A. Bde to 102nd F.A. Bde.

1 Shoeing Smith from 102nd F.A. Bde to 103rd F.A. Bde.

No. 49854 Acting B.Q.M.S. Mitcholl is posted from 103rd F.A. Bde to 102nd F.A. Bde with effect from 29th July 1916.

[signature]
Captain.
Staff Captain, R.A. 23rd Division.

Routine After Order 31st July 1916

By

Brigadier General D Fasson, C.B.

Commanding Royal Artillery, 23rd Division.

FIELD GENERAL COURT MARTIAL.

A Field General Court Martial composed as under will assemble at H.Q. 23rd D.A.C. at 10 a.m. Wednesday, 2nd August 1916 for the purpose of trying No. 36297 Gunner Stephen Tipper, B/105th Bde R.F.A. and No. 50239 Gunner John William Hogg, A/105th Bde R.F.A. and such other persons as may be brought before them.

President

Major B.G. Buchanan, 23rd D.A.C.

Members

Captain W.A.J. Simpson, C/103rd Bde R.F.A.

2/Lieut. J. Palmer, 23rd D.A.C.

Waiting Member

Lieut R.L. Johnson, D/103rd Bde R.F.A.

The accused to be warned and all witnesses required to attend.

Proceedings to be forwarded to Staff Captain, R.A. 23rd Division marked "Confidential"

W. J. Smith.

Captain.
Staff Captain, R.A. 23rd Division.

23rd Divisional Artillery.

C/ R. A.

23rd DIVISION

AUGUST 1 9 1 6

Artillery Orders.
Report on Operations 14.7.16-14.8.16 Appx XLII

Instructions regarding War Diaries and Intelligence Summaries are contained in F. S. Regs., Part II. and the Staff Manual respectively. Title Pages will be prepared in manuscript.

WAR DIARY
or
~~INTELLIGENCE SUMMARY~~
(Erase heading not required.) 23rd Div.

Army Form C. 2118

C.R.A Vol 13

Place	Date	Hour	Summary of Events and Information	Remarks and references to Appendices
W26c.5.5 (W of ALBERT)	1st	Aug	Usual night barrage – otherwise nothing of importance.	
	2nd	"	Special feint bombardments commenced as ordered by R.A 3rd Corps	App XXVIII
	3rd	"	Above bombardment continued – Our Batteries continued to be shelled – at times heavily. Howitzers bombarded MUNSTER ALLEY.	
	4th	"	Assistance given to attack of 34th Division. Howitzer Bombardments of TORR Trench and MUNSTER ALLEY. Unsuccessful attack of 68th Brigade on MUNSTER ALLEY supported.	App XXIX. App XXX
	5th		Usual barrages.	
	6th	"	Howitzer Bombardment carried out. At 4 pm, 69th Inf Bde made a successful attack, at short notice, & established themselves well up MUNSTER ALLEY. A barrage was kept up all night.	App XXXI
	7th	"	Support given to an unsuccessful attack by 70th Bde on elbow of "Intermediate line".	App XXXII

658x
8/3

1875 Wt. W593/826 1,000,000 4/15 J.B.C. & A. A.D.S.S./Forms/C. 2118.

Instructions regarding War Diaries and Intelligence Summaries are contained in F. S. Regs., Part II. and the Staff Manual respectively. Title Pages will be prepared in manuscript.

WAR DIARY
or
INTELLIGENCE SUMMARY
(Erase heading not required.)

Army Form C. 2118

Place	Date	Hour	Summary of Events and Information	Remarks and references to Appendices
W26c55	8th	Aug	15th Division (less Artillery) relieved 23rd Division (less Artillery).	
"	9th	Aug	Howitzer bombardment of portions of switch line carried out	App XXXIII.
"	10th	Aug	At 2pm an "isolation" barrage of switch line was commenced & continued day & night for 56 hours.	App XXXIV.
"	11th	"	Isolation barrage continued – At 10pm certain "lifts" were carried out to allow of patrolling.	App XXXV.
				App XXXVI.
"	12th	"	Isolation barrage continued till 10-15pm. At 10-30pm we supported attack on Switch line by two Brigades of XVth Division – The Left Brigade attack was partially successful.	App XXXVII. App XXXVIII
"	13th	"	Relief of first Sections 23rd Divisional Artillery by 47th Divisional Artillery carried out	App XXXIX.
"	14th	"	Two small bombing attacks by Right Brigade on the switch line supported – Relief of all Batteries completed. G.O.C. R.A handed over command at 6pm and HQRA moved back to BEHENCOURT	

659f

1875 Wt. W593/826 1,000,000 4/15 J.B.C. & A. A.D.S.S./Forms/C. 2118.

Instructions regarding War Diaries and Intelligence Summaries are contained in F. S. Regs., Part II. and the Staff Manual respectively. Title Pages will be prepared in manuscript.

WAR DIARY
or
INTELLIGENCE SUMMARY
(Erase heading not required.)

Army Form C. 2118

Place	Date	Hour	Summary of Events and Information	Remarks and references to Appendices
BEHENCOURT	15th Aug		Batteries moved to camp at QUERRIEU North.	
"	16th Aug		Entrainment of 23rd Divisional Artillery commenced at SALEUX + LONGUEAU – Detraining Stations CASSEL, BAILLEUL, and GODEWAERSVELDE – ~~Units~~	
FLETRE	17th Aug		G.O.C + Bde Major by car to FLETRE. Units began to arrive + were met by advanced parties + conducted to billets in the EECKE area.	
EECKE	18th	"	HQ RA established at EECKE – Remaining units arrived by train.	
"	19th	"	First sections relieved 41st Divisional Artillery in the PLOEGSTEERT sector of 9th Corps front, 2nd Army.	App XLI
"	20th	"	Remaining Sections relieved 41st Divisional Artillery.	
STEENWERCK	21st	"	G.O.C RA took over command from G.O.C RA 41st Divn at 10 am.	660/

1875 Wt. W593/826 1,000,000 4/15 J.B.C. & A. A.D.S.S./Forms/C. 2118.

Instructions regarding War Diaries and Intelligence Summaries are contained in F. S. Regs., Part II. and the Staff Manual respectively. Title Pages will be prepared in manuscript.

WAR DIARY
or
INTELLIGENCE SUMMARY
(Erase heading not required.)

Army Form C. 2118

Place	Date	Hour	Summary of Events and Information	Remarks and references to Appendices
STEENWERCK	22nd Aug		Hostile Artillery very quiet – We strafed a trench mortar at C10 B 5.3 – otherwise no action but registration.	
"	23rd	"	A machine gun engaged & a working party dispersed – Very quiet day.	
"	24th	"	A machine gun engaged – Nothing else to report.	
"	25th	"	Enemy artillery slightly more active – Right Group fired a "test S.O.S."	
"	26th	"	Five working parties dispersed.	
"	27th	"	A good deal of movement seen & engaged – Enemy artillery inactive.	
"	28th	"	Nothing to report.	
BAILLEUL	29th	"	Only registration. R.A. HQs moved back to BAILLEUL.	
	30th	"	No action.	
	31st	"	At 1-30 am we carried out a bombardment, combining with a discharge of gas	App XLII
			A REPORT ON OPERATIONS OF 23rd DIVISIONAL ARTILLERY IN THE BATTLE OF THE SOMME FROM 4TH JULY to 14th AUGUST 1916 – WRITTEN BY G.O.C. R.A IS ATTACHED – MARKED APP. XLII.	661 F

A K Hoy Major RA

BRIGADE MAJOR, R.A. 23rd DIVISION.

1875 Wt. W593/826 1,000,000 4/15 J.B.C. & A. A.D.S.S./Forms/C. 2118.

App XXVIII

SECRET.

S/1/74.

COPY NO: 38

704f

R.A. 23rd Division Order No: 53.

Reference:- Sketch issued 31.7.16.   2nd August, 1916.

1. Preparatory to the attack on the Switch Line, ~~spmtak~~ special bombardments by Field and Heavy Artillery will commence at the following zero hours.

August 2nd	5 p.m.
August 3rd	5 a.m.
August 4th	7 p.m.
August 5th	6 a.m.
August 6th	12 noon

2. Corps Signal time will be repeated to units two hours before zero each day.

3. Programme is attached.

4. From and including the bombardment of 3rd instant, Captain W.J.Simpson and one other Officer of C/103 will watch the bombardment each day, and report to this office, for information of the Corps, on

(a) Distribution of our fire.
(b) Whether all possible cover is searched during the lift.
(c) Accuracy of timing.

For to-day's bombardment, 103rd and 104th Brigades will each detail an officer on the spot to report as above.

5. ACKNOWLEDGE

A.K. Hay. Major,

Issued at 12-5 p.m.   Brigade Major R.A. 23rd Division.

Copy to

No: 1	R.A. IIIrd Corps.		
2	23rd Division.		
3 to 7	102nd Brigade R.F.A.		
8 to 12	103rd	"	"
13 to 17	104th	"	"
18 to 22	105th	"	"
23 to 27	175th	"	"
28 to 32	25th	"	"
33 & 34	Diary.		

B O M B A R D M E N T. L I F T.

HOUR	UNIT	OBJECTIVE	RATE	PROJECTILE	HOUR	OBJECTIVE	RATE	PROJECTILE	REMARKS.
0.18 to 0.25.	102nd Bde:	Switch Line X.6.a.9.2. to X.6.a.5.6.	18 Prs: 3 rounds per gun per minute.	Half H. E., Half Shrapnel.	0.25 to 0.30½.	Search slowly back behind switch line, searching about 50 yards every minute. At 0.30½ all guns drop back on to switch line and fire one salvo	18 Prs: 2 rounds per gun per minute.	S H R A P N E L.	4.5 How: Batteries conform to above exoept that thoy commence at zero instead of 0.18. Rate of fire zero to 0.25 - 1 round per gun per minuto. 0.25 to 0.30½ - ditto.
	103rd Bde:	MUENSTER ALLEY X.6.a. 5.6. to X.6.a.0.4.							
	104th Bde:	Switch line S.1.d.9.9. to S.1.d.5.8.							
	105th Bde:	Switch line S.2.a.3.0. to S.1.d.9.9.							
	175th Bde:	Switch Line S.2.a.6.1. to S.2.a.3.0.							
	25th Bde:	Switch line S.1.d.5.8. to X.6.a.9.2.							

App. XXIX

SECRET.

S/1/75-2.

7036

O.C. 175th Brigade R.F.A.
23rd Division (G) }
1st Divisional Artillery } For information.
34th Division. }

Reference 23rd Division Order No: 57 sent you today:-

1. Your Brigade will assist ~~of~~ the attack of the 34th Division by barraging the SWITCH LINE from S.2.a.0.2. to S.2.a.6.3. as follows:-

From - 1 minute to 0.10 at 4 rounds per gun per minute.

From 0.10 to 1 hour at a gradually decreasing rate, minimum rate of fire being 1 round per gun per minute.

2. Zero hour ~~=~~ is 1.10 a.m., 4th August.
Correct Signal time will be communicated to you later.

3. Particular care should be taken not to drop any shell short into our trenches.

4. The Infantry are arranging to barrage the SWITCH LINE W. of the point S.2.a.0.2. with Stokes mortars.

5. ACKNOWLEDGE.

A K Hay
Major,

3rd August, 1916. Brigade Major R.A. 23rd Division.

App XXX

S E C R E T.

S/1/77-2.

Copy No: 42

R.A. 23RD DIVISION ORDER NO: 54.

699f

Reference :- Sketch Issued.

4th August, 1916.

1. (a) The ANZAC CORPS is attacking O.G.1. and O.G.2., North of BAPAUME ROAD, and O.G.1. between BAPAUME ROAD and RAILWAY on night of 4th/5th August.

(b) The 2nd AUSTRALIAN DIVISION will place a smoke barrage on the Right flank of their attack between zero plus 2 and zero plus 22.

(c) The 5th AUSTRALIAN INFANTRY BDE. will place 4 Vickers guns in position near BLACK WATCH ALLEY to fire on O.G.2. North of the Tramline. After that hour they will maintain a barrage 200 yards in front of O.G.2. until about midnight. The 68th INFANTRY BDE. will co-operate with M.G. fire.

2. On the same night the 68th INFANTRY BDE. will attack MUNSTER ALLEY and will sieze it as far as its junction with TORR TRENCH. They will establish blocks in TORR TRENCH and MUNSTER ALLEY N.W. and N.E. respectively of these two trenches and will join the right of TORR TRENCH up with the HOOP.

3. The Infantry assault will take place at zero plus 1. Zero will be communicated later.

4. The Artillery Programme is as per attached Tables.

5. Lieut: C.L.BOWLEY will be F.O.O. with the Officer in immediate command of the Infantry attack (13th D.L.I.) and will arrange telephonic communication between himself and the Liaison Officer 68th Brigade.

6. The S.O.S. signal of 2nd AUSTRALIAN DIVISION will be three red rockets.

7. Infantry will show flares at 6 a.m.

8. Watches will be synchronized by Signals at 4 p.m. The greatest care must be taken that all Officers watches are exactly set.

9. ACKNOWLEDGE.

A. K. Hay.
Major,

Issued at p.m. Brigade Major, R.A., 23rd Division.

Copies to :-

No: 1 to R.A. IIIrd Corps.
2 - 4 to 23rd Division.
5 1st Divisional Arty.
6. 19th " "
7 34th " "
8 2nd Australian "
9-13 to 102nd Brigade R.F.A.
14-18 to 103rd Brigade R.F.A.
19-23 104th Brigade R.F.A.
24-27 105th Brigade R.F.A.
28-32 175th Brigade R.F.A.
33-37 25th Brigade R.F.A.
38 Liaison Officer 68th Bde.
39 " " 70th Bde
40 Lieut C L Bowley
41-42 Diary

B O M B A R D M E N T.

HOUR	UNIT	OBJECTIVE	RATE	PROJTLE:	REMARKS.
Zero to plus two minutes.	102nd Bde:	TORR TRENCH from X.5.b.8.2. (Junc: with MUNSTER ALLEY) to X.5.b.3.3. (Junction with O.G.2.).	18 Prs: Six rounds per gun per minute. Hows: Two rounds per gun per minute.	18 Prs: S H R A P N E L. HOWS: H. E.	Hows on X.5.b.8.2.
	103rd Bde:	MUNSTER ALLEY from X.5.b.8.2. (Junction with TORR TRENCH) to X.6.a.1.4.			Hows: on X.5.b.8.2.
	104th Bde:	MUNSTER ALLEY from X.6.a.1.4. to X.6.a.5.6. (Junction with Switch line).			Hows: on X.6.a.5.6.
	105th Bde: (less 1 Sec)	Switch Line from X.6.a.7.5. to the railway X.6.a.2.9.			Hows: on X.6.a.5.6.
	175th Bde: less 1 Section.	Railway from X.6.a.2.9. (junction with Switch Line) to X.5.b.4.5. (junction with O.G.2).			Hows: distributed.
	25th Bde:	Switch Line from S.1.b.2.0. to X.6.a.7.5.			Hows: distributed.
	1 Section 105th Bde:	Sweep from S.1.b.0.3. to S.2.a.0.3			
	1 Section 175th Bde"	Sweep Switch Line from S.2.c.1.9. to S.2.a.7.1.			

LIFT.

HOUR	UNIT	OBJECTIVE	RATE	PROJTLE:	REMARKS.
0.2 to 2 hours 16 minutes.	102nd Bde:	Lift on to railway from X.5.b.4.5. to X.5.b.7.7.	0.2 to 0.16 (18 Prs: 4 rds per gun per minute. (Hows: 2 " " " 0.16 to 1.16 (18 Prs: 2 rds per gun per minute. (Hows: 1 " " " 1.16 to 2.16 (18 Prs: 1 rd per gun per minute. (Hows: 1 rd per gun per 2 minutes.	S H R A P N E L. H. E.	Hows: distributed.
	103rd Bde:	Lift on to railway from X.5.b.7.7. to X.6.a.2.9.			Hows: distributed.
	104th Bde:	No Lift - remain on same target.			
	105th Bde: (less 1 Section)	No lift - remain on same target.			
	175th Bde: (less 1 Section)	No lift - remain on same target.			
	25th Bde:	No Lift - remain on same target.			
	1 Section 105th Bde:	Sweep from S.1.b.0.3. to S.2.a.0.3. as before.	0.2 to 1.16 3 rounds per gun per minute. 1.16 to 2.16 2 rounds per minute.	18 Prs: HOWS:	
	1 Section 175th Bde:	Sweep Switch Line S.2.c.1.9. to S.2.a.7.1. as before.			

7014

F I N A L S L O W B A R R A G E.

HOUR.	UNIT	OBJECTIVE.	RATE	PROJECTILE	REMARKS.
2.16 after zero to 5 a.m.	175th Brigade including detached Sect:	S.2.a.0.3. to S.2.a.6.3.	18 Prs: 1 round per gun per 4 minutes. Hows: - ditto -	Proportion of 5 H.E. to 1 Shrapnel changing to all shrapnel in event of an S. O. S.	A L L G U N S M U S T B E E M P L O Y E D O N T H I S B A R R A G E.
	105th Brigade including detached Sect:	S.1.b.0.3. to S.2.a.0.3.			
	102nd Brigade	Railway from X.5.b.2.6. to X.6.a.2.9.			
	103rd Brigade	Switch Line from X.6.a.7.5. to railway at X.6.a.2.9.			
	104th Brigade and 25th Brigade	As per last Table.			

7024

App. XXXI

S E C R E T. Copy

S/1/78.

6988

O.C. 102nd Brigade R.F.A.
" 103rd " "
" 104th " "
" 105th " "

1. A Howitzer bombardment will be carried out tomorrow, 6th instant, By D/102, D/103, D/104 and D/105, shooting simultaneously.

2. The object is to completely flatten out the portion of trench allotted. The remainder of MUNSTER ALLEY is being flattened at the same time by Heavy Artillery.

3. The bombardment will cover two periods, i.e. 9 a.m. to 11 a.m. and 3 p.m. to 5 p.m., during which hours our infantry are being withdrawn from MUNSTER ALLEY to the point X.5.b.4.1.

4. Objectives are as follows:-

D/102:- TORR TRENCH, from its junction with MUNSTER ALLEY at X.5.b.7.2. for 100 yards up TORR TRENCH to the N.W. of that point.

D/103:- All guns concentrated on the junction of TORR TRENCH and MUNSTER ALLEY at X.5.b.7.2.

D/104:- MUNSTER ALLEY from X.5.b.~~8½.3.~~ 7.2. to X.5.b.8½.3.

D/105:- MUNSTER ALLEY from X.5.b.8½.3. to X.6.a.0.4.

5. All shooting to be personally observed by Battery Commanders, who should if possible all observe from places close to each other.

6. From 9 to 9.30 a.m. each Battery in turn will check its range and time, only one Battery firing at a time, a few rounds only.
The actual bombardment will be from 9.30 to 11 a.m. and from 3 p.m. to 5 p.m.
During these two periods each Battery will fire at an average rate of 150 rounds per hour.

7. ACKNOWLEDGE.

A.K. Hall
Major,

5th August, 1916.

Brigade Major R.A. 23rd Division.

App XXXII

SECRET. COPY NO: 23

S/1/79. R.A. 23rd Division Order No: 55.

6971

Reference:- Sketch issued. 6th August, 1916.

1. The 11th Northumberland Fusiliers will attack the "elbow" of the German intermediate line at about S.2.c.8.4. on 7th August, at 8.30 a.m. which will be Zero hour.
They will establish "blocks" in the trench about 30 yards East and 30 yards North of this point.

2. Action of the Artillery will be as follows:-

8.31 a.m. to 9.1 a.m. (1 round per gun per minute.

25th Brigade R.F.A. will barrage communication trench from S.2.c.8.8. to its junction with Switch Line at S.2.a.6.1. - Howitzers between barricade at S.2.c.7.9½. and point S.2.a.6.1.

175th Brigade R.F.A. will barrage Switch Line from S.2.a.6.1. to S.2.c.½.9½.

1st Divisional Artillery will be asked to barrage
(a) Intermediate line for 75 yards to West of the road at S.2.d.3½.6. and as far East of that point as they consider safe.
(b) Switch Line from S.2.a.6.1. for 200 yards to N.E.

9.1 a.m. to 9.16 a.m. Decrease rate to 1 round per gun per 2 minutes.

9.16 a.m. to 9.31 a.m. Decrease rate to 1 round per gun per 3 minutes.

3. Correct time will be issued by telephone at 7 a.m.

4. 2/Lieut: KIRKMAN D/102 will be F.O.O. with the O.C. Attacking Infantry, and will arrange communication through Battalion H.Q. to the Artillery Liaison Officer at Advanced Infantry Brigade H.Q.

5. ACKNOWLEDGE.

A. K. Hay

Major,

Issued at 11.15 p.m. Brigade Major R.A. 23rd Division.

Copy No: 1 to R.A. III Corps.
2 to 4 23rd Division.
5 70th Brigade.
6 Liaison Officer 70th Brigade.
7 2/Lieut: Kirkman.
8 - 12 25th Brigade R.F.A.
13 - 17 175th " "
18 - 22 1st Divisional Artillery.
23 - 24 Diary.

Adjutant 103rd Bde. R.F.A.

On the latest sketch map issued, namely "23rd Div.I" sheet 5 dated 5/8/16, there are several trenches not marked that can be clearly seen and located from WELSH ALLEY or GLOSTER ALLEY.

These are as follows :-

1. A trench runs along just in front of GUNPIT ROAD (namely road from M.25.d.8.6. to MARTINPUICH). This trench is especially visible from about M.25.d.7.3. to M.32.a.2.7.

This is the trench that is so heavily wired, and it is obviously a fire trench and appears to be the next German line of resistance. It may have been overlooked by aeroplanes owing to its closeness to the road.

NOTE. The trench that is marked (from M.25.d.31 to M.32.a.01.) also exists but no wire is visible in front of it and it has more the appearance of a lateral communication trench between COURCELETTE and MARTINPUICH than of a fire trench.

2. A support line trench to the fire trench along GUNPIT ROAD is visible in the corn field behind (where the corn has been trampled down) at about M.26.c.3.0 This trench is plainly visible where it can be seen at all and presumably it runs parallel to the trench along GUNPIT ROAD and about150 to 200 yards in rear after the manner of O.G.1. and 2. No wire is visible in front of this latter trench.

3. There is a big dugout about M.31.b.1.3. and a trench visible on both sides of it as seen from WELSH ALLEY. This trench appears to run to the right along the old track and to join the trench marked on the sketch at M.31.b.4.8. To the left it might join up with the trench that ends at R.36.c.1.6. but it is only visible to about R.36.a.9.1. I am sure of the approximate position of the big dugout and that a trench runs through it both ways but I am NOT sure how the rest of this trench runs.

Two gate posts (brick pillars) are visible on the main BAPAUME ROAD. These mark either R.36.a.9.8. or R.36.a.7.7. where these 2 bye-roads turn off the main one.

The sign post marking cross roads at M.25.d.8.6. is also visible.

The gate posts are visible from WELSH ALLEY and the sign post from GLOSTER ALLEY.

LONE HOUSE at M.25.d.9.6. has disappeared.

(sd)W.MAITLAND-DOUGALLCaptain,
7/8/1916. A/103 Battery R. F. A.

(2).

G.S. 23rd Divn.

Attached report is forwarded for your information. I should think it is worth forwarding to 3rd Corps.

This officer sends in very useful & reliable reports.

(sd) D.FASSON, Brig-Genl.,
7/8/16. Comdg. R.A. 23rd Divn.

RA

Copy

APP XXXIII

696f

CRET.

/1/81.

15th Division.
102nd Bde: R.F.A.
103rd " "
104th " "
25th " "
175th " "

1. The following Howitzer Bombardment will take place tomorrow, 9th instant, with the object of completely flattening out the allotted portions of trench.

2. Each Howitzer Battery Commander will be accompanied by an 18 Pdr: Battery Commander of his Brigade who will be ready to deal with any of the enemy who show themselves.

3. Objectives are as follows:-

D/102 }
D/104 } Switch Line from S.2.a.5.0. to S.1.d.8.8.
D/25 } (each Battery to take a third).

D/103 } Switch Line from S.1.d.3.9. to X.6.a.8.5. (Each
D/175 } Battery to take half).

4. Our trenches, viz "70th Avenue" and the post about S.1.d.2.7. will be cleared of our infantry from 12 noon to 4 p.m.

5. All Battery Commanders will be at their O.P's ready to open fire sharp at 12 noon. At 12 noon Batteries will register and immediately each Battery has registered, bombardment will commence and continue till 4 p.m., at a rate of 150 rounds per Battery per hour. If by 3 p.m. any Battery considers this rate insufficient to flatten the trench by 4 p.m., the rate may be increased from 3 p.m. to 4 p.m. at discretion of the Battery Commander.

6. Reference para 3 above, O.C. D/104 will notify D/102 and D/25 of a suitable meeting place tomorrow morning, and similarly O.C. D/103 will notify D/175.

7. 3rd Corps Heavy Artillery will be bombarding the Switch Elbow at S.1.d.8.8. and 150 yards on either side at the same time.

8. ACKNOWLEDGE.

A.K. Hall

Major,

8th August, 1916. Brigade Major R.A. 23rd Division.

App XXXIV

6924

SECRET.

COPY NO: 40

S/1/83.

R.A. 23rd Division Order No: 56.

Reference:- Sketch issued.

10th August, 1916.

1. With a view to subsequent attack, that portion of the German Switch Line which lies between about S.1.d.9½.9. and X.6.a.4.7. will be isolated as far as possible by Artillery fire day and night from now onwards. This fire will be continuous in order to prevent reliefs, and supply of water, food, ammunition, etc, to the Garrison.

2. Artillery programme is attached.

3. Watches will be checked with R.A. H.Q. at 12 noon and 11 p.m. daily.

4. ACKNOWLEDGE.

A. K. Hay.

Major,

Brigade Major R.A. 23rd Division.

Issued at

Copies No:	
1 to 4	15th Division.
5	R.A. IIIrd Corps.
6	Lahore Artillery.
7	34th Div: Artillery.
8	1st Div: Artillery.
9 to 13	102nd Bde: R.F.A.
14 to 18	103rd " "
19 to 23	104th " "
24 to 28	105th " "
29 to 32	175th " "
34 to 38	25th " "
39 & 40	Diary.

F I R S T R E L I E F.
From 2 p.m. 10th August to 8 p.m. 10th August.

UNIT	OBJECTIVES	RATE	PROJECTILE	REMARKS.
D/125	Block Switch Trench at about S.2.a.6.2.	1 Round per gun per 5 minutes.	H. E.	Each Battery will at once fire an observed series of 100 rounds to establish a block - subsequently continuing at 1 round per gun per 5 minutes.
D/103	Block Switch Trench at X.6.a.4.7.			
103rd Bde:	Switch Line X.6.a.4.7. to S.1.b.0.1.	1 Round per gun per 5 minutes.	5 Shrapnel to 1 H.E.	At 3.10 p.m. / 4.15 p.m. / 5.35 p.m. / 6.20 p.m. / 7.45 p.m. } Search slowly back behind Switch Line in 50 yard searches to MARTINPUICH, returning again suddenly to original barrage
104th Bde:	S.1.b.0.1. to S.2.a.0.1. also 1 gun on track X.6.a.4.7. to MARTINPUICH. 1 gun on track and trench S.1.b.6.6. to MARTINPUICH. 1 gun on railway S.2.a.0.2. to MARTINPUICH.			
175th Bde:	S.2.a.0.1. to S.2.a.6.1. also 1 gun on road S.2.a.3.6. to MARTINPUICH.			

6/13X

S E C O N D R E L I E F.
From 8 p.m. 10th August to 2 a.m. 11th August.

UNIT	OBJECTIVE	RATE	PROJECTILE	REMARKS.
D/102	Switch Trench at about S.2.a.6.2.	1 Round per gun per 3 minutes.	H. E.	Exact points must be ascertained by Battery Commanders from O.C. D/25 and D/103 and registered in daylight.
D/104	Switch Trench at X.6.a.4.7.			
1 Section 46th Bty:	Enfilade Switch Trench from S.1.b.0.1. to X.6.a.4.7.	1 Round per gun per 2 minutes.	5 Shrapnel to 1 H. E.	At 8.50 p.m. / 9.40 p.m. / 10.35 p.m. / 12 midnight / 1.20 a.m. } Lift suddenly 500 yards back, and search slowly back to original barrage dropping 50 yards at at a time.
25th Bde:	Switch Trench from S.1.b.0.1. to X.6.a.4.7.			
105th Bde:	S.1.b.0.1. to S.2.a.0.1. also 1 gun on track X.6.a.4.7. to MARTINPUICH. 1 gun on track and trench S.1.b.6.6. to MARTINPUICH 1 gun on railway S.2.a.0.2. to MARTINPUICH.			
102nd Bde:	S.2.a.0.1. to S.2.a.6.1. also 1 gun on road S.2.a.5.6. to MARTINPUICH			

1369

SUBSEQUENT RELIEFS.

THIRD RELIEF. From 2 a.m. to 8 a.m. 11th August.	Details as for 1st RELIEF except rate of fire to be as for 2nd RELIEF. Hours for lifts will be 2.30, 4.10 5.40, 6.50 a.m.
FOURTH RELIEF. From 8 a.m. to 2 p.m. 11th August.	Details as for 2nd RELIEF, except rate of fire to be as for 1st RELIEF. Hours for lifts to be as for 2nd RELIEF.

FURTHER RELIEFS WILL BE NOTIFIED LATER.

1569

App XXXV

SECRET.

S/1/83-2.

COPY NO: 39

14th August, 1916.

617f

The attached Tables are forwarded in continuation of this office letter No: S/1/83 (Secret) of 10th instant.

ACKNOWLEDGE.

Issued at 8.30 p.m.

A. K. Hay
Major,
Brigade Major R.A. 23rd Division.

Copies to:-

15th Division.
R.A. IIIrd Corps.
Lahore Artillery.
34th Divn: Artillery.
1st Divn: Artillery.
102nd Bde: R.F.A.
103rd " "
104th " "
105th " "
175th " "
25th " "
Diary.

FIFTH RELIEF,

From 2 p.m. 11th August to 8 p.m. 11th August.

UNIT	OBJECTIVES	RATE	PROJECTILE.		REMARKS.
D/25	Block Switch Trench at about S.2.a.6.2.	1 Round per gun per 5 minutes	H.E.		
D/103	Block Switch Trench at X.6.a.4.7.				
103rd Bde: (less D/103)	Switch Line X.6.a.4.7. to S.1.b.0.1.	1 Round per gun per 5 minutes	5 Shrapnel 2. 1 H.E	At 2.50 p.m. 3.45 p.m. 5.0 p.m. 6.10 p.m. 7.20 p.m.	Search slowly back behind Switch Line in 50 yard searches for 600 yards - remaining at each range for 1 minute and increasing rate to 1 round per gun per minute - all shrapnel. After reaching 600 yards behind Switch Line, drop suddenly back to original barrage at normal rate of fire.
104th Bde: (less D/104)	S.1.b.0.1. to S.2.a.0.1. also 1 gun on track X.6.a.4.7. to MARTINPUICH. 1 gun on track and trench S.1.b.6.6. to MARTINPUICH. 1 gun on railway S.2.a.0.2. to MARTINPUICH.				
175th Bde:	S.2.a.0.1. to S.2.a.6.1. also 1 gun on road S.2.a.3.6. to MARTINPUICH.				From 2 to 2.30 p.m. and from 7.45 to 8 p.m. 104th and 175th Bdes: will drop their barrage on to the actual Switch trench itself, that is from S.1.b.0.1. thro' point S.1.d.3.8. to S.2.c.0.9. for 104th Bde:, and from S.2.c.0.9. to S.2.a.6.1. for 175th Bde: Infantry are being warned of this.

S I X T H   R E L I E F.

From 8 p.m. 11th August to 2 a.m. 12th August.

UNIT	OBJECTIVE	RATE	PROJECTILE	REMARKS.
D/102	Block Switch Trench at about S.2.a.5.2.	1 Round per gun per 3 minutes.	H.E.	Stop firing from 11.50 p.m. to 1.20 a.m. when patrols are out.
D/104	Block Switch Trench at X.6.a.4.7.			
1 Section 46th Batty:	Enfilade Switch Trench from S.1.b.0.1. to X.6.a.4.7.	1 Round per gun per 2 minutes.	5 Shrapnel to 1 H.E.	From 1.45 a.m. to 2 a.m. } 105th Brigade will drop their barrage on to Switch trench itself from S.1.b.0.1. thro' point S.1.d.3.8. to S.2.c.0.9. - 102nd Bde: will also drop on to Switch line from S.2.c.0.9. to S.2.a.3.1. Infantry are being warned.
25th Bde: (less D/25)	Switch trench from S.1.b.0.1. to X.6.a.4.7.			
105th Bde: (less D/105)	S.1.b.0.1. to S.2.a.0.1. also 1 gun on track X.6.a.4.7. to MARTINPUICH. 1 gun on track and trench S.1.b.6.6. to MARTINPUICH. 1 gun on railway S.2.a.0.2. to MARTINPUICH.			From 11.50 p.m. to 1.20 a.m. } All fire will be lifted well behind the Switch line - No fire to be nearer Switch line than 300 yards, as patrols are going out. All ground between this 300 yard limit and MARTINPUICH to be searched.
102nd Bde: (less D/102)	S.2.a.0.1. to S.2.a.6.1. also 1 gun on road from S.2.a.5.3. to MARTINPUICH.			

S E V E N T H   R E L I E F.

From 2½ a.m. 12th August to 8 a.m. 12th August.

UNIT	OBJECTIVE	RATE	PROJECTILE	REMARKS.
Same as 5th Relief.	SAME AS 5TH RELIEF.	Same as 5th Relief.	Same as 5th Relief.	5.0 to 5.30 a.m. Barrage of 104th and 175th Bdes: will drop on to Switch [illegible] trench as detailed under 5th Relief. Infantry are being warned. At 2.30 a.m. } 4.10 a.m. } Search back as detailed in 5th Relief. 5.20 a.m. }

E I G H T   R E L I E F.

From 8 a.m. 12th August to 2 p.m. 12th August.

UNIT	OBJECTIVE	RATE	PROJECTILE	REMARKS.
Same as 6th Relief.	SAME AS 6TH RELIEF.	Same as 5.h RELIEF.	SAME AS 5TH RELIEF.	11 to 12 noon. Barrage of 102nd & 105th Bdes: will drop on to Switch Line as detailed in 6th RELIEF. At 9.30 a.m. 10.15 a.m. 11.20 a.m. 12.15 p.m. } Search back as detailed in 5th RELIEF.

NOTE. Details of NINTH and last RELIEF will be issued later.

7169

App XXXVI

6464

U R G E N T & S E C R E T.

S/1/83-3.

15th Division.
R.A. 34th Division.
O.C. 102nd Bde: R.F.A.
O.C. 103rd " "
O.C. 104th " "
O.C. 105th " "
O.C. 175th " "
O.C. 25th : "

With reference to my S/1/83-2 of to-day giving details of the SIXTH RELIEF tonight, i.e. from 8 p.m. 11th August to 2 am. 12th August -

1. The 45th Brigade (left) will send patrols out tonight to the switch line between X.6.a.4.7. and the road at S.1.d.2½.9. at 10 p.m. If the enemy trench is found to be unoccupied, they will seize and consolidate it straight away. If it is found to be held they will withdraw after reconnaissance.

2. This operation necessitates the following alterations to SIXTH RELIEF and also possibly to SEVENTH RELIEF:-

34th Div: Artillery. At 10 p.m. to lift their fire and place a barrage on the railway from R.36.c.4.0. to M.31.d.0.2½, and to maintain this until informed by this office that it may come back to the original barrage.

D/104. To stop firing at 10 p.m. until ordered to re-open.

25th Bde:
Section 46th Bty:
Part of 105th Bde) Will carry out the following programme, 105th Bde: lifting only that part of their fire which is W. of the point S.1.b.5.1.

At 10 p.m. fire will be lifted 100 yards behind the Switch line, that is to the N.E.

At 10.5 p.m. it will lift another 100 yards to the N.E.

At 10.6 p.m. it will lift another 50 yards to the N.E.

At 10.8 p.m. it will lift another 50 yards to the N.E. and will remain here (that is 300 yards behind Switch line) until ordered to return to original barrage by this office.

3. Should the SEVENTH RELIEF have received no further orders from this office they will take it that our infantry are still in the Switch trench, in which case 103rd Bde: and that part of 104th Bde: W. of point S.1.b.5.1. will open at 2 a.m. on a barrage 300x N.E. of Switch trench instead of on the trench itself. D/103 will not open fire till ordered.

4. Patrols from the Right Brigade (46th) are going out to reconnoitre only between 11.50 p.m. and 1.20 a.m., as originally ordered in the Table for SIXTH RELIEF, and during these hours all units firing on or behind Switch line E. of the point S.1.b.5.1. will lift 300 yards to the North whilst these patrols are out, returning to original barrage at 1.20 a.m.

5. ACKNOWLEDGE. by wire.

A. K. Hay.
Major,
Brigade Major R.A. 23rd Division.

11th August, 1916.

App. XXXVII.

SECRET.

S/1/83-4.

COPY NO: 40

684f

The attached Table is issued in continuation of this office S/1/83 of 10th, and S/1/83-2 of 11th August.

ACKNOWLEDGE.

R. K. Hall

Major,

Issued at 8.30 a.m. Brigade Major R.A. 23rd Divn:

Copies to

15th Division	103rd Bde: R.F.A.
R.A. 3rd Corps.	104th " "
LAHORE Artillery.	105th " "
34th Divn: Arty:	175th " "
1st Divn: Arty:	25th " "
102nd Bde: R.F.A.	Diary.

N I N T H and L A S T R E L I E F.
From 2 p.m. 12th August to 10.15 p.m. 12th August.

UNIT	OBJECTIVES	RATE	AMMUNITION	REMARKS.
D/25	Block switch trench at about S.2.a.6.2.	1 Round per gun per 5 minutes.	H.E.	
D/103	Block switch trench at X.6.a.4.7.			
103rd Bde: (less D/103)	Switch line X.6.a.4.7. to S.1.b.0.1.	1 Round per gun per 4 minutes.	5 SHRAPNEL to 1 H.E.	From 5.30 to 6 p.m. 104th and 175th Bdes: will drop barrage on to the switch line itself Infantry have been warned of this.
104th Bde: (less D/104)	S.1.b.0.1. to S.2.a.0.1. also 1 gun on track X.6.a.4.7. to MARTINPUICH. 1 gun on track and trench S.1.b.6.6. to MARTINPUICH. 1 gun on railway S.2.a.0.2. to MARTINPUICH.			At 2.30 p.m. / At 4.10 p.m. / At 7.15 p.m. / At 8.55 p.m. } Increase rate of fire to 1 round per gun per 2 minutes. Lift 100 yards behind switch line - after 2 minutes lift another 50; then after 3 minutes lift another 50 - then drop back after 3 minutes to the original barrage; at normal rate.
175th Bde:	S.2.a.0.1. to S.2.a.6.1. - also 1 gun on road S.2.a.3.6. to MARTINPUICH.			

App XXXVIII

SECRET.

S/1/84.

COPY NO: 47

R.A. 23rd Division Order No: 57. 880/

Reference: (Sketch issued.
(and Special Operation Map No: 1.

11th August, 1916.

1. (a) 4th Australian Division on night 12th/13th August is attacking on the line R.34.a.8.3. - 6.5 - 0.3 - R.33.b.5.5. - 3.2.

(b) On the night August 12th/13th the 15th Division will attack the enemy's switch line from S.1.d.9.9. to point 47 in X.6.a. (MUNSTER ALLEY).
The 4th Australian Division have been asked to assist by forming a defensive flank on the left of the attack.
Zero time will be communicated later.

(c) The 46th Infantry Brigade is attacking on the right, the 45th Infantry Brigade on the left. Dividing line between Brigades 30 yards E. of junction of GLOSTER ALLEY with switch line (SWITCH ELBOW).

2. (a) At zero our Infantry will be formed up 150 yards from the switch trench; at zero they advance and assault close under our barrage.

(b) The position will be consolidated, a double block formed on the right, and a series of strong points established not more than 100 yards in front of captured trench, covering parties being pushed out close under the barrage during their construction.

3. Artillery co-operation is as follows:-

(a) Heavy Artillery. Communications, strong points, etc, North of the switch line and Counter-Battery work.

(b) Right Flank Barrage. 1st Divisional Artillery.

(c) Left Flank Barrage. 34th Divisional Artillery.

(d) Main Barrage. 23rd Divisional Artillery including 175th and 176th Brigades.
A detailed programme of this is attached.

4. Liaison arrangements will be as at present.

5. Watches will be synchronized at the 46th Infantry Brigade Head Qtrs: SHELTER WOOD at 5 p.m. on the 12th instant.
An officer of each Artillery Brigade will be present.

6. ACKNOWLEDGE.

A.K. Hay

Major,

Issued at p.m. Brigade Major R.A. 23rd Division.

Copies Nos: 1 to 5 15th Division.
6 R.A. 3rd Corps.
7 R.A. 1st Division.
8 R.A. 34th Divn:
9 LAHORE Artillery.
10 to 14 102nd Bde: R.F.A.
15 to 19 103rd " "
20 - 24 104th Bde: R.F.A.
25 - 29 105th Bde: R.F.A.
30 - 34 175th " "
35 - 40 176th Bde: R.F.A.
41 & 42 Liaison Officer 45th Brigade.
43 - 45 Liaison Officer 46th
46 & 47 Diary 46th Brigade.
48 Staff Captain R.A.

BOMBARDMENT

HOUR	UNIT	OBJECTIVE	RATE	AMMUNITN:	REMARKS.
- 15 minutes to + 2 minutes.	175th Bde:	Switch line S.2.a.6.1. to S.2.c.0.9.	- 15 to ZERO 18 Prs & Hows: 1 round per gun per 5 minutes. ZERO to + 2 18 Prs: 6 rounds per gun per minute. Hows: 2 rounds per gun per minute.	18 Prs: SHRAPNEL. HOWS: H. E.	Howitzers on point S.2.a.6.1. 1 18 Pr: Section on road S.2.a.3.5. to M.32.c.4.2.
	104th Bde:	Switch line S.2.c.0.9. to road at S.1.d.2½.0.			Howitzers on railway from S.2.a.0.7. to M.32.c.2.2. - also one 18 Pr: gun.
	105th Bde:	Switch line S.2.c.0.9. to road at S.1.d.2½.9.			Howitzers on trench S.1.b.6.6. to M.31.d.8.2. One Section 18 Prs: on road S.1.b.7.6. to M.31.d.9.1.
	176th Bde:	Switch line S.2.c.3.8. to X.6.a.9.1½.			Howitzers on old Battery Position about S.1.b.1½.6½.
	102nd Bde:	Switch line S.1.b.0.1. to X.6.a.7.4½.			Howitzers on old Battery Position about X.6.a.8.6.
	103rd Bde:	Switch Line X.6.a.7½.4. to X.6.a.4.7.			Howitzers on road R.36.c.8½.0. to M.31.d.6.4. - 1 Section 18 Prs: on road M.31.d.0.1. to M.31.d.6.4.
	Section 46th Bty:	Enfilade switch line from S.1.d.3.8. to X.6.a.4.7.			

681f

L I F T S .

HOUR	UNIT	OBJECTIVE	RATE	AMMN:	REMARKS.
At 0.2. (1st Lift)	175th Bde: 104th Bde: 105th Bde:	Lift 100 yards to the North.	From 0.2 to 0.7. 18 Prs: Six rounds per gun per minute. Hows: Two rounds per gun per minute. From 0.7 to 0.10. 18 Prs: Four rounds per gun per minute. Hows: Two rounds per gun per minute.	18 Prs: SHRAPNEL. Hows: H. E.	At 0.2. All Howitzers and 18 Prs: on the communication in rear remain on their targets and do not lift.
	176th Bde: 102nd Bde: 103rd Bde: Sectn: 46th Bty:	Lift 100 yards to the North East.			
At 0.3 (2nd Lift)	175th Bde: 104th Bde: 105th Bde:	Lift 50 yards to the North.			At 0.3. Howitzers of 176th Bde: lift on to Railway about M.31.d.5.3½. Hows: of 102nd Bde: lift on to Trench Juncs: about M.31.d.7.5. Hows: of a 103rd Bde: concentrate on road at M.31.d.6.4.
	176th Bde: 102nd Bde: 103rd Bde: Sectn: 46th Bty:	Lift 50 yards to the North East.			
At 0.5. (3rd Lift)	175th Bde: 104th Bde: 105th Bde:	Lift 50 yards to the North.			
	176th Bde: 102nd Bde: 103rd Bde: Sectn: 46th Bty:	Lift 50 yards to the North East.			
At 0.7. (4th Lift)	175th Bde: 104th Bde: 105th Bde:	Lift 50 yards to the North.			This barrage continued till 0.10.
	176th Bde: 102nd Bde: 103rd Bde: Sectn: 46th Bty:	Lift 50 yards to the North East.			

NOTE. From 0.2 to 0.10, 175th Bde: will keep one 18 pounder Battery on Switch line from S.2.a.6.1. to S.2.a.4.½. Its other two Batteries will lift as per Table.

FINAL BARRAGE.

HOUR	UNIT	OBJECTIVES	RATE	AMMUNITION	REMARKS.
From 0.10 ONWARDS.	175th Bde:	Along road S.2.a.6.1. to S.2.a.3.6.	0.10 to 1.0. 18 Prs: 3 rounds per gun per minute. Hows: 1 round per gun per 2 minutes. 1.0 to 2.0. 18 Prs: 1 rd: per gun per min: Hows: 1 rd: per gun per 3 mins: 2.0 onwards. 18 Prs: 1 rd: per gun per 2 minutes. Hows: 1 rd: per gun per 4 mins:	18 Prs: Shrapnel from 0.10 to 1.0. After 1.0 - 3 Shrapnel to 1 H.E. Hows: H. E.	Howitzers still on point S.2.a.6.1.
	104th Bde:	S.2.a.3.6. to S.2.a.0.5.			Howitzers and 1 18 Pr: gun still on railway S.2.a.0.7. to M.32.c.2.2.
	105th Bde:	S.2.a.0.5. to S.1.b.6.4.			Howitzers still on trench S.1.b.6.6. to M.31.d.8.2. One Section 18 Prs: still on road S.1.b.7.6. to M.31.d.9.1.
	176th Bde:	S.1.b.6.4. to S.1.b.3.8.			Howitzers still on railway about M.31.d.5.3½.
	102nd Bde:	S.1.b.3.8. to M.31.d.2.0.			Howitzers still on trench junctions about M.31.d.7.5.
	103rd Bde:	M.31.d.2.0. to M.31.d.0.3.			Howitzers still on road at M.31.d.6.4.
	Section 46th Battery.	S.1.b.6.4. to M.31.d.0.3.			

6134

App XXXIX

SECRET.

S/3/48.

COPY NO: 34

R.A. 23RD DIVISION ORDER NO: 58. 677f

12th August, 1916.

RELIEF. 1. R.A. 23rd Division will be relieved by Sections on 13th & 14th August by 3 Brigades of 47th Divisional Artillery and one Brigade 34th Divisional Artillery. Relief each day to be completed by 6 p.m. Table of Reliefs attached.

MARCH. 2. On the morning following relief, each Section will march back to Rest Billets under Brigade arrangements. Route will be via ALBERT main road to LA HOUSSOYE and thence to billots. Order of march 102nd, 103rd, 104th and 105th Brigades. First named to start each day at 9 a.m. remainder at half an hour's interval. Billetting parties will proceed ahead on 14th instant reporting to the Town Major at the following places:-

All Brigades and Mob: Vet: Section } BEHENCOURT.

D. A. C. H.Q. Coy: Train } BEAUCOURT.

For allotment of billets see Table.

GUNS. 3. All guns in action (except as below) will be handed over stripped of sights, stores, etc, to relieving Batteries, and an equal number will be taken over at wagon lines.
The following unserviceable guns will not be handed over

No: 4969 of B/103
1602 of C/102
3352 of C/102
2256 of B/104
3451 of A/105.

MAPS. 4. All 1/10,000 and 1/20,000 maps, sketches, photos registrations, etc, will be handed over.

WIRE. 5. All wire laid down will be handed over as it stands and none taken in exchange.

AMMUNITION. 6. All units will move out filled to establishment. Surplus dumped at guns will be handed over, and receipts obtained. Where batteries are not relieved, ammunition will be taken to nearest occupied pits of the Brigade.
23rd D.A.C. will hand over ammunition dumped at Refilling Point and obtain receipts.
Units will report to H.Q. R.A. total ammunition in possession at noon 14th and at noon 15th.

6784

SUPPLIES.	7.	Refilling point B 17 A (Sheet 62 D) on 14th and subsequent days. Supplies to be delivered to present wagon lines on 13th and to new wagon lines on 14th and subsequent days. "X", "Y" and "Z" T.M. Batteries will be attached to 23rd D.A.C. for rations from 13th instant inclusive. Detachment of 23rd Signal Coy: R.E. will be attached H.Q. R.A. for rations from 14th inst:
TRANSPORT.	8.	Baggage wagon horses will join units on evening of 13th.
TRENCH MORTARS.	9.	Two medium T.M. Batteries 47th Division will relieve "X" and "Y"/23 on 13th instant. "X" and "Y"/23 will hand over their mortars to relieving Batteries. Details of exchange of other parts will be arranged between Staff Captain R.A. 23rd Division and D.T.M.O. 47th Divn: Personnel of "X" and "Y"/23 will return to 23rd D.A.C. All 3 T.M. Batteries of 23rd Division with equipment will proceed by lorry to FRECHINCOURT on 14th.
ATTACHED UNITS.	10.	H.Q. Coy: 23rd Divisional Train will march to BEAUCOURT on evening of 13th. 35th Mobile Veterinary Section will march to FRECHINCOURT on morning of 14th.
REPORTS.	11.	H.Q. R.A. close at W.26.c.3.3. at 6 p.m. and re-open at BEHENCOURT CHATEAU at the same hour.
	12.	ACKNOWLEDGE.

A. K. Hay.
Major,
Bde: Major R.A. 23rd Division.

Issued at 7.0 p.m.

Copy: No:			
1 to	R.A. 3rd Corps.	22 to 26	105th Brigade R.F.A.
2	15th Division.	27	23rd D. A. C.
3	1st Divisional Arty:	28	190th Coy: A.S.C.
4	34th Divisional Arty:	29	35' Mobile Vety: Section.
5	47th Divisional Arty:	30	X/23 T.M. Battery.
6	LAHORE ARTILLERY.	31	Y/23 T.M.Battery.
7 to 11	102nd Brigade R.F.A.	32	Z/23 T.M. Battery.
12 to 16	103rd Brigade R.F.A.	33	Staff Captain R.A.
17 to 21	104th Brigade R.F.A.	34 & 35	Diary

6794

TABLE OF RELIEFS.

UNIT OF 23RD DIVISION	RELIEVED BY	TIMES	REST BILLETS	REMARKS.
H.Q. R.A.	H.Q.R.A. 34 Dn:	6 p.m. 14th	BEHENCOURT	
H.Q. 102	H.Q. 238	6 p.m. 14th	BAVLINCOURT	
A/102	A/238	6 p.m. 13th	"	
B/102	B/238	" & 14th	"	
C/102	C/176	"	"	237th Bde: hands over 4 guns to C/102
D/102	D/238	"	"	
H.Q. 103	H.Q. 176	6 p.m. 14th	BEHENCOURT	
A/103	A/176	6 p.m. 13th & 14th	"	237th Bde: hands over guns.
B/103	B/176	"	"	" "
C/103	No one	-	"	Gets guns from workshops.
D/103	D/152	6 p.m. 13th & 14th	"	
			"	
H.Q. 104	H.Q. 235	6 p.m. 14th	"	
A/104	A/235	6 p.m. 13th & 14th	"	
B/104	B/235	"	"	
C/104	C/235	"	"	
D/104	D/235	"	"	
H.Q. 105	H.Q. 236	6 p.m. 14th	FRECHINCOURT	
A/105	A/236	6 p.m. 13th & 14th	"	
B/105	B236	"	"	
C/105	C/236	"	"	In new position
D/105	D/236	"	"	
23rd D.A.C.	47th D.A.C.	12 noon 14th	BEAUCOURT	
H.Q. Coy: 23rd Train A.S.C.	-	-	"	
35 Mobile Vetorinary Section.	-	-	FRECHINCOURT	

NOTE. Earlier on each afternoon 237th Bde: is relieving 176th Bde:, who then come over and relieve A & B 103 and C 102. Guns will be obtained from 237th Bde: in exchange . D 152 is brigaded with 176th Bde:, but it pulls its guns out of present position and hands them over to D/103.

App XI

83

SECRET.

S/3/50-2.

COPY NO: 35

6744

R.A. 23rd DIVISION ORDER NO:60.

Reference: (36 N.W. 1/20,000)
(28 S.W. ")

18th August, 1916.

RELIEF. 1. R.A. 23rd Division will relieve R.A. 41st Division in the Right Sector, IXth Corps front by Sections on nights of 19th/20th and 20th/21st August. No relief to commence before 8 p.m. each night. Details as per attached Table.

GUNS. 2. All guns will be taken over in the pits, stripped. Guns of 23rd Division will be handed over stripped at the wagon lines to 41st Division.

AMMUNITION. 3. (a) All surplus ammunition in gun pits will be taken over.
(b) All ammunition at the Divisional Ammunition Dump (B.1.central) will be taken over.

WIRES. 4. Telephone lines will be taken over as they stand.

MAPS, ETC: 5. All 1/10,000 maps, air photos, trench stores, Panoramas, Defence Schemes, Log Books, Intelligence Reports, Tables of Work on hand and proposed, local orders, and all other documents pertaining to the Sector, will be taken over.

BATTERY COMMANDERS. 6. Battery Commanders and Telephonists will proceed to Group H.Q's and then to Batteries early on 19th instant.

TRENCH MORTARS. 7. X, Y, and Z/23 T. M. Batteries will relieve the 3 Medium Batteries of 41st Division on afternoon of 20th. Relief to be completed by 5 p.m. Mortars will be taken over in the trenches, stripped. Mortars of 23rd Division will be handed over stripped, to 41st Division, at EECKE. Battery Commanders will proceed to 41st Trench Mortar billets at PONT DE NIEPPE (B.23.b.3.1) early on morning of 19th instant.
O.C. Y/23 will take over Heavy Trench Mortars at the above billets.

D. A. C. 8. (a) 23rd D. A. C. will take over ten 15 Pdr: guns and ammunition for same from "B" Echelon 41st D.A.C.
(b) 23rd D.A.C. will detail one officer, 1 N.C.O. and 20 gunners of "B" Echelon, to relieve personnel of 41st D.A.C. at Divisional Ammunition Dump at B.1.central. Relief to be complete by 10 a.m. 20th inst:.
The Officer and N.C.O. will proceed to the Dump early on 19th inst, to learn the work.

6754

REFILLING. 9. On 20th instant, in forward area.

TRANSPORT. 10. Baggage Wagon horses, join units early on morning of 19th, where not already with units.

ROUTE. 11. Sections marching to forward area will proceed by the CAESTRE - FLETRE - METEREN - BAILLEUL road, head of Brigade Columns to pass FLETRE CHURCH as below -

102nd Brigade	at	10 a.m.
104th "	"	10.30 a.m.
105th "	"	11. a.m.
103rd "	"	11.30 a.m.

On the 20th instant, the 23rd D. A. C. will be clear of above point by 9.45 a.m.
East of PONT D'ACHELLES all vehicles will move at 40 yards interval.
East of BAILLEUL, Sections will move at 200 yards intervals.

COMMAND. 12. G.O.C. R.A. 23rd Division assumes command at 10 a.m. 21st instant, at which hour H.Q. R.A. close at EECKE and re-open at the MAIRE, STEENWERCK. Group Commanders assume command of Groups on completion of all reliefs on 20th inst:

13. ACKNOWLEDGE.

G K Hall
Major,
Brigade Major R.A. 23rd Dn:

Issued at 5.30 p.m.

Copy: No:

1 to	R.A. IXth Corps.	15-19	104th Bde:
2	23rd Division (G)	20-24	105th "
3	23rd Division (Q)	25-30	23rd D.A.C.
4	41st Divn: Arty:	31	X/23 T.M.Bty:
5 - 9	102nd Brigade	32	Y/23 - " -
10 - 14	103rd "	33	Z/23 - " -
34	Staff Captain R.A.		
35 & 36	Diary.		

g.r.c. temporarily pt

676f

TABLE OF RELIEFS.

UNIT OF 23RD DIVN:	RELIEVE UNIT OF 41ST DIVN:	TIME	DATES	POSITION	WAGON LINE	REMARKS
H.Q. R.A.	H.Q. R.A.	10 a.m.	20th	THE MAIRIE, STEENWERCK.		
RIGHT GROUP.						
H.Q. 104.	H.Q. Rt: Group.	8 p.m.	20th	B.12. centl:		
A/104.	A/189	8 p.m.	19th & 20th.	C.13.d.1.3.	B.14.a.5.8.	
B/104	B/189	"		C.2.a.5.5.	B.8.c.2.3.	
C/104	C/189.	"	"	C.13.a.9.8.	B.14.a.3.8.	
D/104	D/189	"	"	C.1.d.1.4.	B.7.d.7.5.	
A/102	A/183	"	"	C.14.c.8.9.	B.11.c.8.5.	
CENTRE GROUP.						
H.Q. 105	H.Q.Centre Group	8 p.m.	20th	B.11.d.3.7.		
A/105	A/187	"	19th & 20th	B.6.c.$9\frac{1}{2}$.7.	B.8.c.0.6.	
B/105	B/187	"		U.25.a.6.3.	B.8.c.2.3.	
C/105	C/187	"	"	B.6.a.$9\frac{1}{2}$.7.	A.12.b.8.5.	
D/105	D/187	"	"	U.26.b.8.6. U.20.d.3.1.	B.7.d.7.5.	*
B/102	B/183	"	"	T.24.d.5.5.	B.10.c.3.9.	
LEFT GROUP.						
H.Q. 103.	H.Q.Lft: Group.	8 p.m.	20th	T.23.c.9.5.		
A/103	A/190	"	19th & 20th	T.30.c.7.$9\frac{1}{2}$.	A.24.a.6.4.	
B/103	B/190	"		T.24.c.5.5.	B.8.b.0.6.	
C/103	C/190	"	"	T.17.b.5.6.	A.5.b.7.6.	
D/103	D/190	"	"	U.19.a.5.6.	A.6.c.2.8.	
C/102	C/183	"	"	N I L	A.18.d.10.7.	%
D/102	D/183	"	"	U.19.b.$9\frac{1}{2}$.7.	B.9.b.5.5.	
23rd D.A.C.	41st D.A.C.	12 noon	20th	"A" B.4.c.1.3. "B" B.4.a.6.5.		

* 2 guns in each. % In rest.

NOTE. Batteries of 102nd Brigade are tactically grouped as above with effect from 9 a.m. on 19th inst: Orders for their march to forward area will, however, be issued by O.C. 102nd Brigade.

S E C R E T, & URGENT.

S/1/89

Copy App XLII

O.C. Right Group.
O.C. Left Group.
D.T.M.O., 23rd Div:

---

1. In connection with some gas operations the following Artillery bombardment will take place :-

0.4 to 0.8. Right Group. Concentrate all available 18 Pdrs on enemy's front parapet opposite trenches 96 to 104 and 100 yards further to each flank. Where not possible to fire on enemy's front parapet, fire to be on nearest support trench. Howitzers to be on junctions of communication trenches with support trenches. 1 Howitzer on PONT ROUGE BRIDGE.

Left Group. Concentrate opposite trenches 113 to 117 and 121 to 124 and 100 yards on either flank. Howitzers as for Right Group.

Rate :- 18-Pdrs: ~~5~~ 4 rounds per gun per minute
Hows: 2 " " " " "

0.8 to 0.18 Same targets as above but one 18-Pdr: gun to search each communication trench.

Rate :- 18-Pdrs: 1 round per gun per 2 minutes
Hows: 1 " " " " 2 mins:

0.18 to 0.21. Same targets as for period 0.4 to 0.8.

Rate :- 18-Pdrs: 4 rounds per gun per minute
Hows: 1 round " " " "

0.21 to 0.26 All 18-Pdrsn lift on to support line.
Hows: no change.

Rate :- 18-Pdrs: ~~2~~ 4 rounds per gun per minute
Hows: 1 round " " " "

0.26 to 0.28 All 18-Pdrs: drop back on to same targets as from 0.4 to 0.8. Howitzers no change.

Rate :- 18-Pdrs: ~~3~~ 4 rounds per gun per minute
Hows: 1 round " " " "

0.28 to 0.35 All 18-Pdrs: bombard support line.
Hows: no change.

Rate :- 18-Pdrs: 1 round per gun per 2 minute
Hows: 1 " " " " 2 mins:

0.35. Cease fire.

Rt Group
Say 1040 rounds 18pdr
for B.E. Scheme

2. TRENCH MORTARS. Two-inch Mortars who have suitable positions within range of the portion of the enemy's front concerned and which have registered by evening of 29th, will bombard front trenches between ~~0.4 to 0.21 and 0.26 to 0.35.~~ no bom[bard]... as requested Left group

Total Ammn
18pr: 3456 = 72 rds per gun.
How: 424 = 26½ rds per gun
3880

3. Group Commanders will submit their orders and table of proposed targets both for guns and trench mortars in their Group area to H.Q.R.A. by 6 p.m. on 28th inst:.

A K Hay
BRIGADE MAJOR,
R.A. 23rd DIVISION.

27/8/16

App XLII

CONFIDENTIAL.

REPORT OF OPERATIONS OF 23RD DIVISIONAL ARTILLERY FROM 4TH JULY to 14TH AUGUST 1916.

1. On 4th July, 23rd Divisional Artillery was distributed between BEAUCOURT and FRENCHENCOURT, Headquarters at BAIZIEUX.

2. During night of 4th/5th July, telephone instructions were received from R.A. 3rd Corps to reconnoitre positions for 23rd Divisional Artillery in the vicinity of FRICOURT, with a view to taking part in operations on 7th July.

With 3 Brigade Commanders I motored down to FRICOURT on morning of 5th and found suitable positions in our old front line west of the above mentioned village.

I reported this verbally to R.A. 3rd Corps at about 1 p.m. Owing to sanction of XV Corps having to be obtained to occupy these positions, the order to move was not received till about 3.30 p.m.

The Brigades marched at once, the distance to FRICOURT averaging 13 miles, and although the ground selected was a mass of trenches, all batteries were in action and ready to shoot by daylight on 6th July. I think this was very creditable to all concerned as the difficulty of getting the guns over the trenches and into position by night was considerable.

3. During 6th July, O.P's were selected and Registration carried out.

4. On the 7th the first attack on CONTALMAISON, by the 23rd Division was supported. After the withdrawal of the Infantry from that village it was bombarded and during that night and all the 8th, a continuous barrage was maintained in front of our Infantry positions.

Some good work

Some good work was done by the F.O.O's with the attacking battalions, as was testified in several instances by Battalion Commanders. The telephone lines were of course constantly cut but the F.O.O's and their telephonists never relaxed their efforts to repair them, and much gallantry was shown by all.

5. On the 9th, fire was kept up all day and in the evening the 68th Infantry Brigade were assisted in their capture of BAILIFF WOOD.

6. On the 10th, the attack of the 69th Infantry Brigade on CONTALMAISON was supported.

The G.O.C. 69th Brigade arranged with me the lifts he wanted and these were well carried out. Owing to good observation it was possible when the infantry were observed, to be a bit ahead of the time table and to modify the lifts accordingly.

Some very effective shooting was done on large parties of the enemy as they ran out of the village on the eastern side.

Work of F.O.O's was again good, and three of them got into the village close on the heels of the infantry, it was however impossible for them to keep their lines going except for short periods at a time.

Barrage round the village was maintained all night.

The G.O.C. 69th Infantry Brigade expressed himself as very pleased with the assistance given by the artillery.

Registration on hostile 2nd Line was begun.

During the day, observed fire was obtained on a counter-attack on the village from the N.E., and the enemy suffered a large number of casulaties.

The 23rd Division having been relieved by the 1st

Division

Division, the 23rd Divisional Artillery came under the orders of the G.O.C. 1st Division.

104th and 105th Brigades moved to more forwardx positions.

7. From 11th to 13th batteries were firing pretty continuously day and night, barraging, and registering and bombarding German 2nd Line.

8. On 14th, 103rd Brigade and C/102 went forward to positions near CONTALMAISON and PEAKE WOOD, to cut wire in front of hostile 2nd Line.

The 25th Brigade R.F.A. from 1st Divisional Artillery came under my orders - one battery (114th) was used for wire-cutting, the other two 18 Pr: Batteries and the Howitzer Battery went into action near MARLBOROUGH WOOD to enfilade the German Trenches.

In certain parts, observation for the wire-cutting was not easy, but, showing much gallantry and initiative, the battery commanders concerned surmounted the difficulties, and as was proved on the 16th when the 2nd Line was captured all the wire had been well cut.

9. On the 15th wire-cutting was continued and two unsuccessful attacks by the 1st Division were supported.

102nd Brigade, less C/102, were now in action in front of the 25th Brigade R.F.A. so that there were 26 18 Pr: guns and 8 4.5" Howitzers in direct enfilade of the German 2nd line trenches.

10. On the night 16th/17th, after an intense bombardment by all avaliable guns, the 1st Division successfully attacked the hostile 2nd Line. As before mentioned, the wire was found to be cut satisfactorily, and there were many dead Bosches in the trenches. The value of enfilade

fire was

fire was very marked on this occasion.

The Corps Commander very kindly included the artillery in his congratulatory telegram which was as follows:- "Well done the 3rd Brigade and its supporting Artillery". The G.O.C. 1st Division also expressed his appreciation of the good work done by the R.A.

11. Registration of the German Switch Line commenced on the 17th, and observation now became even more difficult than before. I cannot speak too highly of the manner in which Battery Commanders tackled the job - which often meant lying out for hours in front of our trenches, under sniping fire and with a liability to be rounded up at any moment by an enterprising hostile patrol. Much patience and endurance was required as for every ½ hour's registration anything up to 3 hours had to be spent on mending wires.

104th Brigade R.F.A. moved forward and was followed on the 19th by the 105th Brigade R.F.A.

12. From 17th to 22nd, Registration of Switch Line, and the cutting of wire in front of it continued, with barrages all through the nights and at intervals during the day-time. Air photos were not at this time available and the location of the Switch Line was a difficult proposition.

13. On night 22nd/23rd, an attack on the Switch Line by the 1st Division ~~Ekms~~ was supported. Although the enemy's trenches were entered at places, the attack failed. There were no reports of the Infantry being held up anywhere by wire.

14. From 23rd to 25th - Barrages were kept up day and nights, minor attacks on MUNSTER ALLEY were supported

6674

and counter-attacks engaged. Marked success was obtained on a strong counter-attack in neighbourhood of the WINDMILL, on morning of 25th.

15. On 26th, the 23rd Division relieved the 1st Division. There was, till end of month, no change in procedure, support was given to certain bombing attacks up MUNSTER ALLEY, these attacks did not meet with success.

Feint bombardments ordered by R.A. 3rd Corps, took place from time to time, and barrages as before were kept up. Batteries continued to be shelled, at times heavily.

16. On night of 4th/5th August, an attack by the 68th Infantry Brigade on MUNSTER ALLEY up to it's junction with TORR Trench (inclusive) was supported. The attack did not succeed. TORR and MUNSTER ALLEY Trenches on either side of the objective were bombarded by 4.5 Howitzers during the day preceding, but the objective itself was not fired at, as it was thought that if the junction was flattened out, there would be no trench for our Infantry to occupy.

17. On the 6th, a more serious bombardment by the 4.5 Hows: took place, lasting 3 hours, and one battery was concentrated on the junction. At 4 p.m. the 69th Infantry Brigade made a successful attack and established themselves in MUNSTER ALLEY well to the N.E. of the junction. A barrage was kept on all night, but it was not, I think, at a sufficiently rapid rate, as the enemy was able to make two counter-attacks on the new positions.

The work of the 4.5 Howitzers was good, the portions of trench bombarded were found to be flattened out. TORR ALLEY as a trench had practically disappeared and in the ruins of it were many dead Bosches.

18. On 8th August, the 15th Division (less Artillery) relieved the 23rd Division (less Artillery).

19. On morning

19. On morning of 10th August, orders were received that the SWITCH LINE between MUNSTER ALLEY, and Railway in S.2.a. was to be completely isolated day and night, preparatory to an attack on the 12th.

The barrages to ensure this isolation commenced at 2 p.m. and were continued till 10 p.m. on 12th (56 hours).

Using all available batteries the work was carried out in 6 hour reliefs - each battery having 6 hours on and 6 off.

The rates of fire averaged by day 1 round per gun per 5 minutes - by night 1 round per gun per minute.

20. At 10.30 p.m. 12th, two brigades of 15th Division attacked the SWITCH LINE.

At 0 the infantry were formed up about 150 yards from the objective on which an intense barrage (6 rounds per gun per minute) was opened at the same time.

The Infantry were to go in close under this barrage which at 0.2 lifted by bounds of 50 yards gradually to 250 yards back, where it stayed till the next morning, a good rate of fire being maintained for several hours.

The attack was a partial success only - the left Infantry Brigade got into a good portion of the SWITCH LINE on their front and firmly consolidated themselves there. The right Infantry Brigade did not get in.

This was attributable to several causes - among them, a German attack just previous to ours, and heavy M.G. fire on the right of the attack.

As regards the latter, it is thought that the right flank barrage might with advantage have been stronger.- this flank barrage was undertaken by the artillery of a neighbouring Division, who could not spare many batteries.

21. On the night of 13th August, the relief of the 23rd Divisional Artillery by the 47th Divisional Artillery commenced - it was completed on evening of 14th and on following morning the second sections of all 23rd Divisional Artillery batteries marched back to QUERRIEUX Area, preparatory to entraining on 16th for transfer to Vth Corps.

G.O.C. R.A. 23rd Division handed over his command at 6 p.m. on 14th to G.O.C. R.A. 34th Divisional Artillery and that of 47th Divisional Artillery was to support the Left Division of 3rd Corps.

together with his own Artillery

22. On first coming into the line, 5th July, the 34th Divisional Artillery was also allotted to the 23rd Division and was under my orders. It was later given another task and on 14th July, the 25th Brigade R.F.A. (1st Divisional Artillery) came into action under my orders; 2 days later 175th Brigade R.F.A. (34th Divisional Artillery) was lent to me.

I am greatly indebted to the above units for the assistance given. Very good work was done by O.C. 25th Brigade R.F.A. and his Battery Commanders in rapidly selecting their positions and getting into action. I am sorry to say that the batteries of the 25th Brigade R.F.A. came in for a very bad time from hostile shelling and I was much struck by the way they stuck to their work.

D/25, the Howitzer Battery was practically knocked out in its first position. The remains of it had to be withdrawn, and the battery completely re-organized. As soon as this had been done, it came into action again in a new position.

23. The casulaties in the 23rd Divisional Artillery for the period 5th July to 14th August, were as follows:-

Officers

6707

Officers	Other Ranks
25	310

During the first 10 days the enemy's counter-battery work was very feeble, and casualties were confined almost entirely to F.O.O's and telephonists. From about the 15th onwards, the shelling of our batteries became gradually heavier, all received a share of the enemy's attention, but the worst sufferers at first were 102nd and 103rd Brigades and the 25th Brigade of the 1st Divisional Artillery - these had a very bad time indeed as did the other two Brigades later, and we were extremely lucky not to get more casualties, both in personnel and material.

For about a week or ten days, in addition to the ordinary shelling, all batteries and also Brigade Headquarters came in for gas shell every night. Although only one man was seriously gassed, there was much sickness and inconvenience among the personnel and no rest at night was possible.

24. During the whole period, batteries shot continuously at night, and except for a short time about end of July and beginning of August, they also shot the greater part of the day.

At times, rapid and intense fire was demanded of the Batteries for quite long periods - for example 6 rounds per gun per minute for 20 minutes, 2 rounds per gun per minute for over an hour and 1 round per gun per minute for 3 or 4 hours.

The Officers and men stood the hard work extremely well, though they were undoubtedly rather tired towards the end of our time in action. For some of the attacks which were supported, as many as 15,000 rounds of 18 Pr:

were expended

6714

were expended. The largest expenditure of 18 Pr: ammunition by the 23rd Divisional Artillery wad 30,000 rounds in 12 hours.

25. As regards material, the only serious trouble experienced, has been in connexion with gun springs and it has been practically continuous. Almost every gun has had to go into the workshops once and many of them several times. The supply of new springs is, I understand, very inadequate, and the temporary repairs that the I.O.M. is able to make to damaged springs, are often not of a lasting nature.

Damage to the springs nearly always occurs whenever rapid fire is kept up for more than a minute or two.

Although all the known precautions against prematures with the 4.5 Howitzers are taken, one battery had two very disastrous prematures, in one case the whole detachment being wiped out, and in the other, an officer and several men were killed.

Another battery had more than a dozen prematures, but without serious consequences. The other two batteries had practically none.

26. The system of Liaison between the Infantry and Artillery was as follows:-
The Artillery were under Divisional Control throughout, and were not grouped with Infantry formations. A Liaison Officer was attached to each Infantry Brigade Headquarters, this officer being in direct telephonic communication with R.A. Headquarters. An F.O.O. was attached to each front line Battalion Headquarters, who in turn was linked by telephone to the Liaison Officer at the Infantry Brigade Headquarters.

For special operations, additional F.O.O's were sent with the attacking Infantry, extending the

telephone

telephone communications beyond Battalion Headquarters.

All information, calls for barrages, etc, were thus transmitted direct to R.A. Headquarters, who were thereby able to rapidly concentrate a large number of guns on threatened points.

In addition to the above communications, each front line Battalion had a direct line to one F.A. Brigade, on whom they had an immediate call in case of attack.

27. In conclusion, I would like to bear testimony to the keenness, energy and gallantry shown by all ranks - from Bde: Commanders downwards. The calls I have made on them at times, have been severe tests of courage, initiative and endurance, but I have never failed to get immediate and satisfactory response.

The work, which has been perhaps the most prominent, is that of Battery Commanders, F.O.O's and telephonists, up in and in advance of our front trenches, and I cannot speak too highly of it.

The bringing up of ammunition has had to be done under fire and there have been several occasions when N.C.O's and Drivers have shown up well.

With such a large expenditure of ammunition, the work of the D.A.C. has of course been heavy all the time, but there has never once been any delay or hitch in the supply to batteries and this I think reflects credit on Major Buchanan, Commanding the Column and his officers and men.

Any successful work that the 23rd Divisional Artillery may have accomplished, is very largely due to Major A. K. Hay the Brigade Major.

Circumstances

6737

Circumstances made it necessary to control all artillery action from Headquarters, and his duties have therefore been unceasing. How wholeheartedly he has worked to get the best possible results and how he has never spared himself for one moment, is I think, already well known to the G. O. C.

D. Fasson

Br: General,

16th August, 1916. Commanding R. A. 23rd Division.

Routine Order No. 205 2nd August 1916

By

Brigadier General D Wasson, C.B.

Commanding Royal Artillery, 23rd Division.

584
ACT OF COURAGE. Attention is drawn to Fourth Army R.O. No. 161.

The General Officer Commanding wishes to express his appreciation of the following Act of Courage on the part of the undermentioned non-commissioned officer and man belong to "D" Battery, 105th Brigade Royal Field Artillery, 23rd Division.
On the night of the 14th instant, whilst the D/105th Brigade, R.F.A., was in action E. of Albert a "premature" set fire to a dump of ammunition near the gun emplacement Flames rose to about twenty feet and lit up the whole battery. With ~~xxx~~ great promptitude and presence of mind No. 15005, Sergeant A.W.Edwards and No. 67983, Gunner J Howard rushed up and endeavoured to extinguish the fire. They got it under control but it broke out a second time, when they again set to work and completely extinguished it. A record of the above will be made in the Regimental Conduct Sheets of this non-commissioned officer and man in accordance with paragraph 1919 (xiv) King's Regulations.

Captain.
Staff Captain, R.A. 23rd Division.

N O T I C E

LOST from R.A. Headquarters on 27/7/16 a bicycle No. B.3515. Any information to be communicated to Staff Captain R.A. 23rd Division.

00

Routine Order No. 204 4th August 1916

By

Brigadier General D Fasson, C.B.

Commanding Royal Artillery, 23rd Division.

585
POSTINGS The following having reported their arrival are posted to Brigades and D.A.C. with effect from 4/8/16.

5 Howitzer Gunners to 103rd Bde R.F.A.
6 " " " 105th Bde R.F.A.
3 " " " 104th Bde R.F.A.
6 18-pdr " " 102nd Bde R.F.A.
3 " " " 103rd Bde R.F.A.
2 " " " 104th Bde R.F.A.
2 Shoeing Smiths to 23rd D.A.C.
2 Telephonists to 105th Bde. R.F.A.
1 Fitter to 102nd Brigade R.F.A.
1 Driver to 103rd Bde R.F.A.
8 " " 104th Bde R.F.A.
4 " " 105th Bde R.F.A.

2 Corporals posted from Base to 102nd Brigade will now be posted to 105th Brigade R.F.A.

1 Bombardier 102nd Brigade R.F.A. will be posted to 105th Brigade R.F.A. for promotion to Corporal.

W. J. Smith
Captain
Staff Captain, R.A. 23rd Division.

N O T I C E

LOST. Bay Mare No. 55, 16 hands, Shield on back, off side. 4 Shrapnel wounds off side - 1 on neck, 1 on shoulder and 2 on girth. B/104 off hind 55 near hind

Bay Mare, 14.2 hands, White lip off hind, wounded on rear fore unhealed. B/104 near fore, 52 off fore.

Black Mare, While Nozzle 63 near hoof, C/104 off hoof.

Any information to be communicated to H.Q. 104th Brigade R.F.A.

Routine Order No. 205. 5th August 1916.

By

Brigadier General D Fasson, C.B.

Commanding Royal Artillery, 23rd Division.

586.
HONOURS AND REWARDS. Attention is drawn to D.R.O. No. 1605 of 4/8/16.

The G.O.C. has very great pleasure in publishing the following extract from IIIrd Corps Memo. No. C.R. 3/505/A5/16 dated 3.8.1916.

"The Corps Commanders awards the MILITARY MEDAL to the following:-

A/102nd Brigade R.F.A.

84010 Gunner. H. Bankhead.

587
POSTINGS. The following Officers are posted from 23rd D.A.C. to 102nd Brigade R.F.A. with effect from 4/8/16.

2/Lieut. G.L. Patterson.
2/Lieut. L.A. Dent.

Captain.
Staff Captain, R.A. 23rd Division.

NOTICE.

LOST from R.A. Headquarters, 23rd Division bicycle No. B.3317
Any information to be communicated to the Staff Captain, R.A.

Routine Order No. 206.   7th August 1916

By

Brigadier General D Fasson, C.B.

Commanding Royal Artillery, 23rd Division.

588
POSTINGS. The following officers are posted to Brigades and D.A.C. with effect from 6/7/16.

2/Lieut. C.H. Campbell to 105th Bde. R.F.A.

2/Lieut. W.J.E. Dawson to 23rd D.A.C.

2/Lieut. L.L.Kellie from D.A.C. to 102nd Bde.

589
HONOURS AND REWARDS. Attention is drawn to D.R.O. No. 1614.

The G.O.C. has very great pleasure in publishing the following Extract from Fourth Army No. 62/185/AMS.

"The G.O.C. Commanding-in-Chief has, under authority granted by His Majesty the King, awarded Decorations as detailed below.

MILITARY MEDAL

No. 58641 Gunner J. Bullock, 102nd Bde. R.F.A.

Captain.
Staff Captain, R.A. 23rd Division.

Routine Order. No. 207. 8th August 1916.

By

Brigadier General D Fasson, C.B.

Commanding Royal Artillery, 23rd Division.

590
COMMAND. Lieut. T.J. Craig, 104th Brigade, R.F.A. is posted to temporarilly command "C" Battery, 105th Brigade R.F.A.

591
DISCIPLINE. No. 56297 Gunner S. Tipper, B/105 Brigade was tried by Field General Court Martial and found guilty of "When on Active Service disobeying a Lawful Command given by his superior officer" and sentenced to 12 months Imprisonment with Hard Labour.

No. 50239 Gunner W.J. Hogg, A/105 Brigade was tried by Field General Court Martial and found guilty of "Conduct to the prejudice of Good Order and Military Discipline" and sentenced to 4 months Imprisonment with Hard Labour.

W. J. Smith
Captain
n Staff Captain, R.A. 23rd Division.

Bn 15 Dec

Routine Order No. 208 9th August 1916

By

Brigadier General D Fasson, C.B.

Commanding Royal Artillery, 23rd Division.

592
HONOURS AND REWARDS.

Attention is drawn to D.R.O. No. 1621

The G.O.C. has very great pleasure in publishing the following extract from Fourth Army Memo No. 62/201/AMS dated 7-8-1916.

"The General Officer Commanding-in-Chief has, under authority granted by his Majesty the King, awarded decorations to the Officer and N.C.O. named below.

MILITARY CROSS

Captain E. Maitland-Dougall, D.S.O.

DISTINGUISHED CONDUCT MEDAL

B.Q.M.S. E.E.R. Riddle, B/102nd Bde. R.F.A.

593
POSTINGS. 1 Wheeler of 102nd Brigade R.F.A. is posted to 103rd Brigade R.F.A. with effect from 9-8-1916.

W. J. Smith.

Captain.
Staff Captain, R.A. 23rd Division.

Routine Order No. 209 11th August 1916

By

Brigadier General D Fasson, C.B.

Commanding Royal Artillery, 23rd Division.

594
Honours and Reward. Attention is drawn to D.R.O. No. 1615.

The GO.C. has very great pleasure in publishing the following extract from Fourth Army Memo No. 62/192/AMS dated 8-8-1916.

"The General Officer Commanding-in-Chief has, under authority granted by His Majesty the King, awarded the

DISTINGUISHED SERVICE ORDER

to

Major C. A. N. Hume-Spry, C/102nd Bde R.F.A.

595
Postings. The following having reported their arrival are posted as under with effect from 11-8-16.

6	Drivers	to	102nd	Bde.	R.F.A.
3	"	"	103rd	"	"
7	"	"	104th	"	"
4	"	"	105th	"	"
4	"	"	D.A.C.		
12	Gunners	to	102nd	Bde	R.F.A.
16	"	"	103rd	"	"
10	"	"	104th	"	"
10	"	"	105th	"	"
8	"	"	D.A.C.		

1 Shoeing Smith to 103rd Bde R.F.A.

1 Cold Shoer to 104th Bde. R.F.A.

No. 88556 Fitter Staff Sergeant A.R. Hickling to 105th Brigade R.F.A.

W. J. Smith.
Captain.
Staff Captain, R.A. 23rd Division.

N O T I C E

LOST on night 7th 8th Brown mare, No. 10, with Officers saddle and bridle from A/102nd Bde. R.F.A

Bay Mare, 7 years, 15.3, marked U off hind quarter. C/103 off hind and 66 near hind.

Dark Chestnut Gelding, 8 years, 16 hands. Blaze Three white socks. Marked C/103 hind 80 near hind

Routine Order No. 210 — 18th August 1916

By

Bbigadier General D Fasson, C.B.

Commanding Royal Artillert, 23rd Division.

596 COMMAND. 2/Lieut. H.G. Pring is to assume command of X/23 Trench Mortar Battery during absence of Lieut. J.B.Kyle.

597 POSTINGS. The following having reported their arrival are posted to Brigades and D.A.C. with effect from 18-8-16.

Gunners.

1 to 102nd Brigade R.F.A.
1 to 103rd Brigade R.F.A.
2 to 104th Brigade R.F.A.
5 to 105th Brigade R.F.A.
2 to 23rd D.A.C.

Drivers

1 to 102nd Brigade R.F.A.
2 to 103rd Brigade R.F.A.
3 to 104th Brigade R.F.A.
5 to 105th Brigade R.F.A.
7 to 23rd D.A.C.

Telephonists

6 to 102nd Brigade R.F.A.
5 to 103rd Brigade R.F.A.
6 to ~~XXXX~~ 104th Brigade R.F.A
8 to 105th Brigade R.F.A.

1 Saddler to 105th Brigade R.F.A.

1 Wheeler to 103rd Brigade R.F.A.

1 4.5 How. Fitter to 102nd Brigade R.F.A.

W. J. Smith

Captain.

Staff Captain. R. A. 23rd Division.

Routine Order No. 211 19th August 1916

By

Brigadier General D Fasson C.B.

Commanding Royal Artillery, 23rd Division.

599
DRESS. Attention is drawn to D.R.O. No. 1632 of 14/8/16.
"The practice of cutting down trousers into Shorts is ~~xixkx~~ strictly forbidden and all trousers so cut down will be at once replaced.
Transport drivers are to be properly dressed at all parades and are not to drive in shirt sleeves.

600
FIELD CASHIER. Attention is drawn to D.R.O. 1615 of 15/8/16.
"The Field Cashier will be at 38 Rue de L'Occident, BAIELEUL daily except Sundays from 9.30 a.m. to 12.30 p.m. and from 12.30 p.m. to 4.30 p.m. On Sundays the hours will be from 9 a.m. to 12 noon.

601
HONOURS AND REWARDS. Attention is drawn to D.R.O. No. 1639 of 16/8/16.
"The G.O.C. has very great pleasure in publishing the following Extract from IIIrd Corps Memo. No. C.R.3/505/a7/16.
"The Corps Commanders awards the Military Medal to the following:-

103rd Brigade R.F.A.

No. 48187 Cpl. G.Cooper, "A" Battery.
46376 Gnr. Torrance, "A" Battery.
56054 Dvr. E.Lees, "A" Battery.
39879 Dvr. J. Daniels, "C"Battery
56303 Bdr. J.H. Yates, "D" Battery
56088 Gnr. Campbell "B" Battery.

602
I.O.M. WORKSHOPS. Ref. D.R.O. 15-8-16 para 1616. Workshops of I.O.M. at BAILLEUL are at 156- Rue de la Gare.

603.
BATHS.. Attention is drawn to D.R.O. No. 1648 of 18-8-16.
The Divisional Baths are situated at:-
1. PONT de NIEPPE.
2. PAPOT
3. STEENWERCK.
2. The baths at PONT de NIEPPE and PAPOT will not be available for use until Monday 21st. and full particulars concerning allotment of these baths will be published on Saturday 19th.
3. The baths at STEENWERCK A.11.d.3.8. are now open and units in that area should apply to O.C. Baths, PONT de NIEPPE for an allotment.
4. The Office of the Officer i/c Baths is at the Baths, PONT de NIEPPE B.25.d.3.8.
All correspondence should be sent there except urgent telegrams between the hours of 6 p.m. and 8 a.m. which should be addressed c/o 71st Field Ambulance, STEENWERCK.

FIELD GENERAL COURT MARTIAL. A Field General Court Martial composed as under will assemble at Headquarters, 23rd D.A.C. at 10 a.m. on Monday, 21st August 1916, for the purpose of trying No. 44141 Corporal (a/Sergt.) Alexander McColl, No. 3 Section, 23rd D.A.C.

President

Major R.F. Poiniger, B/104th Bde. R.F.A.

Members

Captain. W.H. Powell, B/103rd Brigade R.F.A.

Lieut. L.R.P.Hindson, C/105th Brigade R.F.A.

Waiting Member

Lieut. E.P. Dale-Harris, D/102nd Brigade R.F.A.

The accused to be warned and all witnesses to attend.

Proceedings to be forward to Staff Captain, R.A. marked "Confidential".

W. J. Arnold

Captain.
Staff Captain, R.A. 23rd Division.

Routine Order No. 212 22nd August 1916

BY

Brigadier General D Fasson, C.B.

Commanding Royal Artillery, 23rd Division.

605
INTELLIGENCE. Group Commanders should study the Corps and Divisional Intelligence Reports very carefully, as from them they can get much assistance in ascertaining enemys' vulnerable points, and selecting targets for their batteries.

Group Commanders are to keep a register of M.G. Emplacements, vulnerable points, and all useful information about their fronts.

606
GAS ATTACKS. Special attention is drawn to a warning order regarding GAS which is being issued by G.O.C. Division.

With a N. or N.E. Wind it is very probable that gas might come into the area where battery positions are, without touching our front line so that batteries would get no warning from the trenches.

Proper protection against Gas is to be fixed up at the entrance to all dug-outs at once.

The examination of Gas Helmets must be frequent and thorough.

607
DISCIPLINE. All units must at once set to work to improve the turn-out and general smartness, which owing to the stress of fighting on the Somme has unavoidably fallen far below our usual standard, and for the moment we compare unfavourably with neighbouring Divisions.

There must now be no relaxation of the order that all vehicles are to be kept clean.

No personnel must ever be allowed to leave their lines dirty or improperly dressed.

The G.O.C.R.A. will give units a short time to get things right and will then inspect all wagon lines and D.A.C. units.

Grooming of horses must be more thorough than it has been lately.

608
DISCIPLINE. Attention is drawn to G.R.O. No. 1716 d/, 18-8-16.

The slackness in saluting referred to in G.R.O. 81 is still noticeable.

A practice appears to have arisen of one soldier only saluting when more than one are passing an officer. This practice is to cease.

When several soldiers pass an office, unless they are being marched as a party, they will all salute, whether there are N.C.Os among them or not. All will take time from the man nearest to the officer.

When a party of men is being marched by a N.C.O. or older soldier, the N.C.O. or man in charge of the party will give the order "Eyes right, or "Left" and himself salute.

When two or more men are sitting or standing about, and an officer passes them, the senior N.C.O. or oldest soldier will face the officer, call the rest to attention and alone salute.

Soldiers will salute in the manner laid down in the training manuals

608 (contd). Officers must return the salutes of their subordinates with a definite motion of the hand and not perfunctorily: if more than one officers is present the senior alone will return the salute.

Officers will check lack of discipline in saluting and will report to the unit concerned the names of men who fail to salute them.

Officers commanding units will deal severely with men whose names are reported to them on this account.

G.R.O. 3 dated 18th August, 1914, is republished:-

(3) SALUTES - The strictest attention of all officers and soldiers should be directed to studying the uniforms and rank distinctions of our Allies and to the necessity of observing the obvious courtesies of saluting and returning salutes.

Quite irrespective of rank, it should be an accepted rule that no officer or soldier passes or is passed by any officer or soldier of the allied army without some act of recognition.

When foreign officers or soldiers salute British officers all the officers so saluted will acknowledge the compliment, irrespective of who is the senior.

J. Smith.

Captain.

Staff Captain, R. A. 23rd Division.

Routine Order No. 213 | 24th August 1916

By

Brigadier General D Fasson, C.B.

Commanding Royal Artillery, 23rd Division.

809
FIELD GENERAL COURT MARTIAL. A Field General Court Martial composed as under will assemble at Headquarters, 103rd Brigade at 10 a.m., Friday, the 25th August, 1916, for the purpose of trying No. 41259 Driver H.Kyle, A/103rd Brigade R.F.A. and No. 44735 Gunner J.Healy, B/103rd Brigade R.F.A. and such other persons as may be brought before them.

President

Major W.M.Shaw, D/102nd Brigade R.F.A.

Members

Captain H.E.Courage, 23rd D.A.C.

Lieut. V.Warden, B/105th Brigade R.F.A.

Waiting Member

Lieut. C.G.L.Dowley, A/104th Brigade R.F.A.

The accused to be warned and all witnesses required to attend.

The Proceedings to be forwarded to "Staff Captain, marked "Confidential"

H Lane Waithead

Lieut.
a/Staff Captain, R.A. 23rd Division.

Routine Order No. 214 — 25th August 1916

By

Brigadier General D Fasson, C.B.

Commanding Royal Artillery, 23rd Division.

610
PROMOTION. Major B.G. Buchanan is to wear the badges of the rank of Lieut. Colonel whilst in command of 23rd. D.A.C.

611
FIELD GENERAL COURT MARTIAL. A Field General Court Martial composed as under will assemble at Headquarters 105th Brigade at 10 a.m. on Monday the 28th inst for the purpose of trying No. 78017 Gunner C. Casson, A/105th Brigade R.F.A. and such other persons as may be brought before them.

President

Major G Badham Thornhill, D/103rd Brigade R.F.A.

Members

Captain A.Hebert, B/102nd Brigade R.F.A.

2/Lieut. E.J.Jackson, B/104th Brigade R.F.A.

Waiting Member

Lieut. E.O.Pryce, D/105th Brigade R.F.A.

The accused to be warned and all witnesses required to attend.

The Proceedings to be forward to Staff Captain, R.A. marked "Confidential"

Lieut.
a/Staff Captain, R.A. 23rd Division.

Routine Order No. 215 26th August 1916

By

Brigadier General D Fasson C.B.

Commanding Royal Artillery, 23rd Division.

612
POSTINGS. The following having reported their arrival are posted to Brigades and D.A.C. with effect from 25-8-1916.

1 Fitter Staff Sergeant to 104th Bde. R.F.A.

1 Bombr. Telephonist to 102nd Bde. R.F.A.

5	Gunners	to	102nd	Bde.	R.F.A.
1	"	"	103rd	"	"
12	"	"	105th	"	"
10	"	"	D.A.C.		

5 Drivers to 105th Bde. R.F.A.

H. Lowe Watchey

Lieut.
a/Staff Captain, R.A. 23rd Division.

Routine Order No. 216

27th August 1916

By

Brigadier General D Fasson C.B.

Commanding Royal Artillery, 23rd Division.

613
POSTINGS. The following Officers having reported their arrival are posted to Brigades and D.A.C. with effect from 27-8-1916.

	2/Lieut.	C.E. Vigor	to 102nd Brigade
	"	N.W.Wise	102 103rd "
*	"	G.E.Tatham	104th "
*	"	C.H.Lapthorn	102nd "
*	"	B.McLachlan	105th "
	"	S.C.Norrington	D.A.C.
	"	F.S.Jones	103rd Brigade
	"	E.T.C.Farr	105th "
	"	A.A.Page	104th "
	"	R.Gilder	D.A.C.
	"	J.Dont	105th Brigade
	"	J.Todd	104th "

* These Officers have had some experience of Howitzer Work.

H. Lane Mathews (signature)

Lieut.
a/Staff Captain, R.A. 23rd Division.

Routine Order No. 217 28th August 1916

By

Brigadier General D.J.M.Fasson C.B.

Commanding Royal Artillery, 23rd Division

614
CORRESPONDENCE Attention is drawn to D.R.O. No. 1697 of 27-8-16.

"With reference to D.R.O. 1628 d/- 12-8-16 communications found in packets of ration cigarettes written from addresses within the British Empire need not be forwarded to Divisional H.Q. in future.

Communications emanating from strangers in neutral countries should however still be forwarded together with a description of the package in which found and date of receipt.

615
POTATOES Attention is drawn to D.R.O. No. 1698 d/- 27-8-16

"It has been reported that troops are digging up potatoes belonging to inhabitants.

O.C. Units will take steps to put a stop to this practice.

Any breach of these orders is to be severely dealt with.

616
SALVUS SETS Attention is drawn to D.R.O. No. 1699 d/- 27-8-16

"Units in possession will at once return these sets to D.A.D.O.S.. They are now superseded by box respirators.

617
A.F. B213. Attention is drawn to G.R.O. No. 1755 d/- 24-8-16

"Para 2 (a) G.R.O. 1461 dated 18-3-16 is cancelled and the following substituted:-

Para 2 (a) Heavy and Medium T.M.Batteries i.e. those composed of Artillery personnel, will render A.F.B 213 to the Officer Commanding The Divisional Ammunition Column, who will embody their returns in the weekly A.F.B213 of the Divisional Ammunition Column.

The Officer Commanding, Divisional Ammunition Column will shew the number of men detached for duty with Trench Mortar Batteries and the designation of the Batteries to which they are attached.

Lieut.
a/Staff Captain, R.A. 23rd Division

87

Routine Order No. 218 29th August 1916

By

Brigadier General D Fasson C.B.

Commanding Royal Artillery, 23rd Division.

618
FIELD GENERAL COURT MARTIAL A Field General Court Martial composed as under will assemble at H.Q. 105th Brigade R.F.A at 10 a.m. on Thursday 31st August 1916 for the purpose of trying No. 81462 Gunner W.Topley, B/104, No. 46323 Gunner J.Kane, B/105th Bde., No. 32766 Gunner H.Concannon B/105th Brigade and such other persons as may be brought before them.

President

Lt. Col. B.G. Buchanan, 23rd D.A.C.

Members

Capt. R.S.P.Wells, A/102nd Bde. R.F.A.
Lieut. J.Abbey, C/103rd Bde. R.F.A.

Waiting Member

Lieut. J.N.Fraser, D/104th Bde. R.F.A.

~~RXW~~ The accused to be warned and all witnesses required to attend.

Proceedings to be forwarded to Staff Captain, R.A. marked "Confidential".

620.
INDENTS. All Indents for R.E. Material are to be approved by O.C. Brigades before being sent in to R.E.

621
GAS HELMETS. Gas Helmets will always be carried by all ranks in IX Corps.

[signature]

Lieut.
a/Staff Captain, R.A. 23rd Division.

Routine Order No. 219 — 30th August 1916

By

Brigadier General D Fasson C.B.

Commanding Royal Artillery, 23rd Division.

622
COMMISSIONS

Attention is drawn to D.R.O. No. 1713 of 30-8-16
Extract from G.H.Q. List No. 96 D/- 19th August 1916 of Appointments, Commissions, etc. approved by the G.O.C.-in-C.

GENERAL LIST

The undermentioned to be temp. Lieut. whilst Commdg. Trench Mortar Battery:-
Temp. 2nd Lieut. C.E.H.Coubrough, Z/23rd Batt. vice Lieut. F.C.George, R.F.A. (wounded) 27-7-16.

623
DEMONSTRATION ON CARE OF WATER CARTS AND TRAVELLING KITCHENS.

Attention is drawn to D.R.O. No. 1715 d/- 30-8-16
The O.C. Sanitary Section will give demonstration on the care of Water Carts and Travelling Kitchens at 3 p.m. as follows:-
Monday September 4th at 69th Fd Ambulance for R.A. & R.E.
As many Medical Officers, Quartermasters, watermen and cooks as possible will attend.

624
FIRES. Attention is drawn to D.R.O. No. 1712 d/- 29-8-16
IX Corps Routine Order No. 38 d/- 26-8-16 is republished.
Fires have occurred recently in huts owing to the heating stove being placed so near the woodwork of the hut as to set it alight.
In future all woodwork, canvas, or roofing within a three foot radius of the stove pipe is to be protected from the heat by a metal screen.
Necessary action to give affect to this order is to be taken forthwith.

W. Fane Blanchard (?)
Lieut.
a/Staff Captain, R.A. 23rd Division.

Routine Order No. 220 31st August 1916

BY

Brigadier General D. Fasson, C.B.

Commanding Royal Artillery, 23rd Division.

625
POSTINGS. The following having reported their arrival are posted to Brigade with effect from 31-8-16.

1 Fitter to 104th Brigade
1 Acting Fitter to 103rd Brigade
1 Acting Bombardier to 104th Brigade
5 Gunners to 103rd Brigade
4 " " 104th "

626
COMMITTALS TO PRISON. A new form (Army Form C.385.B) of Order for the commitment to Prison of persons subject to Military Law sentenced to Penal Servitude or Imprisonment while on Active Service out of the United Kingdom has been approved and will be issued to all units.

627
PROMOTION. Lieut. W.R. Young to wear the badges of rank of Captain while commanding B/105th Brigade R.F.A.

628
HONOURS AND REWARDS. Attention is drawn to D.R.O. No. 1717.
The G.O.C. has very great pleasure in publishing the following Extract from IIIrd Corps Memo. No. OR3/505/A9/16. d/- 26-8-16.
The Corps Commander awards the MILITARY MEDAL to the following:-

No. 40935 Corpl. C.H.Hart, D/102nd Bde. R.F.A.
53275 Bombr. F.Bird [illegible]/104th " "
44874 Gnr. J.Hogan [illegible]105th Bde "
53527 Corpl. S.H.Gr[illegible]/105th Bde. R.F.A.
62739 a/Bombr. J.Gr[illegible] A/105th " "
45653 Corpl W.G. Borne[illegible]/105th " "
42271 Bombr. F.Johnson, [illegible]/105th " "
42131 " [illegible].McGill, D/105th Bde "

W. Lane Mathews

Lieut.
a/Staff Captain, R.A. 23rd Division.

COMMANDER
ROYAL ARTILLERY

www.ingramcontent.com/pod-product-compliance
Lightning Source LLC
Chambersburg PA
CBHW081423300426
44108CB00016BA/2285
* 9 7 8 1 4 7 4 5 1 2 4 5 9 *